The Politics of Women's Work

The Politics of Women's Work

THE PARIS GARMENT TRADES

1750–1915

Judith G. Coffin

PRINCETON UNIVERSITY PRESS

PRINCETON, NEW JERSEY

Library of Congress Cataloging-in-Publication Data

Coffin, Judith G., 1952–
The politics of women's work : the Paris garment trades, 1750–1915 / Judith G. Coffin.
p.   cm.
Includes bibliographical references and index.
ISBN 0-691-03447-8 (alk. paper)
1. Women clothing workers—France—Paris—History.   2. Women—Employment—
France—Paris—History.   3. Clothing trade—France—Paris—History.   4. Needlework
industry and trade—France—Paris—History.   I. Title.
HD6073.C62F733   1996
331.4′887′0944361—dc20   95-25915 CIP

This book has been composed in Berkeley Medium

Princeton University Press books are printed on acid-free paper and meet the guidelines for
permanence and durability of the Committee on Production Guidelines for Book
Longevity of the Council on Library Resources

Printed in the United States of America by Princeton Academic Press

1   3   5   7   9   10   8   6   4   2

For Willy, Zoey, and Aaron

————————————

CONTENTS

ILLUSTRATIONS

MAP

ACKNOWLEDGMENTS

MANY PEOPLE and institutions have contributed to the completion of this study, and it is a pleasure to be able to give them their due. To begin with, I am very grateful to the Danforth Foundation for support in graduate school; to the Social Science Research Council, the Bourse Chateaubriand of the French government, and the Council on Western European Studies at Yale University for dissertation research at the early stages of this project; and to the American Council of Learned Societies and the University of California President's Fellowship in the Humanities for postdoctoral research. That assistance has enabled me to collect the very different kinds of materials on which this book is based.

My most longstanding debt, personal and professional, is to John Merriman. He first introduced me to nineteenth-century French history and has been unflagging in his support ever since. For many years now, he has provided tours of archives and libraries in France, intellectual companionship, editorial advice, professional counsel, and alternating doses of coffee and Calvados as needed. In graduate school and beyond, Peter Gay was also an exemplary teacher, who not only offered expert advice on my work, but passed on materials and references from his own research. It was enormously helpful and a great pleasure to have his guidance.

Four historians of gender and women in the United States, Nancy Cott, Ellen DuBois, Carole Shammas, and Kathryn Kish Sklar have been invaluable mentors, interlocutors, and friends; their work has been an inspiration to my own. I owe special thanks to Tessie Liu, who years ago livened research in Paris and more recently carefully read and commented on the entire manuscript of this book. Many friends and fellow historians have read parts of this manuscript or discussed ideas in various stages and forms. My thanks to all of them: Elinor Accompo, Andrew Aisenberg, Michael Burns, Cissie Fairchilds, Robert Frost, Rachel Fuchs, Ruth Harris, Randy Head, Anne Higonnet, Patrice Higonnet, Seth Koven, Mark Micale, Sonya Michel, Patricia O'Brien, Karen Offen, Simon Schama, David Scobey, Cynthia Truant, and Liana Vardi. I have been lucky to have exceptionally gifted graduate students who also contributed research and editing: Margaret Talbot, Andrea Maestrejuan, and Bill Van Benschoten.

In France, Nancy Green, Nicole Pellegrin, Michelle Perrot, and Monique Peyrière all offered hospitality, informed readings, and references from their own work. I am grateful to Mr. Thierry Devynck and the other conservateurs at the Bibliothèque Forney in Paris and to Mr. Gérard Coulon and the wonderful staff at the Musée de la Chemiserie et de l'Elégance Masculine in Argenton-sur-Creuse for their cheerful help in finding and reproducing illustrations. In Los Angeles, Sally Stein and Amy Dru Stanley were companions through earthquakes and long drives, as well as perceptive readers; Ed Berenson generously read the manusript and related articles, for which I am very grateful; my colleagues at the University of California at Riverside, Lynda Bell, Roger Ransom, and Sharon Salinger, read chapters, made excellent suggestions, and sustained me through hectic times. Daniel Sherman and Paula Sanders have responded to my multiple pleas for help with the irony, humor, and support that one can only get from old friends. My new colleagues at the University of Texas at Austin, especially David Crew, and the students in my graduate seminars have created a stimulating environment in which to work. I would like to thank my editors at Princeton University Press, Beth Gianfagna, Lauren Osborne, and Brigitta van Rheinberg, for shepherding this book through the various stages of publication with such care. Their attentiveness, good judgment, and efficiency made working with them a pleasure.

I owe my love of France and Paris to friends with whom I have a long and particularly wonderful history—above all Catherine Fermand, Jean Philippe Pfertzel, Martine Méjean, Pierre Goldet, and Kattalin and Jean-Michel Gabriel. I thank them and their families for their boundless warmth and hospitality over many years. On this side of the Atlantic, Maria Rivera contributed more than she knows to the sanity and happiness of our household and the delicate balance of parenting and work. So did Darcy Vebber and Andy, Alexandra, and Jordan Romanoff. My own parents, Vi and Ned Coffin, provided me with much-needed "room of my own" during several summers; I would especially like to thank my mother for her expert editing, my father for crucial technical support, and both of them for their helpfulness, love, and encouragement during the long period this book was being written.

My greatest debt is to Willy Forbath, who has done more than any other person to help this book along. He has taken countless hours away from his own work to puzzle through issues with me and suggest better ways of presenting them. His patience, generosity, and historical sensibilities have lit every step of the path this book has taken. Zoey Forbath's empathy and precocious wisdom have buoyed my spirits on innumerable occasions, and Aaron Forbath's boisterous good humor has brought me perspective and joy. I dedicate this book to all three of them. That is surely not enough, but it is a token of my deep gratitude and love.

Material in chapters 1, 3, and 7 has been previously published in somewhat different versions:

"Gender and the Guild Order: Women and Men in the Paris Garment Trades," *Journal of Economic History* 54, no. 4 (December 1994). Copyright

1994 Cambridge University Press. Reprinted with the permission of Cambridge University Press.

"Credit, Consumption, and Images of Women's Desires: Selling the Sewing Machine in Late Nineteenth-Century France," *French Historical Studies* 18, no. 3 (Spring 1994). Copyright 1994 by Duke University Press.

"Production, Consumption, and Gender: The Sewing Machine in Nineteenth-Century France," in Laura L. Frader and Sonya O. Rose, eds., *Gender and the Reconstruction of Working-Class History in Europe.* Forthcoming, copyright 1996 by Cornell University Press. Used by permission of Cornell University Press.

"Social Science Meets Sweated Labor: Reinterpreting Women's Work in Late Nineteenth-Century France," *Journal of Modern History* 63 (June 1991). Copyright 1991 by The University of Chicago. All rights reserved.

The Politics of Women's Work

INTRODUCTION

"UP TO THIS POINT," wrote Jules Simon in 1860, "the needle has been the woman's tool par excellence. . . . More than half of the women who live from their labor are armed with a thimble and needle. That is a very large battalion."[1] As Simon saw it, however, battalion's weapons provided only a paltry defense against the perils of modern life: the inexorable combination of technological change, steam power, and market forces that promised to crush women's traditional work. The needleworkers in *L'ouvrière* (*The Woman Worker*), as Simon's study was titled, vividly illustrated what the author deemed the central drama of his time. In setting the needle against the sewing machine, femininity against the relentless advance of industry, and the organic against the mechanical, *L'ouvrière* inscribed the romantic drama into the literature of social investigation.

Like many of his contemporaries, Simon regarded the needle as an icon of femininity. More than virtually any other industry that employed women, the needle trades bore the weight of larger concerns about the character of modern femininity and the fate of womankind. This business and the "battalions" of women it employed loomed large in the countless nineteenth-century treatises on working women. Even the driest technical or economic studies seemed compelled to address larger social and gender issues, drawing lessons about female labor and poverty, pronouncing on women's fitness for work in industry and their duties as guardians of the hearth, and speculating about the origins and future of the gender division of labor.

If the needle stood as a symbol of femininity, women working in the garment industry exemplified what the nineteenth century first posed as the "problem" of female labor. The problem seemed endlessly fascinating and portentous. As historians recently have shown, gender has very often served as a way of discussing other topics, from definitions of "nature" to the character of political authority and social hierarchies.[2] In the nineteenth century, the broad cultural and metaphorical importance of gender made the topic of women's work nearly irresistible. Moreover, the topic lent itself to any number of approaches, from poetic to statistical or, as Jules Simon's book showed, both. Indeed, the issue of women's work became one of the

[1] Simon, *L'ouvrière*, p. 196. Simon borrowed the title from Jules Michelet's well-known indictment of female labor: "l'ouvrière! mot impie et sordide . . ." [the working woman! blasphemous and sordid word . . .]. Full references for sources cited more than once may be found in the bibiliography.

[2] Especially Lynn Hunt, *Politics, Culture, and Class in the French Revolution* (Berkeley and Los Angeles, 1984); Scott, *Gender and the Politics of History*; and Roberts, *Civilization without Sexes*.

crucial testing grounds for nineteenth-century social theory and a labora-
tory for sociological methods.

This book combines a social history of the "battalion" of needleworkers
with an intellectual history of the increasingly urgent and freighted debates
over female wage labor, and it weaves together several lines of inquiry. The
first concerns the transformation of women's work in this industry: the
changing role of women in the garment trades' labor force, the role of gender in the development and marketing of the sewing machine, manufacturers' eager search for female labor, and the shifting relations between family and market that shaped women's working lives. The second line of
inquiry involves the torrents of research on women's work and the men and
women (publicists, sociologists, working-class spokespersons, and labor
representatives) who navigated those tumultuous waters. Gender was not
always the factor that defined the work women did; how did it become so?
How did "women's work" become the proving ground for political economy
and social theory and the terrain for broader disputes? How were conceptions of gender transformed in the process? Answering these questions en-
tails considering changing forms of social investigation, economic analysis,
and cultural representation. The third line of inquiry examines the links
between the first two: the relationship between economic and cultural
change and how categories of thought generated in the nineteenth century
have shaped our historical understanding of female labor.

The pitched debates over women's work in nineteenth-century France
did not simply reflect changes in the industrial world. Again and again, in
the social research and reform literature, questions specific to the clothing
trade—questions about the organization of production, the division of markets, the acquisition of skills, or hierarchies in the labor force—became the
locus of a wide-ranging debate about industrial society and market culture.
Social scientists, political economists, trade union leaders, and feminists
expounded on the far-reaching social significance of women's wage work,
their theories and speculations informed by their views about markets,
property, the meaning of progress, justice, and so on. In the process,
women's wage work was rendered a symbol of numerous social ills and
injustices. The broader discussion revealed more about the gender and social ideology of the interlocutors than it did about the lives of working
women. As the poorly paid seamstress became the very image of poverty,
women's vulnerability, or the wrongs of market society, the wide variety of
needleworkers moved to the back of the stage. The particular struggles in
the needle trades faded from view. The garment industry provides a particularly interesting and revealing instance of how women's various productive
activities were transmuted during the nineteenth century into the social
question of "women's work."

The categories of thought generated in this process are embedded in the sources on which social historians draw. Examining them not only anchors sources in their historical context, but provides a case study of the production of knowledge. Moreover, it allows us to return to questions about the particularities of women workers, their practices, and their activities with a more critical purchase on the materials that give us access to their lives.

REINTERPRETING THE INDUSTRIAL REVOLUTION

The garment industry was one of the largest employers of industrial labor in France and easily the largest employer of women workers. In the second half of the nineteenth century, the numbers of clothing workers (male and female) more than doubled, rising from 761,000 to 1,484,000.[3] But changes did not take the form contemporaries expected, and they do not conform to popular conceptions of industrialization. New technologies came late, encountered fierce resistance from unexpected quarters, and were used unevenly. The industry remained labor intensive. Production did not move into factories, but instead remained dispersed in cottages and garret apartments, drawing on reservoirs of inexpensive, semi-skilled labor. The tenacity and vigor of *travail à domicile*, the French term for this kind of dispersed production, was one of the most distinctive and often remarked features of the garment trades.[4]

Historians used to consider industries like this one "traditional," and their importance in France as a benchmark of that country's economic traditionalism. This conception meshed with a broader picture of industrialization as an evolutionary process passing through sequential stages: from craft to mass production, from home to factory, and from independent artisan to wage earner. This was the picture sketched by nineteenth-century political economists and reproduced by twentieth-century historians influenced by Marxism and modernization theory alike. In the last ten years, however, this "narrow track" view of industrialization has been pushed aside by a more open-ended approach. Instead of stressing the inexorable logic of industrial development, historians have pointed out the "lurches, reverses, and contingencies" on the paths to modernity.[5] The forces behind

[3] The number of women in the clothing industry rose from 594,000 in 1866 to 1,380,000 in 1906, from 78 percent of the clothing industry's total labor force to 89 percent. Guilbert, *Les femmes et les organizations syndicales*, pp. 13–14.

[4] The term *travail à domicile* was widely used at the end of the nineteenth century to designate all kinds of production in the home, whether artisanal or subcontracted, but usually associated with large-scale manufacturing. For reasons to be considered later, the designation replaced earlier terms like *travail en chambre* or *travail isolé*. I have translated the terms as industrial homework or outwork.

[5] See especially Sabel and Zeitlin, "Historical Alternatives to Mass Production"; Samuel,

this new historiography have been both theoretical and empirical, and the results reinvigorating. Economic historians continue to discover industries, regions, and countries that defied the predictions of classical theory. Boldly sketched national contrasts (between, for instance, an advanced British economy and traditional French industry) no longer seem self-evident.[6] Rather than framing the questions historians ask, the categories of political economy are themselves becoming the subject of historical scrutiny. The technological determinism that has characterized much of the best writing on the industrial revolution, from Adam Smith and Karl Marx to David Landes, is being considered afresh.[7]

The study of gender has been crucial to this newly open-ended conception of industrial development. Women's historians have shown how gender molded hiring practices, manufacturers' strategies, lines of technological innovation, and workers' politics. In many instances, concerns to preserve gender hierarchies trumped economic rationality, technological efficiency, or political self-interest.[8] By demonstrating the power of discursive formations and cultural constructions, historians of gender have underscored that industrial and economic development did not unfold according to any single dynamic—whether that be capitalist or modernizing.[9]

The distinctive twists and turns of the clothing industry's history become doubly interesting in this new historiographical context. The industry quite defies characterization as a traditional trade: it grew too rapidly and changed in fundamentally important ways. Its history provides an opportunity to reconsider our inherited wisdom on the history of labor, women, and economic development, as well as an occasion to explore the unruly,

---

"The Workshop of the World"; and Alain Cottereau, "The Distinctiveness of Working-Class Cultures in France, 1848–1900," in Katznelson and Zolberg, eds., Working-Class Formation. I have borrowed "lurches, reverses, and contingencies" from Scranton, "Market Structure and Firm Size." See also his Proprietary Capitalism. William Reddy's argument in The Rise of Market Culture that nineteenth-century France never developed a "market culture," and his analysis of the clash between the premises of that culture and the social and cultural practices of textile workers points in the same direction.

    [6] The point is no longer that France was "traditional" or lagged behind Britain, but that the British model was "neither the exclusive path to modernity nor a close approximation to the pattern predicted by classical theory." Sabel and Zeitlin, "Historical Alternatives to Mass Production," p. 141.

    [7] Dolores Greenberg, "Energy, Power, and Perceptions of Social Change in the Early Nineteenth Century," American Historical Review 95, no. 4 (June 1990): 693–714; Berg, The Machinery Question; Scott, Gender and the Politics of History (discussed further below); and Reddy, The Rise of Market Culture.

    [8] Joan Scott, "The Mechanization of Women's Work," Scientific American 247, no. 3 (September 1982): 166–88; and Rose, Limited Livelihoods. Sabel and Zeitlin's continuing work does not engage gender except by implication. The best discussion of their thesis and the related literature is Liu, The Weaver's Knot, chap. 2.

    [9] Sabel and Zeitlin, "Historical Alternatives to Mass Production," p. 174.

often centrifugal forces at play in the process of industrialization, and to reflect on the manifold role of gender in that process.

HOME AND WORK

One of the most striking features of the garment industry's history is the resilience of industrial homework, which flourished and grew alongside new modes of production, rapidly expanding markets, and new patterns of consumption. Its role was bound up with a feminization of large sections of the industry's labor force, and in France, with the particularly high participation of married women in industry. Although the legions of outworkers at the end of the nineteenth century included many men, the earlier characteristics of homework, embedded in a different family economy, had changed, and the gender division of labor hardened. This development, with wide-ranging implications for our understanding of the process of industrialization and the position of women in it, forms the center of the book's social history.[10]

Of all the shorthand analyses of the social changes ushered in by industrialization, few have proved hardier than the "separation of home and work." It has loomed large in several generations of research on the reorganization of female labor in the nineteenth century.[11] The centralizing forces of capitalism, the argument goes, removed production from the home, cre-

[10] Cf. the different perspectives in Guilbert and Isambert-Jamati, *Travail féminin*; Cottereau, "The Distinctiveness of Working-Class Cultures in France"; Faraut, *Histoire de la Belle Jardinière*. The introduction to Schmiechen, *Sweated Industries*, discusses the enigmatic character of outwork and its relationship to factory labor on the one hand and older forms of putting out on the other. How *travail à domicile* does or does not fit into the alternative patterns of industrialization sketched by Sabel and Zeitlin is discussed in chapter 4. Boris, *Home to Work*.

[11] The most influential of these has been Ivy Pinchbeck's study of the industrial revolution in England, the conclusions of which have been widely applied. Pinchbeck considered the most important development of the early nineteenth century to have been the expulsion of labor from the household, as, in her words, "one industry after another was taken from the home by invention and the development of large-scale industry." Pinchbeck, *Women Workers*, p. 4; see also pp. 308–9. In her account, industrialization had removed both waged and unwaged labor from the household, creating better working conditions for (usually single) women who worked outside the home and more leisure time for women who stayed inside it. Pinchbeck was writing against the sociological wisdom of her time, which both traced and deplored women's departure from the hearth. She refused to join in the lament, arguing that domestic industry should not be romanticized and that large-scale industry provided better jobs for women. But she did not dispute the description of the process.

Pinchbeck's account of this process was thoroughly revised by Tilly and Scott, *Women, Work, and Family*, who proposed instead a historical succession of different models of a "family economy." For more recent reappraisals, see Maxine Berg, "Women's Work, Mechanization, and the Early Phases of Industrialization in Britain," in Joyce, ed., *The Historical Meanings of Work*; and idem, "What Difference Did Women's Work Make to the Industrial Revolution?" See also Joan Scott, "The Woman Worker," in Fraisse and Perrot, eds., *A History of Women in the West*, vol. 4.

ating new conflict between the work rhythms of industry and the demands of the household. As a result, women were driven from their once-central role in artisanal culture and production; older and married women particularly could not bridge the worlds of home and industry, and their waged labor was interrupted. The gulf between married and single women widened. Historians of the middle class have traced the same dynamic through bourgeois circles, arguing that from the late eighteenth century onward, capitalism extracted economic activity from familial networks, leaving middle-class women, once their husbands' business partners, in economic limbo.[12] According to this view, in both middle- and laboring-class worlds, industrialization separated the spheres of work and non-work. The former was marked "male," the latter "female." This sociological separation then became key to forming the new gender identities of the nineteenth century. Work, production, and the way they were valued forged male identity. The home emerged as the crucible of women's character. This understanding of the separation of home and work and its consequences has become one of the "master narratives" of nineteenth-century European history.

This narrative has provided a map of many developments and has led historians to important insights. Yet it has never done justice to the complexities of labor.[13] To see the home as a sphere of "non-work" begs crucial questions about unwaged labor and the social relations in which it was embedded: the division of labor within the household, struggles between men and women over resources, changing power relations, and the changing cultural meanings of "home."[14] Several historians have recently registered their dissent from the polarization of home and work as the respective

[12] Good representatives of the different generations include: Alice Clark, *The Working Life of Women in the Seventeenth Century* (London, 1919); Olive Schreiner, *Women and Labor* (New York, 1911); Pinchbeck, *Women Workers*; Smith, *Ladies of the Leisure Class*; Lenore Davidoff and Catherine Hall, *Family Fortunes* (London, 1987); and Howell, *Women, Production, and Patriarchy*.

[13] Among historians of women, these diverse criticisms are familiar. The grand narrative, however, remains ready-to-hand, and its powerful synthesis hard to resist. It continues to figure in studies of workingmen's politics or analyses of industrialization that try to integrate gender considerations without really taking on the complexities of women's work. Kathleen Canning has rightly pointed out labor historians' difficulties in coming to terms with research in gender or women's history. "Gender and the Politics of Class Formation."

[14] On households as "mixed economies" and the importance of women's unwaged labor, see Hausen, "Technical Progress and Women's Labour"; Elizabeth Blackmar, *Manhattan for Rent, 1785–1850* (Ithaca, N.Y., 1989), pp. 110–12, 122–24; and Boydston, *Home and Work*. On the continuing importance of the household, see Jean Quataert, "The Politics of Rural Industrialization: Class, Gender, and Collective Protest in the Saxon Oberlausitz of the Late Nineteenth Century," *Central European History* 20, no. 2 (June 1987): 91–124, and Michelle Perrot, Introduction to special issue on "Travaux de femmes au 19e siècle," *Le Mouvement Social* 105 (October–December 1978), p. 3. On struggles within the household, see Liu, *The Weaver's Knot*. On class formation, see Canning, "Gender and the Politics of Class Formation."

sites of female and male gender identity.[15] Moreover, histories that rely on this separation unintentionally reproduce other shopworn assumptions about the dynamics of industrial development: that capitalism by its character tends toward large-scale organization, centralization, and technological specialization, and that these are fundamentally incompatible with family, household, or small-scale production.

The abiding interest of women's work lies in its hybrid character, its melding of paid (industrial) and unpaid (domestic or household) labor, and the way in which it forces us to consider the continuing economic importance of the household as a center of production and of nonmarket resources in working families' budgets and strategies. This hybrid character shaped industrial and economic development, as well as gender roles and the division of labor within the family. In sewing work, where domestic and industrial labor were so intertwined, and in the garment industry, where homework was tenacious and resilient, the distinctiveness of women's work is particularly vivid. This hybrid character of women's work helped to shape the history of technology in the needle trades and, as we will also see, created obstacles for manufacturers to negotiate. In myriad ways, then, making sense of this history forces one to break out of the powerful polarities that have organized much of nineteenth-century working-class history: home and work, family and market, paid and unpaid labor.

CULTURE, GENDER, AND WOMEN

I began this study as a social historian with a strong sense of the importance of culture and representation, a sense powerfully confirmed by the recent work in the field. Despite mounting methodological discord, most scholars would agree that culture produces the forms and categories through which people (individually and collectively) build their sense of self, their work, and their interpretations of the world around them.[16] The subject of investi-

---

[15] To separate the two seriously underestimates the importance of family in transmitting to males work skills, craft status, and class consciousness and ignores the significance of politics, unions, and a hardy "work identity" in the lives of women. Canning, "Gender and the Politics of Class Formation," pp. 752–53; Hilden, *Working Women*, introduction and conclusion; and Kessler-Harris, *A Woman's Wage*, esp. chap. 3. Questions about the formation of women's identity were first raised by Davis, "Women in the Crafts in Sixteenth-Century Lyon," and the centrality of the home for middle-class women's consciousness set out by Smith, *Ladies of the Leisure Class*.

[16] They might, in principle, agree that culture shapes the categories through which historians, in turn, reconstruct and interpret the past. But the new approaches have created real epistemological turmoil in historical circles. Good discussions of these issues may be found in Hunt, *Politics, Culture, and Class in the French Revolution*; "Patrolling the Borders: Feminist Historiography and the New Historicism," roundtable in *Radical History Review*, 43, no. 1 (1989): 23–43; Judith R. Walkowitz, *City of Dreadful Delight: Narratives of Sexual Danger in*

gation, then, cannot be only the history of social structures or activities, but must include the meanings that attach to them.[17] In the case of women's work, that means studying not just the sexual division of labor, but its relationship to changing conceptions of masculine and feminine. In the case of labor history, it suggests not only the need to consider shifting structures of production, but also changing ways of thinking about labor, work, and value.[18]

William Sewell's *Work and Revolution in France*, an analysis of the changing conceptualization of labor and property from 1750 to 1848 and its political ramifications, illustrates both the insights of the cultural approach and its blindness regarding gender.[19] My interests parallel Sewell's in important respects. How the demise of the corporate order and the rise of political economy transformed the social analysis of work is a central question in this study. Similarly, I have set nineteenth-century policy debates, laws, and feminism in the context of century-long developments, inherited discourses, the accretion of precedents, and traditions that go back to the Old Regime. Still it is important to try to answer questions unasked in Sewell's pathbreaking study: how did the rise of political economy and socialism change representations of female labor, relations between working men and women, or women workers' self-understanding from the eighteenth to the nineteenth century?

The production and transmission of new forms of knowledge about society—the emerging discipline of sociology, new forms of social scientific fact and narrative, and, later in the century, the institutionalization of this research—stand among the most important developments of the nineteenth century, with sweeping implications for culture and politics. Bound up as they were with new "ways of seeing," representing, and governing, they have attracted enormous attention from social and intellectual historians.[20] No one interested in the history of social investigation or the trans-

---

Late-Victorian London (Chicago, 1992); Scott, *Gender and the Politics of History*; and Joyce Appleby, Lynn Hunt, and Margaret Jacobs, *Telling the Truth about History* (New York, 1994). The boldest claims about the role of culture are synthesized in Rose, *Limited Livelihoods*. The "culturalists" start from very diverse theoretical stances, from anthropology to postmodern literary theory. Some of their premises (particularly the anthropologists') are commonly accepted, others (above all the literary theorists') have generated enormous controversy.

[17] Judith Newton, "Family Fortunes: 'New History' and the 'New Historicism,'" *Radical History Review* 43 (1989): 6–11; Scott, *Gender and the Politics of History*, p. 41.

[18] Joyce, *The Historical Meanings of Work*.

[19] It is not clear whether or not women workers are intended to fit into the model that Sewell proposes, or what the newly forged language of labor implied for female labor. These observations also apply to Reddy's similarly pioneering *The Rise of Market Culture* and to the excellent collection of essays edited by Kaplan and Koepp, *Work in France*.

[20] In addition to Foucault's work in general; Sewell, *Work and Revolution*; Reddy, *The Rise of Market Culture*; and Scott, *Gender and the Politics of History*; see Coleman, *Death Is a Social*

formation of social paradigms can afford to ignore gender either as a topic or an analytic category. It is well established, for instance, that the "social question" (a broad term for the interlocking issues of poverty, unemployment, and economic inequality) dominated the first half of the century. Here I want to explore how and when the "woman question" emerged as a distinct and distinctly problematic issue.[21]

Gender and women have found exceptionally able advocates among French historians. Indeed, their representation (in the lawyerly sense) has been so brilliant and multifaceted that any new *amicus* brief has to determine which of many different claims to pursue.[22] I am interested, first, in how gender (understood as the cultural significance attached to sexual differences) figured in particular historical processes—in this instance shaping the guilds, manufacturing strategies, technological innovation, and social reforms. I am interested in the emergence of gender as an analytic category in nineteenth-century political economy and social science. Last, I am interested in the history of self-conscious reflection and debates on the social significance of gender from the late eighteenth to the early twentieth century.

Historians in this field, chief among them Joan Scott, have convincingly demonstrated the myriad ways in which gender figures in political discourse, social practices, and power relations. It is worth underscoring that gender thus conceived differs from previous conceptions of patriarchal ideology or prescription. Gender works as a set of assumptions that structure the social whole (in anthropological terms) or signify relations of power (in the terms of literary theory).[23] Thus gender becomes a relevant analytic category in any number of historical matters that are not the conventional province of "women's" history and even in historical episodes in which women do not necessarily figure as social or political actors.[24]

Disease; Robert Nye, *Crime, Madness, and Politics in Modern France: The Medical Concept of National Decline* (Princeton, N.J., 1984); Susanna Barrows, *Distorting Mirrors: Visions of the Crowd in Late Nineteenth-Century France* (New Haven, Conn., 1981); Bertrand Gille, *Les sources statistiques de l'histoire de France* (Paris, 1980); Michelle Perrot, *Enquêtes sur la condition ouvrière*; Institut national de la statistique et des études économiques, *Pour une histoire de la statistique* (Paris, 1977); Gérard Leclerc, *L'observation de l'homme: Une histoire des enquêtes sociales* (Paris, 1979).

[21] Riley suggests the important lines of inquiry in *Am I That Name?*

[22] See Scott's explication of three uses of gender: (1) as a synonym for women, (2) as a topic, and (3) as an analytic category in *Gender and the Politics of History*, pp. 28–31.

[23] As Rose puts it, gender was "built into the fabric of everyday practices, commonsense thinking, and public policies." *Limited Livelihoods*, p. 91. See also Liu, *Weaver's Knot* and Scott, *Gender and the Politics of History*.

[24] By the same token, historians interested in gender need not confine themselves to the topic of women. See Scott, *Gender and the Politics of History*, pp. 45–50. Gender as a "system of signifying" or "web of cultural references" does not have to be grounded in the "social relations between the sexes." Many feminist historians are persuaded that our most important histo-

My project here, however, is to analyze the historically specific ways in which definitions of "male" and "female" shape the lives of men and women and to consider how those definitions change over time. Demonstrations that gender is "always there" risk becoming transhistorical, losing sight of the changing content and significance of gender differences. Gender may play a critical role in a particular historical domain in one period and prove less salient in another. In the eighteenth century gender was understood as a relationship of authority; by the nineteenth it was understood as a division of labor. Moreover, the pace of change in gender codes and relations neither follows from nor neatly parallels changes in other dimensions of a social order. Important tensions arise between social change and inherited cultural formations. In order to trace and explain such processes, this book examines a long period of time, from eighteenth-century battles about the sexual division of labor in the needle trades to early-twentieth-century debates over the minimum wage bill.

Nineteenth-century ideas about women and labor did not stand as a bloc. Nor did they reflect a single ideology of domesticity or "bourgeois ideal." Powerful unspoken premises were shared by all who broached the topic of women's work in the nineteenth-century industrial world, but it would be a mistake to suppress the explosive differences of opinion on the subject, or to ignore the distinctive contours of French debates. Accordingly, I have worked to restore a sense of real debate, exchange, and transformation. The chapters that follow set out a number of key developments that shaped how women's work was defined and discussed: the emergence of political economy and its critics, the institutionalization of sociological research, struggles in the labor movement, and the increased visibility and pressing claims of feminists. In examining these debates and changes over time, this book considers how they contributed to changing what an early-twentieth-century scholar aptly called the "yardstick of value" by which society measured women's worth.[25] It also adds a comparative dimension, showing how French research and debates on women's work differed from those in other countries.

Some may feel that such an intellectual and cultural history short-circuits the agency of women workers themselves. The problems in uncovering

riographical contribution will lie in developing gender as a theoretical concept. Recent work on gender and industrialization, for instance, summons us to go beyond the topic of women's work. See Canning,"Gender and the Politics of Class Formation"; and Baron, ed., *Work Engendered*, introduction. The dangers of prematurely abandoning women as a topic, however, are considerable. See Sonya O. Rose, "Gender History / Women's History: Is Feminist Scholarship Losing Its Critical Edge?"; and Kathleen Canning, "German Particularities in Women's History / Gender History"; and comments by Anna Clark and Marianna Valverde in *Journal of Women's History* 5, no. 1 (Spring 1993): 89–128.

[25] Kim, *Féminisme et travail féminin*, p. 13.

working women's agency are well known, and variously diagnosed as archival (a dearth of sources) and epistemological.[26] Joan Scott's work is routinely criticized for ignoring agency, but her critics often argue in a way that simply assumes the role of agency rather than demonstrating how it might work.[27] At times women's agency (like men's) is registered in words; at other times, in acts. Despite the real constraints of the sources, we can explore the different possible logics of that agency and experience. Many female voices make themselves heard in this history: seamstresses writing petitions, women addressing trade unions, and feminists writing on the minimum wage bill. The growing importance of both women scholars and feminist paradigms in the tradition of social scientific investigation is one of my subjects. Among the small groups of working- and middle-class women who petitioned the government, undertook sociological research, lobbied for laws, and spoke at trades unions congresses, however, there was no single "woman's" voice. Gender by no means assured uniformity, still less unanimity on any of the issues surrounding women's labor.

An Overview

How and when did sewing come to be seen as "women's work?" Jules Simon's conviction that sewing was the most traditional of women's trades has been echoed by countless modern historians. Following the cues of their nineteenth-century sources, historians have attributed the division of labor in industry to the allocation of tasks in the household, and they have explained the feminization of sewing in the nineteenth century with reference to women's duties in the family and the skills they acquired in the household. In fact, sewing tasks, skills, and technologies were gendered in far more interesting ways. Part I of this book traces that process. The first chapter treats eighteenth-century battles between men and women in the needle trades. Chapter 2 sets out the rules of the game elaborated after the collapse of the guilds. An (officially) free market in labor intensified struggles over men's and women's entitlements and their positions in shift-

[26] In addition to the sources already noted, see Berlanstein, "Working with Language"; Canning, "Feminist History after the Linguistic Turn"; Rose, *Limited Livelihoods*, "gender shapes social relations and social practices, it constitutes social agents as men and women" (p. 191). See the exchanges between Laura Lee Downs ("If 'Woman' Is Just an Empty Category") and Joan Scott ("Response") in *Comparative Studies in Society and History* 35, no. 2 (1993): 414–51; between Linda Gordon and Joan Scott, *Signs* (Summer 1990): 848–60; and between Seyla Benhabib, Judith Butler, Drucilla Cornell, and Nancy Fraser in Benhabib et al., *Feminist Contentions: A Philosophical Exchange* (New York, 1995). For a particularly telling example of how representation—in the sense of changing conceptions of "womanhood"—can shape women's agency and politics, see Talbot, "An Emancipated Voice."

[27] Downs, "If 'Woman' Is Just an Empty Category," Scott, "Response," and Judith Butler, "Contingent Foundations," in Butler and Scott, eds., *Feminists Theorize the Political* (New York, 1992), p. 13.

ing economic hierarchies, redefining gender and making it salient in ways that it had not been in the guild world. Chapter 3 shows how decisively both these developments shaped the history of the sewing machine.

As Siegfried Giedion has observed, while the eighteenth century vested its faith in progress in science, the nineteenth century placed its hopes in mechanization.[28] The sewing machine figures prominently in chapters 2 and 3, not as a technological determinant, but as a lightning rod for contemporaries' vaulting hopes and deep fears. By the 1860s, it was beginning to replace the needle as the icon of femininity. Political economists' certainties that technology could eliminate drudgery and lift the human condition encouraged high-flown optimism about the emancipation of womankind. At the same time, newly minted views of what constituted "femininity" guaranteed opposition and cries of outrage from writers like Jules Simon, doctors writing about the female body, and workers themselves—both male and female. These powerful cultural crosscurrents made advertising the sewing machine a revealingly difficult venture. The prevalence of homework in the clothing trades and the poverty of clothing workers further complicated the introduction of sewing technologies. Selling the sewing machine was bound up in a series of nineteenth-century economic and cultural experiments and innovations: the promotion of credit payment plans, new kinds of marketing, and a new science of advertising, with rapidly changing imagery and tactics.

Part Two (chapters 4 and 5) turns away from broad economic and cultural developments to focus on homework itself. The expansion of homework in the late nineteenth century was a response to multiple imperatives: family strategies, manufacturers' contradictory needs, and regional economic development. The principal sources for these chapters are social scientific studies of homework conducted by the French Office du Travail between 1890 and 1914. These studies constitute an important chapter in the history of French sociology and as such are of compelling interest in their own right. They also allow us to explore the workings of the family economy in the late nineteenth century, the meaning of "domesticity" in the popular classes, the balance of waged and unwaged work, and the contribution of both to the household.

The Office du Travail's studies helped to create a furor about "sweated labor," spawning innumerable articles and studies, international reform organizations, and, eventually, demands for minimum wage legislation. This argument raged in all the advanced industrial countries; in France it was inextricable from the cultural crisis of the fin de siècle. In part III (chapters 6–8), this debate also emerges as an unusually rich and important moment

---

[28] *Mechanization Takes Command* (New York, 1948), pp. 30–31.

in the ongoing discussion of female labor. This part follows the politics of this debate through circles of trade unions, feminists, and social reformers, asking how the assumptions underlying this discussion had shifted since the controversy over the guilds in the late eighteenth century or the anxious speculations and prophecies about the sewing machine in the 1840s. The book concludes with the minimum wage bill of 1915. As a legal reform it distilled some of these crucial long-term developments, redefining the terms in which women could participate in industry. Yoked as it was to the social changes of the First World War, it also marked the emergence of new patterns of women's work in the twentieth century.

Any account is partial. The garment industry offers more than enough material for studies of tailors, whose boisterous politics and exceptionally politicized culture put them at the forefront of nineteenth-century artisanal movements. The industry also offers material for histories of Jewish men and women or broad-gauged studies of immigration. Since fashion, taste, and the consumption of clothing have been subjects of extensive study, they take up little room here.[29]

The history of the garment industry per se, then, is not the subject of this book; I am interested rather in aspects of nineteenth-century France which that history throws into relief: the character of industrial organization, the sexual division of labor, and changing representations of work, whether cultural or social scientific.

This is not a uniquely French story. It is about the process of industrialization in Europe and the history of European social science. My interest in it has also been sustained by a concern with recurring dilemmas about women in the labor force that have preoccupied my generation of feminists: why women's work is persistently undervalued, how the labor movement has dealt with difficult issues like part-time labor and homework, and the clash between bureaucratic norms embodied in laws and the day-to-day strategies of working families.[30] These dilemmas, however, have to be confronted in their historical specificity. I bring out the particularly French inflections of this history: the character of French economic development, the arena in which women's reform movements operated, the Le Playan current in French sociology, and the relative absence of the kind of "separate spheres" thinking that flourished in other countries. Part III in particu-

---

[29] Vanier, La mode et ses métiers; Johnson, "Economic Change and Artisan Discontent"; idem, "Patterns of Proletarianization"; idem, Utopian Communism in France: Cabet and the Icarian Movement (Ithaca, N.Y., 1974); Green, The Pletzl of Paris; Roche, La culture des apparences; Philippe Perrot, Les dessus et les dessous; Valerie Steele, Fashion and Eroticism (Oxford, 1985); Elizabeth Wilson, Adorned in Dreams: Fashion and Modernity (London, 1985); Bourdieu, Distinction; Auslander, Taste and Power.

[30] Boris, "Homework and Women's Rights"; Boris and Daniels, eds., Homework.

lar offers rich comparative possibilities with the literature on American and English feminism, reform movements, and welfare state formation.[31] Limitations on space make it impossible to do all those comparisons justice in this book. But those of us who have chosen to study cultures that are not our own always reckon with the constraints of distance. However deep our identification with those cultures, our implicitly comparative perspective may be among our most valuable contributions to their histories.

[31] Including Sklar, *Florence Kelley*, vol. 1; Koven and Michel, eds., *Mothers of a New World*; Pedersen, *Family, Dependence, and the Origins of the Welfare State*; Ellen Mappen, ed., *Helping Women at Work: The Women's Industrial Council, 1889–1914* (London: Hutchinson, 1985).

PART I

Redefining Gender and Work

Chapter One

WOMEN'S WORK? MEN AND WOMEN, GUILD AND CLANDESTINE PRODUCTION IN EIGHTEENTH-CENTURY PARIS

MORE THAN a woman worker, a seamstress is part of a social and cultural enterprise that we have come to consider distinctively feminine. Making clothing, creating fashion, maintaining wardrobes, and dressing families all seem indissolubly gendered. Yet the image of sewing as a womanly activity is relatively recent. So is the gradual feminization of the needle trades, a trend produced by several related developments in the eighteenth century: the expansion of the clothing trades, protracted battles waged by women's guilds, and the growth of clandestine, non-guild, labor. These developments changed the character of women's work in eighteenth-century Paris and set the stage for nineteenth-century economic developments.

The importance of recounting the eighteenth-century history of the garment trades is not simply to provide a foil for dramatic developments during the century that followed. French historians no longer see the Revolution of 1789–1815 as *the* critical threshold of social, cultural, and economic change.[1] The eighteenth century brought rapid changes in the production and consumption of clothing, changes that helped to establish Paris as the "grand foyer du travail féminin," or "great center of female labor." Nineteenth-century writers would charge that the recruitment of women into the labor force, the deplorable "industrialization of women," was wrought by rapacious capitalists in their own day. But the feminization of the clothing trades is a longer and less familiar story, one with more female agency than nineteenth-century writers would acknowledge and with fewer decisive normative conceptions of femininity than we might expect. That history is crucial to understanding nineteenth-century debates and processes.

[1] The now familiar criticisms of the "social interpretation" of the French Revolution; studies of the relationship between the Revolution and the development of French capitalism; and new histories of consumption, industrial production, and the French economy have all, in very different ways, blurred older panoramas and their landmarks. See also Roche, *La culture des apparences*; Kaplan, "Les 'faux ouvriers'"; Fairchilds, "The Production and Marketing of Populuxe Goods"; Sewell, *Work and Revolution*; Maurice Agulhon, *La république au village* (Paris, 1970); Reddy, *The Rise of Market Culture*; Auslander, *Taste and Power*.

Spindle, Shuttle, and Needle

In the nineteenth century, collections of folklore compiled tales, proverbs, and engravings in ways that evoked a simple world, where the respective talents, responsibilities, and crafts of men and women had always been distinct and complementary.[2] With the sweep and conviction of axioms meant to capture the essential order of the social world and the meaning of life, these images seemed to transform women's work into a metaphorical activity, associated with life cycles and fertility. In *Légendes et curiosités des métiers*, Paul Sébillot's 1895 compendium of French folklore about the trades, both sewing and spinning figured, characteristically, as "attributes of womanhood" rather than occupations.[3]

The vast majority of "traditional" engravings and stories involve spinning, not sewing, although later the meanings proved easily transferred.[4] Paintings and popular engravings pictured female figures of all kinds with distaffs. Their associations with generational continuity (the thread of life) gave distaffs and spindles symbolic importance in funerary reliefs and courting and marriage rituals. Villagers gave newlywed peasant couples a spindle or distaff. In the fifteenth and sixteenth centuries, aristocratic suitors gave their brides-to-be distaffs embellished with family emblems and religious symbols. Through a nineteenth-century prism these gifts seemed admonitions to household duties and domesticity, but in early modern France they had sacred connotations involving ancestral traditions and religious values.[5] In traditional Gallic wedding ceremonies, the bride's maid carried a ritual distaff and either placed it in the hands of a saint in the chapel or laid it across the top of a wedding chest. In some regions, custom invited the bride actually to spin during the marriage ceremony, proving her

---

[2] Late-nineteenth-century collections also emphasized the harmony and complementarity of the sexes. Arlette Farge's anthology of writings from the Bibliothèque bleue, where many of the texts are exuberantly misogynist, provides an instructive contrast. *Miroir des femmes*, pp. 13, 15.

[3] Paul Sébillot, *Légendes et curiosités des métiers* (Paris, 1895), "Fileuses," p. 1; "Tailleurs," p. 16.

[4] Natalie Kampen, "Social Status and Gender in Roman Art," in Norma Broude and Mary Garrard, eds., *Feminism and Art History: Questioning the Litany* (New York, 1982), p. 72. Many of these tales and images stem from the Greek myth of Arachne, the master spinner punished for her virtuosity by the jealous Athena. Arachne challenges Athena (goddess of handicrafts as well as of learning and the arts) to a contest. Arachne wins the contest, but is turned into a spider and condemned to continue her trade eternally, spinning the yarn from her own body and weaving her web. *New Larousse Encyclopedia of Mythology* (London, 1959), pp. 107–8; and Marta Weigle, *Spiders and Spinsters: Women and Mythology* (Albuquerque, N.M., 1982), pp. 208–9.

[5] Sébillot, "Fileuses," p. 6; Annette Weiner and Jane Schneider, eds., *Cloth and Human Experience* (Washington, D.C., 1989), pp. 3–4, 21.

competence and, symbolically, her virtue and fecundity, acting out her transition to wife and mother.[6]

Yet these images do not constitute evidence of a timeless association of spinning and sewing with women's duties and the attributes of femininity.[7] They had very different resonances and associations, some ancient, some medieval, and none with any necessary bearing on women's domestic tasks or (even more emphatically) women's role in formal economic activity. The early modern wedding ceremonies evoked fecundity; the distaff as wedding gift referred to ancestral power or lineage; the thread symbolized magical powers. Prescriptive literature recommending needlework as a token of feminine domesticity, or womanly industry (in the early modern sense of diligence) and devotion, seems to have originated with the Counter Reformation's insistence on religious and moral education, when sewing appeared in treatises on female education as "moralizing" work, which taught discipline, patience, and concentration—reinforcing women's sense of their social role and position.[8]

In the nineteenth century, novelists and poets, political economists, and industrialists all summoned these older images of women at the spinning wheel and with needle in hand to show that sewing had *always* been women's work. Sewing machine advertisers in particular tapped into literature and folklore, reappropriated the spinning imagery, and, brashly playing with historical analogies, presented the "Singer girl" as a modern-day Penelope. This worked-over imagery and invented traditionalism, however, is a poor guide to either the early modern history of the clothing trades or changing definitions of gender. It is not simply that the relationship of prescriptive literature to the organization of either household labor or economic activity is tenuous; in this case the prescriptions themselves are absent or contradictory. Once one leaves behind the familiar gender certainties of the nineteenth century, it is nearly impossible to find any single set of convictions, whether elite or popular, about men's and women's respective economic domains. As we will see, in the eighteenth century, tailors' deeply held convictions about the political-economic order clashed with seamstresses' claims about their entitlements, and Enlightened physiocratic writing contradicted corporate (i.e., guild) logic on the sexual division of labor. The assuredness of nineteenth-century popular lore—especially as distilled in collections like Sébillot's—does not even hint at

---

[6] Sébillot, "Couturières," pp. 1–3.

[7] These folktales' resemblance to either unbowdlerized tales, "popular" beliefs, or social practices is hardly self-evident. See, among others, Robert Darnton, *The Great Cat Massacre and Other Episodes in French Cultural History* (New York, 1984).

[8] Roche, *La culture des apparences*, pp. 254, 290–91. For parallels, see Parker, *The Subversive Stitch,* p. 18 and chap. 5.

the complex history of ideas about the sexual division of labor or the long history of fierce disputes between men and women in the garment trades.

Historians often assert that needlework as an industrial occupation for women arose from the sexual division of labor in the household.[9] This, too, is an oversimplification, one that arises from assuming the primacy of household organization in the structure of women's lives and labors. The links between the household division of tasks, craft organization, and, later, the industrial division of labor are less predictable than common wisdom implies.

GUILDS AND GARMENTS

We assume that before the industrial revolution clothing, at least for ordinary people, was made at home. This is not so. By the eighteenth century, even in France's villages, clothing was inextricable from trade and the cash nexus. As far as regional historians have been able to determine, women knit socks and vests for their families. They also invested as many hours as their social standing permitted embroidering, washing, and storing household linens. These items formed a *trousseau*, and maintaining them through life's crucial transitions lent them a sacred and ritual character. The rest of the family's clothing, however, was usually made by village tailors.[10] Those who could not afford cloth or tailoring bought secondhand clothing.[11] For the poor as well as for the better off, then, clothing came from the market, and apart from linens and undergarments, making of clothes in rural areas was dominated by men.

In cities, however, and particularly in Paris, the place of women in clothing production was far larger. Indeed, the expansion of female artisanship and wage labor, tightly bound up with the multiplication of trades for increasingly differentiated markets, was among the most distinctive marks of the Parisian economy.[12] Describing these trades is no simple matter. The

[9] Sally Alexander argues that industrialization drew upon skills women had developed in the family and projected them into a wider arena. "Women's Work in Nineteenth-Century London." Cf. Gullickson, *Spinners and Weavers of Auffay*; and Howell, *Women, Production, and Partiarchy*.

[10] Well into the nineteenth century, women did not sew for their families. Roche, *La culture des apparences*, pp. 252–53; Nicole Pellegrin, "Techniques et production du vêtement en Poitou, 1880–1950," in Pellegrin et al., *L'aiguille et le sabaron*, pp. 252–53; and Bouvier, *La lingerie et les lingères*, pp. 157, 165. See, generally, Verdier, *Façons de dire*, for rural anthropology.

[11] That trade was governed by the fripiers, or used-clothing dealers, who cleaned, remade, and sold secondhand clothes. Inexpensive used clothes could also be had from street peddling "resellers," whose trade was unregulated. Boileau, *Les métiers et corporations*, introduction; Dusautoy, "Habillement des deux sexes," in *Exposition universelle de 1867*, pp. 4–7; Roche, *Le peuple de Paris* and *La culture des apparences*; and Fairchilds, "The Production and Marketing of Populuxe Goods."

[12] See Godineau, *Citoyennes tricoutouses*; Benabou, *De la prostitution et la police*; Roche, *La*

textile and clothing trades included an extraordinary variety of merchants and craftspersons with overlapping specialties: drapers; mercers or dry goods merchants; those who sold trimmings; those who made accessories; the central guilds of tailors, seamstresses, and linen drapers; those who dyed, bleached, and cleaned; the used clothing dealers; and so on.[13] The number of specialized trades alternately expanded and contracted as more powerful guilds first absorbed weaker ones, and then lost them again, or were forced to yield the rights to produce or sell new fashions to new groups of workers and merchants.[14]

Any effort to tally the numbers employed in the clothing business comes up against two problems: the bewildering number of trades and the un-knowns of clandestine production. Next to these difficulties, the absence of reliable general statistics seems a minor issue. Daniel Roche, who has stud-ied the eighteenth-century Parisian economy as carefully as any historian, estimates that at the beginning of the century the clothing trades occupied fifteen thousand masters and mistresses, and about twenty thousand workers. That was approximately twice as many employers and workers as in textiles, and accounted for more than 40 percent of all Parisian employers and workers.[15] Even rough reckonings, then, underscore the weight of this industry in the Parisian economy. In certain districts, especially the central ones around the rues de la Lingerie, Saint-Denis, Saint-Antoine, or Saint-Honoré, clothing overwhelmed all other economic activities.

Paris stood apart from other Old Regime cities. Nowhere else did the fashion industry employ such numbers. Parisian guilds were firmly en-trenched and especially disputatious. Parisian guildswomen were partic-ularly outspoken. Above all, Paris was the case that preoccupied economic thinkers and policymakers. Thus the battles between the men's and women's guilds recounted here assumed singular importance in late-

---

culture des apparences; Arlette Farge, Vivre dans la rue à Paris au XVIIIe siècle (Paris, 1979); Jeffry Kaplow, The Names of Kings: The Parisian Laboring Poor in the Eighteenth Century (New York, 1972); Truant, "The Guildswomen of Paris."

[13] The powerful mercers had the rights to market all kinds of goods made by others, from fabrics to furniture. In the nineteenth century their commerce would be taken over by the department stores. Marchands de modes or, later, modistes specialized in trimmings for dresses, and the trade was often the charge of the mercer's wife. As women's fashion became more elaborate and dress trimmings became increasingly central to design, modistes began to sell gowns that they had designed or trimmed themselves. They were the aristocracy of the fashion world, and in the nineteenth century would dominate the world of haute couture. The term also referred to those who began to sell umbrellas, snuffboxes, and other accessories. Roche, La culture des apparences, pp. 259–61, 264, 281; and Fairchilds, "The Production and Marketing of Populuxe Goods," pp. 28–29.

[14] Lespinasse, Les métiers et corporations, vol. 3, s.v. "vêtement."

[15] That count, however, includes groups such as wig makers, bouquet makers, and laun-dresses. Roche, La culture des apparences, pp. 265–67.

eighteenth-century public debate, and, later, in historical memories of the Old Regime.

THE TAILORS

The tailors' guild believed its domain encompassed all clothing sales and production, and its history is one of incessant battles over that matter. Publicly recognized bodies, the guilds conferred a civic identity on their members and marked them as honorable and creditworthy.[16] The guilds governed the labor market and imposed discipline. Apprenticeship defined skills and regulated their acquisition. The requirements for mastership, enforced by guild officers (*jurés*) were intended to guarantee standards of quality and production, protecting the buying public against fraud. Guild officers therefore had the right to visit members' workshops and to ferret out "clandestine" production. Finally, by patrolling the boundaries between different trades, they regulated competition.

The most powerful guild tailors were merchants, whose wealth and ties to trade contributed to the community's high profile.[17] In production, the guild ranked master tailors, charged with the cut and drape of the fabric, above those who sewed. As the tailoring trades consolidated in the eighteenth century and women were hired as sewers, the trade became more hierarchical.[18] The tailors' guild staunchly defended this ordering of skill and value. A cutter could ruin an extremely valuable fabric with one stroke of the scissors (". . . the slips of a [master] tailor's hand are irreparable. . . .). Sewing labor was an "accessory."[19] The combination of expensive material and cheap labor shaped the form of production characteristic of the clothing industry: merchant capital joined to domestic production.

All of the Parisian trades attempted to police clandestine production, but few worried about it more than the tailors' guild. Tailors accused clandestine workers of driving down prices, making cheap imitations of good clothes, and using shoddy materials.[20] The issue was competition, but questions of legal and political identity heightened the economic stakes. As the

[16] "Réflexions des maîtres tailleurs de Paris, sur le project de supprimer les jurandes." Bibliothèque Nationale, Department of Manuscripts, Joly de Fleury Collection, vol. 462 (1776), fol. 173, p. 3.

[17] For parallels see Simona Cerutti, "Group Strategies and Trade Strategies: The Turin Tailors' Guild in the Late 17th Century and Early 18th Century," in Stuart Woolf, ed., *Domestic Strategies: Work and Family in France and Italy, 1600–1800* (Cambridge, 1991).

[18] Older hierarchies flowed from the market for which an artisan produced and newer ones from the skills he or she brought to the production process.

[19] "Réflexions des maîtres tailleurs," Joly de Fleury, vol. 462, fol. 173, p. 4. On hierarchies in earlier times, see Boileau, *Les métiers et corporations*, introduction; and Lespinasse, *Les métiers et corporations*, p. 178.

[20] "Réflexions des maîtres tailleurs," Joly de Fleury, vol. 462, fol. 173; Lespinasse, *Les métiers et corporations*, pp. 189, 190, 196.

tailors' guild put it, a non-guild tailor was no more than an "unknown artisan, without estate . . . a fickle being, always ready to escape and who will only have to flee the neighborhood in order to escape debt." Clandestine production threatened the "indispensable circulation of trust" basic to the metropolitan economy, merchant capital, and social peace.[21]

The tailors' guild regularly banned women from working in the trade. Yet women's work was more common and visible than such bans suggest. Tailors' wives and daughters were crucial to the business.[22] They could work by their husbands' or fathers' sides, and they could legally make clothing for women and young children. Guild statutes drafted in 1660 tried to clarify policy on women's participation. Tailors were not to employ "clandestine workers, seamstresses or workers from used clothing [fripières]." Such directives were aimed at independent female labor, that is, women who did not belong to guild tailors' families. A widow could continue to practice her husband's trade and to employ apprentices already in training. But the guild strictly limited her rights. Eager to assure continuity and discipline in apprenticeship, the guild blocked the creation of larger enterprises run by women and encouraged widows to remarry within the trade. The political import of the new statutes was unambiguous: however routine women's work might be, it was only acceptable in the context of a patriarchal workshop. Moreover, that work conferred no political rights whatsoever. The guild's stream of injunctions on the subject underscored the point: "no women or girls may have any privileges under any name or pretext whatsoever."[23] The formation of a seamstresses' guild fifteen years later, as we will see, was the next round in the battle between tailors and women, at least those women who would not be their wives.

The patriarchal reasoning behind these guild regulations is clear. Larger questions concerning the logic of corporate thinking about gender and why some trades were "male" and "female" remain unanswered.[24] Some distinctions seem to have been rooted in the household division of labor. Other

[21] "Réflexions des maîtres tailleurs," Joly de Fleury, vol. 462, fol. 173. The political aspects of guild history are particularly well explored by Steven Kaplan, "Social Classification and Representation in the Corporate World of Eighteenth-Century France: Turgot's Carnival," in Kaplan and Koepp, *Work in France*. On the meanings of "estate," see Sewell, *Work and Revolution*, pp. 190–91.

[22] "Réflexions des maîtres tailleurs," Joly de Fleury, vol. 462, fol. 173.

[23] "Statuts des tailleurs pourpointiers," 1660, cited in Lespinasse, *Les métiers et corporations*, 3:195, 197, 198. The developments in Paris seem to have paralleled those in other European cities, which also restricted women's rights in the craft trades. See Merry Weisner, *Working Women in Renaissance Germany* (New Brunswick, N.J., 1986), pp. 160–62.

[24] On this, cf. Lyndal Roper, *The Holy Household: Women and Morals in Reformation Augsburg* (Oxford, 1989), pp. 40–49; and Howell, *Women, Production, and Patriarchy*. Quataert discusses the issue briefly in "The Shaping of Women's Work in Manufacturing," p. 1132. William Sewell lucidly sets out the logic of guild hierarchies, but not how gender would fit into that logic. *Work and Revolution*, pp. 20–23.

distinctions arose from the hierarchy of craft. Tools, associated with craft and jealously guarded as trade secrets, were often off limits to anyone but masters.[25] Still other gender distinctions had less obvious meanings. In Paris, for example, all trades that used silk or gold thread as a primary material were given over entirely to women. The women in those trades may well have been members of wealthy merchant families with access to expensive material through their families' trade. Female guilds resulted from prominent families' efforts to extend their control over different sections of trade and production.[26] Finally, some aspects of the gender division of labor were simply accidental. Household organization often departed from principles. Maintaining patriarchal hierarchies could conflict with the efficient deployment of a family's labor and resources, and a woman might assume an unaccustomed role because she was the only one available to do it, because she was temporarily at the head of the household, or because she was less expensive to hire.

No strict logic governed the gender division of labor in the guild world for several reasons. First, guilds upheld "custom" without having to justify it in higher terms. Second, gender and work had meanings that are unfamiliar to us. In the corporate outlook, the political status of women, subsumed in the household, seemed self-evident; women's place in a gendered division of labor did not. Although the household division of tasks may occasionally have figured in establishing certain traditions of work, that division was not, in principle, a point of reference for the guild order. That women performed certain tasks within the household economy was irrelevant outside the context of that household, in a different economic and political world. Such labor did not give women any title to the civic identity and power established by the guilds, which were, fundamentally, units of *political* power, legitimated as one of the three estates.[27]

In the end, custom, in the sense of the accumulation of precedents and exceptions, reigned, and no principle was definitive. Men's and women's craft and merchant rights were repeatedly redefined in boundary disputes, the outcome of which varied by region. As the corporate order eroded,

[25] Boileau, *Livre des métiers*, cited in Guilbert, *Les fonctions des femmes dans l'industrie*, p. 24. On the links between tools, craft knowledge, responsibility, and liberty, see Kaplan, "Les 'faux ouvriers,'" p. 327.

[26] Howell, *Women, Production, and Patriarchy*, p. 130. See also Cerutti, "Group Strategies and Trade Strategies," pp. 102–47.

[27] Moreover, women's labor in the trades did not, by guild logic, give them any political entitlement. The guilds ordered the world by social standing and occupation, attaching to economic activities meanings that are very different from those created in industrial society. As Steven Kaplan puts it, "Mastership was a system of social classification and representation before it denoted a system of production, distribution, and consumption. Social relations, molded by the corporate code, were anterior to economic relations and in some ways determined or at least significantly shaped them." "Turgot's Carnival," p. 183.

exceptions to rules multiplied, making the privileges left behind seem increasingly arbitrary and unjust.

THE LINEN DRAPERS

The oldest women's guild within the garment trades, and indeed one of the best-established Parisian guilds, dealt not in clothing but linens (*lingerie*).[28] Linens included household linens, layettes for babies and nursing mothers, and, in clothing, breeches for women, shirts and their accessories, night shirts, and handkerchiefs. In medieval times household linens accounted for the lion's share of this commerce and production. In addition to a considerable aristocratic market for these goods, the churches of Paris required ritual linens for mass and consumed enormous amounts of plain linens and bedding for the convents and hospitals.[29]

This was a diverse trade. At its low end, the "poor and pitiable" linen workers whose sheds hung from the wall along what is now the rue de la Lingerie at the center of les Halles caused the guild considerable headaches.[30] The widespread perception that these linen workers were trafficking in sex as well as table linens and shirts had long made the guild particularly emphatic about its moral function.[31] The linen trade also offered a respectable occupation for married and single women of high social standing. At this end of the market, the guild's merchant competition came from the mercers (dry goods merchants) and, later, the *marchands de modes* (who sold dress trimmings), against whom the linen drapers' guild held its own with surprising and disconcerting success.

Unlike the tailors, the linen drapers formed a merchant guild, selling others' goods. Beginning in the late seventeenth century, however, more linen drapers began to produce as well as to sell linens, hiring on women workers. From that time on, both guild statutes and court complaints reflect more differentiation between women with merchant skills and those serving much less expensive apprenticeships in sewing.[32] Jaubert's 1773

[28] Cynthia Truant is studying the social history of the Paris women's guilds. See "The Guildswomen of Paris," pp. 130–38, and "Parisian Guildswomen and the (Sexual) Politics of Privilege."

[29] Bouvier, *La lingerie et les lingères*, pp. 147–53.

[30] Officially, guild members needed to serve three years of apprenticeship and work two years in another's boutique before setting up on their own. Yet these requirements did little to stem the swelling tide of poor peddlers of lingerie. See the 1573 and 1594 statutes of the linen drapers, cited in Lespinasse, *Les métiers et corporations*, p. 63. Bouvier, *La lingerie et les lingères*, pp. 162–65.

[31] The 1485 statutes pledged to guard against women of ill repute (sexual or otherwise) in the interest of protecting the good reputation of the women, their daughters, and the trade in general. "Lettres patentes de Charles 8 confirmant les premiers statuts des lingères," 20 August 1485, cited in Franklin, *Les corporations ouvrières*, p. 92.

[32] The complaints are compiled in the footnotes of Lespinasse, *Les métiers et corporations*, 3:71–74. See also Roche, *Le culture des apparences*, p. 291.

Dictionary of Commerce described familiarity with fabrics (usually acquired by being raised in merchant families) as the highly prized skill, and one that brought access to the upper echelons of the trade.[33] This, then, was a varied commerce, providing livelihoods for peddlers to the popular classes, for those retailing luxury goods to the aristocracy, and for a wide variety of seamstresses. It was associated at the low end with poverty and prostitution and at the other with merchant alliances and respectable women's employment.

By the mid-seventeenth century, the production of underclothing was growing rapidly. Daniel Roche's study of seventeenth-century Parisian wardrobes shows increasing numbers of basic items such as shirts, petticoats, and stockings. Since water was difficult to come by, fresh underclothes took the place of bathing, and rising standards of cleanliness increased demand. Aristocratic armoires displayed a wider array of fine lingerie, made of higher quality fabrics, and garnished with expensive bits of lace and pearls. Gathered wrists and cuffs, sleeves embellished with rows of pleats, and muslin collars were all intended to draw attention to the presence of undergarments, alluding to the body beneath the surface. In Roche's words they were "the visible accessories of hidden cleanliness"; they were also hallmarks of aristocratic sensuality and *galanterie*.[34] New demands and sensibilities encouraged the multiplication of subspecialties in the production of linens, expanding the guild's trade, retailing, and production, creating more work in sewing, and increasing the numbers, visibility, and diversity of women workers.

That the linens trade was female was one of its distinctive characteristics. Unlike tailoring, linens drew on a separate female labor market.[35] Court records show a great many mother-daughter combinations, and the guild's apprenticeship regulations favored daughters of mistresses. Yet the industry did not develop out of a family-based system of household production. Indeed, the guild seems to have been determined to check any development in that direction, to preserve the guild's independence, and to keep male heads of family from encroaching on their wives' business dealings and the guild's prerogatives. Linen drapers' guild statutes specifically forbade linen drapers'

[33] Jaubert, *Dictionnaire*, 2:595–97, s.v. "lingères." For the social history of women in the lingerie trade, see Bernadette Oriol-Roux, "Maîtresses marchandes lingères, maîtresses couturières, ouvrières en linge aux alentours de 1751" (Master's thesis, University of Paris, 1980); and Truant, "The Guildswomen of Paris," and "Parisian Guildswomen and the (Sexual) Politics of Privilege."

[34] Roche, *La culture des apparences*, chap. 7; Lespinasse, *Les métiers et corporations*, 3:63.

[35] Truant uses apprenticeship contracts to estimate that up to 40 percent of the guild members of the linen drapers and seamstresses were single. Two of the four officers had to be single women. See "The Guildswomen of Paris," p. 133. See also James B. Collins, "The Economic Role of Women in Seventeeth-Century France," *French Historical Studies* 16, no. 2 (Fall 1989): 455.

husbands from participating in their business. In the emphatic words of the 1594 statutes, reiterated each time the statutes were reissued, husbands were not to "interfere in any way with [linen drapers'] shops," nor were they to operate other shops in the trade.[36] Likewise, husbands were banned from the bodies charged with administering the trades. All of the women's guilds in early modern Paris registered complaints that men were usurping women's jobs, but few were as outspoken, powerful, or successful in defending their turf as the linen drapers.

For a variety of reasons, then, ranging from tradition to the growth of markets to the wealth and prestige of the trade, by the end of the Old Regime the linen drapers' guild constituted a particularly strong corporation. By all accounts, it governed a large and expanding métier, well connected, well organized, and vocal.[37]

THE SEAMSTRESSES

The seamstresses' guild was much younger than that of the linen drapers, and its existence much more in contention. Unlike the linen drapers, whose principle competition was with other merchants like the mercers, the seamstresses produced as well as sold clothing. Their very existence marked a breach in the tailors' corporate wall. Guild tailors' wives had long sewn clothing for women and children, giving them a more or less distinct trade, but leaving markets for that clothing under the tailors' control. Clandestine tailoring by women also flourished. The tailors' 1660 statutes that insisted only wives of guild tailors could work in the trade signaled rising competition from clandestine women workers.

The tailors' battle against clandestine seamstresses grew increasingly bitter and futile with the changing demand for women's clothing. Eighteenth-century inventories of Parisian armoires registered real changes in women's fashion. The seventeenth-century female "uniform," which had consisted of more or less elaborate bodices, petticoats, and skirts layered to suit the weather and status of the wearer, gave way to dresses. The dress-wearing fashion was expensive and impractical (because the pieces could not be worn, washed, or replaced separately), but was adopted surprisingly quickly, and it helped create an increasingly distinctive branch of the clothing industry, a subspecialty that women workers were able to carve out

[36] "Lettres patentes de Henri 4 confirmant les statuts. . ." (1594) and "Lettres patentes de Louis 14. . ." (1645) in Lespinasse, *Les métiers et corporations*, 3:71–77. See Franklin, *Corporations ouvrières*, p. 87, for complaints of linen drapers. On men in the *jurandes*, see Jaubert, *Dictionnaire*, 2:595–97. Court cases involving many mother-daughter enterprises may be found in Archives Nationales AD XI 20. Howell's research on women's guilds in Leiden and Cologne provides general background and interpretive suggestions. *Women, Production, and Patriarchy*, pp. 152–55.

[37] Lespinasse, *Les métiers et corporations*, 3:64; Jaubert, *Dictionnaire*, 2:595–97.

as their own.[38] Seamstresses could tap a growing market, and many female clients, including wealthy and powerful women of the aristocracy, had a vested interest in the seamstresses' independence and success.

The weight of the new clientele and commerce made itself felt in the 1675 edict creating a seamstresses' guild entitled to make clothing for women and small children. "Women and girls of all social status have become accustomed to having seamstresses make their underskirts, dressing-gowns, bodices and other useful clothing," the edict stated. The incessant fighting between clandestine seamstresses and the tailors' guild had been "vexing" to the clientele as well as to the women workers, and the prospect of serious perturbations in this lucrative commerce may have helped convince the state to agree to a new guild. The promise of new taxes to be collected from that guild was doubtless equally compelling.[39]

The letters patent authorizing the seamstresses' guild also marked an effort to sort out the work domains of men and women. On the one hand, the formal establishment of the guild was said merely to ratify custom: "since time immemorial they [the seamstresses] have applied themselves to needlework to clothe young children and persons of their sex, and that work has been the only means they have had to earn their living honestly."[40] On the other, the edict sought to justify the new division of the commerce in clothing with reference to cultural sensibilities, considering it "within propriety, and suitable to the demureness and the modesty of women and girls, to allow themselves to be dressed by persons of their sex when they deem it appropriate."[41]

Such decrees did not settle the issue. That women workers had a special title to sewing women's clothes was hardly a principle that would cut through the web of regulations and specialties that constituted the clothing industry.[42] Tailors, predictably, found nothing persuasive, logical, or appropriate in the new divisions of the industry. In their view the seamstresses were a "bizarre" guild, and the argument that seamstressing was appropriately feminine was profoundly at odds with corporate norms that the

[38] Roche, *La culture des apparences*, pp. 140–45 and chap. 6 generally.

[39] Lespinasse, *Les métiers et corporations*, 3:231–35. Levansier, ed., *Syndicate de l'aiguille*, p. 20. Seamstresses had the rights to make most women's clothing and clothes for boys under eight but not to make capes, bodices, or corsets. Dusautoy, "Habillement des deus sexes," in *Exposition universelle de 1867*, pp. 24–25.

[40] Cited in Lespinasse, *Les métiers et corporations*; also Franklin, *Les corporations ouvrières*, p. 43.

[41] Franklin, *Les corporations ouvrières*, p. 43.

[42] There were no seamstresses' guilds in Dijon, Coutance, and the Auvergne; seamstresses existed only as an adjunct to the tailoring guild. Abensour, *La femme et le féminisme*, p. 186. Seamstresses' guilds were instituted gradually in Chartres, Alencon, Blois, Orléans, Poitiers, and Nancy. Levansier, ed., *Syndicate de l'aiguille*, pp. 4, 5. On continuing territorial debates in Paris, see "Arrest de la cour de Parlement," (1727) Archives Nationales AD XI 26.

guild should govern the whole trade and that women were subordinate to men. Economic entitlement flowed from social standing and public responsibility, not from economic activity or labor.

The guild seamstresses and their advocates understood the principles differently. They promoted a more "economistic" view that their rights flowed from their labors, a view that clashed with the tailors' assertions of corporate prerogatives. Claims that clothing was properly women's work clearly struck responsive chords among the seamstresses and, combined with their rapidly expanding number, gave the guild a strong public identity. The guild was less restrictive than the linen drapers'. In order to become a mistress seamstress, a girl or woman needed to serve three years as an apprentice, two years as a worker, and be at least twenty-two years old. All these requirements were waived for mistress seamstresses' daughters. In an effort to restrict access to the top of the trade, the guild allowed mistresses only one apprentice in the first three years; other workers in the shop were merely poorly paid assistants (*compagnes*).[43] Over the course of the eighteenth century, between 100 and 150 new mistresses were admitted every year.[44] The upstart seamstresses' guild, less well-established and connected, considerably poorer than the linen drapers' guild, frequently unable to pay its fees to the city, and even more plagued by competition from independent workers, was nonetheless equally combative and self-assured.[45] In the 1760s, when the debate on the guilds peaked, the seamstresses did not hesitate to make their grievances known. A powerful "work identity" and sense of entitlement runs through their many petitions to the government.[46]

CLANDESTINE PRODUCTION

The number of clandestine linen drapers, seamstresses, and tailors certainly kept pace with and probably outstripped those of guild members. By the eighteenth century the guild structure was strained by economic developments and battered by political and ideological broadsides. Even by the rules, the guilds did not control all production under the Old Regime, and

[43] Lespinasse, *Les métiers et corporations*, 3:231–34.

[44] Ibid., p. 233; Roche, *La culture des apparences*, p. 288. For numbers in 1776, see "Observations pour les marchandes et les maîtresses couturières au sujet de l'édit de rétablissement des corps et communautés," Joly de Fleury, vol. 596, fols. 89–91. There were about the same number of master tailors and half as many linen drapers. The linen drapers were a smaller group of well-heeled merchant traders, with larger networks of suppliers and workers. Seamstresses, even more than tailors, were small shopkeepers and artisans.

[45] On the guild's financial woes, see "Observations pour les marchandes et les maîtresses couturières," Joly de Fleury, vol. 596, fols. 89–91.

[46] On women's "work identity," see Davis, "Women in the Crafts in Sixteenth-Century Lyon," pp. 167–97.

within and without the guild structure there were competing and overlapping modes of production and distribution. A non-guild artisan could work either directly for the crown, or in one of the areas that lay beyond the legal reach of the guilds—places like the Faubourg Saint-Antoine, Saint-Germain-des-Près, Sainte-Geneviève, or Temple, which were formerly seignuerial and ecclestiastical fiefs under independent authority, and were now "free zones."[47]

Clandestine workers, both male and female, worked surreptitiously in guild areas. Seamstresses crowded into the central districts alongside *modistes,* flower makers, and fan makers. Some worked independently. Others worked in small shops directed by a seamstress. Linen seamstresses often worked for merchant manufacturers with substantial putting out networks. Hustling small jobs was the key to survival. If we were to follow any individual woman, she would probably be sewing at home one week, peddling her wares in les Halles another, and plying a needle for a small shopkeeper, either a tailor or seamstress, during a third.

By the eighteenth century, there was nothing secret about this "clandestine" labor. Moreover, it was impossible to disentangle guild from clandestine production. Shirts and petticoats were produced legally for large merchants but also peddled illegally by women who sewed them. Aristocrats and bourgeois could purchase elegant linens on the rue Saint-Honoré; the common people could buy cheap imitations legally in the Faubourg Saint-Antoine or les Halles, and illegally just about anywhere.[48]

In principle, the battle against clandestine production lay at the center of the corporate project. Without regulation, so corporate thinking went, there would be anarchy, fraud, corruption, and license.[49] Expensive materials, important tools, and manufacturing techniques would be pirated by clandestine workers. Workshops assured control of workers' behavior and virtue. In striking contrast to their nineteenth-century successors, eighteenth-century commentators considered work done at home (which was called *travail en chambre*) to be undisciplined, and women working beyond the confines of a shop prone to promiscuity. "Apartments, rooms, and garrets hold innumerable crowds of young girls" and were an invitation

---

[47] On the overlapping modes of production, distribution, and consumption, see Auslander, *Taste and Power*; Roche, *La culture des apparences*; and Godineau, *Citoyennes tricoteuses*. Note, though, that none of them even hazards an estimate of clandestine workers.

[48] See Fairchilds on fan making for the overlapping of legal and legal production. Here, the "production and marketing systems [were] truly Byzantine in complexity and so riddled with illegalities that whole neighborhoods in Paris where fans were made and sold lived outside the law." In "The Production and Marketing of Populuxe Goods," p. 31.

[49] "Réflexions des marchands et marchandes lingères de Paris, sur le projet de détruire les jurandes," Joly de Fleury, vol. 462, fols. 128–29, pp. 7–8.

to debauchery, according to the seamstress's guild; by contrast, the watchful eye of a mistress guaranteed the discipline of young workers.[50] Clandestine work was not situated in the "home"; it was seen as outside the order of the workshop. The linen drapers' guild, similarly, argued that morality and discipline were best served by keeping women together under one roof, and writers otherwise critical of the guilds concurred.[51]

In practice, the guild and non-guild worlds were not so starkly separated. Clandestine seamstresses, tailors, and linen drapers in most instances were indistinguishable from their guild counterparts. Clandestine production was not necessarily unskilled. Nor was it more proto-industrial. In the guild and non-guild world artisanal shops prospered alongside large-scale putting out operations. The battle against clandestine production was politically important, but the economic stakes may not have been that high. In the late eighteenth century the tailors' guild acknowledged that easily half of their masters had ongoing commerce with clandestine workers.[52]

Likewise, tailors accommodated women's work. Particularly in Paris, where women's labor was central to the thriving fashion trades, the largely male corporations like the mercers or the tailors had little choice but to tolerate rivals, whether guild linen drapers and seamstresses or male and female clandestine workers. They did so grudgingly. Seamstresses shops were regularly visited by the tailors' guild officers, their apprentices and shop assistants arrested, and their goods confiscated. In a 1764 case that the court considered exemplary, the tailors were reproved for "having taken from the woman Lahaye by force and violence a dress and petticoat that she was delivering to one of her customers, on the grounds that she was a false worker." The court barred tailors from inspecting seamstresses' shops without specific authorization. It also required the guild to print and post no-

---

[50] Clearly pleading for public support, the guild said that the *jurandes* policed the morals of guild shops even more carefully than they did the skills of mistresses. "Supplément au mémoire à consulter des six corps pour la communauté des couturières" (1776), Joly de Fleury, vol. 462, fol. 117, pp. 4–5.

[51] "Réflexions des marchands et marchandes lingères," Joly de Fleury, vol. 462, fols. 128–29, pp. 9, 12. This moralizing was not confined to women workers. The male guilds also considered shopwork to be superior because it allowed them to police work habits, control quality, and reinforce hierarchies of master, journeyman, and apprentice. Steven Kaplan, "The Luxury Guilds in Paris in the Eighteenth Century," *Francia* 9 (1981): 293.

[52] "Réflexions des maîtres tailleurs," Joly de Fleury, vol. 462, fol. 173. These points are underscored by revisionist studies of the guilds, including Gail Bossenga, "Protecting Merchants: Guilds and Commerical Capitalism in 18th-Century France;" Liana Vardi, "The Abolition of the Guilds during the French Revolution"; and Michael Sibalis, "Corporatism after the Corporations: The Debate on Restoring the Guilds," all in *French Historical Studies* 15, no. 4 (Fall 1988); Kaplan, "Les 'faux ouvriers'"; Simona Cerutti, *La ville et les métiers: Naissance d'un langage corporatif* (Paris, 1990); Sonenscher, *Work and Wages*; and Fairchilds, "The Production and Marketing of Populuxe Goods."

tices that tailors would allow seamstresses to "exercise their trade in peace."[53]

The artisanal world of the Old Regime could not exclude women effectively or systematically. Women's labor in those trades ran the gamut from skilled to unskilled, guild to clandestine, and familial to independent. On the one hand, then, women had a visible presence in clothing production and sales, made an essential contribution, and enjoyed specific guild rights. On the other hand, their place in the corporate world was hardly secure: guildsmen considered working women's status ambiguous, and even guildswomen found their title contested in the courts, attacked in petitions to have their corporation abolished, and questioned daily in encounters on the streets. Changes that expanded women's domain thus did not alleviate their sense of vulnerability.

THE CORPORATE ORDER CONTESTED

By the 1760s and 1770s, the struggles between men and women guild members was thoroughly entangled in the battles over the guilds' future. Social critics assailed guild privileges as symptomatic of those of the regime in general: unjust, unnatural, and burdensome. Physiocratic writers argued that abolishing the guilds would unfetter technological development, eliminate regional differences in the organization and regulation of work, and, in general, do away with "arbitrary" conventions and rules.[54] Such arguments found influential supporters in the royal administration, chief among them the liberal A. Robert Jacques Turgot, appointed controller general in 1774. Turgot's rise to power and his 1776 edicts met with a battery of angry petitions from the guilds, including the tailors, seamstresses, and linen drapers. These petitions were written by the guild leadership and their legal representatives. They do not reflect the outlook of common needleworkers.[55] They are nonetheless remarkable documents, and revealing about the crucial ways in which trade issues became intertwined with changing definitions of femininity, new concepts of gender as a division of labor, and the

[53] Sentence de police et arrêt de parlement 7 septembre, 1764 and 27 mars, 1765 for the Communauté des maîtresses couturières de la ville et faubourgs de Paris et la Demoiselle Lahaye, Maîtresse couturière. This and similar arrêts may be found in Archives Nationales AD XI 26. See also Joly de Fleury, vol. 596, fol. 79.

[54] On the enlightened critique of the guilds and corporate self-defense, see Coornaert, *Les corporations en France*, pp. 170–71; Sewell, *Work and Revolution*, pp. 66–77; Fairchilds, "The Production and Marketing of Populuxe Goods"; and Kaplan, "Turgot's Carnival."

[55] Simona Cerutti has warned historians of guilds against assuming any common "language of labor" in a trade, a criticism largely directed at Sewell's approach. See also Hunt and Sheridan, "Corporatism, Association, and the Language of Labor in France." I am interested in what these petitions show about public debate on women's work, a debate which drew on a handful of key ideas and rhetorical devices. The petitions do not adequately represent the point of view of workers, or even "the trade."

intellectual cross currents that began to reshape discussions of women's work.

The master tailors' petition forcefully argued that "competition and liberty," which Turgot hoped to foster, had already progressed too far.[56] The abolition of guilds might be workable in small towns, where "the passions are generally less lively and needs more easily satisfied." In the "capitals," though, such a reform would be "the signal and the food of anarchy."[57] The tailors proposed their own reforms to maintain social order and rationalize the economic world. Chief among these, not surprisingly, was putting all of the clothing guilds back under the governorship of the tailors' guild.[58]

The tailors vigorously defended themselves against charges of "despotism," arguing that guild mastership had never been prohibitively expensive or exclusive. They grounded their privileges in the prerogatives of the male head of household, inextricable from the moral, political, and economic order. A man's craft status was his patrimony. When he died, the guild system assured the orderly transfer of that patrimony, maintaining family hierarchies and providing as well for women within the family. These family hierarchies, the petition continued, were compatible with "enlightened" recognition of women's maternal travails and sacrifices.[59]

Without guilds to guarantee stability, the petition continued, a master's death would leave a vacuum of authority. Journeymen and apprentices would rebel, taking advantage of the master's widow and her children. Such predictions of labor unrest and sedition were accompanied by bleak tableaux of moral decay. Abolishing the guilds portended the collapse of orderly families. "What girl would enter into the solemn act of marriage with a person lacking estate, who has nothing to assure his future, and whom the first accident could reduce to abject poverty?" "Libertinage" would ensue.[60]

The seamstresses' petitions reflected their different and anomalous position in the guild world. They wrote to defend the corporate system, but they also needed to justify their title to a place within it, countering more powerful guilds' arguments that they were trespassers. They did so with reference

[56] "Réflexions des maîtres tailleurs," Joly de Fleury, vol. 462, fol. 173, p. 9.

[57] Ibid., p. 15.

[58] They echoed the petition from the Six corps de Paris (which represented the most powerful guilds) claiming that specialized guilds like the cobblers, *fripiers*, and seamstresses were "bizarre" in the corporate world. "Supplément au mémoire à consulter sur l'existence actuelle des six corps et la conservation de leurs privilèges," Joly de Fleury, vol. 462, fol. 151; and "Réflexions des six corps de la ville de Paris sur la suppression des jurandes," Joly de Fleury, vol. 462, fol. 154, pp. 11–12. Tailors could enforce discipline and order in the trade only if they had the political power and jurisdiction to do so; creating subgroups, grounded in trade specialties, wreaked havoc with corporate logic.

[59] "Réflexions des maîtres tailleurs," Joly de Fleury, vol. 462, fol. 173, p. 13.

[60] Ibid., p. 14. The petition from the *tapissiers*, Joly de Fleury, vol. 462, fol. 176, made the same point.

to the history of the needle trades, to concerns about moral propriety, and, speaking "with an Enlightened accent," they grounded their rights (and monopoly) not in custom and privilege, but in the nature and the character of the sexes. There were, the seamstresses argued, distinctly masculine and feminine responsibilities, honors, and work roles.

> In society there are certain tasks that call for only gentleness, intelligence, and justice; there are honors that could reward peaceful heroism and charity; there are labors that require only a quick and sparkling imagination, only grace and finesse in the execution. Women have had the right to claim these; man has snatched them away because he is stronger."[61]

The seamstresses' petition also borrowed Enlightenment ideas in framing a moralized and "sexualized" denunciation of aristocratic society. To be sure, the seamstresses' grievances against the tailors' guild and male monopolies had been forged in a century of battles and antagonisms in the clothing trades. But their petitions also traded in the currency of larger public debates. Indeed, they provide a good example of the rhetorical "over-bidding" that so marked debates of the late eighteenth century.[62] The 1675 letters patent founding the guild had underscored cultural concerns for modesty (women should dress women), but the linen drapers' petition embellished that theme in a characteristic way:

> For a long time the vulgar hands of men have held the delicate waist of a woman in order to measure it, and to cover her with elaborate clothing; for a long time modesty has been compelled to suffer the prying gaze that prolongs its regard under the pretext of a greater exactitude.[63]

The tailors' pretensions to craft and skill barely disguised their lascivious tyranny, one of the corruptions of privilege.

The linen-drapers' petition struck similar chords, but even more boldly. With perhaps an edge of parody, it opened in an emphatically female voice, speaking as a "community of women," vaunting the community's skills and entitlement.[64] Like the seamstresses, the linen drapers insisted theirs was appropriately women's work. They argued, first, from natural law: nature

---

[61] "Supplément au mémoire . . . des couturières," Joly de Fleury, vol. 462, fol. 117, pp. 1–2. See William Sewell's point that "even [Turgot's] enemies speak with an Enlightened accent." *Work and Revolution*, p. 63. In 1776 and again in the *cahiers de doléance*, many of the guilds defended their organizations while demanding sweeping changes in the state.

[62] The phrase is François Furet's (*Interpreting the French Revolution*), but see also Sonenscher, *Work and Wages*; and Sarah C. Maza, *Private Lives and Public Affairs: The Causes Célèbres of Prerevolutionary France* (Berkeley and Los Angeles, 1993).

[63] "Supplement au mémoire . . . des couturières," Joly de Fleury, vol. 462, fol. 117, p. 3. Again, this borrows from physiocratic attacks on luxury and consumption.

[64] "Réflexions des marchands et marchandes lingères," Joly de Fleury, vol. 462, fols. 128–29.

endowed men with "strength," suiting them for particular kinds of work and it gave women "dexterity," fitting them for others. History and social custom (traditional guild points of reference) powerfully confirmed "nature's" order. Linens had been "in all times" the special responsibility of women. "From their earliest education they are accustomed to make it the goal of their labors and thoughts." If education and families had so honed women's skills and minds, why should the state or corporations ban women from the marketing of these goods or from administering this commerce?[65] The linen drapers argued from professional competence and utility: their continued stewardship of their trade was a guarantee of the highest quality, continuous improvement, and public satisfaction.[66] Finally, they argued for the need to assure womanly industry, lest exclusion from economic activity drive masses of women into poverty. Their guild, which in their view represented the principle of a female monopoly of the linens trade, guaranteed women an occupation and foothold in the industrial world. In a culture where, in their words, "our customs at once forbid women from almost all kinds of work in society and at the same time multiply women's needs," such a monopoly was amply justified.[67] Within the context of the late-eighteenth-century corporate structure, this was the best way for women to carve out a place for themselves.

These "reflections" issued from women at the top of the trade. From their perspective, the greatest danger came from merchant capitalists who debased the quality of the merchandise and shouldered aside women artisans or merchants, turning many into clandestine workers and reducing the wages of workers on the lower rungs of the ladder. "The workshops of these pirates [merchant capitalists] are filled with women reduced to having to scrounge for work."[68] Like the seamstresses, the linen drapers cast the issue not simply as poverty, but also, and more vividly, as women's independence and self-governance. They presented their trade as a last bastion of female artisanship and autonomy in a society that seemed otherwise determined to crush both. In a remarkable turn of phrase, they said that the linens trade was "the only one where she was obliged neither to rent herself to a greedy entrepreneur nor to submit to a tyrannical associate, disguised under the appellation of 'husband.'"[69] The rejection, from this quarter, of the tailors' vision of orderly patriarchal workshops and marital complementarity could hardly have been more decisive.

The seamstresses argued that dismantling the guilds would reduce work-

[65] Ibid., p. 4.
[66] Ibid.
[67] Ibid., p. 3.
[68] Ibid.
[69] Ibid., p. 4.

ing women to prostitutes.[70] In the linen drapers' view, the dangers of free trade and free work appeared even more far reaching. Femininity itself would be corrupted. Turning physiocratic arguments against Turgot, the linen drapers cast their guild as a bulwark against the decadence of aristocratic display and consumption. Their petition read as if it had been written by an austere bourgeois rather than by merchants and manufacturers who traded in embroidered linens for churches or delicate nightcaps and muslin scarves for the aristocracy. Lingerie shops run by mistress linen drapers were both modest and instructive, the petition carefully suggested. "Shelves filled with useful objects teach lessons of economy. There are no decorations other than order and cleanliness." If the guilds were abolished, they warned, the tone of commerce would be quite different. "From the rubble [of the guilds], we will witness the emergence of glittering shops . . . where the attributes of pleasure will eclipse those of labor, where commerce will be conducted by the eyes rather than by the mouth."[71] The image thus evoked of aristocratic galanterie, idleness, and consumption for display, and of a world where pleasures and privileges "eclipsed" labor was a staple of eighteenth-century social and economic criticism; in it women were transformed, literally and figuratively, into objects of desire and consumption. To that unsettling image of feminine and social corruption, the linen drapers juxtaposed a vision of simple, unadorned, and productive womanhood.

"TRAVAIL FÉMININ" AT THE END OF THE EIGHTEENTH CENTURY

However mannered and tactical their arguments, the hardy feminism of the women's guilds' petitions is a powerful reminder of the centrality of gender to criticism of the Old Regime. Recasting women's character and roles, a project that included providing education and teaching skills, encouraging usefulness, and allowing women to work, formed an integral part of the general project of reforming the country and regenerating its *moeurs*. The linen drapers' arguments counterpoising useful womanhood with corrupt femininity were common currency. They circulated freely through the pre-revolutionary press, works of eighteenth-century social critics, and, later, in more republican versions, through petitions from revolutionary women.[72] The linen drapers advanced the arguments considered above on behalf of guild women. But it is symptomatic of women's precarious position in the guild world that critics of the entire guild system found their arguments equally congenial. In the preamble to his 1776 edict abolishing the corpora-

---

[70] "Supplément au mémoire . . . des couturières," Joly de Fleury, vol. 462, fol. 117, p. 6.

[71] "Réflexions des marchands et marchandes lingères," Joly de Fleury, vol. 462, fols. 128–29, p. 13.

[72] Kaplan, "Les 'faux ouvriers,'" pp. 360, 369; and Godineau, *Citoyennes tricoteuses*, pp. 82, 84–86.

tions, Turgot underscored that guilds were male monopolies, excluding women from many occupations that might rightly be considered theirs.[73]

The linen-drapers and seamstresses' guilds were monopolies too, and occasionally came under reformers' fire. Guild fees excluded many women completely and allowed others in only through the intermediary of established mistresses, who became subcontractors paying low wages.[74] Yet most social critics considered "corporate" and "male" privilege synonymous. Systematic discrimination, epitomized by male guilds, had made it difficult for women to get work and deepened women's vulnerability—such was a frequently voiced criticism of the corporate organization of work.

The linen drapers' and seamstresses' arguments about the corruption of women who were denied their productive roles found wide appeal. They resonated with the economic and moral attack on luxury. Many critics of the regime found displays of reified femininity (prostitution, sumptuous fashions, mistresses as symbols of status and social mobility) one of the defining dangers of urban life.[75] Particularly in Paris, the European capital of aristocratic splendor and luxury commerce, the image of idle women was a lightning rod for critics of the government. Negative portraits of aristocratic "feminine character" supplied critics with a vivid image of the regime's defects: it reveled in coquetry and luxury, lacked discipline and a sense of proportion, and had no education in or appreciation for useful skills.

That work was essential for women, that particular trades should be reserved for them, and that "nature" was a sure guide to "feminine" and "masculine" work roles were the seamstresses' and linen drapers' convictions. But they also became increasingly commonplace in the economic and social debates of the late eighteenth century. Searching for principles of social organization encouraged writers and thinkers to explore the "character of the sexes" in a newly systematic fashion; to elaborate on the different biologies, mentalities, and destinies of men and women; and to apply these in-

[73] Abensour, *La femme et le féminisme*, pp. 195–96.

[74] Mercier, *Les tableaux de Paris*, pp. 135–36. On the cost of mastership, see Madeleine Guilbert, *Les fonctions des femmes dans l'industrie*, p. 24. This debate is also discussed in Camille Bloch, *L'assistance et l'état en France à la veille de la Révolution* (1908; reprint, Geneva, 1974), pp. 24–30.

[75] These included philosophes, physiocrats, and "grub street" writers. Mercier lavished attention on fashion, consumption, and women and workers and objects; the play of appearances, the reification of women, and social mobility through imitation and fashion were among his favorite subjects. In addition to passages from *Les tableaux de Paris* cited elsewhere, see his chapter on "marchandes de modes," in 2:212–15. Daniel Roche's arguments about the distinctive *culture des apparences* of late-eighteenth-century Paris take Mercier's themes and observations as their point of departure. See also Nicolas E. Rétif de la Bretonne, *Les nuits de Paris* (London, 1788–94); Elizabeth Fox-Genovese, *The Origins of Physiocracy: Economic Revolution and Social Order in Eighteenth-Century France* (Ithaca, N.Y., 1976), p. 129; and Jones, "Repackaging Rousseau."

sights to the ordering of the social and economic worlds.[76] Any number of
Enlightenment works laid out, with surprising decisiveness, views on the
gender division of labor, nature's prescriptions, and women's capacities.
They used the same dualities that ran through the seamstresses' and linen
drapers' petitions: men were strong and robust, women imaginative, dex-
terous, artful.[77] Rousseau's speculations on the gender division of labor
were enmeshed in his certainties about feminine character. Little girls "love
ornament. Not content to be pretty, they want others to find them so; . . .
no sooner are they able to understand what is said to them than they can be
governed by telling them what one will think of them." In little girls' play
with dolls Rousseau "discovered" both a feminine gift for fashion and,
pressing further, the seeds of desire for self-display.[78]

While no one could consider Rousseau mainstream, similar conceptions
were becoming coin of the realm. Views of women's labor were increasingly
essentialized, or attached to conceptions of feminine nature. Women's innate qualities or inclinations suited them for clothing work. Endowed by
birth with grace and beauty, women had a "natural" sense of fashion—
though no aesthetic sense that would help them in other crafts or arts.
Discussions insisted on the gendered character of crafts and labors. Earlier
guild regulations had described "good" tailoring and seamstressing in identical terms; eighteenth-century dialogue insisted on sharper differentiation.
The Abbé Jaubert's 1773 *Dictionnaire raisonné universel des arts et métiers*,
which appreciatively detailed the skills and knowledge involved in various
trades, said seamstressing required more "cleverness" than skill.[79] The *Encyclopédie*'s engraving of a tailor's workshop presented a well-ordered array
of tools: chalk, tables, marking instruments, weights for making pleats and
folds, thimbles, needles, irons for special cuts, and different patterns. Its
counterpart on seamstressing depicted workers fitting the dress directly to
the body. Women had less capacity for abstraction, the engravings suggested; their trades required fewer "precision" tools and instruments.[80]

[76] On the eighteenth-century redefinition of gender, see, among many others: Offen and
Bell, eds., *Women, the Family, and Freedom*, vol. 1; Hausen, "The Family and Role Division: The
Polarization of Sexual Stereotypes in the Nineteenth Century," in Evans and Lee, eds., *The
German Family*; Carolyn Merchant, *The Death of Nature* (San Francisco, 1980); Laqueur, *Mak-
ing Sex*; Londa Schiebinger, *The Mind Has No Sex? Women in the Origins of Modern Science*
(Cambridge, Mass., 1989); Samia Spencer, *French Women and the Age of Enlightenment* (Bloom-
ington, Ind., 1984); and Abensour, *La femme et le féminisme*.

[77] Abensour, *La femme et le féminisme*, pp. 417–19. The *Encyclopédie* summarized the debate about women's capacities and nature, citing a Hebrew proverb that held women incapable
of using any tools except the distaff (s.v. "Femme"). Voltaire's "nature" forbade women "the
heavy work of carpentry, masonry, metal-work, carting.

[78] Jean-Jacques Rousseau, *Emile ou de l'éducation*, 1874 edition, pp. 443–44, 446.

[79] Jaubert, *Dictionnaire*, 1:571–73.

[80] William Sewell's study of the *Encyclopédie*'s plates remarks that virtually none of them

Louis Sebastien Mercier's indignation at violations of the natural order illustrates the assumptions that informed these discussions. "It is grotesque," he wrote, "to see male hairdressers, men pushing a needle, handling a shuttle, and usurping the sedentary life of women. . . . It is immoral . . . for strong and robust persons to invade areas which nature has particularly designated for persons of the opposite sex."[81] In light of the centuries-old tailors', mercers', drapers', and *fripiers'* guilds, and considering the seamstresses' precarious foothold in the needle trades, the certainty with which "nature" deems everything associated with dress, fabric, and fashion a "feminine" enterprise is striking indeed. The spirit of self-evident rationality and naturalness with which Mercier presents his views illustrates the gulf that divided Enlightenment conceptions of the gender division of labor from corporate convictions about patriarchal authority.

The concern to reserve certain trades for women also marked the growing influence of political economy and the newly systematic discussion of economic questions at the end of the Old Regime. Reform-minded administrators presented manufacturing and labor rather than philanthropy as key weapons in attacking social problems.[82] Women, like men, needed to be productive and to be given work. "Work is the people's only patrimony. They must work or beg," said one reformer, who assailed the guilds for making people purchase the "right to work."[83] Women, especially, could ill afford this indefensible exaction. By the same token, the guildwomen's proud emphasis on productive and independent womanhood echoed changing views of work that we associate with physiocracy and emerging political economy: the critique of hierarchies of craft according to the status and privilege they conferred, increasing respect for mechanical arts, the emphasis on the right to work, and the pervasive criticism of "unproductive" social groups like the nobility and clergy.[84]

Broad currents of eighteenth-century social theory condemned as "unnatural" distinctions of wealth, estate, and privilege. An order of gender that emphasized the natural complementarity of the sexes increasingly figured as a foil to what critics considered radically corrupting social hier-

---

represent women working, that "work was seen as essentially a male activity." "Visions of Labor: Illustrations of the Mechanical Arts before, in and after Diderot's *Encyclopédie*," in Kaplan and Koepp, *Work in France*, pp. 259–60. See also Roland Barthes, "The Plates of the Encyclopedia," *New Critical Essays* (New York, 1980), pp. 23–39.

[81] Mercier, *Les tableaux de Paris*, 9:178–79.

[82] Benabou, *De la prostitution et la police*, p. 462; and Fairchilds, "Government Support for Working Women."

[83] Echoing Adam Smith, cited in Bloch, *L'assistance et l'état*, pp. 24–30.

[84] See Cynthia Koepp, "The Alphabetical Order: Work in Diderot's *Encyclopédie*," in Kaplan and Koepp, *Work in France*, pp. 230, 232, and 240. See also Kaplan and Koepp's introduction on how inherited classical and Christian notions of work combined with Enlightenment reassessments of work, connecting labor to wealth.

archies. At a time when the project of regenerating the country's *moeurs* could compel wide assent, rethinking women's role and character and providing education and work for women proved particularly popular proposals.[85] The image of the useful and independent working women offered an attractive contrast to older models of femininity. These themes dominated the women's guilds' self-defense and the discussion of women's work.

FROM THE OLD REGIME TO THE REVOLUTION

In 1776, opposition to Turgot's edicts had proved overwhelming. Six months after they had been abolished, the corporations were reestablished. They were reformed in minor ways, however, including opening more opportunities to women.[86] All women over eighteen were allowed into the male guilds, including tailoring. Yet they continued to be barred from the assemblies governing those bodies, they could exercise no responsibilities in those guilds, and, in mixed trades, they had to meet in separate assemblies, which drew sharp protest from groups like the seamstresses.[87] In this form the corporations, and the debate surrounding them, continued until the collapse of the regime itself.

By that time, the guilds embraced such diverse methods of production and were so deeply interwoven with "clandestine" labor that their formal abolition made little difference to the workers in the trade, or even to the organization of production. Merchant capital had long since made inroads into garment manufacturing; small artisans, male and female, subsisted alongside wage earners, some of them working in shops, others dispersed in their lodgings. So they continued through the revolutionary period. Dominique Godineau's portrait of the female labor force in 1791 and her "map of Parisian labor" confirms this continuity.[88] That does not mean that the Parisian economy remained stubbornly "traditional," but rather that the dynamism of the eighteenth century had already left its mark, especially in the garment and fashion trades.

By all accounts the most dramatic effects of the Revolution arose from the

[85] See, for instance, "Petition des femmes du Tiers Etat au roi, 1er janvier, 1789," in Harriet Applewhite, Darlene Levy, and Mary Johnson, eds., *Women in Revolutionary Paris* (Urbana, Ill., 1979), pp. 19–20; Groppi, "Le travail des femmes," p. 37, n. 25.

[86] Abensour, *La femme et le feminisme*, pp. 196–97; Coornaert, *Les corporations en France*, pp. 165–77; Kaplan, "Turgot's Carnival"; and Vardi, "The Abolition of the Guilds," p. 708.

[87] "Observations pour les marchandes et les maîtresses couturières," Joly de Fleury, vol. 596, fols. 89–91; patent letters of 1785, in Archives Nationales, AD XI 26.

[88] On the Revolution and women's work, see Hufton, *Women and the Limits of Citizenship*; Gullickson, *The Spinners and Weavers of Auffay*; Godineau, *Citoyennes tricoteuses*; Groppi, "Le travail des femmes"; Raymonde Monnier, "L'évolution de l'industrie et le travail des femmes à Paris sous l'Empire," *Bullétin d'Histoire Economique et Sociale de la Révolution Française* (1979); and Roche, *La culture des apparences*, pp. 272–77. See Kaplan, "Turgot's Carnival," though, on how hard it is to answer precise questions about the effects of abolishing guilds.

acute crisis of the luxury trades, which brought devastating unemployment in the capital until the Empire, when conditions slowly and fitfully began to improve.[89] Hard times heightened the peripatetic character of women's work, forcing needleworkers in all branches of the garment industry to seek short-term jobs from any employer. Thus the economic crisis swelled the ranks of female laborers who could be hired by (usually male) entrepreneurs operating on a larger scale, confirming the earlier fears of guild seamstresses, linen drapers, and tailors. In the guild world these had been called clandestine workers; now they were called home workers, or *ouvrières à domicile*.

Predictably, gender antagonisms rose as employers tried to hire cheap female labor. In one of several similar incidents, the revolutionary commissioners of the Tuileries section had to remind angry male workers protesting the hiring of women that "the corporations had been abolished" and that they had to allow women to work in peace.[90] As far as many "citizens" were concerned, the spirit of male corporatism, privilege, and monopoly remained strong. Trying to relieve distress and keep order during the revolutionary wars, the Convention gave jobs sewing clothes for the army to unemployed women and relatives of soldiers. Some of this work was put out by the government and by popular demand administered through the sections.[91] The rest was routed through private contractors with recourse to large putting out networks. Assemblies of women demanded that the Republic fire these contractors, "bloodsuckers of the people," who had seized control of markets in order to drive down wages. In 1793 their protests registered. By 1795 they fell on deaf ears, and the municipally-run workshops had closed down. The Ministry of Clothing had also set up centralized workshops for the manufacture of tents and overcoats, employing large numbers of seamstresses. Those, too, were handed over to private manufacturers during the Directory.[92]

Neither of these experiments constituted a dramatic departure from past practices; large putting out networks were not new. Nonetheless, in their scale, in the weight of large contractors and capital, and in the deteriorating

[89] There are several studies of the crisis, none of them very precise. Some, like Braesch's influential study, are now being reconsidered. See Roche, *La culture des apparences*, p. 520, n. 65. In 1807 (when the population of Paris was about 580,000), the prefecture of police's "worker-statistics" showed a labor force of 100,000. Of those, 30,651 were in clothing and textiles, a much lower percentage than earlier, and a sign of deep crisis. Roche considers those numbers misleadingly low, however, for these statistics counted only workers with a livret, and thus excluded all casual labor. It is a particularly inaccurate count of female labor; the author of the survey admitted to having counted women only in the trades where they were very numerous (p. 274).

[90] See Godineau, *Citoyennes tricoteuses*, p. 85.

[91] They elected commissioners who supervised the putting out, did the cutting in central shops, and served as a board of appeal for women workers with grievances. Ibid., pp. 86–88.

[92] Godineau, *Citoyennes tricoteuses*, pp. 86–88.

conditions of work, they prefigured developments to come. The crisis took
a heavy toll on small artisans, and the reorganization and slow recovery
accentuated trends already present at the end of the Old Regime. Without
for a moment romanticizing the laboring lives of dressmakers, linen-
workers, or seamstresses under the monarchy, it is fair to conclude that as
the Revolution gave way to the Empire, Paris—*le grand foyer du travail
féminin*—was becoming a more difficult place for women to work.[93]

CONCLUSION

The importance of the clothing trades, the variety of markets for which they
produced, and the range of women's employments in those trades were
among the most important hallmarks of the Parisian economy before the
Revolution. The artisanal world of Old Regime Paris was by no means male;
one found women up and down the guild hierarchy. Much female labor was
clandestine, done outside the control of the guilds. Still, it was hardly concealed from public view and consciousness. On the contrary, seamstresses,
modistes, and working-girls emerged by the mid-eighteenth century as new
urban types, representing to contemporaries both the promise and peril of
life in the capital.

Clandestine work was not necessarily less artisanal than guild work: it
simply lacked legal status. Clandestine work should not be equated with
household production. Some of this work was part of a family economy,
with women working alongside their tailor husbands and fathers. Some of it
was waged or entrepreneurial, though; seamstressing and linens drew upon
a separate female labor force. Last, clandestine production, usually called
travail en chambre, was not associated with the home and domesticity as it
would be in the nineteenth century.

The gender division of labor in the clothing trades did not simply issue
from the division of labor in the household. Nor did contemporary judg-
ments about the appropriate domains of men and women necessarily flow
from convictions about how households were or should be organized. The
guild order defined gender politically, as a relationship of authority. That
definition overlapped and clashed with others. While the guild order provided the normative structure of Old Regime France, the eighteenth-
century guilds bore little resemblance to their early modern (let alone medieval) ancestors.[94] Thus an older logic was overlaid with exceptions and with
concessions to aristocratic demands, new sensibilities and markets, and the
government's fiscal needs. The eighteenth century created new economic

[93] Information on wages is difficult to come by, and the range of earnings makes generalizations virtually meaningless. See, though, Monnier, "L'évolution de l'industrie," p. 55; and the
chart in Godineau, *Citoyennes tricoteuses*, p. 363.

[94] Kaplan and Koepp, *Work in France*, introduction; and Auslander, *Taste and Power*.

and ideological fault lines, making the guild structure particularly fragile and, in the process, changing ideas about women's domain and economic roles. In this context, guild women, with a clear sense of their craft and entitlement, helped to forge Enlightenment definitions of gender as a "natural" division of labor and economic spheres. They drew from the larger arsenal of Enlightenment beliefs about labor, industry, and moral discipline in defending the claim that the sewing trades were theirs.

It is remarkable, though, that none of the various perspectives informing the late-eighteenth-century discussion considered women's work per se to be problematic. Economic theorists, social observers, and opponents and defenders of the guilds alike all emphasized, to different degrees, the importance for women of industry and productivity, and the value of labor and its moral discipline. For all the invocations of nature's order, female labor was not represented as violating a natural order of womanly vocations. Newly minted economistic views seemed straightforward: the right to work ("the patrimony of the people") should be open to all, and "free" work would distribute benefits to industry and the people alike. The discussion of female labor was dominated by political attacks on monopoly and privilege. Female vulnerability and its consequences (prostitution and "libertinage") were issues; so were discrimination against working women and guild or spousal "tyranny." The conflict between labor and family that so troubled thinkers of the nineteenth century hardly figured in this discussion. Only later would the woman worker become an emblem of rampant exploitation, an anomaly, a violation of the "natural" division of labor. Only later would the "patrimony of the people," in nineteenth-century terms the "right to work," be cast in distinctly gendered terms.

Chapter Two

MACHINERY, POLITICAL ECONOMY,
AND WOMEN'S WORK, 1830–1870

THE INDUSTRIALIZING process did not entail just factories or machines. Changes in the labor market, intensified rhythms of work, and new techniques of production all proved equally significant to eighteenth- and nineteenth-century businesses. Still, machinery and technology riveted the attention of nineteenth-century economic thinkers and social observers. The new devices and procedures embodied the mingled sense of newfound power and powerlessness that contemporaries felt in the face of the anonymous forces of industry. They seemed to be the crux of the multiple transformations that so fascinated those who witnessed them: changes in the nature and organization of work as well as in its burgeoning productivity.[1] For these reasons, the sewing machine was at the center of discussions of change in the clothing trades. The first experiments with that machine sparked intense speculation and bitter polemic among workers and observers. The outlines of the debate it touched off are crucial to understanding nineteenth-century social and economic thought regarding gender, women, and labor.

Tracing the emergence and contours of this debate allows us to see how "women's work" became a social problem, a distinct object of social investigation. Eighteenth-century liberal economic thought extolled the benefits of manufacturing and the jobs it would create for women, seeing "free work" as the route to economic salvation. As the first decades of the nineteenth century unfolded, its proponents were forced to confront the inequalties of gender and class created by the new regime of marketplace liberty. Women's work thus became one of the crucial proving grounds for liberal political economy and its critics.

Moreover, this debate reflects a broader transformation whose beginnings were discernible in the battles over the guilds: the process by which gender became a central framework for organizing and making sense of the industrial world and the social division of labor. Where once "women's work" was defined by a number of intersecting norms and social categories of which the sex of those who performed it was rarely primary, now, gender and gender differences seemed fundamental. Not only did they define

---

[1] See Berg, *The Machinery Question*; Giedion, *Mechanization Takes Command*; and, for an excellent French example, Dupin, *Rapport du jury central*, p. 3.

women's as distinct from men's work, they marked the differences between work that was skilled and unskilled, craft and cheap, honorable and demeaning, productive and pathological.

In the eighteenth century, antagonisms between men and women workers had revolved around the guilds, their privileges, and male "tyranny." The abolition of the guilds did little to assuage these antagonisms. On the contrary, the elimination of all guild restrictions intensified clashes over men's and women's respective realms, and these ongoing battles made the early nineteenth-century history of the clothing trades particularly tumultuous. In such a volatile climate, virtually every innovation, from the opening of new department stores to experiments with mechanization, became an occasion to reintroduce longstanding concerns as well as to ask new and pointed questions.

INVENTION AND POLITICAL ECONOMY

The person credited with patenting the first sewing machine is the French artisan Barthélemy Thimonnier (1793–1857). In 1829, Thimonnier applied for a patent on a *cousu-brodeuse*. As the name suggests, the new machine worked on the principle of an embroidery or crochet hook; unlike earlier and unsuccessful models, Thimonnier's sewing device did not try to replicate the movement of human hands.[2] Thimonnier's stitch would be obsolete by 1845. But the French inventor remains in the history books as a pioneer in sewing technology and, more important, as the first person to experiment with its industrial application.

At the end of 1829, with patent and financial backing in hand, Thimonnier moved to Paris and set up, on the rue de Sèvres, a workshop equipped with eighty sewing machines that was intended to make uniforms for the military. Thimonnier's enterprise, the Société Germain Petit, was founded just before the July Revolution of 1830.[3] This was not a propitious moment to launch any venture, and a singularly bad time to experiment in the clothing trades, where unemployment, falling wages, and competition between men and women were the order of the day. Germain Petit apparently encountered hostile tailors on several occasions, and in January 1831, a crowd of two hundred marched toward the shop, demanding work and threatening to smash the sewing machines, which they called *casse bras*, or

[2] The patent was issued on July 13, 1830, to Thimonnier and M. Ferrand, a tutor at the Ecole des Mines, who had financed the patent. See Cooper, *The Sewing Machine*, p. 11; Meyssin, *Histoire d'une invention*; Doyen, *Thimonnier*; and most recently, Peyrière, "Recherches sur la machine à coudre."

[3] The Société de la maison Germain Petit et cie was formed on June 8, 1830. There were eight founders; each contributed eighty thousand francs. Records of the Society, document 735, Conservatoire National des Arts et Métiers.

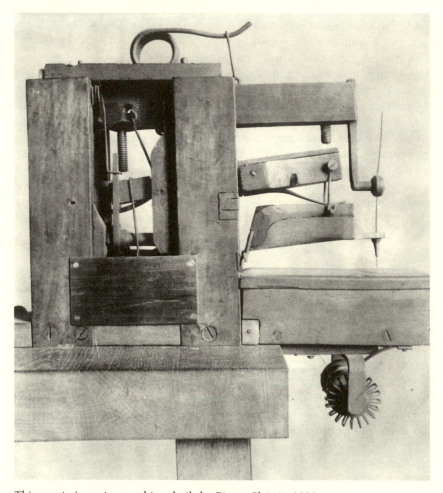

Thimonnier's sewing machine, built by Pierre Clair in 1828.

"arm breakers."[4] The National Guard arrived to break up the crowd, but in July, Thimonnier withdrew from the enterprise, and a few months later his partner died and Germain Petit was dissolved. The closing papers concluded that "experience has shown it is impossible at present to take advantage of the newly invented sewing machine."[5]

[4] *Gazette des Tribunaux*, January 21, 1831. The incident formed part of a wave of tailors' strikes; of fifty-eight strikes in the artisanal trades during the July Monarchy, thirty were led by tailors. Jean Pierre Aguet, *Les grèves sous la Monarchie de Juillet* (Geneva, 1954), pp. 11, 366. For a full account of tailors' militancy, see Johnson, "Economic Change and Artisan Discontent." The incident became a didactic Epinal engraving. Bibliothèque Nationale, Cabinet des Estampes.

[5] Document 735, Conservatoire National des Arts et Métiers.

Speculation about the effects of mechanized sewing was intense and volatile. Concern rapidly shifted from men to women workers, and ongoing
battles between men and women in the clothing trades heightened the un-
certainty and controversy about the possible effects of machines. After the
Paris enterprise of Germain Petit folded, Thimonnier returned to Saint-
Etienne, worked on simplifying his invention, and in 1845 joined forces
with a local lawyer to renew his patent and manufacture machines. The
local newspaper, the *Journal de Villefranche*, hailed his efforts with a combination of economic, mechanical, and aesthetic appreciation. The machine
was "as astonishing in its simplicity as in the grandeur of its results." "Even
in the hands of an apprentice, who has a few hours training," the newspaper
continued, "the machine rivals the delicacy, regularity, and strength of needle work, it can compete with the most skilled hand, and it works as fast as
six workers."[6] From the perspective of many readers, comparing hand and
machine labor in this way could only be provocative.

Three weeks after the original announcement, in September 1845, the
Journal de Villefranche published an angry letter from an anonymous reader.
The newspaper had considered the "industrial question," said the reader.
Now the reader wanted to raise the more important "social question"—that
of the interests of workers whom the machine seemed destined to displace.
In the reader's view, it was clear that the displaced workers would be women
and the social question thus raised was one of distinctly *female* poverty and
vulnerability.

> Of all the troubles which afflict humanity in our time, none is greater than the
> impossibility of a single woman to support herself at work. . . . If the enormous
> group of women whose lives are dedicated to sewing and who are incapable of
> doing anything else is the source of moral concern at present; if, every day,
> some of these poor creatures, disheartened by poverty, succumb to the decep-
> tive promises of debauchery and seduction and debase themselves; and if those
> who have the courage to resist the vices suggested by poverty can only earn
> what everyone knows is not a living wage . . . can you imagine what will
> happen once five in six of these women has been thrown out of work by the
> mechanical stitcher?[7]

Several of these themes strikingly echoed eighteenth-century guildswomen's petitions and women's laments of the revolutionary period: women's
foothold in the world of manufacturing was tenuous; their vulnerability was
at once sexual and economic. The *Journal de Villefranche* reader also linked
the expected displacement of women workers by the sewing machine to a
trend already deplored by guildswomen and eighteenth-century reformers:
"Each day the stronger sex makes new inroads into the trades which should

---

[6] *Journal de Villefranche*, August 21, 1845.
[7] Ibid., September 14, 1845.

be the exclusive domain of women."[8] The "social question," though, was a new point of reference. So was the interpretive web that linked unemployment, mechanization, and systematically low wages. In the *Journal de Villefranche*, unlike the guildswomen's petitions or late-eighteenth-century reform writings, the issues were not the political tyranny of tailors or the privilege of guilds, but the more anonymous forces of industry, the "free market" in labor, and mechanization.

A few weeks after the reader's letter appeared, the *Journal de Villefranche* published a response ostensibly from the inventor himself. (The response may well have been penned by Thimonnier's lawyer partner and financier.)[9] Thimonnier (or his spokesman) vigorously disputed the anonymous reader's predictions that machines would cause female unemployment.

> Why should we assume that these machines are hostile to the female sex? Why not say, instead, that they have come to expand the industrial domain of women, make their forces equal to those of men, and place them at the same level of intelligence? . . .
>
> Rather than proscribe invention, let us demand reform in women's education. Let us create arts and trades schools [*écoles d'arts et métiers*] for working women as well as working men. That way, perhaps we will abolish, or at least reduce, commensurate with their respective needs, the shocking inequalities between brother and sister and the disproportion in their wages.[10]

Here was liberal political economy in its most buoyant and generously universalizing key. The reader's dull and crabbed ideas about women, Thimonnier impatiently argued, merely reflected his contemporaries' limited imagination and, even, their hostility to women's potential. The inexorable changes transforming society made such hidebound conceptions of women's sphere catastrophic. In his memorable words, "The industrial world is changing as if by magic, and people want the fate of the most interesting half of humanity to forever depend on the needle."[11]

The exchange between the reader and Thimonnier in the *Journal de Villefranche* offers a rare glimpse of an incipient nineteenth-century debate on machinery, industry, and gender. Thimonnier's ideas echo arguments advanced by political economists, most strikingly those of the Baron Charles Dupin. By the time of this debate over the sewing machine, Baron Dupin's two-volume *Les forces productives et commerciales de la France* (1827) had become well-nigh unavoidable. Dupin had also written the official report to

---

[8] Ibid.

[9] Peyrière, "Recherches sur la machine à coudre," p. 48.

[10] *Journal de Villefranche*, September 28, 1845. To give women technical training or allow them to operate tools contravened corporate principles of the Old Regime.

[11] *Journal de Villefranche*, September 28, 1845. Thimonnier's confidence that moral and social progress ran in tandem with industrialiation was also reminiscent of Saint-Simon and the utopian socialists.

the industrial exposition of 1834 in France, which disseminated his views in a more accessible form. His advocacy of child labor laws in the Chamber of Deputies had the same effect. Dupin's influence ranked him with Jean Baptiste Say and other prominent French exponents of political economy. By the 1840s Dupin was fêted by the July Monarchy, roundly denounced in the working-class and early socialist press, and attacked by those (like the Christian economist René Louis Villermé) determined to demonstrate the shortcomings of classical political economy. Dupin's work provided a well-spring of ideas for the advocates of technological and industrial progress, and it furnished countless controversial prophecies of prosperity to be pilloried by those concerned with the social question.[12]

Dupin's *Les forces productives et commerciales de la France* included a chapter on women, and that chapter set out clearly all the arguments that Thimonnier would muster on the pages of the *Journal de Villefranche*. Industry offered women new opportunities, freeing them from their confinement to a straitened range of poorly-paid occupations, like seamstressing, laundry, and domestic work. To take advantage of these changes, however, women needed new skills. In the same spirit as Thimonnier, and in defiance of traditional guild culture, which carefully husbanded craft secrets and skills, Dupin suggested women be taught basic geometry and applied mechanics in trade schools.[13] Taking aim at others' tendency to "naturalize" women's capacities, he argued that dexterity and cleverness were not innate female traits. They were acquired skills. Women's industrial work, especially the clothing and textile trades, required precision, regularity, and symmetry. Dupin counseled that women be educated with these demands in mind. Their education could not be abstract: Dupin, like most of his contemporaries, believed that the female mind had difficulty grasping geometry. But women could be taught by pragmatic means—by cutting, measuring, and folding clothes. In this way they would find geometric principles easier to assimilate.[14]

For Dupin the political economist, the question of women in industry was straightforward. Female labor constituted one of France's many forces, like wind, steam, or mule power, and it had to be tapped. Since women's bodies had little physical strength, education and effective deployment of the force they did possess were essential. Dupin was unperturbed by the fear that industrial employment would "unsex" women or violate the natu-

[12] Dupin, *Les forces productives et commerciales*; and idem, *Rapport du jury central*. On Dupin, see Reddy, *The Rise of Market Culture*, pp. 140–44; and Coleman, *Death Is a Social Disease*, p. 252. For working-class views on Dupin, see *L'Atelier*.

[13] Dupin, *Les forces productives et commerciales*, 2:93–94. Dupin taught at an arts and trades school and also wrote a manual on popular education for men. He regretted not having written one for women.

[14] *Les Forces productives et commerciales*, p. 94.

ral order. Beginning from the premise of female inferiority, he argued that industrial work would help women overcome their natural handicaps rather than exploit their vulnerability.[15]

Knowing how controversial his vision of women in industry might be, Dupin painted a grim portrait of the alternative: burly peasant women, hardened by life behind the plow, who looked like "Hottentots" or "Tartares."[16] Whatever uncertainties the industrial future held, women's jobs in manufacturing were bound to be preferable to the backbreaking agricultural work they had done in the past. He optimistically ended his chapter on "improving the strength and destiny of the female sex" with the prediction that better jobs for women would give working-class couples enough money and stability to marry, eliminating common-law unions and strengthening marriage, which he called "l'union entre l'homme industrieux et la femme laborieuse." Marriage, in his sanguine view, offered calculable economic benefits and moral discipline, while bringing out the complementarity of the two sexes.[17]

Dupin's reflections on popular morality did little to still his adversaries. To the contrary, his cool calculations; his enumeration of natural, animal, and human sources of power; and the image of interchangeable bodies he called forth infuriated many contemporaries (like the unnamed reader who wrote to criticize Thimonnier) for whom the nostrums of political economy seemed irresponsibly abstract, inhuman, and, hence, immoral. Women's bodies were not commensurate with men's and certainly not with animals'. To commodify human capacities did a special violence to women, who supposedly embodied a morality that transcended and countered that of the marketplace. These themes would rapidly become staples of socialist and Catholic criticisms of liberal political economy.

Thus the 1845 clash between Thimonnier and the anonymous reader of the *Journal de Villefranche* was but one exchange in a burgeoning debate between political economy and its critics. The arguments of the 1840s carried forward themes from the late eighteenth century: concerns about women's tenuous place in the world of manufacturing, female artisans' worries that they were being shouldered aside, male workers' resentments of female competition, and pervasive uncertainties about mechanization. Thimonnier's memorable ode to technological progress and its capacity to emancipate "the more interesting half of humanity" transposed into a strik-

[15] See ibid., pp. 94–99 on the kinds of work that Dupin considered appropriate for women.

[16] *Les Forces productives et commerciales*, p. 86.

[17] Ibid., p. 97. Attacking concubinage, or common-law marriage, he wrote that "L'esprit conservateur, qui naît d'un lien indissoluble, ne saurait exister dans ce commerce illicite; l'économie est bannie d'un tel commerce" (p. 100). The absence of patriarchal authority in common-law unions was an economic liability as well as a moral one. Dupin neither counseled nor envisioned women leaving the labor force upon marriage.

ing new key the late-eighteenth-century liberal chorus about the benefits of manufacturing for the uplifting of womankind.

Thimonnier's new machine provided an occasion to debate women's capacities for different kinds of labor, both physical and intellectual, to consider their future in the industrial order, and to measure the growing claims of political economy. The arguments made by Dupin, Thimonnier, and their interlocutors remained almost entirely speculative. They nonetheless need to be read in context and set against social and economic changes in the clothing trades in the mid-nineteenth century.

SOCIAL CHANGE IN THE CLOTHING TRADES:
DISTRIBUTION AND PRODUCTION

The first half of the nineteenth century brought three key changes in the making and selling of clothing in Paris. Guild regulations had carefully separated selling fabric from selling clothing. Most customers bought cloth and trimmings from a draper or mercer, took those to a tailor or seamstress, and had the clothing made. Rules barred seamstresses and tailors from stocking fabrics and encroaching on the domain of the textile merchants.[18] The abolition of these restrictions during the Revolution of 1789 gave manufacturers new and potentially lucrative ways to combine the two activities. In 1829, for instance, the textile manufacturer Terneaux opened a shop called the "Bonhomme Richard" on the place des Victoires, which sold clothes made from Terneaux's own fabrics. As one of the leading members of the tailors' association anxiously put it, cloth manufacturers could now bypass tailors and go "straight to the consumer."[19] Similar commercial rearrangements lay behind the emergence of "couture" in the 1860s. Where once women brought cloth and trimmings to seamstresses, with whom they designed the dress, *maisons de couture* began to sell fabric, clothing, and design—and to call the combination "fashion."[20] The principal changes in this sector of the women's clothing trade involved the organization of capital, the relationship of cloth-selling to clothing, and the value added by design—not changes in production techniques.

[18] Dusautoy, "Habillement des deux sexes," in *Exposition universelle de 1867*, pp. 4–7.

[19] Cited in Vanier, *La mode et ses métiers*, pp. 101–3. The *Journal des Tailleurs* represented the views of master tailors. See also Faraut, *Histoire de la Belle Jardinière*, p. 22.

[20] There were several ingredients to the fashion houses' success. The first was credit: only the largest dressmakers could obtain the credit necessary to buy materials and fabrics and to make "models" that customers might want to either buy outright or order for themselves. The second was the addition of "fashion" as a separate element and the designer (often male) as a separate person who added value to the final product. Nord, *Paris Shopkeepers*, p. 70; Auslander, *Taste and Power*; Perrot, *Les dessus et les dessous*; Valerie Steele, *Paris Fashion: A Cultural History* (New York, 1988); Gaston Worth, *La couture et la confection des vêtements de femme* (Paris, 1895), p. 46.

The other important innovation of the early nineteenth century involved ready-made clothing, or *confection*. Ready-made was not entirely new. For more than a century, used-clothing dealers had been selling "ready-made" (in the sense of previously made), altered, restored, and cleaned clothing in popular markets.[21] After the Revolution, this commerce expanded rapidly, and the used-clothing dealers had the connections and markets necessary to begin producing and selling inexpensive ready-made clothes on a wider scale. By the 1820s, the Marché du Temple and the Marché Saint-Jacques had become magnets for the production of ready-made. The neighborhoods surrounding these popular emporia were "teeming with poor men and women, workers and apprentices," as a master tailor observed. "They filled entire houses, from the basement to the attic. In the stairwells, in the windows, on the landings—one could see them sewing everywhere."[22] The tides of immigration to Paris in the first half of the century helped to depress the price of labor. During the economic crisis of 1827–32 in particular, manufacturers of ready-made found underemployed artisanal tailors ready to work for them for egregiously low piece rates. This was the context for the demonstration in front of Thimonnier's Parisian enterprise in 1831.[23]

The final, and most important change of the mid-nineteenth century involved the dramatically new ways of selling clothing made possible by department stores. The *magasins de nouveautés* of the 1820s and 1830s were the first generation of these stores; they sold ready-made items such as shawls and mantles, aprons, jackets, and children's clothing; cloth by the bolt and trimmings for clothes; and "articles de Paris"— snuff boxes, umbrellas, gloves, and so on. Middle-class women purchased fabrics and trimmings there and had dresses made by seamstresses. The first generation of department stores also included the *maisons de confection*, like La Belle Jardinière, which tried to attract customers from the used-clothing markets, selling inexpensive ready-made men's (and some children's) clothing to a working-class public.[24] The second generation of department stores was

[21] Guild regulations had allowed used-clothing dealers to make and sell new clothing as long as it was inexpensive and required no fitting. Dusautoy, "Habillement des deux sexes," in *Exposition universelle de 1867*, pp. 4–7. Roche, *La culture des apparences*, p. 329; Chambre de commerce de Paris, *Statistique de l'industrie . . . 1847*, p. 288; *Rapport des ouvriers parisiens*, in *Exposition de Londres en 1862*, pp. 344–45; and Perrot, *Les dessus et les dessous*, pp. 78–85.

[22] Compaign, "Fabricants et consommateurs," *Journal des Tailleurs*, August 16, 1850.

[23] Chambre de commerce de Paris, *Statistique de l'industrie à Paris . . . 1847*, pp. 108–9; Dusautoy, "Habillement des deux sexes," in *Exposition universelle de 1867*, pp. 12, 13. The rise of ready-made is too familiar to recount in great detail here. See Perrot, *Les dessus et les dessous*; Vanier, *La mode et ses métiers*; and especially, Johnson, "Economic Change and Artisan Discontent."

[24] Vanier, *La mode et ses métiers*, pp. 104–5; Chambre de commerce de Paris, *Statistique de l'industrie . . . 1847*; *Exposition universelle de 1889*, class 36, "Matériel et procédés," pp. 84–86.

formed of *grands magasins* of the Second Empire: the magasins du Louvre, the Bon Marché (1852), Printemps (1855), the Bazar de l'Hôtel de Ville (1860), and the Samaritaine (1869).[25] The *grands magasins* worked according to new economic dynamics, inaugurated new relations between consumers and merchants, and attached a new meaning to goods. Instead of piling fabrics, gloves, and shoes behind counters, department stores displayed them in plate glass windows, in arrangements designed to seduce with their sumptuousness and impress with their abundance and modernity.[26] Signs announced "free entry" to encourage browsing. Store design and architecture worked to underscore the evocative power as well as the use value of the goods for sale.[27]

So much has been written about department stores that they require some demystification.[28] Until at least the 1870s, they did not dominate the market. Elegant mercers and fabric stores held the loyalty of *haute bourgeois*, and the Rotonde du Temple and itinerant used-clothing dealers, with their cries of "marchand d'habits," proved tenacious popular institutions in working-class Paris well into the twentieth century.[29] Department stores' lowest prices were far too high to lure working-class customers.[30] Finally, as concerns the history of clothing manufacture, it is important to note how little the variety of goods thus sold depended on new modes of clothing production. Second Empire department stores were stocked with fabrics, trimmings, and items that complemented custom-made dresses and suits. The abundance of items was the harvest of falling textile prices and the prodigious increase in textile output—not the mechanization of clothing production.

[25] Jeanne Gaillard, *Paris, la ville, 1852–1870: L'urbanisme parisien à l'heure d'Haussmann,* (Paris, 1977), pp. 525–36; Michael Miller, *The Bon Marché: Bourgeois Culture and the Department Store, 1869–1920* (Princeton, N.J., 1981); Perrot, *Les dessus et les dessous,* p. 125; Nord, *Paris Shopkeepers;* Avenel, *Le mécanisme de la vie moderne,* pp. 6–8; Levasseur, *Questions ouvrières,* p. 125.

[26] Nord, *Paris Shopkeepers,* pp. 72–77. See also Miller, *The Bon Marché.*

[27] As the principle of browsing shows, goods had representational rather than simply use value. Williams, *Dream Worlds;* Perrot, *Les dessus et les dessous,* pp. 113–18; Auslander, *Taste and Power,* pp. 513ff.

[28] For this argument, see Auslander, *Taste and Power;* and Nord, *Paris Shopkeepers,* pp. 82–87.

[29] Popular consumption of clothing did expand during the Second Empire. As the price of fabrics dropped, people who could previously wear only cotton or heavy weaves now could afford wool and lighter, warmer clothing. Perrot, *Les dessus et les dessous,* p. 130; George Duveau, *La vie ouvrière en France sous le Second Empire* (Paris, 1946), pp. 363–69; *British Reports on the Paris Universal Exposition: 1867* (London, 1868), 3:364.

[30] Even the lowest priced ready-made houses seemed to reckon with the limits of the popular market. Several of these stores went into custom tailoring, setting up small but very profitable shops alongside the racks of ready-made. There was no linear movement toward ready-made clothes and no simple democratization of apparel. Manufacturers and retailers alike aimed to multiply markets and to combine custom and ready-made.

New modes of retailing contributed to heightened competition in the clothing trades. In the 1850s new markets opened, first in the provinces, then in Latin America; exports tripled from 1851 to 1861. The 1860 free trade treaty drove down the price of textiles.[31] Yet the cheapness of hand-work, the dispersed organization of outwork, and the apparent vastness of the pools of labor on which it drew, still persuaded garment manufacturers that mechanization remained a fool's errand. One manufacturer, voicing the opinions of many of his colleagues, concluded in 1857 that new technologies were irrelevant to the trade. "In our industry, mechanical force is not applicable. . . . Although science has not entirely run out of ideas, nothing yet has been proposed that would allow tools to replace the hand of the worker."[32]

Experiments with machines and factory production were largely government-sponsored. The first of these involved making military uniforms in army regiment shops.[33] In 1853, the Ministry of War set up a shop equipped with twenty Every brand sewing machines to make uniforms for the army. The shop closed down soon afterward, reportedly for fear of social unrest.[34] When the Crimean War broke out, the state again began to promote machine-produced uniforms. It set up a shoe factory in Puteaux and a military clothing plant on the rue Rochechouart in Paris equipped with steel cutting machines, pinking irons, and Every sewing machines. In 1855, the government ordered more machines for the Parisian shop in the hope that it could soon export its products and stimulate technological change in the clothing industry generally. By the late 1860s the rue Rochechouart manufacture, now the privately owned maison Godillot, was not only furnishing uniforms to the French army, but filling orders for the English and Russian armies as well. It was the largest clothing factory in France, and often cited as a model of efficient large-scale production.[35]

---

[31] *Exposition universelle de 1889*; Dusautoy, "Habillement des deux sexes"; in *Exposition universelle de 1867*; Claude Fohlen, *L'industrie textile au temps du Second Empire* (Paris, 1956), p. 293. The clothing industry as a group had favored the treaty, confident that they would benefit from the lower prices of fabrics, but some proved better able to take advantage of the situation than others. See Lémann's testimony before the French Commission on Tariffs, printed in the *Journal des Tailleurs*, August 1, 1857.

[32] Lémann, in *Journal des Tailleurs*, August 1, 1857.

[33] Adelphe Espagne, *De l'industrie des machines à coudre à la maison centrale de Montpellier* . . . (Paris, 1869), p. 4. One of the earliest promotional brochures for a sewing machine featured a drawing of a young soldier sitting at the machine. The engraving captures both the important role of the state in technological change and the prevailing notion that the early sewing machines were for men's use.

[34] According to the *Journal des Tailleurs* (December 16, 1854), the regime feared unemployment among seamstresses working for military contractors.

[35] In Paris there seems to have been only three establishments operating on anything approaching the scale of the maison Godillot and using sewing machines. Dusautoy, "Habillement des deux sexes," in *Exposition universelle de 1867*, pp. 56, 59.

The state also cautiously promoted technological change by experimenting with prison labor. Requiring women prisoners to do sewing work could represent either moral improvement and economic opportunity or punishment and discipline, depending on the point of view of the prison administrator. The new women's prison at Saint-Lazare in Paris purchased thirty-six sewing machines almost as soon as it opened. By 1860, nearly every state penitentiary had set up shops with machines where female inmates sewed corsets, shirts, and other simple lingerie items. French workers had long resented competition from prison labor, and the new machines, which few artisans on the outside could afford, compounded the sense of injury.[36]

Prison administrators were unhampered by the marketplace calculations of entrepreneurs in the clothing industry. George Sheridan has nicely evoked anxieties about overproduction that dogged Lyonnais silk manufacturers and the "terrible responsibility" that the factory, with its relentless output, imposed on the capitalist.[37] Garment manufacturers shared such fears and they too preferred to hedge against the vicissitudes of the market by streamlining their inside production as much as possible. Moreover, from a technical point of view, factory production offered an advantage in only a handful of needle trades, like shoe or hat making, where the complex processes of production could be broken down into simpler, routinized tasks and assigned to different workers using specially adapted machines. The factory's role in these cases was to coordinate the various processes of production and thus to assure that machines were used efficiently. Cutting, too, remained in-house. Specialized cutting machines allowed workers to cut several pieces at a time and, more important, cut different kinds of fabric without binding and tearing. The technological rationale for centralized in-house cutting dovetailed with longstanding workplace hierarchies. Cutters had long been the elite of the trade, with a long corporate tradition, a solid technical culture, and widely recognized design skills.[38] Where sewing was the principal task, however, a very different set of traditions and incentives weighed in. The cheapness of labor and the dispersion of production seemed to militate against any investment in technological innovation.

Through the 1850s, sewing machine manufacturers issued breathless slogans about the time and money the machine could save and lauding the value of technology. They did so without reckoning on the particular dynamics of this industry, the raggedly uneven adoption of technologies, and

[36] Espagne, De l'industrie des machines à coudre, pp. 4, 8, 10. Patricia O'Brien, The Promise of Punishment: Prisons in Nineteenth-Century France (Princeton, N.J., 1982)

[37] George Sheridan, "Household and Craft in an Industrializing Economy," in John Merriman, ed., Consciousness and Class Experience in Nineteenth-Century Europe (New York, 1979), p. 123.

[38] The introduction of specialized cutting machines enhanced cutters' status, skills, and value to the enterprise rather than devaluing them. The effects of technological change on labor and skills are context specific.

the imperatives and lags arising from craft hierarchies and the gender division of labor.

POLITICAL ECONOMY AND LABOR: THE TAILORS' ACCOUNT

Labor relations in the garment trades remained a source of nearly constant
turmoil in the years from 1830 to 1870. The tailors' demonstration in front
of Thimonnier's enterprise on the rue de Sèvres in 1831 was but one explosion in a volatile trade. Tailors and seamstresses marched at the front of
trade delegations and formed workers' cooperatives during the revolution of
1848. Tailors were among the most militant socialist leaders in the 1860s,
and women needleworkers were far the most numerous and vocal of the
women who crowded into Parisian public meetings and working-class congresses. That history is well-recounted elsewhere.[39] Here I am interested in
their political economic outlook, their account of the industry's social history, and how these became entangled in the emerging conversation about
"women's work."

Tailors angrily denounced the changes outlined above, and did so in rhetoric imbued with both corporatist tradition and deeply gendered notions of
skill and craft. From the 1830s through the Second Empire, the most bitter
grievances involved the "free" market in labor, the collapse of the guild
structure of crafts, and the inability to exercise older forms of control. Organized tailors returned repeatedly to the contrast between "bespoke" or custom tailoring, which in their view maintained craft standards, and ready-
made tailoring, which their vision assimilated to the clandestine, non-guild
labor of the past. Like their guild predecessors, they considered the organization of labor in craft shops the key to self-defense, and contracting out the
road to declining skills and wages. That road to ruin and "catastrophe" was
already well-travelled. The Belle Jardinière, for instance, had workshops
that were little more than warehouses where cloth was cut and then shipped
to a vast number of homeworkers.[40] Some of these homeworkers were well-
established entrepreneurs who contracted regularly with manufacturers.
Many more were nomadic "jobbing" tailors who roved from the custom
tailoring to ready-made searching for work. The "empire" of ready-made
was "powerful and deadly," wrote the tailors' delegates to the world's fair of
1867. Subcontracting and the proliferation of small-jobbing tailors under-

---

[39] Johnson, "Economic Change and Artisan Discontent"; Faraut, *Histoire de la Belle Jar-
dinière*, p. 34; Vanier, *La mode et ses métiers*; Scott, *Gender and the Politics of History*, chap. 5;
Dalotel et al., *Aux origines de la Commune*; Judt, *Marxism and the French Left*, pp. 90–91;
Moses, *French Feminism in the Nineteenth Century*; Thomas, *Les femmes de '48*; Faure and
Rancière, *La parole ouvrière*; and Devance, "Femme, famille, et moral sexuelle."

[40] The store employed 116 to 150 cutters depending on the season, and 4,000–5,000 other
workers, most of them homeworkers. Dusautoy, "Habillement des deux sexes," in *Exposition
universelle de 1867*, pp. 44, 45.

mined the standards of quality that the workshops in bespoke tailoring had once sustained.[41] Rather than serving through an apprenticeship, a journeyman tailor would set out on his own in a specialty that required a narrow range of skills: suits, frock coats, jackets, and overcoats. Once in business, jobbing tailors found little opportunity to acquire the array of skills that had been the pride of the trade.

As the tailors saw it, the decline of skills and ruinous competition were inseparable from feminization. The presence of cheap female labor constituted what they considered the most important difference between bespoke tailoring and ready-made.[42] Low wages, intermittent periods of overwork and unemployment, and the uneven rhythms of seasonal production encouraged tailors to forego apprenticeship and set up shop on their own. As jobbing tailors, they could hope to mobilize enough workers to take full advantage of rush orders during the "season" and thereby compensate for the protracted period of unemployment. These pressures and constraints drove artisans to work their wives and children harder, or to hire on women from outside. The multiplication of tasks that involved basic sewing skills simply increased the work that could be done at home by women relying, as one tailor put it, only on their "natural talent for needlework."[43] Women's work was, by definition, "unskilled."

Ready-made manufacturers rarely hired women directly; thus, nearly all of the subcontracted work remained under the control of artisan tailors. That control grew less meaningful as the labor market crowded and competition for contracts from the department stores rose. The tailors were too deeply implicated in women's work to oppose it outright. Instead they bemoaned the squandering of female energies, the degradation of family life, and the corruption of paternal authority.

> As time goes by, the off seasons grow longer, and wages are necessarily reduced. So outworkers, in order to be able to work at home and have the ineffable joys of the hearth, have their wives work with them. This raises the family's budget a little, but when all the accounts are done and one has deducted the time lost running back and forth to the boss and doing these cursed fittings (God knows how much time we spend on them), the cost of heating the irons, and the lighting for the house, there is very little left of the woman's earnings.[44]

[41] *Exposition universelle de 1867: Rapports des délégations ouvrières* (Paris, 1869), 3:19.

[42] Of 3,000 workers that one manufacturer estimated to be employed in bespoke tailoring, 2,500 were men; 500 women. Of the 9,000 who worked year-round for *confection*, 3,500 were women. Ready-made had a vast labor force hired for full season and laid off as soon as the work slowed down. Of 8,000 such workers, 5,000 were women. Estimates given by Lémann, printed in *Exposition de Londres en 1862*, p. 348.

[43] *Exposition de Londres en 1862*, p. 348.

[44] *Exposition universelle de 1867: Rapports des délégations ouvrières*, p. 17; Faraut, *Histoire de la Belle Jardinière*, p. 26.

Even the most Proudhonist tailors found it difficult to flatly condemn women's work. Instead, they repeatedly argued that this labor was un-productive. When sewing machines began to make their appearances in the small shops, in the 1870s, the tailors darkly warned that machine work was ruining women's health and producing sexual disorders.[45]

SEAMSTRESSES AND NEEDLEWORKERS

Women workers echoed many of the grievances of their male counterparts: falling piece rates, rising competition, and long bouts of unemployment followed by frantic weeks of overwork. They also harked back to the dis-tinctly female—and feminist—grievances articulated in the eighteenth-century seamstresses and linen-drapers' petitions. In 1848 seamstresses, like tailors, invoked the republican theme of access to credit as a means to self-organization and independence but gave it their own twist; credit would allow women to run their own shops, and "would free all from bosses who exploit and protectors who dishonor them."[46] Like the linen drapers of the 1770s, they insisted on their rights to run their trade themselves in the face of changes that made it more difficult to do so. Relatively well-positioned women subcontractors (*entrepreneuses*) who designed "models" for manufacturers (and then filled orders for them) found themselves pushed aside by male contractors whose only tasks were distributing piece-work and recruiting new workers.[47] The sewing and design skills that pre-viously afforded the artisan seamstress a relatively privileged position be-came irrelevant in the new market conditions of midcentury. Well-paid inside work still existed, but it was harder to procure. In outwork, the tasks did not become less skilled, but wages declined. Subcontractors sought out women willing to work part time (long hours one month and none at all the next), to wait through the long slow season, and, above all, to accept low wages. From the perspective of Parisian seamstresses, there was less and less work "good" enough to sustain a single woman, let alone one with a family to support.

Men and women workers alike deplored the practice of contracting needlework out to prisons and convents. (Women's prisons produced more commonplace items like linens and shirts; workshops operated by convents

[45] *Exposition universelle de 1873*, pp. 86–89; police reports on meetings in Archives of the Prefecture of Police (hereafter APP), BA 151.

[46] Seamstresses' petition from needleworkers to the Constituent Assembly, June 7, 1848, printed in *La Politique des Femmes. Journal Publié pour les Intérets des Femmes et par une Société d'Ouvrières,* no. 1 (June 18–24, 1848). See also the discussions in the Club fraternel des lin-gères couturières (headed by Desirée Gay) and L'association fraternelle des ouvrières lingères (headed by Jeanne Deroin), cited in Thomas, *Les femmes de 48*, p. 72.

[47] Seamstress designers could still sell their models to manufacturers, but they often found that these designs were sent off to be copied by cheaper hands.

did fine work as well—elaborate stitching for women's dresses and embroidery on silk in gold.)[48] Working-class and republican anticlericalism fueled many of the attacks on convent labor. But the subject also provided an occasion to confront issues of women's education and social position—to strike, again, a feminist chord. One needleworker speaking at a working-class congress, for example, linked the degradation of work not to mechanization, but to the convent's isolation and the ignorance of social relations to which the women who worked there were condemned.

> In the convents' workrooms the division of labor is so advanced that apprenticeship is useless. The working woman, who becomes a machine, earns less, is less intelligent, less active, and easier to exploit. She is at the mercy of her boss, and all the more so because a woman who has been sheltered from the social world is completely unaware of the total transformation of commercial relations in our time. She is ignorant about questions of exchange and transportation. . . . It is imperative to bring women into social life so that they can hold their own as producers.[49]

This comment sounds the same themes put forth by French socialist women like Flora Tristan, Jeanne Deroin, and Louise Michel.[50] Reorganizing work, enabling women to be productive, and ending the corrupting squalor of poverty were the key themes of women garment workers, and ones that, again, linked the demands of the late eighteenth century to those of the mid-nineteenth. Credit would help to make that reorganization and independence possible. So would women's education. So, finally, might technology, at least by the lights of the more "utopian" of women socialists and club members in 1848.[51] Jeanne Deroin, for example, marveled at experiments in the American textile mills at Lowell and the technical expertise of young women who ran the looms. Their skills gave them "a sense of honor and pride."[52] By contrast, she charged, the textile and (especially) garment industry in France simply squandered female labor. Deroin certainly idealized the Lowell mills. Still, that women were excluded from the culture of technology and expertise was a common charge, and one that echoed through needleworkers' speeches long after the more utopian strains of working-class politics had grown faint.

[48] Chambre de commerce de Paris, *Statistique de l'industrie à Paris, 1860*, pp. 282, 283.

[49] Barberet, *Le travail en France*, 7:294, 295.

[50] See Talbot, "An Emancipated Voice," pp. 219–40; Moses, *French Feminism in the Nineteenth Century*; and the works of Edith Thomas: *Les femmes de 48, Pauline Roland* (Paris, 1956), and *Louise Michel* (English translation, London, 1980).

[51] *La Voix des Femmes: Journal Socialiste et Politique, Organe des Intérêts de Toutes*, nos. 1–45 (March 20, 1848 to June 18–20, 1848); *L'Opinion des Femmes*, nos. 1–3 (March–April 1849); *La Politique des Femmes*, nos. 1 and 2 (June 18–24, 1848 and August 1848); Jeanne Deroin, *Almanach des Femmes*, 1853–54.

[52] *Almanach des Femmes*, 1854, p. 61.

Women who worked in tailoring, shoemaking, and other "male" trades could not join the delegations to the world's fairs of the 1860s and 1870s, and the "women's trades," such as lingerie, shirtmaking, dressmaking, and women's ready-made clothing were not encouraged to elect delegations at all.[53] Once, however, in 1876, an association of Paris lingerie workers suggested that they send representatives to the centennial exposition in Philadelphia, proposing to "study the new inventions" in what they wryly called "these great tournaments."[54] They drew up a questionnaire that reveals a keen interest in technology and the sexual division of labor, the social organization of production, and the ways both of these might vary in other nations or cultures. "Is the cloth for women's clothing made by men or women?" "Is work distributed by the manufacturer, or does it pass through the hands of an entrepreneur?" "Do women work in shops or at home?" "Is mechanized work more widespread in the United States than in France?"[55] The Parisian workers' delegation to the Philadelphia exposition decided it could not fund the journey for these women, and so their remarkable inquiry was never undertaken.[56]

As the lingerie workers' queries implied, mechanization in the women's trades was particularly slow and uneven. Both highly skilled work (like fancy overstitching) and certain simple tasks (basting, finishing seams, and applying trimmings) long continued to be done by hand. The machines of the 1850s and 1860s tore fine fabrics, so that in the inside shops of the *maisons de couture* almost all the women's fashions were hand-stitched. Only a few houses owned sewing machines, which they used to stitch trimmings: the "kilometers" of ruching, scallops, and false tucks that surrounded the base of skirts and short jackets.[57] Even in factories like the maison Godillot, where machine production predominated, scores of women handworkers—as many as four to twelve for every machine operator—were employed at preparation and finishing. Mechanization in one sector made for more intense hand work in another.[58]

---

[53] Until the 1880s, women's clothing did not appear at the industrial expositions; it was considered an "art," not an industry.

[54] Barberet, *Le travail en France*, 5:284.

[55] Ibid., p. 285.

[56] Ibid., p. 286.

[57] Vanier, *La mode et ses métiers*, p. 176. By the 1880s petticoats, blouses, and *matinées* could be stitched by specialized machines. Even so, scarcely more than 10 percent of the work that went into a ready-made item of good quality was done by machine. In one Paris cloak-making shop, every twenty hours of machine work required one hundred hours of hand stitching. Aftalion, *Développement de la fabrique*, p. 191.

[58] In both hat and shoemaking, women's work mechanized more slowly than men's. Buttonholes continued to be stitched by hand because the machinery to do them was beyond the means of small jobbing tailors. In 1873, a piece of clothing stitched entirely by machine was still a novelty. Aftalion, *Développement de la fabrique*, pp. 174, 192.

Women workers spoke more tellingly than the tailors of the difference between the tasks that mechanized and those that did not, and the new pressures, dependencies, and imperatives that machine work created. They also evoked with greater vividness the impact of mechanization on work itself: the industrial rhythms at which the sewing machine was run and the exhaustion that resulted from trying to operate a foot-powered machine at factory pace. In order to compensate for the falling piece rates that accompanied machine work, the women had to intensify and lengthen their working day, yet working a ten- or twelve-hour day at a machine was unbearable.[59] In the needle trades, there was an especially acute kind of *usure du travail*, or overwork, that resulted from sporadic mechanization and the coexistence of the domestic system and the factory.

The women needleworkers who formed political clubs, petitioned the government, and spoke at working-class congresses, however, should not be taken to represent an unmediated female outlook or experience. They quoted moral economists like Eugène Buret and René Louis Villermé. They drew heavily from writings of socialists like Auguste Blanqui. They found both data and interpretations in the studies of metropolitan industry conducted by the Paris Chamber of Commerce in 1847 and again in 1860. By the 1870s, their speeches were shot through with references to the influential work of Jules Simon. Their voices, then, while distinctive, were joined with and shaped by the burgeoning writing on and discussion of female labor.

Women's Work and the "Social Question"

From the 1840s on, the subject of women's work occupied an increasingly privileged place in discussions of the "social question." For a growing number of "moral" or "social" economists (as the early critics of classical political economy called themselves), the crucial point of departure was that "production could not be seen as an abstraction independent of the fate of workers."[60] Discussions of national economies and the growth of manufacturing had to reckon with the well-being of men and women workers. As one socialist, Flora Tristan, put it, the "wealth of nations had to be made to confront the distress of nations."[61]

Conservatives and radicals approached this issue with different values. The former were concerned to preserve morality and order, usually by upholding social hierarchies. The latter demanded social justice and articulated the rights of labor and producers. Both, however, started on the same

---

[59] Barberet, *Le travail en France*, 5:287.

[60] Auguste Blanqui, *Histoire de l'économie politique en Europe*, cited in Kim, *Féminisme et travail féminin*, p. 39.

[61] Cited in Talbot, "An Emancipated Voice."

methodological footing: they sought to confront the abstractions of political economy with the particulars of working-class life. The investigators of "social facts" set out, quite deliberately, to counter and subvert the precepts of political economy.[62] The contrasts between "fact" and "theory," or investigation and speculation, constituted a central part of the early social scientific worldview. And the figure of the woman worker was particularly important in highlighting these contrasts.

As many historians have pointed out, the poverty of women and their families provided a readily accepted and easily sensationalized example of industrial misery and its moral repercussions.[63] It was not simply the fact that women were deemed more vulnerable, however, that made the beleaguered female worker a sentimental favorite. In the gendered language of the nineteenth century, to discuss woman was also to evoke her physicality and particularity, by implicit contrast with the universal male individual. To speak, as Baron Dupin had in *Les forces productives et commerciales de la France*, about the interchangeability of resources and labor power was unsettling with regard to humans, but even more so with regard to women. Male bodily labor was more easily elided with the abstractions of "labor power"; women's insistent physicality was considered much more resistant to that exchange of equivalence. The most notorious example of assigning economic exchange value to the female body was, of course, prostitution, and for this reason it proved a touchstone for the era's social critics. Prostitution provided the starkest and most damning instance of what political economy's critics left and right considered the bankruptcy and callousness of the "new habits of mind."[64] Nearly every form of female labor could be made to illustrate the impossibility of exchanging on the market that which was profoundly human and spiritual and, thus, the corrupting aspects of the labor market and cash nexus. Analyses of women's work especially emphasized bodily exploitation, fatigue, and exhaustion; weaving, spinning, and even sewing machines became instruments of torture. "In Lyons in the passementerie shops, some women are forced to work nearly suspended from pulleys, using both hands and feet at the same time," wrote Auguste Blanqui in a passage that was frequently cited.[65] The element of voyeurism and titillation could hardly be denied, and it ran through socialist as well as

[62] Coleman, *Death Is a Social Disease*, p. 91

[63] Katherine Lynch, *Family, Class, and Ideology in Early Industrial France: Social Policy and the Working-Class Family, 1825–1848* (Madison, Wis., 1988); Scott, *Gender and the Politics of History*; Reddy, *The Rise of Market Culture*; Coleman, *Death Is a Social Disease*.

[64] The phrase is Coleman's, *Death Is a Social Disease*.

[65] Blanqui cited in Kim, *Féminisme et travail féminin*, p. 39. Blanqui's passage, repeated in several texts, evoked a scene reminiscent of medieval tortures and was clearly used as a contrast to the image of work as either ennobling, creative, or efficient. Human work was meant to allow men to transform nature; with women's work nature was deformed. The sexual disorders allegedly wrought by the sewing machine are discussed in the next chapter.

conservative writings. Discussing capital's exploitation of labor, even in the writings of socialists, was technical and abstract; shifting gender gears made that exploitation much more vivid.

By the 1860s, the notoriously low wages of women needleworkers had earned them a prominent place in reform literature. Those seeking an example of an overcrowded trade with substandard wages, chaotic organization, and fierce competition between workers had to go no further than the garment industry, one of the largest employers of female labor. If one wanted to argue, as Blanqui did, that women's work generally was a "criminal waste of human capital," the garment industry—not the shop labor of dressmakers, but the travails of needleworkers earning piece rates—made the case powerfully. Marx's passages on the "sheer brutality of exploitation" and "monstrous overwork" of women in the needle trades were intended to underscore the particular dynamics of the industry and women's work within it, and here as elsewhere Marx was following French critics of political economy.[66] Women's labor defied political economists' predictions (Dupin's are a good example) about rising productivity, the labor-saving promise of machinery, and the material well-being of the working classes: none of this had come to pass in the garment industry. The clothing trades illustrated the moral chaos and economic inefficiencies that Marx so powerfully indicted.

The partiality of this portrait is evident, as are its pitfalls for women workers who plied their living in the trade. It accentuated their vulnerability, recommending them to the custody of others: social reformers, the church, or their husbands in the conservative view; the protection of trade unions in the socialist version. As other historians have noted, Marx used women workers to illustrate only some aspects of his indictment of capitalism: women's work dramatized the waste and degradation wrought by capital, but women rarely figured in Marx's discussions of alienated labor, nor did they appear in any of his classic portraits of independent producers and artisans from whom control over production had been wrested.[67] From Blanqui to Marx and Proudhon, women wage earners appeared as exploited bodies rather than as underpaid producers or disenfranchised citizens. When feminists like Flora Tristan, Jeanne Deroin, Paule Minck, and Julie-Victorie Daubié tried to approach the issue differently, insisting on female productivity and the importance of women's contribution to the "wealth of nations," they were swimming against a powerful current.[68]

[66] *Capital* (New York: Random House ed., 1977), 1:599–608.

[67] Ann Phillips and Barbara Taylor, "Sex and Skill: Notes towards a Feminist Economics," *Feminist Review* 6 (1982).

[68] See Talbot, "An Emancipated Voice," on Tristan; Moses, *French Feminism in the Nineteenth Century* on Deroin; Scott, *Gender and the Politics of History* on Julie-Victorie Daubié; and chapter 8 below on late-nineteenth-century feminists.

JULES SIMON, *L'OUVRIÈRE*, AND FRENCH "VICTORIANISM"

In 1860, the title of Jules Simon's *L'ouvrière* (*The Woman Worker*), announced that the "problem" of women's work had come into its own. Simon's uniquely influential book was not a larger study of pauperism, the
dangerous classes, or the condition of labor. He refused to debate the morality of capitalism or the exploitation of labor. Women's labor, he argued,
constituted the only serious social question, and one that concerned all
interested in France's industrial future. Simon tied the subject into Second
Empire debates about tariff reform, industrial policy, and the social consequences of different routes to modernity—to what he saw as the moral
future of the nation.[69] His approach joined a romantic, Michelet-like concern with the principle of "femininity" and its bearing on the character of a
society to a growing body of empirical evidence—in the case of the needle
trades, a study conducted by the Paris Chamber of Commerce in 1847–48
and published in 1851.

The book's enormous influence stemmed from Simon's position in the
post-1848 reform establishment, its authority from his solemnly proclaimed distance from the "dangerous" political currents of his time. Simon
staked out a resolutely antisocialist position. He nonetheless repudiated
conservative nostalgia for a preindustrial world. At the juncture where
France found itself, nostalgia was irresponsible. The revolutionary turmoil
of 1848 lay in the not-so-distant past. The reduction of tariffs signed into
the 1860 free trade bill with England urgently posed the issue of France's
industrial future.[70] Simon did not share the lowered tariffs' supporters' be-
lief in the self-evident moral benefits of free trade. Still, he clearly intended
his arguments to be taken seriously in those circles and to situate his study
at the center of the earnest debate.[71] The moment, he said, called for hon-
esty and realism, for treating difficult moral questions in a new way. Conservatives and socialists alike, he suggested, could find in "women's work" an
opportunity to do so.

Simon could not simply oppose women's labor. Working-class families
needed money, and women would work. "When they are not spoiled by our
cultural prejudice, women like work; they are industrious; the slackness
and languor into which their spirits and bodies [bodily organs, actually]
have fallen comes from us and not from nature."[72] At the same time, and in
the light of the newly signed free trade treaty, large-scale manufacturing was
"not going to retreat. We need to accommodate ourselves to it, and to re-

---

[69] See Joan Scott's brilliant analysis of Simon and French political economy in *Gender and
the Politics of History*, chap. 7.

[70] *L'ouvrière*, p. 87.

[71] Ibid., pp. 72, 80.

[72] Ibid., p. 10.

store what we can of family life in the shadow of the factory."[73] Simon's survey of women's wages and work across France showed that larger workshops and factories paid better, more regularly, and offered considerably better working conditions than did the home industries.[74] Still, Simon refused to follow the logic of his findings, which would favor factory work. Passages on factories seemed calculated to horrify.[75] Demonic descriptions of machinery joined warnings about the promiscuous intermingling of men and women workers and denunciations of sexual advances made by supervisors. Simon abruptly concluded that if women had to work, they should do so in their homes.

The garment industry, however, demonstrated the difficulties of any such return. The impending destruction of women's "traditional" work formed the principal theme of Simon's anguished chapter on needleworkers. "With the recent economic innovations, there is no longer any way to spin or sew." The "natural industry of women"—particularly married women—has been entirely destroyed.[76] "If a woman counts on making a living with her needle, she will either die of hunger or go into the street."[77] Competition from convents and prisons, the rise of ready-made with its expanding networks of putting out, and the introduction of sewing machines were destroying the livelihoods of married women in domestic industry.

Here as elsewhere, Simon eschewed argument entirely, making his points through vivid contrasts: the organic and the industrial; the peaceful spirituality of womanhood and the violent disruptiveness of the machine; demonic automatons and icons of feminine traditionalism—distaff, spinning wheel, and needle. He presented the mechanization of sewing as something nearly inconceivable. "Notices are posted in Paris of clothing factories. We are starting to sew with steam."[78] The argument that women had labored in the bosom of the family until rudely interrupted by the inexorable demands of industry cannot withstand historical scrutiny. Simon's conviction that garments produced by seamstresses at home in small, dispersed shops constituted a "backward," "dying" trade was equally mistaken. And however compelling his exposition of classically Victorian themes, Simon offered no programmatic agenda. As Joan Scott has observed, the book was an "exercise in prescription and idealization."[79]

---

[73] Ibid., p. 103.

[74] Ibid., pt. 1, chap. 4, on "les avantages du travail isolé." As Simon said in the preface, "If we deplore the employment of women in manufacturing, it is not because the material conditions there are poor" (p. iv). See also pp. vii, xiv.

[75] L'ouvrière, pp. 107, 194.

[76] Ibid., p. 192.

[77] Ibid., p. 193.

[78] Ibid., p. 276 (Simon's emphasis).

[79] Scott, Gender and the Politics of History, pp. 148, 154–58.

"The Working Woman," June 1861. Exhausted womanly virtue. The accompanying article on the drama of the impoverished, "honest" seamstress borrowed freely from Jules Simon's just published book, which it praised as "the testimony of a man with talent and a heart, who has himself studied the fate of the working woman."

The idealization remained enormously influential, however, capturing the imaginations of contemporaries across the political spectrum. *L'ouvrière*, as Scott also says, "drew on (and preempted) the views of earlier critics of capitalism," romantic Catholics, moral economists, Christian socialists. The text became a point of departure for socialists in the 1860s and 1870s; at the end of the Second Empire, Parisian workers came to public meetings citing Simon and demanding discussions of "women's work." From working-class congresses to the French Academy of Moral and Political Sciences, *L'ouvrière*'s findings and arguments became common currency. By 1871, Simon's book was in its seventh edition. More than any single text of its time, it defined the subject, dramatized the stakes, and announced themes reformers would pursue over the second half of the century.[80]

PAUL LEROY-BEAULIEU: POLITICAL ECONOMY RESTATED

Simon's powerful indictment of women's industrial work, then, stood at the confluence of several currents of social and political thought. Many writers and social thinkers offered different perspectives; interest in the topic exploded. The most influential counterpoint, though, came from Paul Leroy-Beaulieu.[81] Leroy-Beaulieu stood solidly in the tradition of English political economy and its French practitioners, like Charles Dupin and Jean-Baptiste Say. He was a much-honored writer, member of the editorial board of the *Journal des Débats* and *L'Economiste Français*, and professor of political economy at the Collège de France; in Richard Kuisel's words he was both the popularizer and the "high priest" of orthodox liberalism. Leroy-Beaulieu had begun writing on "the question of labor" in the mid-1860s and, like so many others, he turned his pen to the subject of women's work. The disconcerting success of Simon's book and, later, the Franco-Prussian War and the Commune delayed his book.[82] Leroy-Beaulieu's *Le travail des femmes*, published in 1872, aimed to dislodge *L'ouvrière* from its nearly canonical status in reform literature and to still the rising chorus of concern on the left.[83]

Leroy-Beaulieu's was a critically important restatement of the classical liberal position. To consider women's work a new social drama, he began, was utterly misleading. Like Charles Dupin in the 1820s, Leroy-Beaulieu reminded his audience of the harsh history of female labor. He refused to

[80] See Cochin, *Paris*; Corbon, *Le secret du peuple de Paris*; Fribourg, *Le pauperism parisien: Ses progrés depuis 25 ans* (Paris, 1872); Cere, *Les populations dangereuses*; seamstresses' speeches in Barberet, *Le travail en France*, s.v. "Couturières;" and Dalotel et al., *Aux origines de la Commune*, p. 174.

[81] Leroy-Beaulieu's work represents the most direct confrontation with Simon's. For other contrasts, see Scott, *Gender and the Politics of History* on Julie Daubie; Dalotel et al., *Aux origines de la Commune*; and Thomas, *Les femmes de 48*.

[82] Richard F. Kuisel, *Capitalism and the State in Modern France* (Cambridge, 1981), pp. 1–5. The book on women began as part of a series on "La question ouvrière au 19e siècle" in the *Revue des deux mondes* in the spring of 1870. See Dan Warshaw, *Paul Leroy-Beaulieu and Established Liberalism in France* (DeKalb, Ill., 1991) (though Warshaw says little about *Le travail des femmes*); and Mitchell, *The Divided Path*, pp. 13–16.

[83] In addition to *L'ouvrière*, Leroy-Beaulieu named Cochin, *Paris*; Corbon, *Le secret du peuple de Paris*, and the public meetings of the last years of the Second Empire as examples of the new thinking he deplored.

wax nostalgic for small industries like weaving and needlework or to nourish illusions about "occupations dear to the hearts of poets."[84] Nothing in these occupations made them particularly fulfilling, manageable, "sedentary." or in any other way appropriate for women.[85] He found his contemporaries' poetic notions about femininity and women's unsuitability for industrial labor ridiculous, singling out Michelet especially for ridicule.[86] In passages strikingly reminiscent of Dupin's work and Thimonnier's 1845 letter to the *Journal de Villefranche*, he mocked his contemporaries' views of women's limited capacities and their image of women as perpetual convalescents bound to the protective custody of a husband or father. Such views, he said, shaped the social literature of his time; they were the "common base of all our dissertations, reports, and inquiries."[87] The romantic conviction that women were unsuited for labor, when combined with ignorance about female physiology, he observed, had worked the French medical profession into such fits of anxiety that they produced exaggerated and wildly contradictory accounts of the health hazards of machine labor.[88]

Leroy-Beaulieu considered the "problem" to be women's low wages, which, in the style of classical political economy, he attributed to the low productivity of women's labor. The garment trades occupied the same key position in his analysis as they had in Simon's. Overcrowding depreciated female labor. The prevalence of outwork made technological advance or large-scale organization impossible. In the highly skilled branches like millinery, hand labor impeded mechanization and reduced productivity. As long as women languished in these backward, unmechanized, and chaotically organized trades, their wages would continue to fall.[89] Leroy-Beaulieu dismissed other explanations for women's limited earning power. Female "docility" did not account for women's exploitation and neither did competition from married women earning only a "secondary wage." The issue, he argued, boiled down to the "static, and unprogressive" character of the women's trades.[90]

Indeed, the technological backwardness of women's sphere became Leroy-Beaulieu's overriding theme. He emphatically dissented from Simon's idealization of the "home." For Simon and the other moral economists, the

[84] *Le travail des femmes*, pp. 182–83.

[85] Ibid., pp. 185–86.

[86] Specifically, Michelet's opinion that a woman was constitutionally unsuited for "the work that contemporary civilization imposes on her." *Le travail des femmes*, p. 216.

[87] *Le travail des femmes*, p. 216.

[88] Ibid., p. 228. He attacked the moral economists for contradicting themselves on issues of prostitution, illegitimacy, and so on.

[89] *Le travail des femmes*, chap. 3.

[90] Ibid., pp. 136–37.

home gave women their value and figured as a sphere of social redemption; for Leroy-Beaulieu it was an isolated trap. Household labor was unrationalized and unproductive. Families could neither transmit "savoir-faire" nor prepare women for the world of industry. "Women seem disoriented in the middle of our automatic civilization and our marvelously specialized tools."[91] Domestic industry or homework partook of the home's general backwardness.

Like Simon, Leroy-Beaulieu emphatically ruled out labor legislation or restrictions on economic liberty and set his face against the growing demands of labor. His diagnosis dictated his prescription: better education, more apprenticeship opportunities, and design schools for women. Training in the domestic arts and the rationalization of the household were imperative, he said, announcing a theme that would become important later in the Third Republic.[92] Finally, evincing his enthusiasm for technology and his concerns with the backwardness of the garment trades, he devoted a whole chapter to the anticipated benefits of the sewing machine, which would rescue women and their trades from stagnation and, he seemed to suggest, break the male monopoly of technological know-how.

Like Simon, Leroy-Beaulieu believed the "traditional women's trades," particularly hand sewing, to be dying. Handwork, whether skilled or unskilled, and domestic industries were doomed by the rise of the factory. For Simon, this was a moral drama: women were being devalued and their importance had to be reconceived as spiritual. For Leroy-Beaulieu, it simply illustrated the laws of political economy: unproductive industries or modes of industrial organization either would be fundamentally reorganized or pass away. To say homework was a dying trade, of course, was to deny any basic correlation between capitalism and the kind of squalid exploitation that the garment trades seemed to instantiate. The repeated and misleading references to the garment trades as "small" as opposed to large industry (a distinction repeated in many of the surveys of industry) also served to underscore the supposed marginality of these trades and their doomed historical character. By presenting these trades as the quintessentially "female" trades, Leroy-Beaulieu made the issue women's technological backwardness rather than the character of the trades or capitalism.[93] Rather than dramatizing the shortcomings of political economy's harsh and abstract catego-

[91] Ibid., p. 295. Women's physical incapacities made education that much more imperative. He put this bluntly, ". . . la femme qui est une force materielle presque nulle" (p. 293).

[92] He noted women's "incapacité de diriger d'une manière rationelle et efficace les choses de la maison et de la famille." *Le travail des femmes*, pp. 178–81 on education; p. 340 on design schools.

[93] The argument quickly became circular: women's work was unskilled and unproductive because it was women's, and women were backward.

ries of mind, as moral economists and socialists charged, women's work provided ample evidence of its powers of explanation.

CONCLUSION

Leroy-Beaulieu's study forcefully returned to the themes sounded earlier by Baron Dupin and Barthélemy Thimonnier, dissolving gender troubles in the solvent of free labor and technological progress. Although he rejected the moral economists' trope of the women worker as emblem of capitalist exploitation and moral anarchy, he contributed to the new centrality of gender in the general conversations over capitalism, social order, and the role of the state in society. *Le travail des femmes* underscores how insistently this theme commanded the attention of mid-nineteenth-century writers. It also records changes undergone. In its earlier and more utopian moments, nineteenth-century liberal economic thought held out the promise of limitless expansion, the emancipation of labor, the conquest of nature, and thereby the expansion of women's capacities and the lightening of their burdens. Dupin's writings distilled these expectations and promises in hard-boiled economistic prose. Thimonnier's letter to the *Journal de Villefranche* presented them in a popular idiom and in a specific case, turning the appearance of his sewing machine into a parable about the capacity of technology and human ingenuity to eliminate inequalities, sweep away old barriers, and lift the human condition.[94] Leroy-Beaulieu's *Le travail des femmes* represents a retreat from that earlier optimism, and its defensiveness is a sign of liberalism's receding confidence as economic crises and social unrest began to erode its premises. In the 1870s even a doctrinaire political economist had to recognize implicitly that industrialization and technological change had created more dramatic inequalities between men and women. As a result, Leroy-Beaulieu acknowledged, nineteenth-century France had to reckon with a "woman problem" as well as increasingly urgent class issues.

If his tone and expectations of attainable felicity were a good sight lower, Leroy-Beaulieu's remedies remained much the same as Dupin's. The slow and uneven application of technology in the needle trades meant that Leroy-Beaulieu could invest his own more muted hopes in the sewing machine. More technological change and new technology for *both* sexes would vindicate political economy's claims that moral and industrial progress proceeded in tandem and that government did best when it did least. The sewing machine became the *deus ex machina* of liberal political economy as it confronted the problem of women's work and strove to respond to the

---

[94] For more examples of the progressive outlook, see the *Exposition universelle de 1855*, especially the passages by the former Saint-Simonian and future architect of the Cobden Chevalier treaty, Michel Chevalier, in 2:722–29; and Adolphe Guéroult, "La poésie de l'exposition," cited in Vanier, *La mode et ses métiers*, pp. 180, 181.

increasingly articulate scorn of workers like those who penned the "counter-jury reports," to socialists clamoring for legal restraints, and to romantic critics like the annoyingly influential Simon.

As the controversy between Simon and Leroy-Beaulieu suggests, by the 1870s the question of women's work had become not only a distinct object of research and debate, but also one of the key proving grounds for political economy and its critics from all sides. Increasingly, the subject became mandatory for anyone addressing state policy and France's industrial future. It was a topic with broad appeal, for several reasons. It invited those with deep convictions to philosophize about the character of femininity past and future or to debate the legacy of the revolutionary tradition and the promises of socialism. It joined arguments about France's industrial future to investigations (in some cases quite detailed and specific) of social conditions. Above all, it could be used to dramatize, as few other subjects could, the differences between classical political economy and the developing discipline of social science. In this newly charged context, the particular issues of the garment trades became increasingly inextricable from seemingly remote and deeply political concerns: women's labor was either evidence of the spiritual bankruptcy of capitalism or proof of the emancipating possibilities of economic modernity.

Chapter Three

SELLING THE SEWING MACHINE: CREDIT, ADVERTISING, AND REPUBLICAN MODERNITY, 1870–1900

AN 1880 PAMPHLET published by the Singer sewing machine company doubted whether "the history of the entire world" could "furnish an instance in which any single house . . . has had a growth so stupendous within an equal amount of time."[1] In France as elsewhere, such pamphlets were distributed at world's fairs, given out in department stores, and carried by traveling salesmen or dry goods merchants into the countryside. Imitating the style of popular broadsheets and almanacs, brochures like *Les merveilles de l'industrie* exulted in the "miracles" of technology and tried to conjure them up for their readers. And the Singer company attributed the extraordinary success of its product to what it deemed an unassailable fact: "In every corner of the inhabitable world" sewing was women's work. In their view, the sewing machine was destined to become "the gentle and docile companion of any working woman—whether her skin be white, red, black, or yellow."[2] It could stitch together a far-flung empire where the common and "civilizing" bonds were the universality of women's essential roles and an admiration for modern technology.[3]

By the 1860s the sewing machine had become an especially compelling symbol of women's "modernity." It bore the burden of deeply conflicting expectations about women's work, expectations that were all the more charged with cultural meaning as a result of the era's rising debate about femininity, industry, and labor. Singer's advertisements of the 1860s and 1870s, like the writings of liberal political economists, celebrated technology's particular promise to women. Doctors in the 1860s and 1870s, sounding the same themes as Jules Simon, anguished about women's suitability

[1] John Scott, *Genius Rewarded*, p. 40.

[2] *Les merveilles de l'industrie à l'exposition de Lyon: The Singer Manufacturing and Co* [sic]. Brochure distributed at the 1872 industrial exposition of Lyon. From the files of the Singer company, avenue de l'Opéra, Paris.

[3] See advertisement for Singer, with the word SINGER floating confidently down what is intended to represent the Nile. Bibliothèque Forney, collection of advertisements. Another advertisement shows a crowned woman named "Civilization" standing before an African king. One of her hands points across the ocean to a large manufacturing plant spewing smoke; the other points to a small model sewing machine at the king's feet. Davies, *Peacefully Working*; also Brandon, *A Capitalist Romance*.

Calendar advertising Singer sewing machines, with a Victory figure honoring the machine with palm fronds and France and "Paris" shown on the globe below, 1891. Singer's global empire was a favorite theme in the company's advertisements.

for industrial labor and the effects of technological change on women's distinctly spiritual mission and destiny. By this time, sewing was so thoroughly
wrapped up in a more generalized image of femininity that no less than the
fate of womankind seemed at stake.

Singer's product also confronted economic obstacles. Garment manufacturers remained nearly indifferent to sewing technology, discouraged by the
clumsiness and expense of early sewing machines and reluctant to invest in
factories. Jobbing tailors and seamstresses on a shoestring budget could not
afford to purchase machines for themselves. Thus manufacturers who
sought to "conquer the world" with sewing machines faced the heady challenge of tapping a market for the machine among buyers who seemed unable to pay for it.

The introduction of this new technology was a complex undertaking, and
one that contributed to far-reaching changes in working-class consumption:
not only the availability of new kinds of goods, but the creation of wider
networks of credit, changes in the family economy, new kinds of advertising, and the promotion of different cultural ideas, including a new and
more modern(ist) gender imagery. The mobilization of a female labor force
for the garment industry was bound to the formation of a working-class
buying public. In this case particularly, the history of labor needs to move
beyond that of the workplace, for the introduction of the sewing machine is
a story about the interlocking transformations of production, consumption,
and gender.[4]

TECHNOLOGY, MASS PRODUCTION, AND CONQUEST: THE SEWING MACHINE INDUSTRY

From the beginnings of the new industry, around 1870, French sewing machine makers lagged far behind their American and English counterparts.
In the 1930s French technological experts were still ruing the extent to
which foreign sewing machine manufacturers dominated the world market.
One of them, with a combination of envy, admiration, and typical hyper-
bole, remarked that a single Singer plant employed forty thousand workers
and supplied sewing machines to "half the universe."[5]

Histories of technology traditionally ascribe the American advantage to
its sophisticated machine-tool industry. Indeed, the sewing machine has
provided the principle case history of how the "American system" of mass

---

[4] On sewing machines and production, see Michelle Perrot, "Machine à coudre et travail à
domicile," *Le Mouvement Social* 105 (October–December 1978); Hausen, "Technical Progress
and Women's Labour"; and Pellegrin, "Femmes et machine à coudre," pp. 65–71.

[5] *Le centenaire de la machine à coudre*, in *Exposition universelle de 1900*, p. 14. Bariquand,
"Matériel et procédés," in *Exposition universelle de 1878*, p. 2. Bariquand headed one of the first
French sewing machine companies, and he provides a good account of the first years of sewing
machine production in France.

production traveled to Europe. While the technology of the sewing machine itself was simple, the argument goes, the processes of its production were exceptionally complex, and this complexity propelled manufacturers toward assembly lines and automated machine tools.[6] The sewing machine was one of the first small precision instruments to be produced with interchangeable parts on an assembly line. The process demanded rigorously exact measuring instruments, automatic lathes with as many as eight cutting tools, and milling machines that combined cutters with swivels so they could grind out virtually any shape.[7]

This display of technological virtuosity impressed many contemporary observers. The 1873 Larousse's entry on "machines à coudre" lavished attention on novel aspects of the manufacturing process and was decidedly more concerned with advanced production techniques than with how sewing machines were used. "The plants are built on a very large scale and their organization can only be compared to that of big armories in the United States and England. The equipment is magnificent and admirably adapted to production; the parts are made by strictly mathematical processes so that two machines of the same calibre are absolutely identical." The Larousse article considered interchangeable parts significant for two reasons. First, they made assembly lines possible. Second, they were essential to the success of the home model, which needed to be easily and inexpensively maintained. "If customers break a piece of the machine, they can simply send the name of the part and the caliber of the machine to the manufacturer and receive a piece that will fit."[8]

This account of American technological prowess and expansion needs

[6] See Bariquand, "Matériel et procédés," in *Exposition universelle de 1878*; *Exposition universelle international de 1889*; *Exposition universelle de 1900*; *Musée rétrospectif de la classe 79*; Picard, *Le bilan d'un siècle*, 4:300–304; Granger, *Thimonnier et la machine à coudre*, p. 36; and the short notices in *Exposition de Londres en 1862*, p. 339; *Exposition de 1867: Rapports des délégations ouvrières*, p. 20; and *Exposition universelle de 1873*, p. 77. Visual evidence is also crucial, and I have drawn on engravings, posters, postcards, and pamphlets at the Bibliothèque Forney, Bibliothèque du Musée des Arts Décoratifs, and the Cabinet des Estampes at the Bibliothèque Nationale.

[7] David Landes, *The Unbound Prometheus* (Cambridge, 1969), pp. 307–17, on the technological preconditions for assembly line production. French manufacturers did not acquire the technical capacity for this kind of production until the 1870s. Goodyear pioneered important new technologies, but his most important contribution was to have demonstrated how factory organization assured efficient use of these machines. See Bariquand, "Matériel et procédés," in *Exposition universelle de 1878*, p. 25. The principal critic of this account is Hounshell, *From the American System to Mass Production*. Relations between French and American sewing machine manufacturers, the very complex developments of patents, and French companies' slow acquisition of manufacturing techniques are carefully analyzed by Peyrière, "Recherches sur la machine à coudre."

[8] "Machines à coudre," in *Le grand dictionnaire du 19e siècle*, by Pierre Larousse, 1873, pp. 864–65; "Rapport de la délégation des tailleurs," in *Exposition universelle de 1873*, p. 77.

revising. Sewing machine manufacturers did pioneer the use of machine tools that would later be used to build bicycles, typewriters, and, ultimately, automobiles; they wrote a crucial chapter in the history of mass production.[9] But that history is less linear and simple than we have thought. Ironically, the Singer company built its reputation and extended its reach over the world market while hewing to very traditional techniques. The Larousse may have extolled the technological wizardry of American manufacturers, but in 1873, as David Hounshell has demonstrated, Singer machines were built according to the "European system"—that is, by skilled machinists, who fitted the parts individually with files and hand tools—rather than assembled in mass production. Singer advertisements may have boasted interchangeable parts, but in reality, those parts were barely uniform, and machines had to be repaired, individually, in shops. Singer did not switch to the "American system" of assembly line production until the 1880s. And even then, the sparkling new factory in Elizabethport, New Jersey, described as "the largest establishment in the world devoted to the manufacture of a single article," was much less modern and efficient than we might expect. Singer was able to reduce the number of skilled "fitters" he employed, but hardly to dispense altogether with their files and handiwork.[10]

In this industry, as in others, rising demand created contradictory technological imperatives. On the one hand, manufacturers needed the speed and output of rationalized and more mechanized production. On the other, to maintain their market share, they required the certainty and quality of skilled hand work. The sewing machine industry and the garment industry might stand at opposite poles of a spectrum, but both had this in common: expanding markets had no single and predictable effect on processes of production.

Likewise, technological innovation did not offer the key to success in this industry. The French sewing machine manufacturer Edouard Bariquand, reporting from the world's fair of 1878, claimed that foreign manufacturers had made no contribution to sewing technology. Any visitor to the exposition who was truly interested in that subject, he remarked acerbically, could simply skip the American exhibits. His fellow French industrialists were bolder and more energetic in the realm of technological innovation; they had concentrated their efforts on developing specialized machines to be used in the hundreds of different branches of the garment industry. But this strategy exacted a toll: high costs and low profits.[11]

[9] Landes, *Unbound Prometheus*, p. 308; Hounshell, *From the American System to Mass Production*, pp. 75–82.

[10] One of Singer's production engineers thought that rising demand, far from pressing Singer toward mechanized production, had set the company even more firmly in its older ways of "dubious hand work." B. F. Spalding quoted in Hounshell, *From the American System to Mass Production*, p. 107.

[11] He attributed these problems to indifference in the case of garment manufacturers and to

Initially, foreign manufacturers fared no better in France. The French market had been one of Singer's first targets. The Parisian garment industry in particular, with its hundreds of branches and thousands of workers, beckoned enticingly; Paris was also a logical beachhead on the European continent. The Singer company sought out agents in the city's needle trades, and in 1854, for thirty thousand francs, sold a franchise to a Monsieur Callebaut, vice president of the Tailors Association. While Singer considered the price too low, the company expected fast results, estimating several thousand sales in the first year. Callebaut sold only 426.[12]

In 1858, embarking on new strategy, Callebaut requested a new French patent for a small model Singer, an industrial machine adapted to home use. Callebaut cited the crucial need for a "machine de famille" that could do industrial work while conforming to domestic interiors decorated with "tasteful" pieces of furniture.[13] The decision reflected several cultural as well as economic calculations. To concentrate on the home model was a gesture toward the organization of the garment industry in which outwork predominated. It was also a decision to cut costs; a "family" machine meant an inexpensive one. Finally, it marked an effort to define the Singer as a "woman's" machine.

From the late 1850s on, Singer and the American manufacturers channeled their energies into the small model sewing machine and marketing. "The best foreign houses have started to advertise in gigantic proportions," Bariquand wrote, "—far beyond anything we are accustomed to in France. They have practically imposed certain names on the public."[14] Singer in particular poured money into advertising and lavishly decorated showrooms staffed by women who demonstrated how to use the machine. Other manufacturers offered courses that introduced the machines to consumers, and they encouraged the development of patterns with explicit and detailed directions.[15]

In the 1870s, both production and sales soared. Specialized machinery to be used in factories provided some of the stimulus. Still, it is clear that the

---

hostility in the case of families. Bariquand, "Matériel et procédés," in *Exposition universelle de 1878*, p. 2.

[12] Davies, *Peacefully Working*, pp. 24–25.

[13] *Exposition universelle de 1900*, pp. 18, 19. In 1855, Singer tried to set up a factory in Paris. Hounshell, *From the American System to Mass Production*, p. 88. This effort may or may not have involved Callebaut.

[14] Bariquand, "Matériel et procédés," in *Exposition universelle de 1878*, pp. 2–5. Bariquand singled out Singer's aggressive advertising. On the American sewing machine industry, see Hounshell, *From the American System to Mass Production*; Cooper, *The Sewing Machine*; William Ewers and H. W. Baylor, *Sincere's History of the Sewing Machine* (Phoenix, Ariz., 1970); Brandon, *A Capitalist Romance*; James Parton, "The History of the Sewing Machine," *The Atlantic Monthly*, May 1867.

[15] The appearance of such patterns can be traced in *Journal des Demoiselles*, *Petit Echo de la Mode*, and *Moniteur de la Mode*. Most of these patterns were used by seamstresses.

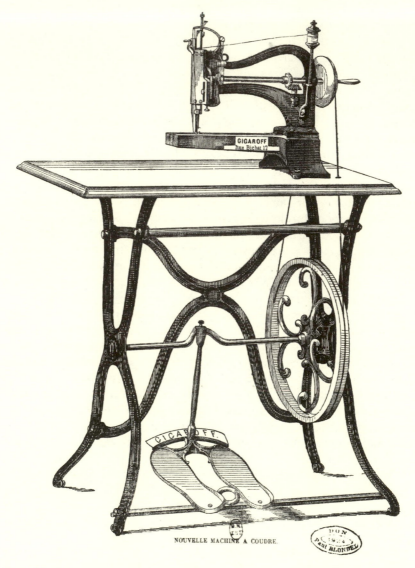

NOUVELLE MACHINE A COUDRE.

Gigaroff's "new sewing machine," 1864. Intended for "families," this machine closely resembled Singer's model A machine.

better part of this retooling was financed by small tailors and seamstresses adapting the machine to their tiny shops. In 1872, almost 50 percent of the sewing machines sold in Paris were purchased by workers, and nearly 20 percent went to "families."[16] The rest went to convents.[16] The "family" mar-

[16] Chambre de commerce de Paris, *Enquête sur les conditions du travail*, pp. 42–43. On sales,

ket made cutting prices crucial. In the late 1860s, a good machine mounted on a table cost four hundred francs; by the late 1870s, the price had fallen to two hundred francs retail.[17]

CREDIT AND WORKING-CLASS CONSUMPTION

Even two hundred francs remained, in the Larousse's words, "inabordable." Few working women or men could purchase such an expensive device outright, and certainly not tailors and seamstresses. In the late 1870s an ordinary family model cost anywhere from one-fifth to one-half of a seamstress's extremely unstable yearly earnings. Only more widespread use of credit, which came in the 1890s, permitted many persons of "humble fortune" to acquire the newfangled device, starting with a down payment of twenty francs.[18]

Credit was by no means a new institution or practice. The peasant economy had long run on a combination of credit, barter, and payment in kind, all supplemented by infusions of cash from heartily detested local moneylenders. By the late eighteenth century, the urban economy had spawned highly developed customary credit practices. In the cities, working people rarely paid cash for their food. Families owed money to the neighborhood butcher, the wine merchant, and, of course, the baker (the "banker of the neighborhood"), whose role as a source of credit gave him enormous power over urban housekeepers.[19] After neighborhood merchants, the principal source of credit for the popular classes were the pawnshops, where a loan could be procured at 6 or 7 percent interest against any item of value. Pawnshops piled high with mattresses, linens, wool blankets, jewelry, and the

---

see Bariquand, "Matériel et procédés," in *Exposition universelle de 1878*, pp. 37–39; Picard, *Exposition universelle de 1889*, 7:113–15. Between 1873 and 1889, sales in France rose from 20,000 to 150,000 annually.

[17] Bariquand, "Matériel et procédés," in *Exposition universelle de 1878*, pp. 2–5. On pricing and patents held by the Sewing Machine Trust, a patent pool of at least four American manufacturers, see Cooper, *The Sewing Machine*, and Peyrière, "Recherches sur la machine à coudre."

[18] Despite high tariffs, Singer held the lion's share of the French market until the late 1890s, when German companies took its place. Fewer than one in seven of those machines bought in France were produced there. Du Maroussem, *Le vêtement à Paris* in Office du Travail, *La petit industrie*, p. 34. See also Walter Kohler, *Die Deutsche Nahmaschinen-Industrie* (Bielefeld, 1912), p. 279; and Hausen, "Technological Progress and Women's Labour." France and Russia were the largest export markets for German machines.

[19] Couture, *Des différentes combinaisons*, p. 5. On the history of credit, see Chambre de commerce de Paris, *Enquête sur les conditions du travail*, questionnaire A, no. 12, pp. 13–14; Roche, *Le peuple de Paris*, p. 85; Sonenscher, *Work and Wages*; Guy Thuillier, *Pour une histoire de la vie quotidienne au 19e siècle en Nivernais* (Paris, 1977), pp. 382, 386; Eugen Weber, *Peasants into Frenchmen: The Modernization of Rural France* (Stanford, 1976), pp. 38–40; Avenel, *Le mécanisme de la vie moderne*, 4:364, 365, 373; Henri Leyret, *En plein faubourg* (Paris, 1895), pp. 49–50; and Williams, *Dream Worlds*, pp. 92–94.

occasional piece of family silver testified to increasingly complex networks of credit. Workers used pawnshops, but so did small manufacturers and merchants, for interest rates were lower than those of other financial institutions. These institutions remained embedded in daily life and finances. By the mid-nineteenth century, state officials, working-class leaders, and novelists were all calling attention to French (and especially Parisian) workers' "inveterate" habit of spending beyond their means and buying everything—from groceries and coal to clothes—on credit. Workers who replied to a government survey on the subject in 1872 said that the difficulty of depositing and withdrawing money from banks made it impossible to save in the way that economists thought that they should, and that the absence of any regular credit establishments contributed to the long lines outside the pawnshops. Others claimed that working people simply refused to save and that practices were too deeply anchored in French life to change.[20]

Installment payment plans pioneered by the sewing machine industry in the 1870s, then, hardly entailed a new attitude toward money; it would have been a far greater novelty to persuade working people to pay for even small items with cash. Still, the last third of the nineteenth century witnessed significant changes in how working people borrowed and bought. Workers were paid more frequently, shortening the long waits between paydays and reducing the need for small, short-term loans. Merchants and café owners who previously had extended this kind of credit to all comers became less willing to do so. At the same time, the new consumer items of the late nineteenth century, like furniture, sewing machines, and bicycles, required much larger sums of money. In the words of one economist, desires were multiplying more rapidly than "the spirit of foresight, or saving."[21] The result was a continuing crisis in the working-class family economy, which, combined with the ambitions of large retailers, produced a newly organized and large-scale credit industry. That industry expanded beyond the boundaries and control of neighborhood grocers or wine bars. Instead of running a tab and borrowing small amounts to buy everyday necessities, working people made larger purchases on credit. Credit transactions became more formal. Over the course of a few decades, new credit institutions transformed the relationship between manufacturers of consumer goods and the people of France.

The leader among these new institutions was the "Grands Magasins Dufayel." The enterprise was launched in 1856 by a Monsieur Créspin who, after a short stint in the army, established himself in Paris selling photographic portraits on credit. Créspin's success encouraged him to start sell-

---

[20] Chambre de commerce de Paris, *Enquête sur les conditions du travail*, questionnaire A, no. 12, pp. 13–14.

[21] Couture, *Des différentes combinaisons*, pp. 4, 8. Couture's book was virtually a brief for establishing popular savings banks.

ing other merchandise, like clothing and linens, and to expand his credit operations. Créspin sold credit in the form of coupons (*bons d'abonnement*) which his clients could use at designated merchants' stores. For a down payment of twenty francs, a customer purchased a Créspin coupon worth one hundred francs of merchandise. In return for being supplied with customers, those merchants discounted their bills to Créspin 10 to 20 percent from the retail price.[22] Combined with the interest charged to the client, this produced a profit so handsome that the enterprise was accused of fraud.

Créspin's business thrived. His successor, Georges Dufayel, added new operations, including, in the 1880s, a department store on the Boulevard Barbès in working-class Paris. The plebian counterpart of department stores like the Bon Marché or the Magasins du Louvre, which accepted only cash, Dufayel's was the first department store to offer all its wares on credit. Dufayel next opened a store in the suburb of Versailles, and by 1904, he had outlets in all the principal cities of France.[23] "The largest department store in the world; and the best bargains in all of Paris!" claimed the company's catalogue.

The main store sprawled across several blocks from the rue de Clingnancourt to the Boulevard Barbès. Its domes towered over the neighborhood, and its credit networks extended into nearly all the popular quarters of Paris, which were divided into rounds (*tournées*) of two streets and assigned to a Dufayel salesman (*abonneur*), who sold "subscriptions." Anyone who had been living at one address for at least six months could apply without even venturing into the store. The salesman carried a booklet that recorded information on his clients, including the initial deposit, how many payments had been made, and the reliability of the customer. In order to allay Parisians' long-standing suspicions of authority, Dufayel had to reassure his customers that this information was in secret code, and could not be used by the police.[24] By 1907, three of every seven working-class families in Paris had taken out subscriptions to Dufayel.[25]

The system bridged old and new forms of commerce. Obviously aimed at a national market and marshaling enormous capital, Dufayel's credit network nonetheless relied on local contacts, word of mouth, and face-to-face encounters. Concierges, for instance, were crucial sources of information for the salesman, their tendency to gossip coaxed along by "giving them

[22] Ibid., pp. 67–71; Avenel, *Le mécanisme de la vie moderne*, vol. 4, chap. 18, pt. 2, "Les bons Crépin-Dufayel"; Miller, *The Bon Marché*, pp. 178–79; and Berlanstein, *The Working People of Paris*.

[23] See Couture, *Des différentes combinaisons*, p. 79, and Dufayel brochures in the Service Recueil at the Bibliothèque Nationale.

[24] Couture, *Des différentes combinaisons*, p. 73.

[25] What was more, families spent as much making their credit payments as they did on clothing. Perrot, *Les ouvriers en grève*, 2:211, n.36. The history of credit and popular notions of thrift and economy still need to be investigated.

easy terms for their payments."[26] But the company also used the information these salesmen thus gathered to strike out in new directions. Dufayel became one of the first French advertising agencies, conducting market research, publishing surveys, and compiling mailing lists.[27]

Dufayel was vital to the economic terrain of the "new Paris" of the fin de siècle, built up by large-scale commerce, retailing, credit, and advertising. His success created a compelling model for retailers with a variety of markets.[28] Department stores had aimed to break with the practices of traditional markets: to set prices, eliminate bargaining, and get customers to pay cash. Ironically, by the end of the nineteenth century the same magasins, pressed by Dufayel's example, had raised the credit system to "the heights of perfection."[29] Dufayel clearly relished its revolutionary role. The company's brochure was illustrated with an engraving of the cash registers, which, the text breathlessly explained, "seem to extend as far as the eye can see. The bustle of the enormous crowd offers a glimpse of only a small part of the prodigious business of this enterprise."[30] Long receding rows of tellers' booths suggested the vastness of Dufayel's operations. The entire scene, including the throngs of people and the track-like perspective lines, evokes a railroad station—an eloquent reference to the expanded horizons, the new vistas, and the (social) mobility made possible by payment on credit.

The sewing machine was Dufayel's most widely advertised item. It figured prominently in engravings and views of the interior, in advertisements, and in descriptive pamphlets. The "immense department" of sewing machines stood at the top of the central staircase, just below four stained glass windows emblazoned with the store's slogan: "Saving, Confidence, Abundance, and Work."[31] It was a key item in the store's self-presentation, an emblem of its appeal and possibilities. That appeal was partly practical: Dufayel offered credit to buy expensive necessities, and the catalogue offered a wide range of industrial and "home" sewing machines alongside, for instance, coal stoves. Dufayel's promise was also cultural. Brochures for the Barbès store,

---

[26] Couture, *Des différentes combinaisons*, p. 72.

[27] By 1904, Dufayel had 3,500 regular subscribers. Ibid., p. 75. In 1893, Dufayel's trade journal, *L'Affichage Nationale*, offered, for example, lists of 600,000 Parisians classified by profession, *milieux*, or *situation*. (Brochure found in Service Recueil at the Bibliothèque Nationale, p. 26.)

[28] Couture, *Des différentes combinaisons*, pp. 79–81. The collections of the Musée de la Publicité, now in the Musée des Arts Décoratifs, document the rapid expansion of stores selling on credit to working- and middle-class people. Stores with names like "Au Classes Laborieuses," "Le Bon Génie," "Les Phares de la Bastille," and other cheap clothing stores promised "everything on credit": small down payments, and fifteen to thirty months to pay. See series in the Bibliothèque du Musée des Arts Décoratifs on "grands magasins."

[29] Couture, *Des différentes combinaisons*, p. 10. First other stores accepted Dufayel's coupons, then they adopted his methods.

[30] *Une visite aux grands magasins Dufayel*, 1902.

[31] Ibid.

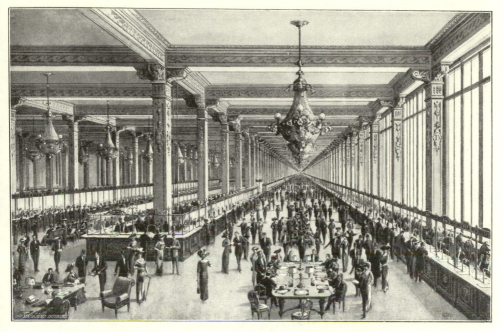

"The new central arcade for making payments at the Dufayel department store."
Engraving from promotional brochure, *Visite aux grands magasins Dufayel*, 1902,
p. 15.

striking a different chord, showed working-class families ogling sewing machines in elegant cases on the store floor along with imposing furniture,
decorated mirrors, clocks, and pianos; all of these, even the most utilitarian,
could be considered furnishings to upgrade a household. As one economist-
critic remarked, "the whole [credit] industry gives the appearance of luxury
for cheap."[32] But what Dufayel offered and promoted was a more specific
cultural ideal: the working-class version of a middle-class *foyer*, or home.
Such a place was more than a shelter; it was a center of leisure and self-
expression. It was not simply a locus, but a mood and a sign of status, and it
had to be *created*, through careful purchases, chez Dufayel. Credit made it
possible for working-class women to make their homes in the same way
that their middle-class counterparts had done for decades. Pictures and descriptions of Dufayel's interior deliberately mirrored those of the Bon
Marché and other middle-class stores.[33] Thus Dufayel's cultural innovations

[32] Couture, *Des différentes combinaisons*, pp. 3–4.

[33] See text and illustrations in *Journal illustré des grands magasins Dufayel*; *Une visite aux
grands magasins Dufayel*; and Williams, *Dream Worlds*. On middle-class consumption and its
relationship to ideas of the home, see Auslander, *Taste and Power*; Adrien Forty, *Objects of
Desire: Design and Society, 1750–1980* (London, 1986); and, still, Halbwachs, *La classe ouvrière
et les niveaux de vie*, esp. pp. 130–35.

Advertisement for Créspin offering, on credit: clocks, jewelry, furniture, sewing machines and pleating machines, novelties, and different kinds of coal, 1891.

and messages were intimately linked to the enterprise's economic and social significance. It was a celebration of modernity, consumption, and the "home," and it offered all of these to the popular classes via credit. It held out a working-class version of modern domesticity.

Dufayel's success helped make traveling salesmen and installment payment plans commonplace. Sewing machine manufacturers tried to reach the public directly by sending out their own salesmen. In some regions, salesmen also helped clothing manufacturers recruit workers by traveling from house to house in search of families needing extra income. They claimed virtually any woman could learn to sew a straight line and then hire herself to one of the many shirt manufacturers nearby. This work would allow her to make payments on her machine and earn a little extra money as well. Labor organizers charged that such tactics had helped to create a small army of barely skilled seamstresses working part time in the garment industry.[34]

In areas where clothing manufacturers had large networks of hand-workers, they "tried with all their power" to make women use machines and raise their productivity.[35] Employers lent machines out to women, but discovered to their irritation that doing so increased their workers' independence and bargaining power; temporarily equipped with their own machines, seamstresses could secure work from other manufacturers who offered better or steadier pay. For the same reason, workers purchased their own machines whenever possible, saying that doing so allowed them to work for whom they pleased.[36]

But the price of this independence was indebtedness. Wage-earning seamstresses faced a dilemma. Not to have a sewing machine doomed one to the cheapest kind of hand work, but low wages and very high seasonal unemployment made embarking on a credit payment plan a risky venture. In some regions and trades, workers calculated that a machine simply did not justify the risk, and they refused to abandon hand work, no matter how poorly paid.[37] Promises and hopes notwithstanding, in many cases debt added to the burden of overwork, long days, and low wages in the garment trades.

Credit from Dufayel and from the sewing machine manufacturers was expensive. Workers in the garment industry reckoned that sewing machines were sold at over twice their value, and surprisingly, manufacturers agreed with that estimate.[38] Moreover, Dufayel and other retailers sold sewing machines *à tempérament* (lease-to-buy plan), which meant they waived the

[34] Office du Travail, Enquête . . . lingerie, 3:421–23; 5:54, 68. See also Aftalion, *Le développement de la fabrique*, p. 68. We will consider the question of regional development and women's employment in the next chapter.

[35] Enquête . . . lingerie, 5:66. Charitable and religious societies set up programs teaching poor women how to machine stitch and helping them to buy or rent cheap machines. Brochure from the "Association pour faciliter aux ouvrières l'achat d'une machine à coudre," in Bibliothèque Marguerite Durand, dossier, "Machine à coudre"; Espagne, *De l'industrie des machines à coudre*, p. 22; and Pellegrin, "Femmes et machine à coudre."

[36] Enquête . . . lingerie, 5:101. See worker monographs, nos. 44, 68, 77, and 90.

[37] Enquête . . . lingerie, 5:66–67. See also 3:421–23.

[38] Ibid., 5:68.

down payment, offered free delivery, and required no payment for the first month. But this practice was considered a rental, which meant that when customers could not make payments they lost their machines, and none of their money was reimbursed.[39]

Expanding networks of credit and salesmen transformed the market for sewing machines, the garment industry, and women's work. The abundance and cheapness of labor in the garment industry had long created powerful disincentives to mechanization. They were the principal reasons for garment manufacturers' relative indifference to new sewing technologies. Women's labor in the household was similarly cheap, or undervalued. Thus mechanization only happened when widespread credit enabled workers, whether as small subcontractors or pieceworkers, to shoulder the burden of the transition themselves.

GENDERING THE SEWING MACHINE:
ADVERTISING AND DESIGN

Sewing machine manufacturers were among the most aggressive advertisers of the nineteenth century. Yet how to advertise their machine, and how to represent their market, posed real dilemmas. Some of the problems arose from the nexus of ideas surrounding women, technology, and the home. Medieval and early modern guild regulations had specifically banned use of machines in the home and prohibited women from operating them. The aim of those regulations had been to combat "clandestine," non-guild, home production and to guard trade secrets and craft hierarchies. Nineteenth-century taboos were different, more concerned with preserving the tranquillity of the *foyer* and with separating the home, a sphere of privacy and family life, from a more intrusive industrial economy.[40] But older and newer ideas overlapped and reinforced each other.

Nineteenth-century advertisers began with inherited cultural imagery and traditional depictions of women in the workplace. Several conventions seemed to govern these inherited images. Eighteenth-century engravings of women workers in the clothing trades were often a pretext for pornographic

---

[39] Couture, *Des différentes combinaisons*, pp. 8, 87. The working-class press of the late nineteenth century frequently denounced the *maisons d'abonnement*, arguing that the onus of credit perpetuated the enslavement of labor. "If a family is late in its payments, the problems begin; the interest piles up, so do the costs, and these enormous 'treasure houses' become enormous centers of usury." *Le Cri du Peuple*, as cited in Perrot, *Les ouvriers en grève*, 1:211. See also "Honteuse Exploitation," *L'Eveil Démocratique*, December 8, 1907; and Bonneff, *La vie tragique des travailleurs*, pp. 288–90.

[40] Smith, *Ladies of the Leisure Class*; Forty, *Objects of Desire*, pp. 118–19 and chap. 5 in general.

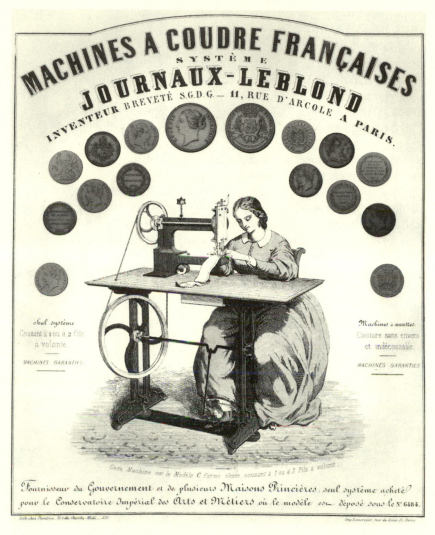

Advertisement for Journaux-LeBlond, the "only French device accepted for the London Exposition of 1862."

or erotic fantasies and merged depictions of the commerce in fabrics and clothing with evocations of prostitution. Eighteenth- and early-nineteenth-century engravings of the lingerie trade, for instance, showed women flirting with their male clients and provided voyeuristic peeks at groups of women together behind closed doors. Seamstresses' fantasies (romantic, materialistic, or both) were also favorite themes and likewise can be read as projections of the viewers' desires. Unlike representations of male labor, which focused on the worker and the work process, those of female labor centered instead on commerce and sales and on women as vendors or beautiful objects. The "artistry" of working "girls" was the closest any came to acknowledging skill. Intimate conversations, gossip and rumors, and flaunting workshop rules and discipline were represented as the core of seamstresses' "work culture."[41] Representations of femininity endowed women with qualities like dexterity, taste, intuition, and artistry, but sharply distinguished those from craft, skills, and technological mastery, which were acquired and maintained in the masculine world of the shop. Artisan elites worked with machines, operating and repairing them; it was difficult to imagine "Jenny l'ouvrière," gazing dreamily out her garret window, doing anything of the sort. The iconographic storehouse from which advertisers and designers drew did not associate women with machinery.

In principle, the sewing machine had many possible destinations, or markets, for the garment industry had a male as well as female labor force and a mix of home and shop trades. In its infancy, then, the sewing machine was polymorphous. But particularly in marketing and advertising, these tendencies were repressed in favor of a more gendered identity. Manufacturers almost immediately began to differentiate machines and markets, multiplying the number of models available and advertising various specialized machines as male and all-purpose or "family" ones as female. These categories hardly meshed with the actual division of labor in the garment trades, but they did comport with the culture's gendered notions of skill: men were trained to be specialized, they acquired expertise, and they could handle complicated technologies, while women did "all-purpose" work. The "Singer girl," who appeared in the company's advertisements from the beginning, became the trademark of Singer's aggressive effort to associate itself with the home model.[42] An engraving used in early Singer advertisements illustrates this effort nicely. Scores of men are drilling holes, stamp-

[41] The visual material on lingères and couturières is enormous and scattered through various archives. The largest collections are at the Bibliothèque Nationale, Cabinet des Estampes, "métiers" (Md 43) and "moeurs" (Oa22) collections and at the Bibliothèque du Musée des Arts Décoratifs, Maciet collection, series 330 ("métiers") and 35 ("boutiques et magasins").

[42] Tailors' journals were virtually the only ones to run advertisements in this early period. In these early years of distribution, tailors and entrepreneurs were clearly expected to buy them for their wives and women workers.

Visual materials and advertising archives offer the best evidence for the evolution of design. Drawings of Thimonnier's early machine can be found in Meyssin, Histoire d'une invention, p. 9, and in the Bibliothèque du Musée des Arts Décoratifs, series 330.23 "couturières." An early Singer, in the middle of its metamorphosis toward the home model, with what is clearly a working-class woman operating the machine, can be seen in the Journal des Tailleurs (December 15, 1856), p. 7. The ornamental painting and ironwork are well illustrated in an advertisement for Pfaff, 1901, in Bibliothèque Forney. Forty, Objects of Desire; and Penny Sharpe, An Introduction to Design and Culture in the Twentieth Century (New York, 1986); Susan Strasser, Satisfaction Guaranteed: The Making of the American Mass Market (New York, 1989).

ing out parts, molding bases, and manipulating lathes. The female figures sit in the showroom demonstrating the use of the sewing machine.[43] Manufacturing these machines was men's work, the advertisement made clear, but operating them was women's.

A pamphlet distributed by one of the first French manufacturers had been illustrated with a soldier sewing at a machine, but within a few decades references to men sewing became few and far between. The exceptions are interesting. A poster, issued around 1900 for the Compagnie française de la machine à coudre showed a tailor sewing a Prussian flag. "Women of France, take notice!!" the caption reads, "No more foreign competition! Victory!" The "competition" was ostensibly the German sewing machine industry, represented by the Prussian tailor, but the advertisement also drew on reservoirs of hostility to men competing in the "women's trades." The other advertisements depicting men—the colonialist "civilizing mission" images cited in the introduction and an advertisement for Singer's outlet in Tunis—portrayed "picturesque" or "exotic" scenes. By the late nineteenth century, a man at a sewing machine became a kind of anthropological flash card; instantly recognizable as foreign.[44]

The Victorianism of the mid-nineteenth century, with its intense preoccupation with home and femininity, produced some very strange efforts to gender the machine "female." Manufacturers offered sewing machines that incorporated elaborate sculptures into the simple machinery: a squirrel (suggesting frugality and prudence), a cupid with a bow drawn, and a golden scissors.[45] During the Second Empire, machines were advertised in fashion plates, where they seem particularly out of place perched delicately on table tops, resting under the gloved hands of elaborately dressed ladies. Advertisements exaggerated the machine's femininity, as if it were trying on a gender for the first time. The fussiness of these models, and the pictures of them, are reminders of how strange such a machine seemed, at least to a middle-class home, and how forced was the connection between a sewing machine and femininity in the 1860s.

Most advertisements from this early period (1850s–1870s), though, seem less contrived. To the contrary, they contributed to creating and disseminating the now-familiar tropes of nineteenth-century domesticity: the contrast of public and private, industry and home, and male and female. They commonly juxtaposed descriptions or engravings of sewing machine factories with their blast furnaces, smokestacks, and brawny men carrying rods of pig iron with the world of women, needlework, family chores, and the home.

[43] See the two-page engraving advertising Callebaut's enterprise in *Journal des Tailleurs* (January 1862): 4–5.

[44] Espagne, *De l'industrie des machines à coudre*, p. 4. The collection of postcards at the Bibliothèque Forney is full of picturesque or "folklorique" scenes: "the old tailors of Finistère," "Egyptians and Arabs [sic] knitting," and so on. See "couture."

[45] See the illustrations in Cooper, *The Sewing Machine*, p. 48.

French Sewing Machine Company advertising poster, circa 1900, part of a nationalist response to marketing and sales of German sewing machines in France.

"The machine pictured . . . is manufactured by the company called Singer . . . 10 percent off for cash payment. . . . The price of this sewing machine is 110 francs or more depending on features. . . . Insist on the Singer trademark, here on the right." Advertising poster for Singer outlet in Tunis. 1892.

Advertisement for "Le Follet," showing "silk dresses from the Union des Indes and sewing machine from André et Fontaine," 1860.

They acclaimed the excitement of progress, industry, and technology, "celebrating the mass in mass production"; at the same time, they strove to wed that excitement to the reassuring imagery of separate spheres.[46] Engravings showed the whole family going into a machine showroom or a woman alone at her machine, framed, more often than not, by a window looking onto the

[46] Scott, *Genius Rewarded*; advertisements for the "Compagnie française de la machine à coudre" in the Musée National des Techniques; Strasser, *Satisfaction Guaranteed.*

Advertisement for Hurtu, French sewing machine manufacturer, showing the Hurtu factory and gold and silver medals from the 1878 Exposition.

world *outside*. Most advertisements also had a broader appeal than the fashion plates and the golden-scissors machine, whose sensibility was so unabashedly middle class. The "sewing machine girl" who figured in advertisements from Singer, LeBlond, Gigaroff, and other French manufacturers, was simply dressed, with a small lace collar, long dark skirt, and hair fastened neatly. She could easily have been a working woman, but not surprisingly the advertisements cast her as a paragon of domestic industry and womanly virtue who transcended social class.

The 1880s and 1890s, however, marked an important turning point in the history of advertising and brought important innovations in both techniques and images. The transformation of large-scale commerce and retailing was so dramatic that several late-nineteenth-century writers wrote of witnessing a "second industrial revolution," fueled not by electricity and oil, but by credit and advertising.[47] Fin-de-siècle Paris stood at the center of this revolution, for the increasingly aggressive presence of department stores and a series of world's fairs made the city the largest advertising

[47] "The transformation accomplished through credit was as dramatic and significant as the replacement [sic] of handwork by machine work." *La Publicité* (1903–4): 12.

"New machines for sewing, quilting, and embroidery, from LeRoy and Company, 1864," a characteristically 1860s advertisement.

market in the world.[48] Forms of advertising multiplied. Handbills passed out on corners gave way to expensively produced mail-order catalogues and

[48] See Avenel, *Le mécanisme de la vie moderne*, 3:174. On advertising, see Auslander, *Taste and Power*; Marjorie Beale, "The Politics of Public Persuasion in France, 1900–1939" (Ph.D. diss., University of California, Berkeley, 1992); Marc Martin, *Trois siècles de publicité en France* (Paris, 1992); Nord, *Paris Shopkeepers*, pp. 69, 75–78; Miller, *The Bon Marché*, pp. 173–79 and 181–83; Roche, *Le peuple de Paris*, pp. 229–33; and Williams, *Dream Worlds*. I have also consulted histories of poster art: Max Gallo, *The Poster in History* (New York, 1972); Roger Marx, *Masters of the Poster, 1896–1900* (New York, 1977); Ernest Maindron, *Les affiches illustrées* (Paris, 1896); Abdy, *The French Poster*; Conservatoire National des Arts et Métiers, *Exposi-*

to posters—hallmarks of the belle époque. (These were intended primarily to make brand names familiar, enhancing the value of the company's catalogue, with more detailed information on the products and prices.) "Advertising is the soul of commerce," explained a brochure mailed out by Dufayel, capturing the new thinking on the subject, and it went on to list the various venues in Paris where merchants could hang their posters for a fee. In addition to street walls (listed by arrondissement), railroad stations, and kiosks, Dufayel offered space in urinals (exterior or, one hopes less expensively, interior), at the Bastille on the hundredth anniversary of its fall, in the "brightly lit chalets of the world's fairs," or on the "allegorical curtain" at the Folies Bergères.[49] As with credit, Dufayel played a key role in developing advertising. The selling of credit and the making of names and products familiar all helped create and attract a new buying public.

At the end of the century, too, the basis of advertising was shifting; advertising sought to become more "scientific" and to connect its techniques to studies of potential consumers. Dufayel's pioneering market surveys classified thousands of Parisians by the level of rent they paid, and Dufayel sold those rolls to merchants. Trade journals that critically reviewed advertisements emerged and articulated the "basic laws of advertising." Those "laws" became increasingly psychological, although few could agree on what psychology entailed. Articles discussed the importance of repetition and clarity, debated whether "harmony" or "intensity" would more effectively imprint a message, reviewed the use of symbols, and counseled advertisers about how to use associations and images to link their product to their target audience among a new group of consumers.[50]

That target audience was increasingly female. One article in *La Publicité Moderne* claimed to have found that 80 percent of all department store purchases had been made by women.[51] Many of the subsequent studies of women's needs were remarkably straightforward. Articles explained that women liked sales and that they carefully compared prices and models, working through both visual and written detail in advertisements.[52] Journal articles (often incorrectly) considered women to hold the key to household

---

tion de l'affiche en couleurs de Chéret à nos jours (Paris, 1939); and Alain Weill, ed., *Trois siècles de l'affiche française: 1ère exposition du Musée de l'affiche* (Paris, 1978). On Europe in general, see de Grazia, "The Arts of Purchase," pp. 221–57.

[49] Dufayel, *L'Affichage Nationale* (1889): 42–57.

[50] As one of these new trade journals put it, "L'affiche est sortie de l'empiricisme et est devenue une véritable science dont il importe de préciser les lois." *La Publicité Moderne* (March 1908). See also, in the same journal, "Six principes de la psychologie" (November 1907); "Les bases scientifiques de la publicité" (October–November 1908). Writers took pains to point out "ce qu'il faut dire, ce qu'il faut taire." On psychology and its relationship to advertising, see Silverman, *Art Nouveau in Fin-de-Siècle France*, chap. 5.

[51] "Conquerez les femmes," *La Publicité Moderne* (May 1908).

[52] Ibid.

spending. As one article on women and advertising summarized its find-ings, the "home" was "the umbilical cord of our economic and social world."[53] How, exactly, the author envisioned this anatomy and the rela-tionship it represented is not clear, but the metaphor is revealing about gender and the economy in the era's developing social thought. Money spent on or channeled through the home (newly adorned as a well-appointed interior) was the emergent economy's lifeblood, and it flowed through an unmistakably gendered vessel.

Developments of the 1890s also helped refashion advertising imagery. The home as a center of display and consumption, modernity, and the "new woman" who embodied all of these, supplied an extraordinary variety of new themes to manufacturers, industrial designers, department stores, and poster artists.[54] Even the most practical consumer good could signify some-thing about its owner's class or status. Catalogues advertised sewing ma-chines' "beautiful cabinetry," and their "mahogany wood." They elevated their class standing, describing them as "rich" "furnishings," "extremely elegant," that could grace "bourgeois interiors" and be suitable "in any mi-lieu." Almost all advertisements underscored the machine's dual purpose as a *gagne pain* (breadwinner) and *beau décors* (handsome furnishing). One particularly emphatic line of catalogue copy asserted, "The sewing machine will be valued as a mode of existence [*moyen d'existence*] as well as an appliance with so many uses in the home."[55]

The catalogues highlighted this association of the sewing machine with a new "mode of existence," and downplayed its links to a mode of produc-tion. By the 1890s, domesticated sewing machine advertisements beckoned to working- and lower-middle-class families as well as to the more elite bourgeois. Many of them showed cozy, well-furnished parlors in which these instruments of toil were displayed; they were images that represented ways in which lower-middle- and working-class households could become "homes." Advertised, as it was, along with bicycles, the sewing machine stood for modernity, freedom, and technological advance. Like the piano, with which it was often compared, it symbolized self-expression, evoking images of female crafts and domestic activities. The sewing machine was marketed as a vehicle of an emerging popular consumerism, presented to

[53] "Les femmes et l'annonce," *La Publicité Moderne* (1920–21): 301–2. They used the En-glish term "home."

[54] The new woman was "modern" in that she was unconstrained by traditional prescrip-tions about domesticity and virtue; her ties to the home were as a consumer who embellished that home.

[55] Pfaff brochure, 1901. See catalogues from Erda and Griga, Howe, Hurtu, Panneton frères, A. Petit, Pfaff, Singer, Stoewer, and Wallut in the collection of catalogues at the Bibliothèque Forney and advertisements for Gigaroff in the Bibliothèque Nationale, Cabinet des Estampes, R4560 and R4599. Cabinets often cost double the price of the machinery, underscoring that the product's value was not simply utilitarian.

"The best sewing machine is Howe's," postcard advertisement, 1905.

"Athos, a new sewing machine, with a circular bobbin." "Don't cry, little Pierre, Martha is fixing your trousers!" Postcard advertisement, 1910.

women as a symbol of modern femininity and framed in a picture of a new and distinctly modern popular domesticity. In that picture, industrial labor (as piecework) could be done in the home and, time permitting, sewing skills could be directed toward work for the family; the "labor saving" machine seemed to promise sufficient time to make fashionable clothes for oneself. These ideals had real resonance in wide circles of workers, artisans, and clerical employees.

The new aesthetics and gender imagery of modernity pressed belle époque advertising in many different directions. Graphic artists began to reinterpret the rich iconographic tradition involving women spinning and sewing. They used sorcerers and magicians, harking back to Rapunzel and to seamstresses' folklore about fairies who inhabited their workshops. Familiarly "Victorian" imagery remained popular: mothers sat at sewing machines while their daughters gazed up admiringly, learning important skills in a familial setting—the commercial progeny of more exalted artistic lin-

"Neva: The best for families and workshops." Advertising poster by Tamagno, 1880s, also distributed as a postcard.

eage, like Millet's seamstresses.[56] Still, by the 1890s sentimental domestic scenes were obliged to share the stage with more "modern" images of femininity. Advertising produced new icons like the woman now emblematic of belle époque art: "half fairy princess," as a late-nineteenth-century writer

[56] See Bibliothèque du Musée des Arts Décoratifs, Maciet collection, series 330.23.

described her, "half 'gigolette,' lips parted, eyes promising, . . . enticing passers-by with sewing machines, chicory drink, petrol lamps, and sulphur waters."[57] This siren/prostitute, her drinks and soaps, bodily luxuries, material comforts, and labor-saving devices combined to project a euphoric vision of abundance, eroticism, and freedom that the belle époque defined as "modernity." Many sewing machine advertisements from this period featured the "new woman": self-confident, showing her ankles, wearing skirts in light and billowing fabrics. Visions of fashion, freedom, and self-expression eclipsed representations of work.

Other advertisements relied on different modernist allusions. Machines themselves were designed so that the wheel on the side of the machine suggested the wheel of a bicycle or car. Drawings placed women at whirring sewing machines as if they were driving a locomotive or riding a bicycle; sometimes their children were shown helping to guide the fabric through. The juxtaposition brilliantly banished images of stasis, confinement, and necessity, replacing them with those of movement and freedom and making work look more like recreation. One Singer advertisement showed a winged sewing machine flying over the Eiffel Tower and a rainbow. "Marianne" figures (then deployed as symbols of the modernizing Third Republic) flew or danced with machines in their arms. New Home's boast that their machine was "light and fast" had a similar purpose: by the century's end the exhilaration of speed and freedom from industrial or domestic drudgery had become more compelling sales pitches than the virtues of needlework and the duties of domesticity, staples of 1860s advertising. In this fashion, advertising revealed its flair for more ambiguous, erotic, and anarchic fantasies.

Yet the exhilaration of speed—and the image of the "new woman" that accompanied it—also produced currents of anxiety, which run through many of these images. Magician figures who promised to conjure away toil could also call to mind stories of the sorcerer's apprentice and of magic and machinery out of control. In a widely reproduced "New Home" ad, a woman sews up a boy's pants, but with him in them, dangling head first off the table, and pumping the machine's pedal with his arms. The picture refers to a story by the very popular Comtesse de Ségur, *Le bon petit diable*, where a wicked Madame MacMiche takes revenge on her mischievous orphan nephew Charles, and the machine assumes some of the playful, or diabolical aspects of the characters. The advertisement could be interpreted as a spoof on maternal tenderness or as a comic vision of folk characters hurtling into the modern world. In either case, it seems menacing as well as whimsical.

[57] Avenel, *Le mécanisme de la vie moderne*, 4:176. Many of these belle époque advertisements were undifferentiated by product; the "gigolette" was there as "a euphoric dream of a social class," or paradigm of desire. *Trois siècles de l'affiche*, introduction.

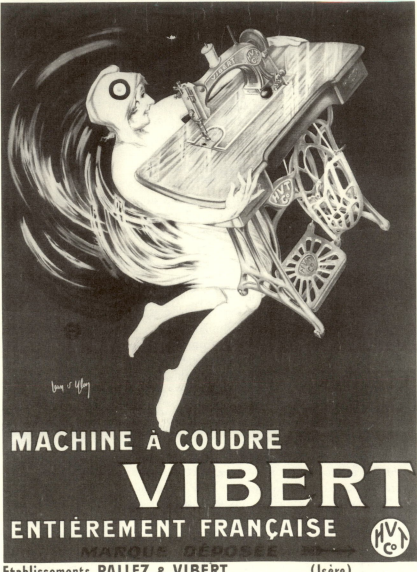

"Vibert sewing machines, entirely French," 1921.

Other advertisements used caricature, which likewise turned on elements of the grotesque or worrisome. The machinery was so simple, advertisements proclaimed, that a monkey or an elephant could use it. Advertisements showed elephants clambering onto sewing machine chairs as they would onto circus pedestals, operating the sewing machine with their

Advertising poster for New Home sewing machines, 1889. Also printed in smaller format, and in black and white, in fashion magazines.

trunks, or monkeys, balanced atop the machines, hurtling down roller coasters. These images offered a fantastical vision of machine labor as a spectacle of dexterity, something akin to a circus performance. Yet just as the circus featured performances that were at once marvelous and freakish, so these advertisements could quickly become hostile and demeaning, belit-

MACHINES A COUDRE
ELIAS HOWE
Agent
Régional

Advertisement for the American sewing machine company, Elias
Howe, 1906.

tling women's domestic skills and domestic duties. The possibility did not
escape notice at the time. In 1903, *La Publicité Moderne* anxiously identified
caricature as a larger trend; the journal chided commercial artists for their
tendency to ridicule their subjects and for what the journal perceived as a
rash of "bad" mothers and ugly, frightening, or "devouring" women in advertisements. The New Home sewing machine advertisement was singled
out for criticism, and so were the circus images. The journal's editors may
have objected to the irreverent portrait of domesticity. They may also have
sensed that commercial artists were satirizing rather than celebrating the
new consumerism and turn-of-the-century materialism.[58]

[58] *La Publicité Moderne*, September 15, 1903. In May 1907, *La Publicité Moderne* took up the
subject again, criticizing strange and jarring images, depictions of products doing odd things
in order simply to call attention to themselves.

To move from the commercial art of the 1860s to that of the fin de siècle, then, is to chart a rebellion against older models of domestic virtue. The sources of that rebellion were diverse. By the 1880s and 1890s, public health officials, trade union women, and social reformers began to denounce "sweating" in the needle trades. Feminists began to voice their impatience with the sentimentalization of needlework and domestic crafts.[59] Thus manufacturers, designers, and advertisers were forced to contend with what they considered women's new needs and discontents.[60] Sewing machine manufacturers cast the machine as great emancipator, or the bearer of women's fantasies; advertising artists tried to visualize and "package" those fantasies. If some of these images were whimsical and exhilarating, the real gender antagonisms of the period inevitably made other depictions of women's desires seem frightening or ugly. Those fears took on a characteristically belle époque cast: that femininity on wheels might careen out of control, escaping domesticity altogether. Finally, as the next section will show, it is not far-fetched to find sexual or erotic imagery in these advertisements—release, weightlessness, and being transported with pleasure—that was at once exciting and troublesome.

The anxieties represented and provoked by these images help explain the surprising success of the Singer company's advertisements.[61] Today we might find them dull. But La Publicité Moderne commended these advertisements for their "verve" and legibility.[62] Their message was straightforward and clearly aimed at working women: the text promised that purchasers could make payments of three francs a week, with no down payment, and receive free lessons at home. Chéret's design cleverly negotiated some of the ideological shoals created by the appearance of the "new woman," most notably that the promise of emancipation and the lure of new consumer goods aroused fears of female flight and a materialist weakening of the social fabric and nation. A page-sized Singer S, like a dollar sign, marked the machine's national origin. It created an image of movement and ease (like

[59] See chapters 7 and 8, below.

[60] The feminist Madeleine Pelletier was appalled that schools taught girls skills that headed them toward crowded and poorly paid trades. She found the glorification of handicrafts ridiculous. "We should be careful not to teach knitting, crochet, lace making, and embroidery. Over the course of their lives, women spend thousands of hours dulling their minds on these activities. If people have money, they can easily buy these products ready-made. If they cannot buy them, they can perfectly well do without." L'éducation féministe des filles (1914) cited in Martin-Fugier, La bourgeoise, p. 171. Marie Guillot called needlework "a useless, exhausting, and dull chore." L'Ecole Emancipée, May 24, 1915. She insisted that "education should simplify rather than romanticize housework." Tribune Féministe, June 7, 1913, p. 444. See also Bouvier, Mes mémoires.

[61] Jules Chéret did eight posters for Singer. Lucy Broido, The Posters of Jules Chéret (New York, 1980). These advertisements were done by other artists in other countries; the Russian one was framed by a Russian Z.

[62] La Publicité Moderne (1906–7): n.p.

One of many versions of the classic Singer advertisement, published from the late 1870s onward.

the roller coaster). And it also wrapped itself reassuringly around the woman sitting at the sewing machine—connecting her to the table and the task before her.

Sex and the Sewing Machine

The disturbing and distinctly eroticized imagery of the advertisements found a striking counterpart in medical writings about women's work. Indeed, the medical profession generated a discourse about women, their erotic energies, and their relationship to the machine that was as elaborate and freighted as the representations produced by commercial artists whose business lay in selling the machine. The discourses of advertising and medicine were, in some respects, quite different, produced in different circles and addressed to different publics—learned medical men on the one hand and potential consumers on the other. Yet they were, in important and unusual respects, strikingly reminiscent of each other. The parallels between the two help to explain the apparent surfeit of meaning in the advertising; they also underscore the startling "modernity" of the sewing machine, with its seemingly unlimited capacity to capture contemporaries' attention. They are a closely related instance of late-nineteenth-century culture and its reworking of images of labor, femininity, and women's desires and needs.

"The medical community has become very worried about the physiological repercussions of the new sewing machine industry," wrote one French physician in 1869, "and all the more so because machine sewing is almost exclusively women's work."[63] Machine sewing was not exclusively women's work. But only the gendered aspects of this work interested the medical profession. By raising and then attending to worries about women's machine work, the medical profession buttressed its expanding claims to be guardians of the nation's health and future—a future that France's increasingly natalist physicians pegged almost exclusively to women's reproductive roles and capacities. Doctors' concern about the "physiological repercussions" of the sewing machine also followed from and confirmed their views of the distinctive vulnerabilities of the female body and psyche.[64]

Doctors, like their contemporaries in other professions, had long disagreed about how mechanization might change women's sewing work. One enthusiast, writing in the 1860s, sounded the "great emancipator" theme that ran through so many of the Singer advertisements. The sewing machine, he proclaimed, would "end the white slave trade," ending the poverty

---

[63] Espagne, *De l'industrie des machines à coudre*, p. 4.

[64] Ibid., pp. 11, 12. On public health and labor, see Cottereau, "L'usure au travail," pp. 71–109; Michelle Perrot, "Three Ages of Industrial Discipline," in Merriman, ed., *Consciousness and Class Experience*; Robert A. Nye, *Crime, Madness, and Politics in Modern France: The Medical Concept of National Decline* (Princeton, N.J., 1984); and Anson Rabinbach, *The Human Motor: Energy, Fatigue, and the Origins of Modernity* (New York, 1990).

that drove needleworkers to prostitution.[65] Such promises, whether issued by manufacturer or doctors, were vigorously contested. In 1869, Dr. Adelphe Espagne devoted an entire book to doing so. Espagne made an interesting effort to compare what most deemed incommensurable: men's and women's bodies, efforts, and labor. He calculated that the foot movements of a woman sewing on a treadle-operated machine for an average working day were the equivalent of a trek that would weary even the sturdiest soldier. The treadle caused leg and abdominal cramps; the machinery shook the operators' arms, chest, and abdomen. Espagne went on to explain that sewing machine work required "not only a real deployment of energy and strength, but close attention and a certain degree of intelligence."[66]

Espagne was writing about sewing work in prison, and he believed that the mental challenge was therapeutic: such demanding labor would discipline women prisoners whose lives had been "disorderly."[67] But many of his colleagues clearly believed that such work exceeded the capacities of most women. The shaking of the machine, they said, gave women tremors. The noise, especially in workshops, caused "fatigue and irritability"—at least in women. In the medical debate, as in the sewing machine advertisements, references to men virtually disappeared. Likewise, physicians linked sewing machine work to health problems such as agitation, excitability, tension, and "menstrual problems" (heavy periods and vaginal discharges [leucorrhea]). The list of symptoms is typical; nineteenth-century medicine viewed nervous and gynecological problems as being of a piece. The presumed connection encouraged doctors to label the maladies that they discovered in sewing workshops (like fatigue and irritability) as characteristically "female," to ignore "ungendered" forms of stress and overwork, and to move swiftly from treating sewing machine operators' aches and exhaustion to studying their reproductive organs.

For the same reasons, physicians riveted their attention on female sexuality. An astonishing number of doctors seem to have believed that the action of rubbing the legs together while pedaling the machine was sexually arousing—though not surprisingly, they hastened to add that only women were thus aroused.[68] A Dr. Eugène Gibout, writing for a Parisian hospital bulletin in 1866, described in vivid detail how this happened:

As you know, these machines are propelled by two pedals, one for each foot. They are driven by the rapid up and down motion of the lower limbs, in partic-

[65] Cited in Espagne, *De l'industrie des machines à coudre*, pp. 5–6.

[66] Espagne, *De l'industrie des machines à coudre*, pp. 11–13. Espagne was one of the few doctors to suggest that sewing machines could be run by men as well as women, and he pointed out that the first machines were run by soldiers.

[67] Ibid., p. 13.

[68] See Ibid., pp. 4, 15; Leroy-Beaulieu, *Le travail des femmes*, pp. 407–9; and Karen Offen's collection of these writings: "'Powered by a Woman's Foot,'" pp. 93–101.

ular the thighs. Sometimes the movement is simultaneous and isochronic for the two limbs, which rise and fall together, thereby giving the entire body a continual and regular rocking motion. Sometimes, however, with differently constructed machines the driving motion of the two limbs alternates, that is, when one thigh rises, the other descends. In this latter case the body doesn't bear this regular rocking motion easily, but experiences a jolt, a general agitation, ceaselessly repeated, resulting from this rapid friction of the thighs against one another.

For this young woman, these different movements produced a considerable genital excitement that sometimes forced her to suspend work, and it is to the frequency of this excitement and to the fatigue it produced, that she attributed her leucorrhea, weight loss, and increasing weakness.[69]

Gibout presented such evidence as the testimony of women workers themselves. He cited women's testimony that their co-workers stopped in mid-seam to douse themselves with water, or left the workshop to conceal their sexual excitement. His article illustrates how this testimony was constructed and how authoritative professionals received and diagnosed women's complaints about vaginal discharges or menstrual aches. A patient "complained of having her period much too often, twice per month, and each time flowing abundantly during at least five or six days." "Positive proof," Gibout asserted, "with regard to the intensity of the aphrodisiac excitement and its frequency."[70] The diagnosis aptly distills nineteenth-century confusion about the relationship between reproductive biology and sexuality. The menstrual period was considered to be a woman's most fertile time, and also the time when she was apt to be aroused sexually—like a female animal in heat. Gibout, like many of his contemporaries, saw the uterus as the key to women's overall health and as an organ that was at once reproductive and erotic. Anything involving menstrual discharge must be related to sexual desires or needs. Seen through such a lens, women's industrial labor readily seemed immoral as well as unhealthy, exposing women to temptations that were beyond their (feeble) powers of resistance. Women were exhausted and made sick not just from overwork, but from the strain of battling their errant erotic impulses.

Not all medical professionals followed Gibout's thinking on the subject. One year later, in 1870, a more skeptical doctor, Emile Decaisne, questioned 335 women workers on the subject of sexual arousal at the sewing machine. Of those who responded, 141 could not imagine what he was talking about; 126 believed that *other* women had such experiences, though they had not; and 68 reported "great excitement, though only during their

<hr/>

[69] Gibout, "De l'influence des machines à coudre sur la santé et la moralité des ouvrières," *Bulletin et mémoires de la sociéte médicale des hospitaux de Paris*, 3:107–10, translated and cited in Offen, "'Powered by a Woman's Foot,'" pp. 95–98.

[70] Ibid., p. 97.

menstrual periods." (It is impossible to tell whether he suggested the link between arousal and menstruation or whether women reported it that way.) A few of these women were willing to speak frankly with him, and their testimony was straightforward: "masturbation was possible with the machine, but one had to work at it." Like the doggedly antiromantic Leroy-Beaulieu, Decaisne chided his colleagues for their demonization of industry and machinery, and for their ignorance about female sexuality.[71]

These worries moved from medical journals into the broader public discussion of women's work, vexing boosters and advertisers of sewing machines. While sewing machine advertisements promised an end to drudgery and banished images of labor in favor of those of handsome furniture, joyous consumption, and unfettered motion, medical discourse returned to themes of work, pain, and corruption. Medical findings like Gibout's fueled the fires of those already persuaded that women's industrial labor signaled moral decay. In the 1860s and 1870s, tailors advised women to use machines with only one pedal; otherwise, they intoned darkly, "the deplorable effects we are warning you about are inevitable."[72] The *Journal des Demoiselles* counseled its readers interested in purchasing a home model to chose "la pédale magique," which was more "hygenic."[73]

This discussion continued from the 1860s through the end of the century. As the turn of the century approached, and paralleling the shift traced in the sewing machine advertisements, the concerns became less moral and more distinctly erotic. It was characteristic of this change that the issue of sex and the sewing machine resurfaced, not in studies of women's work, but in discussions of female sexuality like physician and sexologist Thésée Pouillet's *De l'onanisme chez la femme*, which went through seven editions in the 1880s and 1890s. Pouillet's observations, picked up by Havelock Ellis and incorporated into the chapter on "autoeroticism" in his *Studies in the Psychology of Sex*, were as follows:

> During a visit which I once paid to a manufactory of military clothing, I witnessed the following scene. In the midst of the uniform sound produced by some thirty sewing machines, I suddenly heard one of the machines working with much more velocity than the others. I looked at the person who was working it, a brunette of 18 or 20. While she was automatically occupied with the trousers she was making on the machine, her face became animated, her

[71] Emile Decaisne, "La machine à coudre et la santé des ouvrières," *Annales d'Hygiène Publique et de Médecine Légale* (1870), cited in and translated by Offen, "'Powered by a Woman's Foot.'"

[72] *Exposition universelle de 1873*, "Rapport de la délégation des tailleurs," pp. 78–80. See also *Exposition universelle de 1867: Rapport des délégations ouvrières*, p. 21; the report from the *Congrès ouvrier* of 1867, cited in Barbaret, *Le travail en France*, 5:297; and Bariquand, "Matériel et procédés," in *Exposition universelle de 1878*, p. 2.

[73] *Journal des Demoiselles* (1881): 23; Mme Cocheris, *Pédagogie des travaux de l'aiguille* (1882), cited in Pellegrin, "Femmes et machine à coudre," p. 69.

mouth opened slightly, her nostrils dilated, her feet moved the pedals with constantly increasing rapidity. Soon I saw a convulsive look in her eyes, her eyelids were lowered, her faced turned pale and was thrown backward; hands and legs stopped and became extended; a suffocated cry, followed by a long sigh, was lost in the noise of the workroom. The girl remained motionless a few seconds, drew out her handkerchief to wipe away the pearls of sweat from her forehead, and, after casting a timid and ashamed glance at her companions, resumed her work.

As I was leaving, I heard another machine at another part of the room in accelerated movement. The forewoman smiled at me, and remarked that that was so frequent that it attracted no notice.[74]

Here was an extremely odd account of how machines set loose women's erotic natures: in a military clothing factory, against the backdrop of the uniform sound of thirty machines, first one woman and then another suddenly whirred out of control, having orgasms at their machines. What understandings of the body led doctors to produce "facts" like these? Under what conception of erotic energy would work at the sewing machine seem to be arousing? And how does the imagery of this passage connect back to representations of women's desires and models of the body in the advertising?

Pouillet's account of factory women having orgasms sounds much like contemporaneous descriptions of attacks of hysteria, and like the medical literature on hysteria, it is revealing about late-nineteenth-century medicine's conceptualization of the female body.[75] As Pouillet's "observations" (like Gibout's) amply illustrate, a woman's body appeared to be in the thrall of biological and sexual rhythms only half-understood by modern medicine. In writings like these, medical experts projected their inability to master the dynamics operating in the female body onto their female patients,

---

[74] Thésée Pouillet, *Essai médico-philosophique sur les formes, les causes, les signes, les conséquences et le traitement de l'onanisme chez la femme* (1st ed., 1876) cited in Havelock Ellis, *Studies in the Psychology of Sex,* 3d ed. (Philadelphia, 1927), 1:176–77. Ellis referred readers to Henri Fournier, *De l'onanisme, causes, dangers et inconvénients pour les individus, la famille, et la société, remèdes* (Paris, 1875); and Hermann Rohleder, *Vorlesungen über Sexualtrieb und Sexualleben des Menschen* (Berlin, 1901), p. 132. On Pouillet, see Gay, *The Bourgeois Experience,* 1:301. Pouillet's book was a panic-stricken chronicle of the erotic dangers of modernity. Ellis's was a matter-of-fact catalogue of a variety of sexual experiences, and one that pointedly replaced the biblical "onanism" with the clinical "autoeroticism," suspending moral judgment and granting women a sexual agency that others denied.

[75] See Mark Micale's excellent and comprehensive review: "Hysteria and Its Historiography: A Review of Past and Present Writings," *History of Science* 27, nos. 3–4 (September and December 1989). See also Michel Foucault's observations on the "hysterization" of women's bodies that accompanied the emerging science of sexuality. *The History of Sexuality* (New York, 1978), vol. 1. Tailors sometimes referred to women's alleged health troubles as "délire hystérique." See Pellegrin, "Femmes et machine à coudre," p. 69.

presenting women as bewildered and "tyrannized" by their sexuality.[76] This tyranny subjected women not only to menstrual pain and miseries but also to sporadic attacks of sensual agitation or "nervousness," which the medical profession considered more or less synonymous.[77]

These writings should also be understood in the context of changing models of the human body mapped out by Anson Rabinbach. In the late nineteenth century, an earlier and predominantly moral approach to labor discipline gave way to a new discipline of scientific management. Exhortations to work and denunciations of sloth (common features of traditional political economy) were supplanted by scientific studies of fatigue and invalidism. Views of the body as a proving ground of human conscience and free will gave way to visions of the "human machine." The change paralleled shifts in advertising imagery; depictions of womanly virtue (like the Singer woman from the 1860s) gave way to evocations of womanly pleasure and desire—unleashing, as we see here, worries about nervous as well as erotic exhaustion and disorder.[78]

In other ways, too, the medical models at work here are closely linked to advertisements featuring sewing machines hurtling down tracks and the "new woman" in constant and dizzying motion; indeed, the Pouillet passage plainly resembles some of the advertising imagery. Womanhood itself was often envisioned as a "biological roller coaster,"[79] sporadically exhilarated or depressed by eruptions of nervous or erotic energy. It is not surprising, therefore, that images of automated femininity (like women on bicycles, or at sewing machines) carried strong sexual associations and that female sexuality seemed so utterly unpredictable. The seductive and erotic associations promoted in modernist advertising and the broader currents of modernism with which women's new activities were associated helped to shape medical perceptions, producing anxieties about how the nation's reproductive and maternal energies were being wasted. Alarmist writings like these obliged advertisers to assuage public health worries by taming the image of their machine. At the same time, advertising could not help but register some of the excitement and energy these discussions generated.

[76] Laqueur, *Making Sex*, pp. 214, 217, 207–27; Gay, *The Bourgeois Experience*, vol. 1, chap. 4.

[77] Doctors warned that puberty was a particularly difficult time for girls and could lead to nervousness and erotic disorders. See Yvonne Knibliehler, "Le discours médical sur la femme: Constantes et ruptures," *Romantisme* (1976): 54, 55.

[78] Rabinbach, *The Human Motor*, pp. 291–92. Scientific management was close kin to the new "science of sexuality," of which Gibout and Pouillet were practitioners. They shared an interest in managing the body and its energies, and both advocated a resolutely materialist approach to these questions. Like scientific management, the science of sexuality remapped moral anxieties as malfunctions of the body, now seen as a machine. Pouillet's women workers appeared neither lazy nor sinful; instead their energies had gone haywire, making them at once overstimulated and exhausted.

[79] The phrase is Laqueur's, *Making Sex*, p. 221.

These "findings" about the health hazards of women's sewing work issued from a staunchly antifeminist and pro-natalist medical profession. In the profession's diagnosis, women's latent sensuality, their lack of self-control, and their physiological vulnerability combined to make impossible all kinds of public activity, from working at machines to travel, sports, education, and politics.[80] Fearful about the declining population, persuaded that the industrial employment of women imperiled the future of the French nation, eager to deploy new scientific models of understanding, and, no doubt, fascinated by their own quasi-pornographic writings, medical researchers and commentators returned insistently to the erotic and reproductive body, even in the most seemingly remote arenas of women's lives. In so doing, the medical profession contributed mightily to defining the "problem" of work as one of physical incapacity and as one afflicting *women's* bodies. If the debate between liberal political economists and writers like Simon began the work of making gender and sexual difference a defining feature of the social division of labor, the doctors helped put that work on a new and seemingly firm footing: the problematic character of women's work was rooted in the very nature of women's bodies and bodily functions.

CONSUMPTION, CLOTHING, AND THE FAMILY ECONOMY

The startling modernity of the sewing machine and its introduction to French consumers needs to be understood in a final context. If that machine seemed such an emblem of social change, of the civilizing process, and of women's emancipation from drudgery, that was due in no small measure to the conditions of household labor.[81] Household working conditions varied according to class, region, and locale (urban or rural). But everywhere, changes came slowly. One early-twentieth-century observer declared that work in contemporary homes recalled the middle ages.[82] Water was not piped into bourgeois households until the 1860s. Gas ranges for cooking

---

[80] Medical evidence was a staple of arguments against admitting women to universities or giving them the vote.

[81] See Guy Thuillier's brilliant and suggestive *Pour une histoire du quotidien au 19e siècle en Nivernais* (Paris, 1977), p. 153.

[82] Erich Lilienthal, "La réforme du travail ménager," *Documents du progrès* (October 1911). One report to the Exposition of 1900 remarked that "The feminine routine still rules the foyer uncontested. In all classes it shortens lifespans and saps physical and moral energies." Cited in Thuillier, *Histoire du quotidien*, p. 157. The underdevelopment of household labor was frequently cited as an illustration of the general "backwardness" of female labor and the women's trades. See Bebel, *La femme et le socialisme*; Leroy-Beaulieu, *Le travail des femmes*. Such concerns gave rise to *écoles ménagères* and expanded programs in home economics in the early twentieth century.

On housework, see Caroline Davidson, *A Woman's Work Is Never Done: A History of Housework in the British Isles, 1650–1950* (London, 1982); and Ruth Schwartz Cowen, *More Work for Mother: The Ironies of Household Technology from the Open Hearth to the Microwave* (New York, 1983).

marked an enormous improvement over coal or wood stoves, but they did
not appear before the end of the century. Electric lighting was long priced
beyond reach of most consumers. Domestic technology advanced at a snail's
pace in the nineteenth century, delayed by an abundance of inexpensive
hands.

Thus if the sewing machine was one of the first consumer durables to
make its way into French (and European) homes, it was primarily because
it offered women access to wage earning. The popular and thoroughly practical household manual, *La maison rustique des dames*, in 1888 recommended sewing machines to all women. But the author acknowledged that
the expense might be prohibitive. Her recommendation that "one sewing
machine easily replaces the work of four persons" inadvertently highlights
the problem. Such a replacement might make sense to a subcontractor; it
would not to an ordinary *mère de famille*.[83] The deeply ideological *Journal
des Demoiselles* also recommended general purpose sewing machines to its
audience, and the *Journal*'s editors expected that these machines would be
used in "les arts de la femme" and "womanly crafts," that is, unwaged domestic work. Even if ready-made clothes could be purchased, women's magazines tirelessly reiterated, many sewing tasks remained: *trousseaux* made at
home could save a family considerable expense; little girls could work embroidering household linens, smocks, or blouses; socks and shirts needed to
be repaired, seams restitched, holes darned, and buttons replaced.[84] The
Journal's editors hoped that sewing machines would help extract women
and the home from the cash nexus: sewing for the family would encourage
self-sufficiency, bracing women against the seductive power of cheap fashions and buying on credit.

Any number of sources, however, suggest that most women who sewed
did so for wages. The prospect of making higher quality clothes for the
family, fashioning a bit of finery for oneself, or having the time to do either
had wide appeal.[85] Some who bought machines seem to have hoped to
withdraw from the labor force, taking in less piecework, devoting more
time to household chores. Still, most of the women who wrote to the *Journal des Demoiselles* about their sewing machines were seamstresses working
for wages and customers. This is not surprising. The clothing of French
families had long been inextricable from the cash nexus. Middle-class

[83] Millet-Robinet, *Maison rustique des dames*. This is from the 1888 ed., p. 37. This manual
was an encyclopedia of farm life and gave recipes, medical treatments, and detailed instructions on how to make sheets and preserve vegetables.

[84] See, for instance, *Journal des Demoiselles* (1870): 222; (1872): 27; (1873) 296; (1879) 20.
Millet-Robinet, *Maison rustique des dames*; and Valette, *Travaux manuels pour les filles*; idem, *La
journée de la petite ménagère* (Paris, 1884).

[85] On this subject, see the suggestions in Joanna Bourke, "Housewifery in Working-Class
England, 1860–1914," *Past and Present* 143 (May 1994): 167–97; and Carolyn Steedman,
Landscape for a Good Woman: A Story of Two Lives (London, 1986).

women paid seamstresses to make their clothes if they could afford to do so, or hired a day worker (*femme de chambre*) to copy a seamstress' designs. In the late nineteenth century, they supplemented custom-made clothing with items purchased from the mail-order catalogues. Patterns published in the fashion magazines of the Third Republic—*La Mode Illustrée, La Mode Pratique, Le Journal des Demoiselles*—do not testify to their subscribers' domestic zeal or sewing skills; they were usually taken to seamstresses. Women from the laboring classes had neither time nor skills to do much sewing at home. Working-class families clothed themselves via the thriving trade in used clothes or, by the late nineteenth century, at inexpensive clothing stores like La Belle Jardinière. On the eve of World War I, a working-class newspaper asked Marie Guillot (a feminist and union activist who frequently wrote on women's issues) to comment on recent changes in working women's domestic routines. Guillot wrote that the sewing machine had been a great boon, for it had reduced the purchase price of ready-made clothes. She made it clear that unless they were seamstresses, most women did not sew clothing for their families.[86] When working-class families bought sewing machines, they usually did so for piecework.

It remains impossible, however, to neatly separate women's waged and unwaged work. Third Republic debates about how sewing could be taught in French schools illustrate the problem. Under Jules Ferry, the Third Republic took up a characteristically "modernizing" project of teaching schoolgirls important domestic skills, chief among them sewing. The project proved controversial, for its critics claimed that these skills would inevitably be turned to wage earning.[87] In response, the project's defenders tried to distinguish between teaching girls a "trade," which they conceded would be inappropriate, and imparting "useful general knowledge," which would serve girls in domestic life and was rightly part of Republican womanhood. School programs were not providing vocational training, they argued, only teaching modern domesticity.[88] Efforts to draw such distinctions were futile. Women's work in the family economy ran on a continuum from paid to

---

[86] Marie Guillot, column in *La Vie Ouvrière*, July 5, 1913, p. 4. On clothing practices and budgets, the best discussion is Pellegrin et al., *L'aiguille et le sabaron*, p. 151. See also Martin-Fugier, *La bourgeoise*, pp. 175–77; Pierre Pierrard, *La vie ouvrière à Lille sous le Second Empire* (Paris, 1965), pp. 169, 213; and the household manuals cited above.

[87] Cocheris, *Pedagogie des travaux à l'aiguille*; Koenig, *La couture en classe*; Bibliothèque de la tante Marguerite, *La coupe et la couture*; Moll-Weiss, *Le foyer domestique*; idem, *Le manuel du foyer domestique* (1923). As Moll-Weiss noted, one of the crucial issues at stake here was whether girls should be educated by their families or by the state.

Critics of the program included inspector of primary education Drouard, *Les écoles de filles*. While it was important to keep women from being idle, he said, they should not engage in wage work.

[88] Piffault, *La femme au foyer*. On similar debates in Germany, see Quataert, "The Shaping of Women's Work in Manufacturing," pp. 1136–38.

unpaid labor. "Industrial" and "domestic" did not stand at opposite ends of a spectrum. Skills acquired in the schools would be turned to industrial use, and then brought back to the home, where seamstresses could make for themselves or their daughters the dresses illustrated in ready-made catalogues and fashion magazines.

Historians, following the cues of nineteenth-century writers, think of sewing as a skill that women routinely learned in the family and then turned, in the nineteenth century, to industry. This image forms part of a larger historical picture in which the origins of the gender division of labor in industry lie in the household. As we have seen, this picture is distorted in important respects, and it takes as its own the nineteenth century's construction of the past and women's natural occupations. As the late-nineteenth-century shirtmaker and union leader Jeanne Bouvier observed in her unsentimental autobiography, sewing entailed skills that were not routinely acquired in homes.[89] More often than not sewing skills were acquired and honed in industry, and only then brought to the home. Nineteenth-century depictions of daughterly apprenticeships, sentimentalizing a self-enclosed family unit, obscure the extent to which wage work also "nurtured" women's skills—although, as in the family, within strict parameters. If women were able to fashion clothing for their families, that was usually because they had trained and worked as seamstresses.

In sewing work, the distinctively hybrid character of women's work is particularly obvious. Women's unpaid household labor cannot be understood without reference to their industrial involvement. Skills were not cultivated in a hermetically sealed household or separate "women's sphere," and women could rarely afford to acquire skills solely for domestic purposes. For that reason, the sewing machine remained a "mule"—its domestic and industrial purposes and markets inescapably intertwined.

CONCLUSION

The development and dissemination of a sewing machine that could be used at home made an important contribution to the feminization of the garment trades. That dissemination was immensely complicated by the poverty of all garment workers, but especially women and the particular undervaluing of women's labor (waged and unwaged, industrial and domestic).[90] Negotiating these obstacles encouraged manufacturers to pioneer new practices, like credit payment, which would expand the market for consumer

[89] Bouvier, *Mes mémoires*; Pellegrin et al., *L'aiguille et le sabaron*. One reading of the household manuals—Valette, *Journée de la petite ménagère*, or Millet-Robinet, *Maison rustique des dames*—is a healthy reminder of the skills involved in even the most basic sewing. Women were more likely to learn embroidery or knitting. Historian Nicole Pellegrin has underscored the point.

[90] Tabet, "Les mains, les outiles, les armes," pp. 5–61.

goods and help create a working-class buying public as well as restructure the labor force in the garment industry.

Manufacturers' and advertisers' appeals to this new female market were complicated by the knot of prescriptions, taboos, and anxieties surrounding women's work and particularly women and industrial machinery in the second half of the century. The medical literature on sex and the sewing machine is an arresting reminder of just how tangled that knot could become. If technology could galvanize utopian aspirations, it was also a lightning rod for powerful fears and widely arrayed hostilities. The curious medical warnings about the erotic dangers of sewing at machines echoed the moral economists' descriptions of the tortures of women's machine work and the romantic anguish of Jules Simon's *L'ouvrière*. In both instances, these fears drew on and helped to fuel an anxious essentialism, an understanding of femininity as incompatible with technological modernity. Again, as we saw in chapter 2, the female body and its insistent physicality figured prominently in the critique of market culture and political economy.

Much nineteenth-century advertising was frankly experimental. Advertisers groped both for a new "language of goods" and effective ways of selling unprecedented products, and for a new language of gender. The search for a "science" of advertising, the emergence of a modernist visual culture, class differences, and contradictory expectations of women pulled advertising in wildly different directions. Advertisements veered from sentiment to caricature, from promises to emancipate women from domestic and industrial drudgery to reminders of the hard-nosed calculations required in working families. These were not simply scenes of sentimentalized domesticity. Yet many did anchor themselves in what we have seen in the last two chapters to be increasingly fundamental points of reference by the end of the nineteenth century. The first of these was the "home," invested with new economic as well as cultural significance as a center of consumption, "mode of existence," and self-expression. The second was the centrality of gender understood as a division of labor—in other words, the conviction (quite foreign, as we have seen, to the guild world) that the organization of the household mirrored that of social relations outside, and that both household and social world were structured around different economic roles for the sexes.

Sewing machine manufacturers understood the actualities of working-class family economies and the importance of easing industrial labor. The lion's share of their advertisements appealed to what we might identify as a distinctively working-class vision of "domesticity." Withdrawing from wage labor was not an option for the overwhelming majority of French women. But this most utilitarian and modern of home furnishings democratized, after a fashion, the department store's promise of domesticity. If this proved a dubious democratization, it was nonetheless one that was forged in the minds of working-class women as well on the drawing boards of commercial artists and industrial designers. It held out the hope of access to better wage work and a measure of independence as well as to the world of "modern" women, with better homes, clothes, and improved standards of living.

Physician's histrionics about the laboring female body notwithstanding, working families needed at least two wage earners. And despite cultural ambivalence about women's work, the garment industry's labor needs continued to multiply. We now need to consider the nexus of industrial organization, wage work, and "domesticity" as it emerges in the social history of *travail à domicile*.

PART II

The Factory in the Home

Chapter Four

THE REVIVAL OF HOMEWORK:
MANY ROUTES TO MASS PRODUCTION

ECONOMIC HISTORIANS of early industrial Europe have long assigned home-work—in this context called putting out or cottage industry—a central role in the preliminary fits and starts of the industrial revolution.[1] It is also common knowledge that putting out was the predominant form of industrial organization in the early nineteenth century, although nineteenth-century historians often describe it as a lingering "traditional" form of production—a halfway step on the road from household manufacturing to large-scale factory organization.[2] If we are to understand the changing landscape of industrial Europe, grasp the dynamics of industrialization, or appreciate the centrality of female labor to families' and manufacturers' strategies alike, we have to part with the "traditional" label. Centralized and dispersed manufacturing grew side by side, and the expansion of homework was as essential to the second industrial revolution as it had been to the first.[3]

This chapter traces and explains the resurgence of homework in the late nineteenth century, placing developments in the garment industry in a

[1] The "rural" environs of towns like Lille, Rouen, and Barcelona were among the "most industrial landscapes in 18th century Europe." See Charles Tilly, "Did the Cake of Custom Break?" in John Merriman, ed., *Consciousness and Class Experience*, pp. 17–41. The literature on proto-industrialization is well reviewed by Gay Gullickson, "Women and Protoindustrialization: A Review of the Literature and the Case of Caux," in Maxine Berg, ed., *Markets and Manufacture in Early Industrial Europe* (London, 1990); Hudson and Lee, *Women's Work and the Family Economy*; and especially Liu, *The Weaver's Knot*, chap. 2. See also Myron P. Gutmann, *Toward the Modern Economy: Early Industry in Europe, 1500–1800* (Philadelphia, 1988); Maxine Berg and Pat Hudson, "Rehabilitating the Industrial Revolution," *Economic History Review* 45 (1992): 24–50; Thomas Dublin, "Rural Putting Out Work in Early-Nineteenth-Century New England: Women and the Transition to Capitalism in the Countryside," *New England Quarterly* 64 (1991): 531–73; Accampo, *Industrialization, Family Life, and Class Relations*; and Vardi, *The Land and the Loom*.

[2] Tilly and Scott, *Women, Work, and Family*. There are many terms for the phenomenon, all with different connotations. By the end of the nineteenth century, the most common French terms were *travail à domicile*, *industrie à domicile*, or *travail en chambre*, which translate as homework. Cottage industry suggests small-scale production and artisanship. "Dispersed production" may be the most neutral term, free of the baggage that encumbers debates about artisanship and small industry. (See Liu, *The Weaver's Knot*, pp. 4–10.) But the term is awkward, so I use either outwork or homework, with the understanding that both are embedded in large-scale manufacturing.

[3] Liu suggests that historians of industry and labor look "less for systematic answers (in the sense of searching for a generative logic) and more toward modeling the dialectics of strategy and human action." *The Weaver's Knot*, pp. 22–23. See also Sonenscher, *Work and Wages*.

larger context. The tremendous growth of the consumer goods industries, economic crisis, improvements in hand technologies, legislation regulating factory hours, and waves of immigration combined to reinvigorate homework at the moment when observers like Simon and Leroy-Beaulieu were predicting its demise. The revival, in fact, was so remarkable that it prompted the economist Albert Aftalion to wonder if factory production were not some "transitional" form of economic organization, fulfilling a specific, short-term function, and soon to pass from the historical stage. "Perhaps the historical function of the factory will be . . . to surge forward in periods of transition, pressing home industry to renovate its manufacturing processes, equip home industry with more productive machinery, put more formidable weapons in its hands, and then disappear."[4]

Other late-nineteenth-century French sociologists and legislators interpreted the vigor of homework in France as a hallmark of the country's economic traditionalism. This is misleading. Home industries were no less dynamic and innovative than large-scale and centralized manufacturing. The adaptability of homework cannot be adequately explained by referring to the unevenness of technological progress, although that progress certainly was uneven, and laborious hand work persisted alongside extremely sophisticated machines.[5] The nineteenth century saw as much science, invention, and entrepreneurial energy channeled into outwork as into large plants or assembly lines. In this case, the dichotomy between traditional and modern is largely a false one. In order to understand the interests that sustained homework and established its modernity, we need to review the interplay of the economy and nineteenth-century society in particular and the nature of industrialization in general.

THE INDETERMINANCY OF TECHNOLOGY AND THE EXPANSION OF HOMEWORK

The history of the mechanization of sewing harnessed to dispersed production was hardly unique. As any number of industrial historians and sociologists, most prominently Jonathan Zeitlin and Charles Sabel, have insisted, technology itself was indeterminate. Technological innovation did not follow any "inevitable logic of interest or efficiency."[6] In the late nineteenth century, new technologies fortified homework as often as they encouraged centralized factory production. The hosiery or knitting trades offer a close parallel to the clothing industry. Until the mid-nineteenth century, stock-

[4] Aftalion, *Le développement de la fabrique*, p. 207. Another labor reformer echoed Aftalion. "Who can tell where it will stop? . . . We may well witness a sudden and complete change in conditions of production, and sooner than we think." Cited in Valentine Paulin, "Industrial Homework in France," *The International Labor Review* (February 1938): 207.

[5] See Hudson and Lee, *Women's Work and the Family Economy.*

[6] "Historical Alternatives to Mass Production," p. 174.

ings, slips, and camisoles were made at home by peasant families who subsisted on agriculture and domestic industry. These were not independent artisans, for hosiery very early in the century had come under merchant control; they were producing for a manufacturer and not for the local market. Cotton hosiery was centered in the Aube, silk hosiery in the Midi (the Gard and Hérault), and wool hosiery, the oldest of the specialties, in the Nord and the Somme. A visitor to the Nord in 1850 would find homeworkers in nearly every cottage along the roadside, most of them working with the same looms their ancestors had used: a "French" loom (with a circular frame) for stockings and socks, and an "English" one (the flat stocking frame invented by William Lee in the sixteenth century) for hunting vests, camisoles, and slips. Men worked at the hand loom while their wives and little girls did sewing, mending, and winding.[7]

The years after 1860 brought two kinds of technological progress: the introduction of machinery to be used in factories and, simultaneously, the invention and improvement of small machines destined to revitalize homework in the industry. The Paget loom, introduced in the 1860s, represented the first effort to hitch steam power to a circular frame; the more challenging problem of applying steam power to the flat frame was solved by the Englishman William Cotton in the 1880s. The Cotton frame could spin out a dozen hose at a time, promising substantial economies of scale. But those who predicted the triumph of the factory and the demise of home industry reckoned without countervailing technological advances like the development of small gas motors, allowing workers in the Aube to use even Cotton frames at home, and the *tricoteuse*, a small knitting machine which was home-sized, versatile, inexpensive, and perfectly suited to the needs of domestic industry. The *tricoteuse* sold for the same price as a sewing machine and was marketed in much the same vigorous and determined way. Its dissemination revived homework in communities of framework knitting and even spread it into new regions; Lille, Roubaix, and Tourcoing became new centers of home wool knitting.[8] In 1900, the hosiery trade employed fifty-six thousand workers, and 70 percent of the labor force worked at home. A survey of the trade in that year reported that homeworkers equipped with *tricoteuses* and Cotton frames powered with small gas motors had found a niche in the world of factory industry.[9]

---

[7] Gabriel Desert, *Une société rurale: Les paysans du Calvados, 1815–1870* (New York, 1977), p. 412. On the gender division of labor in familial production, see Martine Segalen, *Mari et femme dans la société paysanne* (Paris, 1980); Gullickson, *The Spinners and Weavers of Auffay*; Liu, *Weaver's Knot*; and, on England, Maxine Berg, "The Mechanization of Women's Work in Early Industrial England," in Patrick Joyce, ed., *The Historical Meanings of Work*.

[8] Aftalion, *Le développement de la fabrique*, p. 31.

[9] Levasseur, *Questions ouvrières*, pp. 120–23; Aftalion, *Le développement de la fabrique*, pp. 38–46.

Science and technology had no single effect on industrial organization. The Third Republic gave France the Bessemer converter, Goodyear machines for stitching shoes (and blueprints for the factories they were to be used in), hydraulic presses, rolling mills, and machines for lifting and transmission. Between 1864 and 1913 the number of steam-powered machines tripled, as did the number of factories equipped with them.[10] But the late nineteenth century also brought scores of inventions that rendered small industry more productive and encouraged the decentralization of production: the sewing machine, the small gas motor, the band saw, and the turning lathe. The development of machines with immense productive capacities was matched by the rapid dissemination of small machines, especially in the consumer goods industries, where manufacturers were reluctant to invest much capital, and the cheapness of homework made it competitive.

At a more general level, a new source of power like electricity could produce apparently contradictory effects on the organization of industry. On the one hand, electric power brought electrolysis as a chemical process, electric ovens for the iron industry, and fully automated rolling mills. On the other, it prompted experiments with electrically powered motors in household watchmaking, ribbon weaving, and silk weaving. In the towns of Saint-Etienne and Lyon, where home industries were particularly well entrenched in the local economies and where independent artisans (like the *canuts* of Lyon) were still a powerful social force, several companies were set up to organize the distribution of power to working-class neighborhoods for the purpose of supplying power to household manufacturing. "The Lyons Society for the Development of Weaving" was one such organization. Similar experiments occurred in the Aube (for hosiery) and in Paris, where manufacturers encouraged their home workers to move into new "industrial buildings" provided with electricity. During the first decade of the twentieth century, scores of articles and books drew attention to these experiments. Every study of women in industry mentioned them.[11]

Improved transportation also made it easier to put work out. Little more than assembling was carried out in the shops; the other tasks, once done

[10] In mining, surface work mechanized and steam-driven pumps allowed engineers to drive shafts deeper into the earth, but down in the shafts workers still carved coal out of the earth with picks and dragged it to the elevator in hand-drawn carts. In the building and carpentry trades, new chemical processes changed the way materials were prepared; the introduction of wood veneers gave cheap furniture a more expensive look, but the same hand methods of assembling it prevailed. Michelle Perrot, "Les questions de la main d'oeuvre," in Daumas, ed., *Histoire générale des techniques*, pp. 479, 480; and Samuel, "The Workshop of the World," pp. 6–72.

[11] Gonnard, *La femme dans l'industrie*, pp. 219–40; Mény, *Le travail à domicile*, pp. 130–35; Ernest Dubois and Armand Julien, *Les moteurs éléctriques dans les industries à domicile* (Paris, 1902); Henri de Boisseu, "L'usine au logis à Paris," *Questions Pratiques de Législation Ouvrière et d'Economie Social* (November 1902): 321–26; and Levasseur, *Questions ouvrières*, p. 884.

under the same roof, could now be separated out and sent to homeworkers. Shopwork was streamlined, and homework "reconquered" new domains of production.[12] Thus outwork rooted itself in new regions and new industries: ribbon weaving in the Puy-de-Dôme and the Creuse, brush making in the Calvados and the Oise, embroidery in the Saône-et-Loire and the Vosges, muslins and comb making in the countryside around Lyon.

These developments were by no means incompatible with economic consolidation.[13] French economists in the late nineteenth century frequently reminded their readers of the modernity of networks of dispersed production. As one put it simply, "Collective manufacturing is part of large-scale industry. In other words it only expands to its fullest with the appearance of this essentially modern form of production." The concentration of capital and industrial growth multiplied the numbers of outworkers. "Capital is centralized, but laborers are dispersed."[14]

FLEEING THE WORKSHOPS: "PROTECTIVE" LABOR LEGISLATION

One of the reasons for the keen interest in small machines and outwork lay in the labor legislation of the 1890s that limited women's and children's factory hours. Prompted by the anxieties, convictions about gender, and public-health worries outlined in part I, the 1892 labor reform and the so-called Millerand-Collier law of 1900 sought to redefine the terms of female and child participation in industry, to distinguish the acceptable from the inappropriate, and to encourage specific kinds of "traditional" manufacturing.[15] They also provided a powerful incentive for manufacturers to have work done outside workshops and factories, heightening the appeal of technologies that promised to free industry from the confines of factory walls and the constraints of state-imposed limits on toil. Factory hours legislation also contributed to feminizing the ranks of homeworkers, helping to establish outwork as "women's work."

"No manufacturer understands the provisions of the labor laws," commented a factory inspector in his yearly report for the Conseil supérieure du travail (CST) (Higher Council of Labor).[16] The laws were confusing: they

---

[12] Gemahling, *Travailleurs au rabais*, pp. 241, 243.

[13] The Third Republic was a period of striking industrial concentration; in the five years from 1896 to 1901 the number of plants employing more than one hundred persons increased sixfold, and the number employing more than five hundred more than doubled. By the turn of the century, one-third of the French labor force worked in large plants. Levasseur, *Questions ouvrières*, pp. 275, 279.

[14] Boyaval, *La lutte contre le sweating système*, pp. 20–21. Le Play coined the term "fabrique collective" to distinguish industrial homework from independent artisanship.

[15] The 1900 law was urged on the government by Alexandre Millerand, minister of commerce and the first socialist to participate in a "bourgeois" government. Debates over such legislation are discussed in chapter 8, below.

[16] *Rapport . . . réglementant le travail*, 1902, p. 11.

rested on contradictory ideas about what work was "fit" for women, and they endeavored to reconcile medical worries, ideas of the "home," and natalist concerns with manufacturers' needs. The factory law of November 2, 1892, banned all children under thirteen from manufacturing work and limited children thirteen to sixteen to ten hours of work a day. Women of all ages and boys sixteen to eighteen were limited to eleven hours a day. Adult males, however, still fell under the law of September 1848, which set the working day at twelve hours. The 1892 legislators also created a department of work inspection, charged with the daunting tasks of enforcing the laws and deciding which statute governed each particular case. The Millerand-Collier law of March 1900 was intended to reduce hours further and to simplify enforcement by sweeping away some of these distinctions. It placed boys under eighteen and women and girls of all ages under the same rubric, limited their workday to eleven hours immediately, and scheduled a gradual reduction to ten and a half hours in 1902 and ten in 1904. In cases where men and women worked together, their hours were subject to the same restrictions. The new simplifications created new confusions, for working men were now subject to three different regimes. Those employed alongside women or children in shops could work eleven hours, those in single-sex shops could work for twelve hours, and those engaged in outwork or "home industry" were governed by no limits at all.

The exceptions to the law were revealing. Hours legislation did not apply to "family shops" except under special circumstances.[17] Determining whether or not a shop could be classified "familial" became one of the work inspectors' regular nightmares. Even in family shops, employers took on extra workers at high season. Industries were also eligible for temporary exemptions in the form of *veillées*: legally permitted nights of extra work during the full season.[18] Every branch of the garment trades automatically received sixty permissions for such night work a year, and industrialists could apply for more if they needed them.[19] Manufacturers regularly requested and were granted permissions to compensate for time lost during strikes. The combination of exemptions for family industry and generously accorded exemptions for the clothing industry made hours legislation largely ineffective as far as most women's work was concerned. This was not simply a case of intentions thwarted by realities. French legislators believed

[17] Hours legislation only applied to family shops if the industry in question was classified as "dangerous" or "unsanitary," or if the shop used power machinery. Small sawmills, steam-powered weaving and spinning, lathe turning, and grain mills came under the law; lock making, blacksmithing, and carpentry did not. Levasseur, *Questions ouvrières*, pp. 440–44.

[18] *Veillées* were the traditional gatherings of village folk on long winter evenings for work, storytelling, and keeping warm at the collective fire. Weber, *Peasants into Frenchmen*, pp. 413–18.

[19] For a discussion of these practices, see the introduction to the 1903 *Rapport . . . réglementant le travail*. This policy ended in 1911.

that sewing was, and ought to remain, "women's work," that families needed women's labor, and that regulating women's hours or working conditions might drive clothing manufacturers to replace women workers with men whose labor was unencumbered by restrictions. One of the ironies of protective labor legislation is that much female labor fell outside of the law's provisions. In the end, the law operated in narrowly circumscribed areas of industry, and in 1905 the Office du Travail (Office of Labor) estimated that only two in seven workers fell under its protection.[20]

Late-nineteenth-century labor laws may appear paltry in retrospect. They nonetheless met with concerted resistance from manufacturers at the time. French industrialists only gradually came to accept the principle of limits on the working hours of women and children; even when they did so, the Office du Travail observed, they found it very difficult to comply with the law.[21] Employers used a variety of tactics to "get back" the working time the legislation had taken away. In mechanized factory industry, they sped up machines, controlled workers clocking in and out more carefully, and set up night shifts, when teams of men could work longer. Where there were no machines to speed up, or where workers ran their own hand tools, employers resorted to the old device of substituting piece rates for daily wages in order to make their employees work faster. The Office du Travail reported several strikes protesting this practice. Work inspectors also described forms of banditry such as tinkering with clocks—employers literally stealing back from their workers what they felt the law had stolen from them.[22]

In many industries, however, and especially those deeply dependent on female labor, the simplest way to avoid the law was to put work out. Factory inspectors from almost every region of France recorded startling increases in outwork after 1900. "Family workshops that are not covered by the law . . . are spreading more and more. This is not fortuitous, it is planned, with an eye to avoiding the law." Thus wrote the work inspector from Limoges, echoing the findings of his colleagues in Dijon, Rouen, Marseilles, and Saint-Etienne.[23] By 1904, the CST acknowledged that the "rapid and ever increasing rise in the number of these shops is indisputable," and it officially asserted that limited protective labor legislation had spawned a new

[20] I will return to these policies and the dilemmas surrounding them in part 3.

[21] Rapport . . . réglementant le travail, 1910, p. 52.

[22] For general reactions to the law, see Rapport . . . réglementant le travail, 1901, pp. 45–48, and 1904, pp. 27–30. Since the law limited men's hours when they worked alongside women, it encouraged the division of factory space into "protected" and "unprotected" areas. In the eleven years following the passage of the Millerand-Collier law, the number of shops employing women and men together rose 20 percent, while those employing only men rose 50 percent. See Rapport . . . réglementant le travail, 1904, p. 30; and 1911, p. 9.

[23] Rapport . . . réglementant le travail, 1903, p. 23.

form of industrial organization intended to subvert the law.[24] Work inspectors discovered that enforcing labor legislation proved more difficult than
they had expected. As one observed in 1910, the high number of fines
handed down for violation of the law in that year showed that manufacturers either could not or would not change their practices regarding female
and child labor. Industry remained less "rationalized" than many believed,
and still dependent on drudgery and excessively long hours rather than
labor-saving devices or more sophisticated forms of discipline.[25]

In the clothing trades, where homework was already widespread, the
small sewing machine made it relatively simple for manufacturers to con-
vert their limited factory operations to home production. In areas outside
Toulouse, for instance, industrialists drove wagons up to their factories,
loaded in the sewing machines, and carried them to their laborers' homes,
where women could work without any limits on their hours.[26] The inspector from Limoges noticed that manufacturers in his area began peddling
sewing machines to rural families in anticipation of the new reductions in
working hours scheduled for 1904.[27] A lingerie manufacturer in Lille, fined
for employing girls under sixteen as machine operators, simply sent the
girls, with their machines, home to work.[28]

The increases in homework, however, were not limited to the clothing
trades; the work inspectors were witnessing a broader phenomenon. In every industry where homeworkers were employed their numbers rose, and
trades previously confined to shops began to put work out. The records of
the Office du Travail between 1900 and 1910 document a marked resurgence of homework in any number of industries: wood turning, comb
and brush making, and the manufacture of musical instruments. By classify-
ing rag sorting as an "unsanitary" trade, which meant that children under
eighteen could no longer work in the shops, the 1892 law created yet another clandestine home industry. In this case, the "unsanitary" classification
meant that rag sorting outwork was not officially "familial" and therefore
not officially exempted from hours laws. Still, putting out remained the
surest way to avoid the watchful but greatly outnumbered representatives of
the state.

Similar developments took place in brush making: once protective legislation limited child labor, boys and girls were given the hogs' bristles to sort
at home. Manufacturers of laundry detergent likewise had soap packaged by
women homeworkers rather than in workshops. The law (or rather the

---

[24] Ibid., 1904.

[25] Cross, *A Quest for Time*. Proponents of Taylorism and new forms of work discipline
would label such practices backward and inefficient.

[26] *Enquête . . . lingerie*, 4:363.

[27] *Rapport . . . réglementant le travail*, 1903, p. 16.

[28] Levasseur, *Questions ouvrières*, p. 883.

determination to avoid it) provided a powerful spur to invention. Thus, in 1903 a work inspector found a team of engineers hard at work developing a machine run by pedals, like a bicycle, which would allow the cleaning and winding of silk—among the oldest of shop trades—to be done at home.[29]

Most of the so-called family shops did not fit even a loose definition of family industry. "People call this home industry," explained the work inspector from Paris, "but usually it is subcontracting, and the shops are set up in the 'homes' of sweaters who work for department stores or large industrialists. The sweaters have little contact with the public. They take great care not to draw notice to their businesses . . . and they prefer to set up their operations in the back parts of courtyards, in hallways, or on the top floors of buildings, so that it is very difficult to discover them. Sometimes they employ several other workers in their shops, sometimes they distribute work to other 'homeworkers,' creating yet another intermediary and driving down wages."[30] Many of these shops were nomadic, lasting long enough to fill a rush order—a week, perhaps, or a season, if business was good—and then closing down or moving to another building. In addition to helping manufacturers skirt the law, then, outwork permitted them to pass on to subcontractors the terrible responsibility of finishing orders for impossible deadlines. "We no longer need to fear visits from the work inspectors . . . and, what is more, we no longer have to struggle with our customers' unreasonable demands. Who cares if we get an order that has to be done right away? We put the work out and it is up to the subcontractors to manage as best they can."[31] The net effect of the labor legislation was to endorse the economic dynamics of the industry, making it doubly attractive to manufacturers to subcontract and heightening the clandestine, nomadic character of homework.

OLD AND NEW HOME INDUSTRIES

Our images of the decline of home industry in the nineteenth century arise from the dramatic and moving accounts of the demise of handloom weaving. The French handloom weavers survived longer than their English counterparts—well into the second half of the nineteenth century. But the 1880s dealt a crushing blow to the dispersed weaving of cotton, wool, and linen (in that order), stripping some regions of their livelihoods and populations, and dramatically altering the economic landscape of others. Household cotton weaving in the environs of Roanne disappeared in the ten years

---

[29] *Rapport . . . réglementant le travail*, 1903, p. 16; 1904, p. 16; 1906, pp. 22, 24; and Levasseur, *Questions ouvrières*, p. 883. After the Matignon agreements of 1936 imposed a forty-hour work week and paid vacations, some industries dismantled their operations and reconstructed them in workers' homes. Paulin, "Industrial Homework in France," p. 220.

[30] *Rapport . . . réglementant le travail*, 1906, p. 4.

[31] Ibid., 1902, p. 9.

from 1872 to 1882, as did the weaving of cotton velours around Amiens. The Norman villages surrounding Elbeuf and Louviers had been enclaves of domestic workers weaving wool for the manufacturers in the towns; these rural trades were momentarily revived in the 1870s, but by the end of the next decade they had virtually vanished, felled by the fully automatic loom and insuperable competition from cotton, now less expensive and much more popular than wool.[32] In the Calvados, employment in the different textile trades dropped a stunning 75 percent in the half-century from 1850 to 1900 as mills sprang up in the region, producing more, and better quality goods than home industry. What became of the families in those regions once sustained by rural industry? The displaced male homeworkers generally found work in the mills, but women, except for a few young girls, did not, and the most enduring consequence of rural industry's exodus was chronic female unemployment in the region. Wages in lace making, a staple form of female employment in the Calvados dropped by two-thirds, leaving women the choice of low earnings at homework, employment in increasingly commercial Norman agriculture, or going off to domestic service in the towns. And thus the exodus of families began. Few households could survive without the woman's wages. Men and children went to work in the mills, daughters were placed in maid service, and finally, the entire household left.[33]

Yet the protracted decline of some home industries created conditions in which new ones could flourish. Regional labor markets and manufacturers' strategies shaped the alliance of factory and homework. In many regions female unemployment resulting from the dwindling fortunes of weaving households or the demise of women's hand spinning merely created an opportunity for a new generation of industrialists who wanted to put work out. Tessie Liu's recent history of manufacturers' and laboring families' strategies in the Cholet (western France, in the Maine-et-Loire) shows that the protracted decline of handloom weaving in the region was far from the end of the story.[34] To begin with, handloom weaving was not simply doomed.

[32] On new hand technologies, see Paulin, "Industrial Homework in France," pp. 203, 204; on the Northrop and women's work, see Levasseur, *Questions ouvrières*, pp. 93, 94, 104, 105.

[33] In the lace making trade alone thirty thousand women lost their work in the years between 1830 and 1880. "Le prix de la domesticité étant considérablement élevé, beaucoup de jeunes filles abandonnent la chaumière de leurs parents pour aller habiter les hôtels des grands," wrote the prefect ruefully in his report of 1878. Désert, *Une société rurale*, p. 413; see pp. 399–431 on deindustrialization.

[34] Edward Thompson made the decline of handloom weaving central to the story of European industrialization. *The Making of the English Working Class* (New York, 1963), chap. 9. Thompson's moving chronicle centered on the themes of a disappearing community, culture, and way of life. Several historians have pointed out the partiality of Thompson's analysis. But Tessie Liu has gone further, uncovering new themes in the familiar story: how the labor market was tangled in the "knots" of family life, and how wives' and daughters' discipline and self-

The population of weavers dropped off sharply in the 1880s but then stabilized. Handloom weavers carved out a place for themselves by producing, on the one hand, luxury linen products too fine to be done by machine and, on the other, low-end linens of poor quality materials, where the selling price of the final product did not warrant investment in relatively expensive machinery.[35] The livelihoods thus preserved were precarious, though: productivity declined, earnings fell, and familial relationships were rearranged to accommodate new hardships. Weaver fathers defiantly held on to their weaving work, but their wives and daughters (largely in the name of saving the "family's" weaving identity) turned to other sources of income. Rural spinning had collapsed as a female livelihood, and the commercialization of agriculture, with its demand for more intensive labor, offered few good jobs for women. Under these conditions, saving the family's livelihood (again, as Liu shows, deeply bound up with the father's skills, craft, and work identity) meant taking the new kinds of outwork that were becoming available in the growing shoe and needle trades. Women did the outwork tasks in the manufacture of the light and cheap shoes and slippers for which the region became known. Ever-rising numbers of women in the Cholet began to do finishing work in lingerie, especially household linens—an industry that was spreading like wildfire through the French countryside.[36] From the interstices of these changing family economies there emerged a new source of labor for local shoe and lingerie entrepreneurs with links to Paris. In the Cholet and elsewhere, the protracted decline of homework in textiles was matched by its rise in a whole range of industries, most of them consumer goods like clothing, shoe and glove making, and umbrella making, including several trades where it had never before taken hold.

Within the same industry, too, factory production and homework coexisted. In some cases, they competed directly with each other. But more frequently the relationship was indirect, with outwork specializing in certain tasks, products, or markets. In order to understand the division of tasks, we need to recall that factories never appropriated artisans' trades all at once, and the division of labor (sexual or otherwise) in factory work rarely reproduced that of either the household or dispersed manufacturing. The most valued tasks (in the garment trades, for instance, cutting) were generally the first to be brought in; undervalued ones stayed out. "Initially the factory is uninterested in accessory tasks, especially tedious and poorly paid work. . . . Those are left to home industry."[37] This "tedious and poorly

---

sacrifice were shaped by economic hardship, limited opportunities, and an intense identification with the father's livelihood as the family's patrimony and identity. *The Weaver's Knot*, esp. chap 7.

[35] Liu, *The Weaver's Knot*, pp. 54–56.

[36] Ibid., chap. 7.

[37] Aftalion, *Le développement de la fabrique*, pp. 128, 129. See also Liu, *The Weaver's Knot;*

paid work" was sometimes detailed hand work, like embroidery. Sometimes it was cheap finishing. Throughout the 1870s and 1880s, finishing tasks continued to multiply. Until a second or third generation of machines allowed for the mechanization of those tasks, the demand for working hands increased exponentially. This finishing work was usually described as "unskilled." It would be more accurately described as multi-skilled; in the case of sewing it involved tacking down seams, finishing hems and buttonholes, sewing on buttons, and so on. Some of these tasks were difficult, others not. As I argued earlier, French women did not routinely acquire such skills in the course of family chores. The designation of this work as "feminine" had more to do with low levels of pay than with its alleged fit with either womanly qualities or skills developed in the household.[38] Men did finishing work as well—provided they were willing to accept low wages, do different kinds of work by hand or with simple machines, and accept the bouts of seasonal unemployment. The late-nineteenth-century demand for "female" labor to do finishing needs to be understood against this backdrop.

The division between factory and outwork ran along market or product as well as task lines. Factory production proved especially well suited for medium quality goods, but homework provided reserves of craftsmanship for high quality products (like fine embroidered linens or good shoes) and, at the same time, cheap labor for extremely inexpensive goods (like the Choletais slippers and shoes). Again, cheap labor was not necessarily unskilled. To the contrary, in many cases only experienced weavers or seamstresses were able to work with the poor quality yarns and cloth used in bottom-of-the-line fabrics and clothing; these materials would be mangled or broken by larger, factory-run machines. Manufacturers also used outwork to be able to vary their product lines (in the case of rapidly changing fashions) or to have recourse to extra hands during busy production runs in the high season. In the clothing industry manufacturers built factories on a frankly experimental basis and for many years continued to give the *buches*, or bundles of pieces to be sewn, to homeworkers as well as inside shops. The protracted economic crisis of the 1880s and 1890s made all manufacturers, but especially those in the volatile and competitive consumer goods trades, anxious to avoid risks. They tenaciously hung on to products where the French reputation for "taste" and "cachet" had helped secure their position in an increasingly international market.[39] At the same time, they tried

Gullickson, *Spinners and Weavers of Auffay*, and Harden-Chenut, *Formation d'une culture ouvrière féminine*.

[38] Anne Phillips and Barbara Taylor, "Sex and Skill," *Feminist Review* 6 (1982).

[39] "La maison de bonneterie de soir à Ganges, la maison de belle bonneterie de laine dans le Santerre, la maison Lillois que tente de manufacturer, grace au système de l'usine des produits moins grossiers qu'auparavent, continuent en même temps à faire confectionner à domicile les mêmes marchandises que naguère." Aftalion, *Le développement de la fabrique*, pp. 132, 133.

out new products to establish their names and avoid being outstripped by new rivals. Doing so required holding onto reserves of skilled hand labor in regions where reserves ran deep, expanding into new areas where cheap labor might be available, cutting costs, and minimizing investments.[40] In this hothouse atmosphere, manufacturers' labor needs multiplied both in number and in kind. As a result, they simultaneously expanded centralized production and outwork. They sought out new kinds of factory equipment and small machinery that could be used at home.[41]

Manufacturers' complex labor needs are well illustrated in their interviews with government sociologists around the turn of the century. Makers of shoes, linens, garments, and other consumer goods offered contradictory testimony about the place of homework and factory production in their manufacturing processes and strategies. They were increasingly certain that factory labor was more productive, predictable, and in the end, more profitable. Factories assured that machines would be used efficiently and under careful supervision, providing work of reliably good quality. But even those who held to those certainties told government investigators and committees that under the present conditions they either preferred or felt obliged to simply turn over to subcontractors (*entrepreneurs* and *entrepreneuses*)[42] the entire process of recruiting, paying, supervising, disciplining, and laying off workers via outwork.[43] "The manufacturer has too many concerns to add those of recruiting, keeping, and varying the number of workers," as one put it.[44] The problem of finding enough workers (at low wages) seems to have weighed most heavily on manufacturers' minds.[45] Nearly all spoke of chronic labor shortages. One linen manufacturer's words to his local contractor in the Sarthe captures the urgency that others expressed: ". . . we have a great deal of work; every year we have more, and you have to organize yourselves to take lots of work. Above all, only take very good [women] workers."[46] Manufacturers acknowledged that contractors' familiarity with local labor markets was essential to recruiting workers, a fact that gave them considerable bargaining power vis à vis the manufacturer.

For all its attractions, however, homework also had distinct disadvantages—employers of men and women alike were voluble on this score.

---

[40] See interviews with manufacturers in all three of the Office du Travail's studies of homework: *Enquête . . . lingerie*; *Enquête . . fleur artificielle*; and *Enquête . . . chaussure*.

[41] The exposition reports of 1889 and 1900 are particularly good on this point. On labor shortages, see Cottereau, "L'usure au travail," p. 105.

[42] When I have not translated these terms, it is to preserve the gender of their referents.

[43] *Enquête . . . lingerie*, 1:24–50; and *Enquête . . . chaussure*, pp. 533–35.

[44] *Enquête . . . lingerie*, 1:28–29.

[45] Shoe manufacturers complained about the expense of factory machinery and the difficulties of obtaining it, which increased their dependence on large numbers of out workers. *Enquête . . . chaussure*, pp. 327, 543.

[46] *Enquête . . . lingerie*, 5:22–24.

They complained about the quality of the work produced by unskilled, distracted, workers. Women and men grew tired and sloppy after hours at a foot-powered machine. Still others "recoiled" at the prospect of long hours behind such a machine.[47] Homeworkers never got a proper technical education. Machines were not well maintained. Particularly in regions where agricultural work was still available, it was impossible for manufacturers to exact regular hours from workers. They "drop their needles each time there is anything to do in the fields."[48] In short, homework by no means solved all problems; manufacturers' strategies did not neatly fit with labor's availability. Some manufacturers clearly rued their inability to lure labor into well-organized shops or factories. Others were happy to avoid the headaches entailed by direct relations with workers. No single logic dictated manufacturers' tactics. They improvised, pursuing strategies that varied according to the region and local customs, product, and the size of their operations.[49] Multiplying and often contradictory needs helped to shape the alliance of outwork and factory production and assure the resilience of both.

FROM FAMILY WORK TO WOMEN'S WORK?

The newly invigorated homework of the late nineteenth century differed in important respects from earlier forms of cottage industry, or putting out, and one of the principal differences was that it was no longer "familial" in character. Under a surface appearance of continuity, the organization of many homeworking households had changed. In the case of the handloom weavers, shoemakers, and household linen workers of Cholet, men and women, sons and daughters moved into separate occupations.[50] Falling wages were the principal factor in this transformation. Families could no longer eke out a living with domestic industry; in this sense a self-contained household economy came apart. In framework knitting, for example, household production broke into its constituent parts; the factory appropriated knitting on a large frame, which had been a male job, and left women workers at home knitting with the *tricoteuse* or sewing seams, mending meshes of stockings, and putting on buttons. In all but a few centers of knitting, male homework vanished, but women's homework flourished and crept into new regions. The growth of large-scale manufacturing accentu-

[47] Ibid., 1:33–35.
[48] Manufacturers testified that needleworkers in rural areas generally would not go to factories. *Enquête . . . lingerie*, 1:49, 50. After Easter, one manufacturer testified, 30 percent of workers did not bring in their goods. Ibid., p. 32.
[49] Liu underscores this point in *The Weaver's Knot*. See also *Enquête . . . lingerie*, 5:59–60.
[50] Liu, *The Weaver's Knot*. Cf. the different perspectives on feminization in Alain Cottereau, "The Distinctiveness of Working-Class Culture," in Katznelson and Zolberg, eds., *Working Class Formation*; and Guilbert and Isambert-Jamati, *Travail féminin*.

ated the sexual division of labor that had characterized cottage industry, but it did not take production out of the home.

In the Nord, the demise of handloom weaving left families stranded on the land without industry; as a result, the department became a stronghold of late-nineteenth-century homework. In other areas homework was seasonal, following the rhythms set by male employment. The Office du Travail's representative in the Oise described nicely the movements of rural populations and the patterns of work those created. "When the bad weather closes down the stone quarries, families left without work leave the area and move back toward the region where brush making and button factories are located. While the men work in the clay pits, the women and children package brushes and put buttons on cards. . . . This kind of supplementary income allows families to stay in the regions."[51] Outwork also took hold in the impoverished rural areas of the south at the time of the phylloxera infestation, which devastated agriculture and ruined families dependent on the grape harvest.

The feminization of homework was not as thoroughgoing as the late-nineteenth-century debate would suggest. In the poor and mountainous regions of the Jura, Savoie, and Massif Central, men made toys and shoes and turned out the tiny sprockets and shafts used in watchmaking. Male cutlery workers around Thiers used small, electrically powered machines to harden and grind knives. Men also made pipes, cut diamonds, and turned wood at home.[52] In the Indre, Cher, and Allier, men took up sewing outwork for shirtmakers and manufacturers of household linens when agricultural and forest work contracted.[53] The handloom weavers of the Cholet held on by their thumbs. So did small jobbing tailors in Paris, and by much the same means: their wives and children took in extra piecework from different trades to compensate for falling rates and in the name of keeping the family shop afloat.[54] The overall trend toward feminization needs to be kept in perspective.

Outwork trades flourished in the Parisian region. Since the beginning of the century, the nation's capital had served as the center of the consumer goods industry, providing the largest market in the country, access to shipping and rail, and large reserves of labor. The developments of the century strengthened the affinities between the capital's economy and the outwork trades. The last two chapters have described the most important of these developments: the revolution in retailing and distribution ushered in by the department stores, which in turn expanded the market well beyond the

[51] *Rapport . . . réglementant le travail*, 1907, p. 13.

[52] See Paulin, "Industrial Homework in France," p. 205. Association nationale française pour la protection légale des travailleurs (ANFPLT), *Le minimum de salaire*, p. 93.

[53] *Enquête . . . lingerie*, 1:33, 34.

[54] Office du Travail, *Le vêtement à Paris*, vol. 2 of *La petite industrie*.

horizons imagined in the early nineteenth century. The variety of miscella-
neous trades this booming market created is staggering: for instance (be-
sides an infinite variety of needle trades), making jewelry, packing candy,
making funeral wreaths, attaching the ends to safety pins, assembling umbrellas, and plucking the feathers used in "boas," the snakelike mantles that
fashionable women draped around their necks.[55] What is more, the multiplication of consumer goods created a considerable subspecies of industries
related to their display and distribution such as wrapping hats, shoes, and
shirts and packing them for shipment to other stores; manufacturing paper
bags and cardboard boxes; and attaching hooks, eyes, and buttons to cards.
Like the industries that spawned them, these were simple manufacturing
trades, drawing on cheap labor from local outworkers. It is to developments
such as these that Jeanne Gaillard refers when she asserts that "the department store turned Paris into the capital of the sweating system."[56] Combined, the various consumer goods industries constituted one of the most
significant growth sectors of the urban economy.

The other important factor in the development of the Parisian economy
was immigration. The tides of newcomers from the provinces that had
poured into the capital in the first half of the century played a key role in
establishing Paris as a center of small scale, labor-intensive manufacturing.
Two kinds of industries took root in the city. One, growing in the periphery,
took advantage of reserves of skilled labor and proximity to the market. The
other continued to tap, first, the pool of skilled and semiskilled female labor
that was mobilized for the clothing trades, then, later in the century, new
immigrant populations. In fact, it seems that in the 1890s, just as female
labor was beginning to prove less abundant (largely because clerical work
offered some women jobs with considerably better wages and working conditions), Parisian manufacturing was revived by a new infusion of cheap
labor through immigration.

In 1907, the Office du Travail began to call attention to the dimensions of
the change, confirming "the rapidly rising number of foreign workers in
French industry" noticed in earlier reports. "In the clothing workshops of
Paris," the Office stated, "foreigners constitute the majority of the labor
force, and in some specialties, like cap making, they count for 75% of all
workers."[57] Most of these workers came from Romania, Poland, Bulgaria,
and Russia; the majority were Jews fleeing pogroms and persecution after
the failure of the revolution of 1905, as well as cholera, hunger, and unemployment in the underdeveloped regions of central Europe.[58] The garment

---

[55] This evocative list comes from Guilbert and Isambert-Jamati, *Travail féminin*, p. 18. See
also Bythell, *The Sweated Trades*, pp. 127–38.

[56] Jeanne Gaillard, *Paris: La ville* (Paris, 1976), p. 537.

[57] *Rapport . . . réglementant le travail*, 1907, p. 2.

[58] On the causes of emigration and immigration, see Nancy Green, "Ouvriers juifs de Paris
en 1900," *Le Mouvement Social* 110 (January–March 1980): 52–53.

trades were by no means the only ones to depend heavily on immigrant labor. A 1908 report pointed out that the manufacture of luxury jewelry, which was always, in the words of the government inspector, "un métier bien parisien," had been "overrun" by foreigners. "At least one-quarter of the workers are now Russian, German, or Turquo-Greek." Most of the workers in the distilling of sugar beets were Belgian, and manufacturers in brick and glass making made a practice of hiring Italian and Spanish children, pretending not to know that they were under age.[59] The report of 1911 offered a backhanded but significant acknowledgment of the important role late-nineteenth-century immigration played in the capital's economy. "We should be very pleased about the expansion and prosperity of industrial enterprises in Paris, but there is also cause for concern, for the growing number of companies and the increases in the labor force depend far too much on foreign immigration, which has reached startling proportions in Paris."[60] Immigration also helped industrial recovery, coming as it did, on the heels of a recession. This same pattern of immigration, revival of urban manufacturing, and mounting unease about the ways that industrialists seized upon new arrivals characterized the metropolitan areas of New York and London as well as Paris. The development was international.[61]

In France as elsewhere, the nationalist and labor press linked immigration and the decline of sturdy artisanship into sweated labor. Wherever immigrant workers go, wrote one syndicalist, they demoralize the nation's workers, stealing away their jobs and driving wages down. The working-class movement heaped most scorn on Turkish and Jewish peoples: "ce sont de forts vilaines gens, sans foi ni loi."[62] Other writers asserted that the sweating system originated from immigration; clearly they forgot, or conveniently ignored, the fact that homework was widespread outside Paris and among workers of native "French" extraction.[63] It did not take long for shops with immigrant workers to become notorious for disregarding the law or for trying to take advantage of exemptions by virtue of their (extended) family status. The following excerpt from one report describes the way these shops cropped up and their encounters with the state.

> I have just visited 243 shops. . . . Almost all of them are newly installed, and most of them are in the neighborhood of Clingancourt, which seems to have a monopoly on subcontracting and piecework in garments. Most of the workers here are foreigners—they flock to this trade in ever-growing numbers. Each group expands as more or less distant relatives are summoned to Paris by those who came to try their luck. They call their shops "family shops," hoping to

[59] Rapport . . . réglementant le travail, 1908, pp. 4, 5; 1909, p. 13.

[60] Ibid., 1911, p. 9.

[61] On immigration, see Green, The Pletzel of Paris.

[62] Cited in Schirmacher, La spécialization du travail, p. 92.

[63] Boyaval, La lutte contre le sweating système, p. 49; Gemahling, Travailleurs au rabais, p. 197; and Mény, Le travail à domicile, p. 118.

avoid the laws. They are sly and tricky, and since they do not understand French (or pretend not to), we have to repeat our questions and explain everything ten times. In the end, we always discover that the members of the family in question are not relatives at all, or that they are so distantly related that the shop is not entitled to exemptions.[64]

Work inspectors and other social researchers tended to attribute the miseries of sweating to immigrant culture, suggesting that their houses were particularly squalid or, more often, that foreigners were fundamentally unscrupulous and therefore accustomed to exploiting each other. Inspector Thibault of the first district (Paris) returned shaken and angry from a visit to a filthy basement shop in Montmartre. "'The owners of this establishment are foreigners,' she wrote, 'They have a big, clean store to receive customers, but they find it natural to close their workers away in this cave, with hardly any air and only a small, artificial light, and to tolerate sanitary conditions that are almost unbelievably awful.'" She continued, her offended sense of domesticity activating her views about industrial hygiene: "you want to go in there and clear it out, remove the debris, organize. . . . The abuses we are condemning are also those of domestic life."[65] In this way connections between the miseries of sweated labor and immigrants' traits and habits were spun out, and such connections account for much of the force and frenzy of the anti-sweating campaigns across Europe and the United States at the turn of the century.

The attractions outwork held for immigrants are not difficult to find. Since the early nineteenth century, the garment industry had drawn on migrant workers—German and Belgian tailors who came to Paris to be hired for the season and who then returned home to work for their own customers when it ended. The intense seasonality of the clothing market encouraged such comings and goings. Some of the new arrivals, then, came along roads already well traveled by itinerant artisans en route to the world center of high fashion and tailoring. Few of these newcomers had channels into "inside shops." Only a handful could set up as independent tailors, for workspace was prohibitively expensive, and few merchants would give them credit sufficient to buy the costly fabrics for fine tailoring. Instead, they signed on with a local contractor.[66] They were similarly blocked from lingerie and women's couture, where most shop managers would not employ foreigners and the labor force was almost entirely native-born French and female. Immigrant families usually went on the labor market as a unit, the wife working in the same occupation as her husband.[67]

---

[64] *Rapport . . . réglementant le travail*, 1907, p. 2.

[65] Ibid., 1912, p. 15.

[66] See Schirmacher, *La spécialization du travail*, p. 65.

[67] In 1901, the garment trades employed more immigrants than any other industry. Offi-

The immigrants' cultural isolation—their ignorance of French, their seg-regation in separate neighborhoods, and the prejudice of native-born workers or bosses—contributed to closing them off in the outwork trades. But we should not exaggerate cultural factors or lose sight of the economic or commercial motives that led manufacturers to use outwork. Immigration held out an opportunity; outwork allowed them to seize that opportunity and at the same time avoid the costs and complications that employing such a mass of workers would normally involve. Contractors had long been vital to the garment industry's organization, but at the turn of the century they became even more so, partly to bridge the cultural gap between manufac-turers and the labor force.[68]

This overview of the kinds of regions in which homework became anchored—lands of subsistence agriculture and seasonal male employ-ment, regions where patterns of household manufacturing were shifting, areas with growing numbers of immigrants, and cities where there was a glut of labor and an absence of factory work—helps to explain the re-silience of homework. Observers at the turn of the century attributed the surprising tenacity of homework to "the existence of groups which the fac-tory cannot absorb, groups found in very different surroundings, from the very large cities to the remote countryside."[69] "What could be easier for manufacturers," wrote one economist, "than to resort to these vast sectors of the population? It seems that the reservoir of labor is so deep it will never run dry."[70] Tapping that labor was actually not so easy, and the process embroiled industrialists in complicated transactions with truculent sub-contractors and workers who were alternately desperate and reluctant. That manufacturers so vigorously continued to do so underscores their interest in the reservoirs of outworkers.

By the late nineteenth century, outwork or dispersed production was in-creasingly viewed as "women's work." The designation was a shorthand term for labor that was poorly paid and multi-skilled (able to do hand as well as machine work, and to switch specialties when product lines called for it). But it served as more than a convenient expression; it naturalized the existence of a vast pool of cheap labor—in much the same way that the

---

cially, 11 percent of the male and 5 percent of the female labor force was foreign; the real proportions were undoubtedly much higher. Office du Travail, *Le vêtement à Paris*; see also Paula Hyman, *From Dreyfus to Vichy: The Remaking of French Jewry* (New York, 1979), pp. 74, 75.

[68] "Irritating relations of subordination," one commentator wrote, "are replaced with purely commercial transactions; instead of supervising the worker, the boss can simply refuse to accept the product of his labors." Gemahling, *Travailleurs au rabais*, p. 243. Lewis Levitski Lorwin, *The Women's Garment Workers: A History of the ILGWU* (New York, 1924), pp. 12–15.

[69] Cited in Mény, *Le travail à domicile*, p. 120.

[70] Aftalion, *Le développement de la fabrique*, p. 15.

work inspectors "explained" the miseries of sweating with reference to immigrants' supposed indifference to cleanliness. Women accepted low-waged work because they were women, so the assumption ran, with fewer needs. Women worked at home because of the division of spheres between the sexes. Gender as a division of labor and as hierarchy of needs became a catch-all explanation for the kinds of manufacturing strategies surveyed in this chapter. How and why labor remained cheap were questions easily answered at the time. We need to revisit them, looking more closely at the households involved in these developments; the women, men, and children who worked in them; and their economic and cultural strategies.

Chapter Five

MARRIED WOMEN'S WORK: WAGE EARNING, DOMESTICITY, AND WORK IDENTITY

THE LEGIONS of homeworkers formed what one early-twentieth-century observer called a "second industrial army."[1] It is impossible to measure with any precision the size of this army. Much homework was hidden away from census takers, industrial surveys, and work inspectors. The seasonal variations in the labor force were so dramatic that manufacturers could not say how many persons they employed at any time of the year.[2] Finally, the census never used the same categories from one count to the next; at some times it grouped homeworkers with industrial laborers, at others the government created a separate rubric called "isolated workers." The most reasonable estimate is that at the end of the century there were eight hundred thousand homeworkers, male and female, in an industrial labor force of twelve million. Among women, the proportions were far larger, about one in six.[3]

The revival of homework in the late nineteenth century fits uneasily into a narrative that tracks the unraveling of a once integrated family economy

[1] Mény, *Le travail à domicile.*

[2] "Depending on the time of the year, the number of workers we employ varies by a factor of ten." Cited in Barberet, *Le travail en France,* "Couturières," 5:323.

[3] Levasseur, *Questions ouvrières,* p. 276. According to the 1906 census, for every one hundred women in industry there were eleven *chefs d'établissement,* forty-nine *ouvrières salariées,* thirty-eight *travailleuses isolées,* and two *chomeuses.* But *travailleuses isolées* was a broad category, which included maids, charring women, and midwives, as well as homeworkers of all kinds. Every discussion of the issue began with the author trying his or her hand with the figures, and estimates ranged from 250,000 to 1,500,000. To my mind, Fagnot, *La réglementation du travail en chambre,* provides the most reasonable discussion of the issue. According to the *recensement professionel* of 1896, the garment industry—*travail des étoffes, confection, couture, lingerie, modistes*—employed around 1,300,000 persons; about half of these were homeworkers. Very likely there were more, for factory inspection records showed that only 355,000 of the labor force in the clothing industry worked in shops covered by protective legislation, leaving 1 million working alone or in "family shops." Using a conservative estimate of 700,000, Fagnot adds 100,000 from figures on employment in other home trades: shoemaking, weaving, box making, toy manufacture, book binding, etc., which brings him to 800,000 in an industrial labor force of 12 million. See Fagnot, *La réglementation du travail en chambre,* p. 5; and Levasseur, *Questions ouvrières,* pp. 271–76.

On the issue of how women's work was counted and categorized in various censuses, see E. Higgs, "Women, Occupations, and Work in the Nineteenth-Century Censuses," *History Workshop Journal* 23 (1987); Folbre, "The Unproductive Housewife"; Scott, *Gender and the Politics of History,* chap. 6; and Hudson and Lee, *Women's Work and the Family Economy,* pp. 20–21.

into what are assumed to be its constituent parts: production and reproduction, male and female. It is impossible to situate homeworkers in a terrain customarily mapped out as either "public" or "private," in which "home" and "workplace" are the two poles of social life. Yet those same difficulties help define the central issues: the constitution of a feminized labor market, the overlapping of paid and unpaid work, the home as a workplace, and the power of nineteenth-century definitions of gender to shape the meanings and experience of labor. In the first decade of the twentieth century, the French government's Office du Travail commissioned studies of homework in three industries. This chapter uses those studies, primarily that of the lingerie trade in Paris, to explore these issues.

INVESTIGATORS IN SEARCH OF A METHOD

The Office du Travail's first study of industrial homework was published in 1911. Its introduction recognized that anxieties about working conditions and wages in home industries had been rising for ten years.[4] In other nations, reformers had sounded calls for government investigations and legislative remedies far earlier. The first and best publicized study of homework was the English Report from the Select Committee of the House of Lords on the Sweating System—a massive, seven-volume survey issued in 1888 after years of research and seventy-one sessions of hearings and testimony before the House of Lords. In the following decade the governments of Canada, the United States, New Zealand, Belgium, and Germany commissioned studies of their own.[5] French legislators, however, remained reluctant to consider homework a matter within the purview of the law. Their reticence arose partly from hostility to state intervention in the economy, particularly in light of the exceptional importance of the clothing trades and of industries employing women in the French economy.[6] It was also a measure of the attachment to traditional French industries, of the strength of conservative social thought, especially social catholicism, and of the moral and ideological investment in the authority of the family. Many commentators believed

---

[4] *Enquête . . . lingerie.* The *Enquête . . . fleur artificielle,* done between 1908 and 1910 and published in 1913 was much smaller, and confined to Paris. The *Enquête . . . chaussure* covered eighteen departements; it was done between 1909 and 1911 and published in 1914.

[5] See Office du travail de Belgique, *Bibliographie générale des industries à domicile* (Brussels, 1908).

[6] In France women constituted 34.5 percent of the active population and 33.7 percent of the industrial labor force—much more than Belgium, England, Germany, or the United States. Levasseur, *Questions ouvrières,* p. 276. The importance of women in the French labor force flowed directly from the numbers employed in the clothing industry. Precise comparisons between countries are difficult to establish, but see Daric, *L'activité professionelle des femmes,* chap. 5; and Deldycke et al., *La population active et sa structure,* p. 169.

that what the French called *travail à domicile* had nothing in common with the "sweating system" discovered by the House of Lords.[7]

Conundrums about government policy on women's wages, work, and home industries obliged the government to introduce its study of homework gingerly, as an inquiry involving a "particularly difficult question." Had it not been for nearly constant pressure from international reform groups and the Office du Travail, a bastion of reformism since its founding in 1891, the French government might have tabled the issue indefinitely. Factory inspectors' reports, which repeatedly demonstrated that "family industry" was a fiction and that manufacturers put work out in order to subvert hours legislation, helped to provide the final impetus for the Office du Travail's investigation.[8] The Office had already studied wages and working conditions in the Parisian clothing trade.[9] The study of the lingerie trade, however, represented the first effort to deal specifically with the problem of homework.

Since the eighteenth century, lingerie had ranked among the largest and fastest growing of the clothing trades. Over the course of the nineteenth century the number of specialities multiplied. Changes in middle- and lower-middle-class consumption, promoted by department stores and their celebrated "white sales" helped to fuel a striking expansion. Fine lingerie for women (night and day gowns, camisoles, breeches, corsets, garters, and slips) provided the bulk of the industry's exports and also its largest profits. Men's shirtmaking, the most rapidly growing branch of "lingerie," aimed principally at a domestic market. So did the commerce in household linens, from sheets and pillowcases to bandages. Combined, the different branches of the lingerie industry employed nearly nine hundred thousand men and women workers at the time the survey was conducted—as the authors of the census remarked, "5 percent of the working population of France."[10]

---

[7] See Fagnot, *La réglementation du travail en chambre*, for a summary of political economists' views.

[8] *Enquête . . . lingerie*, 1:11. The Office du Travail was established as part of the Ministry of Commerce and charged with gathering statistics on labor and labor-related issues. During the first two decades of its existence, it compiled an impressive variety of reports: surveys of industry, monthly bulletins summarizing factory inspectors' reports, statistics on strikes, and the multivolume *Associations professionelles*, based on union papers.

[9] *Le vêtement à Paris*. The study was conducted by Pierre Du Maroussem.

[10] That "working population" includes those in agriculture. Statistique générale de la France, *Résultats statistiques du recensement général: 1901*, 4:148.

Combined, all of the clothing trades (lingerie, men's tailoring, women's tailoring, and so on) employed nearly 1.5 million men and women, or 7.5 percent of the French labor force. About 20 percent of these clothing workers were in Paris. The clothing trades employed 19 percent of all women in the French labor force (including those in agriculture) and an imposing 61 percent of all women in French manufacturing. Ibid., 4:124, 148. See also Statistique générale de la France, *Résultats statistiques du recensement des industries . . . 1896*, 4:39.

The Office du Travail underscored that its study of homework in lingerie was only a partial

The trade continued to be overwhelmingly female. It drew very heavily on outworkers, and by the end of the nineteeth century had become notorious for poor working conditions.[11] Manufacturers and workers alike described a trade in crisis: pressed by foreign competitors, struggling (with uneven success) to hold onto its traditional products while developing new ones, and all the while searching for more hands.

Between 1905 and 1907, the government's investigators interviewed 129 lingerie manufacturers, 112 subcontractors (*entrepreneuses* and *entrepreneurs*), and 2,012 workers. All were chosen from a range of departments and cities: (1) traditional regions of homework in lingerie, namely, Paris (by far the largest group with the most diverse specialties) and the central region (Loir-et-Cher, Indre, Cher, and Allier), which specialized in men's shirtmaking and undergarments for all; (2) areas of the Nord (Saint-Omer, Lille, Amiens, Saint-Quentin, and Rouen), where lingerie had fast replaced weaving as the chief home industry; and (3) other centers in the east and the Midi, where lingerie tapped into longstanding networks of home embroidery. Although Paris remained the principal place of production, sections of the countryside were laced with networks of domestic workers. The investigators spoke to workers and contractors from four categories: (1) women's lingerie—wedding trousseaux, fine lingerie, babies' clothing, pleating, and blouses; (2) men's lingerie—shirts, shirt fronts, collars, cuffs, and vests; (3) household linens; and (4) philanthropic and state organizations (notably Public Assistance), which gave work out to needy women.[12]

The process of gathering information proved long and complicated, for the Office du Travail's investigators had to track down maddeningly elusive workers. Factory inspectors had long known the frustrations of such research. As one explained, "You only discover these shops by accident. . . . You have to contend with nasty concierges, knock on any number of wrong doors, and climb six or seven flights of stairs—only to find nothing when you reach the top. You have to grope through dark, back staircases because in central Paris *entrepreneuses* set up their shops in the rafters of buildings next to the ready-made establishments."[13] The authors of the report on homework encountered the same difficulties. They reported futile afternoons spent exploring "eccentric" (and dangerous) quarters of Paris and hurrying home, their notebooks empty, before the sun went down, "because

---

view of a much larger industry. It also emphasized the difficulty of distinguishing home from shopworkers in a trade where shops were small, many employing fewer than five persons. *Enquête . . . lingerie*, 1:xi.

[11] "In the clothing and lingerie industries, abuses are most marked." Office du Travail, *Rapport . . . réglementant le travail*, 1904, p. 15.

[12] Public Assistance in Paris gave out hospital linens and babies' clothing as piece work to some twelve hundred women in the capital. *Enquête . . . lingerie*, 1:51–53.

[13] *Rapport . . . réglementant le travail*, 1902, p. 5.

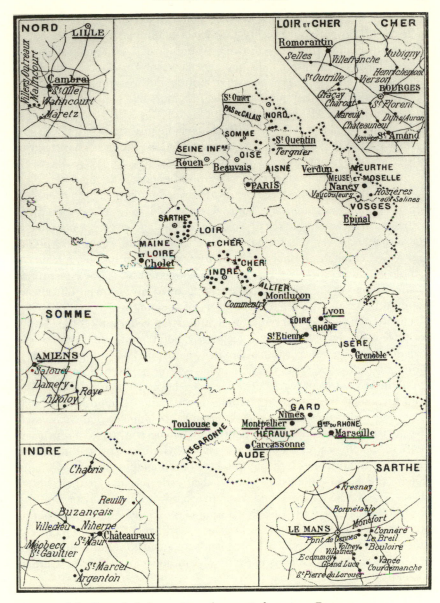

Centers of the lingerie industry in early-twentieth-century France.

for several reasons, the investigators did not want to continue their research after dark."[14] It proved especially hard to ferret out part-time workers. Not surprisingly, small subcontractors often refused to give the names and addresses of their employees and they concealed information or (the report said) simply lied about profits, wages, hours, and working conditions. In the end, the government estimated that inspectors had to make 1,500 visits in Paris to fill out 510 questionnaires.

The questionnaires followed from the sociological tradition of Frédéric Le Play's "family monographs," or budgets and case studies. That tradition valued analytic detail vastly more than statistical panoramas. As Pierre Du Maroussem, Le Play's student and certainly the most influential of the Office du Travail's sociologists, colorfully described the project, the process of constructing monographs and family types could be seen as "sounding a turbulent and changeable sea of working, urban, and rural populations."[15] He warned, however, that the goal was not to "illustrate" theoretical points, and it was emphatically not to be "picturesque." Each monograph was "a sample which permits . . . to assess with near certainty . . . the constitution of the whole."[16] The monograph aimed to open up a crucial but elusive family economy to the scientific scrutiny of sociologists.

The French sociological tradition of "industrial geography" offered a descriptive overview of the region's geography, population, and economy, and it painted workers' and peasants' families against this backdrop.[17] Le Play's monographic approach stood at the other end of the methodological spectrum: the environment practically disappeared. And Du Maroussem pressed even further in this direction, zeroing in on family structure rather than surveying regional character and economic development. Du Maroussem also insisted on the differences between what he considered French and German sociological methods. In his view the Germans spent all their time on history, did little research, and produced monographs that simply "illustrated" the broad conclusions they had already reached in their library chairs. Du Maroussem's method was remarkably antihistorical and antitheoretical. "A careful study of one working-class family, one which "photographs' every detail, is sufficient to give a surprisingly accurate picture of other families in the area."[18] He defiantly claimed to admire the French novelist Zola, famous for his portraits of families, more than any German sociologist.

---

[14] *Enquête . . . lingerie,* 1:12.

[15] Du Maroussem, "Les instruments."

[16] Ibid., p. 63.

[17] Especially the work of Audiganne, *Les populations ouvrières.*

[18] Cited in Perrot, *Enquêtes sur la condition ouvrière.* See Du Maroussem, "Les instruments," and idem, *Les enquêtes,* pp. 9, 19–20. See Levasseur's assessment of the value of "monographs" in *Questions ouvrières,* pp. 890–94.

Like the work inspectors and the interviewers at the Office du Travail, Du Maroussem underscored the difficulty of getting into working-class households. Workers were reluctant to let interviewers in the door, and they feigned ignorance about their household economies, especially the contents of the "woolen sock" in which their savings were stored. Still, the advantages of "direct observation" outweighed the complications of carrying it out. Moreover, Du Maroussem considered no obstacle insurmountable. He described the techniques of a good sociologist in the tone of a persistent suitor: one could win a subject's confidence and loosen his or her tongue by asking about the family's history. "At the end of his recollections, he will be yours." However stubborn popular resistance, then, and however time-consuming the monographic method, Du Maroussem seemed utterly confident that a patient sociologist would work his or her way into the working-class family. "Everything eventually reveals itself, however; everything will be known."[19]

Would it? The questionnaires assembled in the studies seem to be curiously inhibited results of such zealous sociological pursuit. The monographs were short. In an effort to make the project more quantitative, the budgets were standardized and the detail removed. The Office du Travail's concerns followed immediate political imperatives, chief among these articulating a wage policy for the government. The questionnaires, accordingly, aimed to muster data on workers' earnings and their purchasing power. They neither intended nor allowed a more open-ended study of the family economy.[20] Given their methodological starting point, the investigators did not feel compelled to track down every worker. Even so, the questionnaires offer an illuminating view of the nexus of economy, work, and household; the dynamics that conferred value on women's paid and unpaid work; and the operation of labor markets. Moreover, they offer a glimpse of women homeworkers and their work identity.

MARRIED WOMEN'S WORK

In almost every region covered by the study of the lingerie industry, the great majority of homeworkers were married or widowed. The percentages varied slightly according to the regional economy and labor market; but in Paris, where young girls could find jobs in the workshops of the rue de la Paix, Sentier, or Montmartre, very few were willing to do homework. Of the homeworkers interviewed in the capital, 51 percent were married and 33 percent widowed; only 16 percent were single, and many of these were middle-aged women living with their parents or married sisters and

[19] These passages come from Du Maroussem's very interesting instructions to prospective interviewers in *Les enquêtes*, pp. 74–79.

[20] Changes in sociological method and theory will be discussed in chapter 7.

brothers.[21] In an industrial labor force that was overwhelmingly young, and in a world where girls worked intensively as teenagers, the number of older women doing homework is striking; 20 percent of the Parisian lingerie workers interviewed were over sixty. By contrast, of the women working in the garment industry's workshops, 32 percent were under eighteen, 65 percent under twenty-five, and almost 75 percent were single.[22] One manufacturer set out his understanding of working-class custom this way: "It is the rule almost everywhere that married women do not do lingerie work in shops."[23] And single women would not work at home.

This "marriage bar" structured the female labor market as much as did the gender division of labor. The material pressures created by the combination of wage labor, household work, and child care were enormous. Factory and workshop days officially ran ten to twelve hours, and unofficially much longer. In addition, working women spent time cleaning house, caring for children, marketing, carrying water, cooking, and doing laundry. In the textile cities of the Nord, married women nonetheless continued at the mills, barely stopping for childbirth; in Paris, where small commerce and industrial outwork were so central to the city's economy, women left workshops and went into industrial homework.[24]

The marriage bar was created by cultural expectations as well as material pressures.[25] Needlework at home, like taking in laundry or charring, was

[21] In a few areas, like Walincourt, Malincourt, and Saint-Omer, the majority of homeworkers were single. *Enquête . . . lingerie*, 5:33–34. In the Cher, Indre, Allier, and Haute-Garonne, however, the survey reported that young, single women clearly preferred shopwork. In the Cher, young women traveled several hours to work in factories making military clothing, shirts, porcelain, and jewelry rather than take poorly paid homework. Ibid., pp. 39–40. Much the same happened in the Allier; once a factory making detachable collars had been established, local contractors found that only housewives were willing to do homework. Ibid., p. 42. Manufacturers from the countryside around Toulouse told government researchers that peasant families would rather send their daughters into domestic service in cities than have them do homework. Ibid., p. 50. There were considerably more single women in the artifical flower making trade—57 percent married, 20 percent widowed, 21 percent single. *Enquête . . . fleur artificielle*, p. 103.

[22] Girls regularly began to work in the clothing trades at fourteen or fifteen. *Résultats statistiques du recensement des industries . . . 1896*, 4:305, 313. Only 5 percent of the flower workers were over sixty.

[23] *Enquête . . . lingerie*, 5:62.

[24] Patricia Hilden emphasizes that women worked in textile mills throughout their lives; see *Working Women*, pp. 34–40, 278–79. Kathleen Canning makes some of the same points about textile workers in regions of Germany. Like Hilden, she argues that historians have exaggerated married women's withdrawal from both the labor force and politics; see "Gender and the Politics of Class Formation." See also Harden-Chenut, *Formation d'une culture ouvrière*.

[25] On the marriage bar, see Tilly and Scott, *Women, Work and Family*. Sonya Rose speculates that more compulsory schooling made it increasingly difficult for married women to go "out" to work, since school-age children could no longer run errands and care for younger siblings at home. Rose, "Gender Antagonism and Class Conflict: Exclusionary Strategies of Male Trade

typecast "married women's work," similar in nature to routine chores and fitting into those rhythms. All these tasks were recommended to wives and mothers as "light" work—a wonderfully ambiguous characterization that concealed the real exertions of ordinary household tasks—and as a form of employment that allowed them to stay near their children. Reformers, philanthropists, and the clergy prescribed homework as suitable for married women; so did Public Assistance, which gave married women only lingerie work that they could do at home; and so too did working-class men, whose opinions might be reckoned most influential of all. Laboring men in France knew full well that their daughters would have to earn wages throughout most of their lives. Still, they expected them to leave the workshop when they married.[26] Workingmen's opinions on this score joined concern for their children's well-being with a proprietary interest in their wives' sexuality. At the working-class congress of 1879, a delegate from Bordeaux explained:

> A woman's place is in her home and not in a factory or shop, where bosses and supervisors will not show the proper respect and restraint. A little girl should learn only those trades that she will be able to do at home when she marries; then, instead of abandoning her children, exposing them to pernicious influences and dangerous accidents, she will be able to keep them under her kind and watchful eye.[27]

Nineteenth-century Parisian tailors commonly referred to a garment workshop as "Saint-Lazare," a prison where prostitutes were incarcerated; the expression distilled tailors' judgment of the character of women who worked in them.[28]

Such fiercely voiced opinions, frequently buttressed by women's own complaints about sexual harassment, shaped families' plans and expectations. It is worth underscoring, however, that no one expected working-class women to withdraw from the labor force. Marriage was not an alternative to wage labor; both were economic strategies. A seamstress who married into a family that could loan her money could contemplate moving from a workshop to her own business. Marriage served as a lever for moving up in the working world, and good work could be an advantage in the marriage market. The long-term strategies of combining marriage, a family economy, and waged labor, which made industrial homework seem suitable to a woman's married

---

Unionists in Nineteenth-Century Britain," *Social History* 13, no. 2 (May 1988): 191–208. On married women's work, see also Meacham, *A Life Apart.*

[26] Perrot, "L'éloge de la ménagère," p. 110.

[27] Ibid., p. 119.

[28] Aftalion, *Le développement de la fabrique,* p. 287. Like most women's prisons, St. Lazare did serve as a clothing factory; see Patricia O'Brien, *The Promise of Punishment: Prisons in Nineteenth-Century France* (Princeton, N.J., 1982).

life, also help to explain why families would send their daughters into a trade as poorly paid as needlework in the first place.[29]

When the Office du Travail's investigators turned to Parisian lingerie workers and their families, it became plain that the need to care for children did not pertain to many of the women actually doing homework in this trade. The investigators were startled to find that a great many of the home-workers had no dependent children at the time of the survey. Half of the married women without children were under thirty-five and, therefore, of an age where they would typically have children in their homes. The au-thors suspected that what they called "Malthusian calculus" had come into play, a sign of the declining fortunes of the trade and falling wages of lin-gerie workers. Although they did not gather enough data to press the anal-ysis, they considered their rough findings significant to the ongoing debate about the causes of France's worrisome depopulation, the quality of family life, and the relationship of these concerns to *la femme au foyer* or the future of home industries.[30]

The monographs show that working at home was hardly an inevitable choice among working women with children. The government only uncov-ered a handful of instances in which mothers were able to work and also take care of their offspring. One of them was Mme F, thirty-five years old, wife of a carpenter, mother of five children (including a set of twins), and lingerie worker, who finished shirts for an *entrepreneuse* in the neighbor-hood of Epinettes. The investigators saw her as a model worker-mother: by finishing shirts five or six hours a day, she could earn 250 francs a year or enough to pay the rent and still take excellent care of her children, whom the survey glowingly described as "all chubby and pink." "She was able to bear and then nurse her twins without stopping work for a minute, and although she did get tired, she never fell sick."[31] The very next monograph in the survey, however, described an equally characteristic family, one of a day laborer, his wife (a lingerie worker), and their five children. Since the woman had to work full time, it proved more economical to send the chil-

---

[29] Mothers who were themselves lingerie workers, however, refused to apprentice their daughters in the trade. On marriage and wage work, see Ferree, "Between Two Worlds."

[30] *Enquête . . . lingerie*, 1:732, 733. The investigators did not ask if women had ever had children, which, when combined with the small size of the sample, makes it impossible to say anything about fertility. On those issues, see Accampo, *Industrialization*; and Gullickson, *The Spinners and Weavers of Auffay*. That the study did not collect this data is telling about its singleminded preoccupation with women's wages and how many people they were supporting at that moment, rather than how family economies worked over longer time periods. On the one hand, the absence of dependent children was reassuring, for it suggested that low wages were not sending families with children into poverty. On the other hand, readers could find in these figures cause for alarm about the vitality of family industries and their ability to sustain a healthy and expanding French population.

[31] *Enquête . . . lingerie*, 1:688.

dren to wet nurses in Brittany, which cost 30 francs a month, than to have them at home where they would certainly be under foot.[32] In this instance, as in many others, family arrangements undermined the ostensible rationale for working at home.

To simply cite the dual imperatives of mothering and wage earning does not do justice to the conflicts and duties with which women homeworkers contended. Their problems emerge more clearly in the Office du Travail's study of Parisian artificial flower makers, because investigators questioned these women more carefully on this subject than they did the lingerie workers.[33] Two of the flower makers stated frankly that they worked at home because they needed more money than they could earn in the shop, where legislation limited working hours. Flower makers employed in shops took extra work home at night for the same reason.[34]

The study of homework in artificial flower making provides a revealing panorama of the Parisian labor market and different workplaces. The study makes it abundantly clear that women considered almost any job better than domestic service and that many felt the same way about charring, even though in Paris charring paid better wages than many alternatives.[35] Women gave mixed and telling testimony about their experience in workshops. Almost all said that shopwork was strenuous, but better paid and less isolated than working at home. Several flower workers would have preferred shopwork but for the demands of pace and skill, and for the gulf that separated them from younger working girls. As one older woman wistfully noted, "The workshop is more cheerful than it is here in my room. But when you get older, they make fun of you. In my time, we all got along; but the kids of today are another story."[36] The well-known work culture of women's shops, whether flower workers' or *midinettes*' (dressmakers in the couture shops of Paris), was exclusive and tight-knit, driving away older workers. Other women voiced unspecified fears, and routine sexual harassment probably contributed to their wariness. "In the shop we're afraid," or "we are freer at home," they said, to explain why they found shops, their employers, or their fellow workers troublesome.[37] The government studies

[32] Ibid., p. 689.

[33] Since flower-making work was more evenly divided between shop and home, working at home might appear to be more of a choice. Moreover, the Office du Travail's interviewers considered flower workers more skilled and, hence, purposeful and likely to make choices.

[34] These practices confirmed the predictions of feminist opponents of protective legislation. *Enquête . . . fleur artificielle*, pp. 113, 169, 170. See also chapter 8.

[35] See *Enquête . . . fleur artificielle*, p. 192. The report on the Cholet recounted that women in the area refused domestic service. For a summary of similar findings in Germany, see Barberet, *Le travail en France*, 5:359.

[36] *Enquête . . . fleur artificielle*, p. 187.

[37] Ibid., p. 112. On concerns about factories and sexual harassment of women, see CST, *Rapport sur le travail des femmes à domicile*; and Octave Gérard, *L'enseignement primarie à Paris*

also highlight dilemmas of women who found themselves cast into the world of wage work without any preparation. One such woman, a young widow of a police officer, took up homework because she was frightened of the shop. "She knows how to sew quite well, but she does not have the ease and speed or experience of professional workers. She insists on working at home, because she has never frequented the shop." Her skills, but more important, her culture, class, and self-understanding put a gulf between her and the "working girls."[38]

Finally, irrespective of household duties or cultural norms, few women withstood the pace of workshop production for more than ten years. Among the elite of women workers—the seamstresses in couture around the rue de la Paix—fears of aging, slowing down, or losing one's edge were central to work culture. One of them, Jeanne Bouvier, described in her autobiography her fear and anger when she lost her workshop job. She was fired for voicing her strong union sympathies and for running afoul of a mercurial supervisor, both common examples of the strict, often capricious, and deeply resented discipline of the elite houses. ". . . My hair was turning grey. In those days, that made it virtually impossible for a seamstress to find work. 'Too old!' I would be told in the houses where I introduced myself."[39] Across the spectrum of the women's trades, from elite to sweated, low piece rates and intense bouts of labor pushed workers beyond their endurance and contributed to *surmenage*, or overwork.[40]

Of the flower workers interviewed, 14 percent told the investigators that they preferred homework, despite lower piece rates and correspondingly longer hours. Several of them worked "in a family setting," alongside their parents or children, and the extra hands helped to compensate for lower earnings. The tradition of familial labor was attenuated in the lingerie trade,[41] but several lingerie workers' testimony shows that they shared the flower workers' calculations and preferences. One explained that she

---

et dans le département de la Seine (Paris, 1878); Cottereau, "L'usure au travail," pp. 100–101; and John W. Shaffer, "Family, Class, and Young Women: Occupational Expectations in Nineteenth-Century Paris," in Robert Wheaton and Tamara Hareven, eds., *Family and Sexuality in French History* (Philadelphia, 1980).

[38] *Enquête . . . lingerie*, 1:649. Women in the shoemaking trade said much the same about their experience in shops. See *Enquête . . . chaussure*, p. 537. Many men in the shoemaking trade said that they worked at home because their health was failing, pp. 536–37.

[39] Bouvier, *Mes mémoires* (1983 ed.), p. 114.

[40] One flower maker began her apprenticeship at fifteen, apprenticed for three years, and then did shopwork. "During the busy season, she took work home in the evening, which is a common practice among flower-workers." At twenty-five, she had become so worn down that she had to leave the shop and do homework. *Enquête . . . fleur artificielle*, p. 169. On the intense pace of labor in all the women's trades, see Cottereau, "L'usure au travail," p. 91.

[41] In Paris, of 510 workers interviewed, only 26 involved other members of the family, and of these, only 16 were mother-daughter teams. *Enquête . . . lingerie*, 1:730.

"would rather work only nine and a half months a year at 2,50 francs a day at home than the whole year at 4 francs a day for someone else.[42] Another, Mlle B, told the investigators that she would rather work at home—not because it simplified her family duties (she was single)—but because she felt it gave her some autonomy. Her story highlights the ambiguous advantages of homework.

> Mlle B "rolls" her machine from 6 o'clock in the morning until 10 o'clock at night, stopping for three hours to eat and do her housework. She spends another three hours or so each morning and evening preparing her work. Her working day comes out to be 16 hours long.
>
> When asked about these hours, Mlle B points out that she hardly works longer than she did during her time in the shop, when she repeatedly stayed well into the night. What is more, she no longer has to travel enormous distances to her job, and she can stay in her home, which is the most important thing to her, even if it means she is obliged to work harder in order to earn the same amount of money.[43]

Homework, then, provided some respite to those weary with the banter and pace of work in the shop, or with traveling alone across the city; the irony is that Mlle B, like many of her fellow laborers, seemed to have brought other aspects of the factory home with her.

By many women's reckonings, even with very low wages their presence at home created savings for the whole family. One shirtmaker estimated the three francs a day she earned at home to be the equivalent of four and a half a day in the shop.[44] It was not simply that, as several workers said: "We spend less on clothing and eating out." The balance of paid work and domestic chores was crucial to the fragile equilibrium of working-class family economies. Working at home enabled women like Mlle B to do three hours of housework in addition to her sewing. Male outworkers in shoemaking echoed all of these points, including the costs of men going "out to work." Yet the crucial calculus involved women's dual labor. Homeworkers in the shoe industry explained the chief advantage this way: unlike factory work, industrial homework did not "disorganize working-class families and their economies." A woman who could not spend ten hours a day in the factory could, via homework, nonetheless contribute to her household's resources. Separating waged from unwaged work compromised women's efforts to do both, and was seen and felt by some women as well as men as a powerfully corrosive force.[45]

---

[42] Ibid., p. 672. She also worked as a concierge in her building, a tenement in La Butte aux Cailles.

[43] Ibid., pp. 648–49.

[44] Enquête . . . fleur artificielle, p. 112; and Enquête . . . lingerie, 1:688.

[45] Enquête . . . chaussure, p. 319. Several male shoemakers worked at home because they

The Office du Travail's investigators recorded very little of what lingerie or flower workers said about women's role or place, perhaps because their comments seemed so self-evident. Likewise the studies offer only a few fleeting glimpses of family discussions and husband's views. Several home-workers made it clear that they were bowing to another's opinions. In one instance, "her husband's jealousy and possessiveness kept her from going out to work," and in another, the worker said she detested shopwork because "when a woman's husband comes home in the evening, everything should be ready."[46]

The government study showed, however, that many of the reasons for working at home had nothing to do with any deeply felt obligation to cultural ideals of *la femme au foyer*. The homeworkers' testimony reveals mixed motives, a straitened range of alternatives, hidden economies, and ambiguous advantages of homework. The narrow range of choices, savings, and advantages of homework were in many ways the material effects of discrimination against women in the labor market, harassment in shops, and family hierarchies that assigned women unpaid as well as paid labor. At the same time, ideas of "women's place," or definitions of gender as a division of labor and spheres, made these family arrangements seem "natural" and presented homework as an obvious way to combine family duties and wage earning.

"Je ne suis pas ouvrière": Class, Gender, and Work

Although the study's view was partial, it cast a searching light on little-discussed members of the labor force, like wage-earning mothers and hard-working widows. It also showed that women's wage work spanned the social spectrum. Its most surprising finding involved the number of women from the petty bourgeoisie in the labor force. This was the aspect of homework most commented on by contemporaries, astonished and dismayed to learn how widespread wage work was among married women in the lower middle classes.[47]

The table below (taken from the study) provides a rough guide to the

had been expelled from shops during strikes. Others invoked their freedom to work according to their own rythms and habits—smoking, for instance, if they wanted to (pp. 536–37). I discuss male homeworkers in the section on unions in the next chapter.

See Jean Quataert's interesting discussion of how German families resisted bureaucratic requirements to account for the time each member of the family spent in paid and unpaid work. "The Politics of Rural Industrialization: Class, Gender, and Collective Protest in the Saxon Oberlausitz of the Late Nineteenth Century," *Central European History* 20, no. 2 (June 1987): 91–124.

[46] *Enquête . . . fleur artificielle*, pp. 112, 157.

[47] Poisson, *Le salaire des femmes*, p. 144. Similar findings from German studies were summarized in Barberet, *Le travail en France*, 5:356.

TABLE 5.1

Occupation of Spouses of Married Women Homeworkers Surveyed
in the Lingerie Trade

Husband's Trade	Women's Lingerie I	Shirtmaking II	Household III	Charities IV	All Groups
*Employees in commerce and administration	13 (20%)	1 (3%)	3 (6%)	3 (5%)	20 (9%)
*Employees in public services	6 (9%)	5 (13%)	6 (11%)	6 (11%)	23 (11%)
*Transportation, railroads, shipping	4 (6%)	4 (11%)	5 (9%)	16 (29%)**	29 (14%)
*Police officers	3 (4%)	—	3 (6%)	—	6 (3%)
Workers	17 (26%)	17 (46%)	22 (41%)	17 (31%)	73 (35%)
Day laborers, carters, errand "boys," etc.	16 (24%)	7 (19%)	11 (21%)	13 (24%)	47 (22%)
Miscellaneous	7 (11%)	3 (8%)	3 (6%)	—	13 (6%)
TOTAL	66	37	53	55	211

Source: Enquête . . . lingerie, 1:734–35.

Note: The government study used the asterisks to designate trades or occupations with high wages and stable employment. It summed up this table as follows: of the married women in group I, women's lingerie, 39 percent were married to regularly employed, relatively well-paid men; in group II, shirtmaking, 27 percent; in group III, household linens, 32 percent; and in group IV, Public Assistance and other organizations, 45 percent. The figures for group IV, however, are misleading, because the category includes the Economat, an organization distributing lingerie work to the wives of men who worked on the railroads. Hence the high number (**) of husbands in group IV in transportation.

spouses' earnings and trade. The majority of the families were working-class, and the worker husbands represented a broad range of Parisian trades and industries. Few were tailors, for tailoring wives worked alongside their husbands rather than in the separate "women's trades," and the family's identity was bound up with the joint enterprise. The study of shoemaking showed many husband-wife teams as well, but here patterns were changing; in almost half of the households women worked in separate trades.[48] Other artisans, however, like farriers, masons, and stove setters figured prominently among the lingerie workers' husbands. So did drivers, deliverers, and

[48] On patterns of family work in shoemaking, see Enquête . . . chaussure, pp. viii, 348, 475, and 503–5. On tailoring, see Office du Travail, Le vêtement à Paris.

other workers connected with the capital's enormous transport business.[49] Skilled artisans and elite (*hauts*) workers—painters, photographers, type-setters, printers, brewers, and so forth—were also well represented.

The most "industrial" of the lingerie trades, shirtmaking, was also the most solidly working class. Shirtmakers usually were recruited from the neighborhoods of Belleville and Menilmontant, where the big shops were located and where work was distributed daily. Women's lingerie, a less "in-dustrial" trade, attracted many women anxious to maintain their status and embarrassed by their involvement in the labor force. More than one-third of homeworkers in this branch were married to men with typically petty bour-geois occupations: clerks or shop assistants in small businesses, clerical employees in warehouses, and so on. Specific government professions reap-pear frequently on the list of spouses: public service workers, policemen, and military officers. Wherever there was a military school or post, or a detachment of gendarmes, the Office du Travail found groups of women ready to do lingerie (or lace making) while their husbands were away or after they had retired, for pensions did not provide enough to live on. Rail-road companies provided another pole around which networks of home-workers formed. Several manufacturers said that they only hired women married to a specific company's drivers or employees. One railroad com-pany ran a program that distributed lingerie work to their employees' wives.[50]

This description of the labor force offers a glimpse of important eco-nomic changes in Paris and its social hierarchies. The families of govern-ment employees, clerks, and transport workers were the ones who peopled the capital and its suburbs in the late nineteenth century. They formed the largest part of the new urban classes in Paris, where industry had been declining and administration, commerce, and transportation expanding since at least midcentury. They also constituted the poorest section of this new social stratum, standing closer to the "people" than other middle-class groups. Since the garment industry was one of the few offering employment to women, it found in these households a plentiful supply of female labor.[51] Organized in a semi-nomadic fashion, the industry could pursue these

[49] These included movers, tramway mechanics, delivery drivers, tramway carpenters, car-riage drivers, gas deliverymen, and so on. Flower workers came from solidly working-class families; 58 percent of their husbands were skilled workers, most of whom, the survey pointed out, were paid good wages. *Enquête . . . fleur artificielle*, p. 106.

[50] *Enquête . . . lingerie*, 5:45.

[51] "Employees are more and more numerous, and appear to be victims of a global evolution from which they profited very little." Cited in Alain Corbin, *Les filles de noce* (Paris, 1978), p. 292. On women's employment in Paris, see Tilly, "Women and Work in French Cities"; Ber-lanstein, *The Working People of Paris*; and Centre de documentation d'histoire des techniques, *Evolution de la géographie industrielle de Paris et de sa proche banlieue au XIXe siècle* (Paris, 1976).

households into new working- and lower-middle-class neighborhoods. According to an earlier survey of the garment industry in 1896, subcontractors made a point of setting up their shops in the suburbs, "right next to the factories, depots, and warehouses, close to groups of women married to skilled workers and clerical employees."[52]

For women from these households, that they worked at home was crucial to their identity. Homework provided a way of earning wages without the stigma of the factory and even, in some cases, a way of disguising that they had to work at all. They frequently told investigators that they did not need their wages. One, married to a salesman, insisted that she did lingerie "to keep busy more than to add to the family's resources."[53] Another, the wife of a police officer in Belleville, said that she worked when she had the time, half an hour here and there, to keep from getting bored, and then added emphatically, "je ne suis pas ouvrière" [I am not a worker].[54] Issues of social class and respectability emerged obliquely. A few women claimed not to be "professionals," and, with a mixture of pride and apprehension, reported they had never "spent any time" in a workshop—obviously the crucial mark of class identity.[55] When investigators pressed them for details about their work, they avoided answering. Mme H provides a good case in point:

> Her husband is a clerk and earns 2,920 francs a year. The family, which has no children, thus has a total of 3,350 francs to spend each year. Their housing reflects this situation: it is a typical small apartment of a comfortably off employee, well-furnished, spacious, and bright, located in a modest building in the neighborhood of Plaisance.
>
> Mme H says that she works to keep busy, for she is alone all day long, but she complains of falling piece rates in a way that suggests these rates are a matter of concern—the family is probably in financial need.

This woman estimated that she worked around ten hours a day and earned 420 francs a year, and she claimed to know nothing about other aspects of the trade, such as off-seasons, *entrepreneuses'* practices, or other workers' earnings.[56]

Mme H exemplified what working men and women associated with the trade union movement cruelly called "surreptitious women workers," who were afraid of being "caught red-handed in the proletariat."[57] Only a small group of shop assistants and clerks was able to work itself free of the "people" and into the middle classes. That the women in these families were

[52] Office du Travail, *Le vêtement à Paris*, p. 666.
[53] *Enquête . . . lingerie*, 5:32 from the column "Observations."
[54] Ibid., 5:28.
[55] Ibid., 1:649.
[56] Ibid., pp. 702, 703.
[57] Cited in Barberet, *Le travail en France*, 5:292.

earning wages marked the social distance they still had to travel, and it provides an important measure of the importance of women's wage earning in French family economies.

ENTREPRENEUSES AND THE LIMITS OF FEMALE ARTISANSHIP

There remains one more group of women homeworkers to discuss. The expanded production of ready-made clothing and the availability of inexpensive sewing machines (with quick lessons from their salesmen) had eroded apprenticeship and made many women with pressing needs and no particular skills into wage earners. As one woman lamented, "No sooner does a girl know how to make a correct stitch on a machine than she thinks she's a real worker."[58] Above these legions of the untrained, however, stood former dress designers or seamstresses now working as *entrepreneuses*, or contractors.[59] Contemporary writings and cartoons—many of them viciously anti-Semitic—portrayed subcontractors as immigrant tailors.[60] In the lingerie trade, however, as in artificial flower making, outwork did not build on traditions of male-headed family production, and most of the contractors were female. Women with talents for design or special sewing skills found in home industry an alternative to the factory and workshop, neither of which had use for her abilities, except as a "first hand" in a *maison de couture*. Homework, then, was a refuge for the skilled as well as the unskilled.[61] In Paris, which was the center of fashion and quality production, craft traditions remained strong, and even outwork required expert supervision, assembling, or repairs. The group of skilled "artisanal" *entrepreneuses* bulked especially large in the capital, where they designed models of particular items of clothing and then contracted with houses to produce them.

Scores of women testified that the dream of becoming an *entrepreneuse* kept them in an otherwise difficult trade. One of the crucial differences between tailoring and the "women's" trades, like lingerie, was that mobility

---

[58] *Enquête . . . lingerie*, 5:54. The study showed that half of the lingerie workers had begun in the trade after twenty-six years old and had no "apprenticeship" (1:729). In flower working, by comparison, more than half started working between twelve and fourteen, and almost all had some shop experience. *Enquête . . . fleur artificielle*, pp. 110–11. Workshops and family-based home production kept apprenticeship alive.

[59] Again, I use the French term because it is gender-specific.

[60] Many considered subcontracting the defining characteristic of "sweated labor," for middlemen insinuated themselves between manufacturers and workers, driving down rates and wages. It was easier to focus on those dynamics than to untangle the web of family economics, child care, and paid and unpaid labor. Immigrant jobbing tailors were a convenient scapegoat. See, for instance, Descoust, *Marchandage et sweating-system*, p. 13. At least one firm tried to do without *entrepreneuses*, distributing work directly. Wages went down, probably because the contractors were not there to negotiate. Mény, *Le travail à domicile*, p. 74. In Paris and New York tailoring, contractors were often the leaders of strikes.

[61] Aftalion, *Le développement de la fabrique*, p. 293. For more analysis of the relationship between producers, entrepreneurs, and merchants, see Liu, *The Weaver's Knot*, chap. 3.

was possible. It was very common for a newly married couple to buy a sewing machine and take an apartment with enough room for the woman to work at home; the former shophand's dream of opening a small business dovetailed with her husband's determination that she should not have to "go out" to work. If the couple had more money, or the man could get a loan, the woman might set herself up as an *entrepreneuse*. The dynamics of the industry endorsed these ambitions, for in order to get by, women workers explained, one had to take in more work than one person could possibly accomplish. Uneven rhythms of work and unemployment made it crucial to find helpers to take advantage of the "season."[62] Women's aspirations and the industry's economics combined to multiply constantly the number of *entrepreneuses*, increasing competition among them and driving down rates, yet, at the same time, sustaining a sense of artisanship and possibility.[63]

If upward mobility was a hope, downward mobility was a realistic expectation. The line separating artisanal or entrepreneurial status from something less was easily passed over.[64] A once-independent seamstress without a shop or a home with enough space to welcome and fit customers fell back into *entreprise*, bidding for contracts from big houses. Likewise an *entrepreneuse* who could no longer afford to maintain several sewing machines and workers fell back into simple homework, dependent on others to set rates. It is striking to notice how many of the homeworkers were former *entrepreneuses* who had not been able to keep up their businesses after their husbands died. Their numbers dramatize women's economic dependence in the family and the limits of female artisanship and autonomy. Single and widowed women rarely crossed the border out of the proletariat.[65]

The fine line that separated workers from contractors may explain why relations between the two were better than in other outwork trades. Many workers pointed to their common vulnerability ("she is not rolling in gold either") and to small kindnesses that give a fleeting impression of neighborhood relations: an invitation to work at the entrepreneuse's house in the winter to save money on heat and light, a willingness to pick up and deliver clothes, a contractor who is "a little bit of a friend."[66] The complaints, however, were equally telling. *Entrepreneuses* regularly threatened to cut women out of their networks if they did poor work or delivered it late. A

[62] In many cases, large houses would only contract with workers who could take on a large order. *Enquête . . . lingerie*, 5:21.

[63] The survey underscored that the number of subcontractors was constantly growing. Ibid.

[64] The lives of these workers make it very hard to assign them to categories of "artisans" or "sweated workers." An independent seamstress might work for her own customers one day, and on the next, if that work slowed down, go to the *entrepreneuse* next door. Mény, *Le travail à domicile*, p. 15.

[65] In shirtmaking, which was organized on a larger scale, more of the contractors were male.

[66] *Enquête . . . lingerie*, 1:688.

few workers hoped that the government's investigation was directed against their *entrepreneuses*, who were described as "cold, arrogant, and pitiless." Real friendships were rare. Workers were more likely to say that their (and *only* their) *entrepreneuse* was honest, if only in her dealings with them, and that they did not allow themselves to be exploited—mixing pride, defiance, and anger.[67]

The Office du Travail's survey makes only one reference to immigrant workers, and that is to Italian women in Marseilles.[68] Factory inspectors' reports show that tailoring, fur making, and cap making—again, predominantly male trades—were "colonized," as they put it, by recent immigrants from Alsace, Germany, and, later, Russia.[69] But the different specialties were very sharply defined and the labor market extremely localized. Homework was not limited to immigrant neighborhoods or to impoverished families locked in the slums; instead it was a much broader phenomenon, answering a variety of diverse and contradictory needs.

THE FACTORY IN THE HOME

The investigators' descriptions of the *lingères'* homes and shops do not have the visual impact of Jacob Riis's photographs of tenements and sweatshops in early-twentieth-century New York. The interviewers, though, were clearly preoccupied with public hygiene, disease, and their relationship to housing and work, and to judge by public reaction, the descriptions were riveting to contemporaries. Some of the workers' dwellings seemed only semi-urban, like the sprawling *cité ouvrière* in La Butte-Aux-Cailles in southeastern Paris behind the Gare d'Austerlitz. The investigators depicted the place as "a kind of encampment . . . formed by a series of barracks surrounded by little gardens and chicken coops. Twenty-five families live in these hovels, which are crawling with children."[70] In centers of home industry in the capital, like the vast expanse of tiny shops and courtyards that stretched east of the Bastille, lingerie workers and their families lived and worked alongside cabinet makers, fur pullers, and rag pickers. Buildings used for industry accumulated fumes and dirt. The sawdust from cabinet makers' shops settled on the stairways. "There are piles of rags, of old boxes, of old bottles, of garbage of all sorts, mice multiply . . ."[71] Most of Paris' shirtmaking was quartered in the tangled streets and unpaved alleys that combed the northern hills of the city in Belleville and Menilmontant. In

[67] Ibid., 1:759 and 5:149.

[68] Ibid., 4:273, 304 and 5:132.

[69] Gemahling, *Travailleurs au rabais*; and *Rapport . . . réglementant le travail*, 1907, 1908, 1911, and 1912.

[70] *Enquête . . . lingerie*, 1:672–73. On the rising sense of crisis about housing, see Berlanstein, *The Working People of Paris*, pp. 46–47.

[71] *Enquête . . . lingerie*, 1:663.

these crowded and heavily working-class neighborhoods, housing conditions—and therefore workplaces—were terrible, as one investigator described in a journey down "a narrow and insalubrious alley of Belleville, where a carriage could hardly fit, past narrow cracked houses . . . a few wine merchants, a fruit-seller, a tripe-seller, one after another. A dark lane leads to a darker stair to shaky steps; two flights climbed by the light of matches too soon out, and the visitor arrives at the door of the working-woman's lodging."[72]

The study judged few of the homes "unhealthy" (the Belleville tenement was one of the few), but it did find them to be terribly small and crowded. Of the 520 homes that the investigators visited, 135 consisted of only one tiny room, and half of these had more than two persons living in them.[73] Gas lamps threw little light, so homeworkers desperately needed sunlit rooms, a luxury in most Parisian buildings, and they often paid disproportionately high rents to get them.[74] In the United States, laws prohibited workers from using their bedrooms or kitchens as workplaces, but in France no such rules applied, and it was just as well, for the sewing machine was always pushed up against the largest (or the only) window in the home, wherever that might be. Here is a telling description of the home of a woman who worked as a concierge as well as in lingerie: "The kitchen is arranged so inconveniently that in order to get light from the window, Mlle S has to hold her head over the burner of the stove. . . . During the day, when she needs to sit near the window to have light, she places a little mirror on a chair so that she can see anyone who goes by or knocks at the door."[75] Light and space were at a premium, and so was fresh air, for poorly ventilated buildings did not dispel bad odors. Mlle S's ground-floor kitchen opened out onto the courtyard, and the stench was so awful that as soon as the spring came, she moved her work out onto the sidewalk, leaving the odors and the stove and mirror behind.

After so many descents into hellishly dark and cramped homes, the authors of the report found the shops lining the boulevards of the city well-lit, spacious, and orderly. "The workshop is lit by a very big window; the machines are in front, next to the window, the irons on the left, next to a big table."[76] Such descriptions nearly breathe with relief. But conditions in the Paris garment shops were not enviable; in fact, they were notoriously bad,

---

[72] Ibid., 1:676. The survey also found homeworkers far from the industrial centers of the city, tucked away in seventh-floor maids' rooms in the Faubourg Saint-Germain.

[73] Almost half of these one-room apartments measured less than thirty *cubic* meters. Ibid., pp. 753–54.

[74] "The rent is 230 francs a year. That is a lot of money for a woman of her means. But it would be hard for her to find another room with good lighting, which is essential to her work." Ibid., p. 702.

[75] Ibid., 1:66.

[76] Ibid., 1:82.

especially in the pressing rooms where the irons gave off noxious fumes. Work inspectors transferred to Paris after a year or so in the provinces were appalled by conditions in the capital's workshops. Tight quarters made it impossible to install machinery correctly or to comply with health regulations. In the opinion of one inspector, the housing crisis made the problem of working conditions utterly intractable: "Transforming industrial Paris would be a Herculean undertaking. In order to do so, one would have to move the center to the periphery—transport it to the suburbs."[77] The contrast between homework and workshop was not as striking as the report contended. Still, as the story of Mlle S shows, poor housing conditions devalued paid and unpaid work, making both immeasurably more time consuming, tiring, and inefficient, which in turn compounded the miseries of homework.[78]

The differences between homework and factory labor were sharp along some lines and illusory along others. Several historians have argued that the autonomy homework allowed women made this work more attractive than one would expect. The study's monographs, however, suggest that in many respects that bore on workers' autonomy, homework did not differ from factory work. Most of the Office du Travail's respondents testified that they only worked for one establishment or contractor. Those who sought to enhance their independence by serving more than one master or mistress usually suffered the consequences. The shirtmakers made frequent rounds, picking up and delivering work often two times a day, and "If you tried to work for two *entrepreneuses* at once," said one woman, "you would displease both of them and lose all your work."[79] Nor was the division of labor much less advanced in outwork than in the factory. One homeworker guessed that a shirt went through nine pairs of hands before being finished. In the provinces, boasted one manufacturer, the division of labor had so developed that "some villages specialize in right sleeves and others in left sleeves."[80]

[77] *Rapport . . . réglementant le travail*, 1905, pp. 12, 17. "In the Center, especially in the buildings around Bonne Nouvelle and les Halles, tiny rooms were expensive to rent." Ibid., 1911, pp. 17, 18.

After 1904, workshops had to allow seven cubic meters per person. A 1911 investigation found that 39 percent of the shops were in violation of the law. *Enquête sur le cubage d'air dans les ateliers de la confection*, Archives Nationales, F 12, box 571. The capital was not the worst of the metropolitan areas; in Rouen 62 percent of the homes visited were unhealthy. *Enquête . . . lingerie*, 1:6, 7.

[78] The Office du Travail insisted on housing conditions to make a point: urban hygiene was not simply a question of housing and public health, it was a question of work and wages. The point was lost on most contemporaries, who saw the squalor of homes as signs of domestic disarray, poor housekeeping, and the inevitable result of combining industry with family life. See chapter 7.

[79] *Enquête . . . lingerie*, 1:674, 675. The autonomy argument is powerfully made by Boxer, "Women in Industrial Homework."

[80] *Enquête . . . lingerie*, 1:40.

The case studies amply illustrate what one reformer meant when he dubbed homework "the factory in the home."[81] One woman "rolled" her machine, as the expression went, so relentlessly that her husband did the house cleaning, cooked the meals, and picked up and delivered the table-cloths she sewed.

> Mme M is an excellent and well-respected worker, and her unusual strength permits her to do an almost incredible amount of work. There are times when she sits at her machine for 8 days at a stretch without going out, making her bed, sweeping the floor which is piled high with scraps of material, or looking after herself. She eats only cold foods from the *charcuterie*.[82]

The flower making study provides several cases that similarly dramatize the "infernal cadences" of homework and the intense work discipline to which women submitted themselves. Mme C, for instance, had been in rose making for fourteen years and was a determined worker.

> In order not to lose any time when she is making roses, she puts her alarm clock on the table next to her to spur her on. She allows herself a given amount of time for each task, and if she even begins to slow down, the ticking of the clock accelerates her movements. . . . Her housework does not distract her at all from her work, for that is strictly her mother's job.[83]

Mme C's day was more typical than one might think, for as one of her fellow workers told the investigators, "You really have to work hard. If you let up, even a little bit, you get nowhere."[84] A woman worker could not allow the household and its routines to break her concentration.

Monographs like these, with the deliberately telltale details about clocks, unmade beds, and unswept floors, were written to dramatize how the factory had come to the home. They also caution against simple views of homework and women's autonomy. As we have seen, cultural and material constraints made the autonomy that homeworkers so prized a largely counterfeit kind of freedom. They gained no leverage vis à vis their employers and were certainly not free to work fewer hours. They could intersperse waged with unwaged labor, but to say that this enabled them to work according to their own rhythms is to ignore how piecework brought the "speed-up" and long hours from the factory into the home.[85] At the same time, perhaps unwittingly, the monographs underscore how the insertion of wage labor into the home undercut what we wrongly assume to have been

---

[81] Henri de Boissieu, "L'usine au logis à Lyon et à Saint-Etienne," *La Quinzaine* 230 (May 1904).

[82] *Enquête . . . lingerie*, 1:661.

[83] *Enquête . . . fleur artificielle*, p. 182.

[84] Ibid., p. 160. See also "Mme B," p. 167.

[85] Cf. Boxer, "Protective Legislation"; and Boris, "Homework and Women's Rights," pp. 19–21.

women's domestic priorities.[86] When their wage labor demanded, and when it was valuable, women's unwaged work stood aside—to be done by their mothers or husbands. The *entrepreneuses'* family monographs in particular showed many husbands doing household chores while their wives made bids or deliveries, sewed, or did the books.[87] It is paradoxical that a study of homework should show the malleability of the division of labor. Although gender structured the low value assigned female labor, both in the labor market and in the family economy, it did not always dictate that women perform such labor. Gender set constraints, but it did not strictly govern women's lives and families' strategies.[88]

THE FAMILY ECONOMY AND THE "SECONDARY WAGE"

The issue of wages proved the thorniest matter that the government's investigation of homework had to address—not for any lack of information, but because of the profusion of muddled theories about why wages remained so low. The letter from the Minister of Labor prefacing the study repeated what reformers throughout Europe had been saying for a decade or more: "starvation wages" were not the exception but the rule. Fifteen percent of the workers interviewed earned more than six hundred francs a year; 25 percent earned between four and six hundred francs; the majority, 60 percent, earned less than four hundred francs a year.[89] Homeworkers usually received piece rates slightly lower than those paid to their counterparts in garment shops, but by the time their costs and, above all, days lost in the

---

[86] For a critical reconsideration of "separate spheres" thinking and whether it shaped women's strategies or their sense of social justice, see Kessler-Harris, *A Woman's Wage*, esp. chap. 3.

[87] See also *Enquête . . . chaussure*, pp. 536–37, for examples of men engaged in child care.

[88] Female labor was devalued in the sense that neither paid nor unpaid labor were worth much unless combined. Since women's wage labor was so poorly paid, their unwaged work took on greater importance. That women's work in the market was worth so little added to their burdens at home.

[89] A group of homeworkers' representatives calculated that a minimum living wage was between 888 and 961 francs per year.

	Francs
Rent	180
Food	475–548 (1,30–1,50 daily)
Heat and light	70
Clothing	100
Cleaning	63

Cited in F. J. Combat, *Le travail des femmes à domicile: Textes officiels avec commentaire explicatif et étude générale sur les salaires féminines* (Paris, 1916), p. 10. See also "Salaires de famine," *La Fronde*, February 3, 1898.

"dead" season were accounted for, their yearly earnings totalled only half those of shopworkers.[90]

Women combined homework with other ways of making money, like house cleaning, taking in boarders, doing laundry, or taking care of a building (44 of 540 Parisian workers were also concierges). Industrial labor fit awkwardly into the economy of makeshift, however, and during full season, most women found it impossible to do anything but homework.[91] Forty-three percent of those interviewed in Paris said they worked ten to twelve hours a day, and 13 percent worked more than twelve hours. Eighty percent testified that lingerie was not a second job but their principal livelihood—an important finding, and one that potentially put the study on a collision course with the theory of the "secondary wage."

The study reported that in certain areas, like the Cher and the Indre, wages fell so low that women refused work. In others, particularly Paris, manufacturers could find "an inexhaustible reservoir of labor." A Parisian *entrepreneuse* had seen as many as five hundred women coming to look for work from one clothier. "Rates are very low, but women will be content with them as a secondary wage (*salaire d'appoint*), for at least they are regular," she explained.[92] In the Office du Travail's 1892 study of the clothing trade, Du Maroussem described the way that working-class families made their calculations:

Everyone knows that women's work in the clothing trades is only supposed to bring a secondary wage. The head of the family earns wages which are meant to meet the needs of all its members. The woman is supposed to supplement this wage—she is concerned with the rent, the family's clothing, pocket

[90] Long periods of unemployment help to account for these figures. Homeworkers and shop shop rates were higher. But the principal advantage of shopwork was that it was more regular. Aftalion sketched this out as follows:

Skilled Worker	Shop	Homework
Daily earnings	2.85 francs	2.70 (three vests @0.90)
Weekly earnings	17.00	14.40 (time lost in deliveries)
Net weekly earnings	17.00	11.10 (cost of thread, machine, heat, and light)
Net annual earnings	825.00	415.00 (unemployment)

Source: Le développement de la fabrique, pp. 262, 263, 274–75, 280.

[91] Enquête . . . lingerie, 1:742–43. Hufton, "Women and the Family Economy." On the informal economy, see the articles collected in Hudson and Lee, Women's Work and the Family Economy.
Monograph #151 in the lingerie survey gives an idea of how women survived on such wages and the workings of the informal economy. This worker earned 300 francs a year at lingerie, made 120 francs a year in addition to housing and light for being a concierge, and the residents of her building brought her food and wood when they came back from the country.
[92] Enquête . . . lingerie, 1:162–63.

money, and little things [*menus plaisirs*]. Under these circumstances 500 or
600 francs a year is enough to make it worth her while to work.[93]

According to this theory, women's wages reflected neither skills nor conditions in industry; they corresponded instead to the woman's position as a
"secondary wage earner." The passage above illustrates some of the theory's
ambiguities: Du Maroussem holds, on the one hand, that women's wages
supplied such essentials as rent and clothing and, on the other, that they
provided only *menus plaisirs*. The confusion about the nature of the needs
that women's wages met stems from contradictory assumptions about their
proper role in the family. Before taking on these assumptions and the ways
in which they distorted analyses of homework, let us consider the study's
evidence about the place of women's wages in the family economy.

Many of the lingerie workers interviewed could specify exactly what their
wages were intended to pay for. Rising rents alone sent many married
women in cities into the labor force.[94] After rent, the household expenses
homeworkers cited most frequently were food and clothing, also a rapidly
growing expense in nineteenth-century working-class budgets. Even a
skilled worker's wages did not feed a family of five. One lingerie worker,
married to a carriage and coach carpenter who brought home twenty-two
hundred francs a year, said that she and her mother needed to earn between
them twenty-two francs a week to put food on the table.[95] Accidents and
sicknesses (often work-related) recur in the monographs with a frequency
that points up the chronic insecurity of working- or lower-middle-class life.
A painter was injured on the job and pensioned at one thousand francs a
year; in his household, "the woman's wages provide the support without
which life would be impossible." Another tradesman, employed by a mirror
maker, fell through one of the mirrors. "His employer offered him 120
francs a year, he refused the offer, sued, lost in court, and now he earns 3
francs a day as an errand boy. The woman's wages are essential to the household." One lingerie worker said that her earnings used to be a secondary
wage, but since her husband, a cook, had contracted tuberculosis, they had
become "the family's only reliable source of income."[96]

We have already noted the remarkable number of women from the lower
middle class among homeworkers, which suggests the importance of
women's wage work at different social levels. One of them, a former seam-

[93] Office du Travail, *Le vêtement á Paris*, p. 189.

[94] In late-nineteenth-century Paris, rent was the fastest rising expense in working-class
budgets. On an index of 100, bread rose from 36 to 42 between 1875 and 1913, and rent rose
from 77 to 99. Statistics cited in John Weiss, "Poor Relief in the Third Republic, 1871–1914,"
French Historical Studies 13, no. 1 (Spring 1983): 70.

[95] *Enquête . . . lingerie*, 1:128–29.

[96] Ibid., 1:641, 674–75. The necessity of women's contribution to the family economy is
amply documented in Office du Travail, *Salaires*. See also Sowerwine, *Sisters or Citizens?*, p. 10;
and Gemahling, *Travailleurs au rabais*, p. 183.

stress, whose husband and son earned together 2,925 francs a year, continued to work "to make a contribution and to help make the family a little better off." Another testified that her husband supported the family and that she intended her wages "not for necessities, but for small enjoyments."[97] This does not mean that these women took their work casually. Take, for instance, a pleater, who told the investigators that her wages allowed her husband and two children "to have some recreation." It is jolting to discover that the work supporting this "recreation" occupied three hundred days a year and brought in 750 francs, which was exceptionally high for lingerie work.

> Mme N's work is well paid and requires special skills. . . . She is paid 55 centimes a meter, and in one eleven-hour day she can sew between 3 and 8 meters of pleats, depending on the length of the strip of material. . . . This is very tiring work, and she has to stop from time to time; occasionally she pierces her thumb with the needle and cannot work for several days.[98]

Nor were all lower-middle-class women easy game for unscrupulous employers, as many in the labor movement claimed. Well-defined needs set at least some limits to their exploitation, allowing them to work only four or five hours a day, or to refuse work they found badly paid. One testified that since "her wages were only an *appoint*, she did not let the manufacturers take advantage of her. Once she decided how much she needed to make, she absolutely refused to lower her rates."[99]

Whatever Mme N's wages paid for, her family clearly considered her earnings essential. Whether petty bourgeois or working class, women worked because their families needed the money—not in the great majority of cases for "small enjoyments." All three studies on homework and other studies of earnings and wages conducted by the Office du Travail made it abundantly clear that even in the lower middle class, and even without the accidents that regularly disrupted life, most men's wages simply did not meet the needs of a household.[100]

The theory of a "secondary wage" had little explanatory value. It concealed the significant number of self-supporting needleworkers: of 540 workers interviewed in Paris, 103 were single, or divorced or widowed women living alone. It also ignored married women who were supporting families in the fashion we have described and, needless to say, women who might have supported themselves if they were better paid. In short, there were more than enough "genuinely needy" women to define a different

---

[97] *Enquête . . . lingerie*, 1:685 and 219.

[98] Ibid., p. 665.

[99] Ibid., p. 656.

[100] In shoemaking, for instance, fewer than 20 percent of male wage earners interviewed by the Office du Travail were supporting their families alone. See *Enquête . . . chaussure*, pp. viii, 348, 503–5 for results on Paris, and on France generally. Of the men with working wives, 56 percent brought in less than three-quarters of the family's resources (p. 506).

labor market, if that market were defined by need. The popularity of the secondary wage theory stemmed from the way in which it ratified cultural convictions about women's lesser needs and the protective role of men in the family. In its bluntest, most ideological form the theory encouraged complacency about women's wages by trivializing—or simply falsifying— the needs they covered. "These earnings should only be considered an extra for the family," wrote one publicist, "they comfort, *as we say*, the family wage."[101] Manufacturers, on the defensive about their labor relations, argued that wages in the clothing industry were not exploitative and comported with expectations for women.[102] And although the Office du Travail was not complacent about these issues, the report's presentation subtly echoed the dominant interpretation. Fewer than one in five married women, the study said in summarizing its findings, contributed more than one-third of the family's resources. When one considers that women's wages were half (at most) of men's, the women's contribution—in terms of hours, efforts, and intensity of labor—seems significantly more than the report implied.[103]

CONCLUSION

The Office du Travail's study of homework in the lingerie industry took no position on the question of wages. Surprisingly, the survey ended with only a cursory summary of its findings, as if the authors deliberately shied away from any conclusions about the broader significance of homework's persistent vitality and resilience, or as if their budgets and "monographs" spoke for themselves.[104] They did not. The investigators had tracked clandestine workers through warrens of tangled streets only to lose them again in well-ordered columns of budgets. Discovering much about women's views of the Parisian labor market, the workings of the family economy, or the workers' understanding of their own labor requires reading between the study's lines. In important respects, the method and preoccupations of these reports were as significant as their findings, and how the reports fit into the changing discussion of women's work forms the subject of part 3.

Changes in the social history of women's work came slowly. The year 1906 stands as a watershed in the history of women's employment in

---

[101] Poisson, *Le salaire des femmes*, p. 117, referring to an article from *La Réforme Sociale*, 1898 (my emphasis).

[102] CST, *Rapport sur le travail des femmes à domicile*, pp. 69, 70.

[103] *Enquête . . . lingerie*, 1:753. For a striking example of how social scientific conclusions could be uninfluenced by statistical evidence, see Susan Pedersen's discussion of Rowntree's studies in "The Failure of Feminism."

[104] By contrast, in the introduction to the survey of artificial flower making, Minister of Labor Fontaine endorsed proposals for minimum wage legislation covering women homeworkers.

France, marking structural changes in the economy that significantly altered the patterns of women's work described in this chapter. After 1906, the textile and clothing industries and domestic service, which had historically employed the vast majority of women, began gradually to decline. Between 1906 and 1936, the proportion of working women employed in industry fell from 57 to 42 percent, and the proportion working in the tertiary sector increased correspondingly, from 44 to 56 percent.[105] Although the proportions of married women working did not change, the kinds of work they engaged in did; we find more clerical workers and fewer small employers and "isolated workers"—more women in the commercial sector, the post office, and other civil service jobs and fewer tending the family café or taking in needlework. How those changes reshaped the fit between waged and unwaged labor or the routines of household work remains to be explored.[106]

The Office du Travail's study of homework in the lingerie industry, conducted between 1905 and 1907, captures the precise moment when women's employment in the various clothing trades peaked: the high point of the process of expansion and feminization in that industry that began in the eighteenth century.[107] It records the world of women's work in the period before slow structural shifts in the economy began. Whether that world was a "belle époque" is an open question. If, like many late-nineteenth-century commentators, one's point of reference is the Le Playan image of family industry, where members of the family worked together and craft skills were a patrimony passed through generations, that ideal was hopelessly debased: most lingerie workers testified that they would never teach their daughter the trade, and the monographs leave us with a striking impression of women working *alone*. If, like a brilliant generation of twentieth-century social historians, one's point of reference is independent artisanship, these women homeworkers will exemplify the degradation of that type, the constraints on female artisanship or, perhaps, the limited usefulness of these categories in analyzing the history of women's work. To understand the point of view of women homeworkers or to help present-day sociologists grappling with issues of part-time work, the informal economy, and the balancing of paid and unpaid labor, it is crucial to recognize the choices,

[105] Married women, however, found it difficult to secure clerical work—again, the "marriage bar" shaped the labor market. Between 1906 and 1936 married women tended to move from the clothing industry into other kinds of waged, industrial employment. Daric, *L'activité professionelle des femmes*, pp. 52–60.

[106] On the United States, see Alice Kessler-Harris and Karen Brodin Sacks, "The Demise of Domesticity in America," in Catherine R. Stimpson and Lourdes Benería, eds., *Women, Households, and the Economy* (New Brunswick, N.J., 1987).

[107] The clothing trades' labor force was about 60 percent female at midcentury, and about 88 percent female in 1900. Guilbert, *Les femmes et les organizations syndicales*, pp. 13–14.

experiences, and calculations that have made homework so attractive and tenacious.[108]

Literally rooted in their households, homeworkers exemplified to late-nineteenth-century observers women's economic and emotional ties to their families; thus the *salaire d'appoint* seemed a ready-to-hand answer to questions about their earnings. If women were willing to work for such low wages, however, that was not because their earnings were secondary. Nor was it due to the power of prescription. Domesticity as a moral imperative was less compelling than the material calculus that combined domestic and industrial labor. Because she was tethered to domestic chores, a woman's work was cheaper to manufacturers. Yet because it enabled her to combine wage work with household labor, homework had the paradoxical effect of making home the site where women's wage work had the greatest overall value. Mindful of their indispensable dual contributions, a great many of the study's respondents also seem to have found in homework a hard-won source of pride. A homeworker from rural France summarized these calculations nicely, and she captured as well the bewildered response those calculations elicited from most observers. When approached by an investigator, she said that she did not think that married women should have to give up their work—by which she meant homework. Why not? "Because of habit, and custom, and, also, on account of a certain dignity that no one understands."[109]

[108] See, for instance, Boris, "Homework and Women's Rights."
[109] Mény, *Le travail à domicile*, pp. 9–11.

PART III

The Gender Politics of Sweated Labor

THE RESURGENCE of homework in the late nineteenth century was an international phenomenon. Throughout Europe and across the Atlantic, regional shifts in industry, changing patterns of work in family economies, new markets for consumer goods, protective legislation for female factory labor, and waves of immigration from east to west contributed to the high profile of industrial homework. Rising concern about this situation was also international. By the time the French Office du Travail published its studies in the 1910s, there were already hundreds of English, American, Belgian, and German studies of what was called home industry or manufacturing, *heimarbeit*, *travail à domicile*, or "sweating."[1] The amount of attention devoted to the issue was staggering. The writings ranged from social scientific studies to journalism, from the scholarly to the sensationalistic, and they were published in forums as different as the *Journal des Economistes* and *La Libre Parole*. The Office du Travail's study was, I have argued, oddly laconic and reluctant to draw any conclusions from its findings. Yet scores of trade unionists, progressive reformers, social catholics, conservative nationalists, and a variety of feminists eagerly stepped into the breach, determined to mine the data for their own purposes and present their own studies of the social question.

They did so in the context of a deep crisis of national identity. The outlines of the fin-de-siècle malaise are familiar: a protracted economic crisis through the 1880s and 1890s, anguished awareness of a falling birth rate, intensified foreign competition, and deteriorating international relations.[2] Parliamentary instability in the face of impatient right-wing nationalists and an increasingly militant working-class movement created constantly nagging fears punctuated by panic and serious political crises. In this political and cultural conjuncture, the Office du Travail's studies of industrial homework, with their bare-boned monographs of working-class family life, could be and were read as alarming narratives of national decline.

In the 1860s, tariff issues had posed pointed questions about how France would compete in the world market, the price it might pay for modernizing, and how to avoid the unraveling of the social fabric. In that period the "problem" of women's industrial work, so influentially framed by Jules Simon in *L'ouvrière* and then taken up by others, became one of the crucial

---

[1] Boyaval, *La lutte contre le sweating system*. "Sweating" and "homework" are not synonymous. Sweating refers to the particular exploitation involved in systems of contracting and subcontracting. Not all sweated work is done in homes. Homework designates all kinds of production in the home, whether artisanal or contracted. By the end of the nineteenth century, most homework was contracted, or "sweated," so commentators often used the terms interchangeably.

[2] Karen Offen, "Depopulation, Nationalism, and Feminism in Fin-de-Siècle France," *American Historical Review* 89, no. 3 (June 1984): 648–76.

terrains on which those questions were to be joined. Questions about economic competition, industrial organization, and their social consequences
continued to gnaw at Simon's turn-of-the-century successors, who worried
in print and in the parliament about how to preserve their country's
strengths and traditions while making a firm commitment to the industrial
future.[3] Economic crisis and social movements had combined to erode the
liberal certainties of Simon's times. By the 1890s, state intervention and
labor reform were squarely on the parliamentary agenda, and concerns
about how labor legislation might reshape forms of industry, women's participation in the labor force, and what many economists and social scientists considered distinctively French gender relations emerged at the forefront of the political and cultural struggle.

The turn-of-the-century battles over women's work were distinctive in
other crucial respects. The heightened prestige of the social sciences provided new paradigms for interpreting the issues at hand. Socialism, social
catholicism, and nationalism contributed new voices to the debate. So did
feminism, a movement that incorporated all of these other outlooks. Last,
the turn-of-the-century sociological research, social movements, and debates about women's work were international and self-consciously so, unlike their counterparts in the earlier periods we have considered. French
reformers interested in women's industrial work, labor legislation, and wage
policy worked in close contact with labor and feminist reformers in the
United States, Belgium, Austria, England, and Germany. For this reason, an
analysis of the wide-ranging debate over sweating accentuates some of the
distinctive features of French reformism and political culture while also
casting light back across a century's developments in France itself.

[3] Judith Stone, *The Search for Social Peace: Reform Legislation in France, 1890–1914* (Albany,
N.Y., 1985).

Chapter Six

UNIONS AND THE POLITICS OF PRODUCTION

IN 1898, Aline Valette, factory inspector, feminist, member of the Guesdist Parti ouvrier français, and delegate of a seamstresses' union, penned a series of articles on women in trade unions for Marguerite Durand's newly founded feminist newspaper, *La Fronde*.[1] Valette had been an inspector in Paris, and she sought to explain the obstacles to organizing Parisian working women. She did so following her version of Marxism, tying social consciousness to the social organization of production. Match and cigar makers, sugar workers, printers, weavers, glove makers, spinners, and so on were attentive to union appeals. "Laboring collectively, suffering collectively, they are naturally, ineluctably, led to organize themselves, and to see a union as a collective body responding to their needs for collective justices: shorter working hours, minimum wages, and equal wages for both sexes." By contrast, needleworkers (who constituted such a large portion of Parisian working women) could never develop such a collective consciousness or agency. "Their isolation leads them to believe that they are utterly and forever helpless, and they recoil before any initiative that needs to be taken." Isolated and vulnerable, they might address themselves to friendly societies and employment bureaus. They were unlikely to stay in a union.[2] Valette was sympathetic about the problem, but firm in her convictions: those who did not conform to her model of a proletariat could never be drawn into the labor movement.

The prevalence of homework in the garment industries heightened unions' difficulties. The reform literature on home industry contributed mightily to fixing the image of the homeworker as immune to the appeals of trade unions and socialist politics. "She represents the opposite of the atheist, materialist worker of the revolutionary committees," wrote Pierre Du Maroussem. Another reformer called home industries the "nursery of strike

---

[1] *La Fronde*, or "the sling" (a reference to David's attack on Goliath and the seventeenth-century French aristocratic revolt) was a feminist daily founded in 1897 by Marguerite Durand (1864–1936). In 1903, it became bimonthly, and it closed in 1905. Steven Hause, *Women's Suffrage and Social Politics in the French Third Republic* (Princeton, N.J., 1984), pp. 32–36.

[2] "Le travail des femmes: Ouvrières et syndicats," *La Fronde*, July 10, 1898. Valette served on the administrative council of Parti ouvrier français and was one of several late-nineteenth-century feminists who tried to bring Marxism to bear on questions of women's work and gender relations. See Hilden, *Working Women*, pp. 197–99, 212–13, 218–19; Sowerwine, *Sisters or Citizens?*, pp. 59–66; and Zylberberg-Hocquard and Diebolt, eds., *Femmes et travail au XIXe siècle*.

breakers."[3] That women homeworkers were hostile to organized labor seemed an amply illustrated sociological truth.

By the late nineteenth century, homework had become one of the single most important issues to confront unions, especially unions in urban areas. As a perceptive analyst of the French labor movement wrote, "When homework runs rampant, it brings such disorganization, and so saps working-class forces that not only is there no resistance, but the seriousness of the question goes practically unnoticed." He went on to say that the guilds of Old Regime France had been better able to handle competition from clandestine workers than late-nineteenth-century unions were to understand and organize the swelling ranks of "cut-rate workers."[4] In addition to weakening strikes, homework threatened apprenticeship programs, which could only be effectively carried out in the shops, under the supervision of skilled workers. Like the clandestine workers of guild days, homeworkers were enmeshed in a web of detested practices that drove wages down: subcontracting, piecework, and bitter competition. And last, homework undermined the late-nineteenth-century labor movement's hard-won political gains, such as hours laws and protective legislation.

Homework was not solely a gender issue. It was equally bound up with ethnic antagonisms and shifting hierarchies within the trade. The question of homework was inextricable from that of women's place in industry, and labor's anti-homework campaigns were infused with hostility to women in the labor force. Yet it is important to ask how "men's" and "women's" interests were defined vis à vis this particularly thorny issue. The years before World War I marked a particularly tumultuous and important moment in the history of gender relations in the labor movement. The rise of syndicalism (or industrial unionism) pressed labor leaders and the rank and file toward new theories and practices. Bracing examples of female militancy in the garment trades (and others) shook commonly held preconceptions about womanly quiescence. So did the rise of feminism, although it also met with ambivalence and hostility. Finally, the dramatic feminization of clothing and textiles forced the labor movement to accept and to try to organize women workers.[5] But even the most sympathetic and open-

---

[3] Du Maroussem, *Ouvrière mouleuse*, p. 177; Mény, *Le travail à domicile*, pp. 199, 200.

[4] Gemahling, *Travailleurs au rabais*, pp. 253, 257–58. Late-nineteenth-century industrial unions tried to break with the corporatist past to reach a broader constituency and to organize the unskilled rather than simply excluding them. In this, Gemahling argued, they had failed.

[5] Guilbert, *Les fonctions des femmes dans l'industrie*, pt. 1; and idem, *Les femmes et les organizations syndicales*; Gemahling, *Travailleurs au rabais*; Hilden, *Working Women*; Sowerwine, *Sisters or Citizens?*; Scott, *Gender and the Politics of History*, chap. 5. For parallels, see Christine Stansell, *City of Women: Sex and Class in New York, 1789–1860* (New York, 1986), chap. 7, and pp. 130–54, 138–39; Milkman, "New Research in Women's Labor History"; and Sonya O. Rose, "Gender Antagonism and Class Conflict: Exclusionary Strategies of Male Trade Unionists in Nineteenth-Century Britain," *Social History* 13, no. 2 (May 1988): 191–208.

minded union militants were far from sure about how this might be accomplished. How the unions wrestled with those issues, how "male" and "female" interests were articulated in the process, and how these battles were different from the conflicts between guilds and clandestine workers under the Old Regime are the subjects of this chapter.

THE GARMENT TRADES "AWAKEN"

The decades before World War I brought a string of explosive strikes in the Parisian garment trades. These seemingly unplanned strikes caught the world of organized labor by surprise. Three strikes in particular, in 1901, 1910, and 1911, marked for many observers the emergence of female militancy in the clothing trades. They became the backdrop against which union debates about wage policy, labor legislation, and women's role in the union movement played out.

The first of these strikes began in February 1901 and was centered in women's clothing. The initial sparks came from workshops in the area around the avenue de l'Opéra, the boulevard Haussmann, the place Vendôme, and the rue de la Paix, which served the "grands couturiers" in women's clothing.[6] As in any strike, strategic timing was essential. February was the time when "models" for the season's fashions were made and priced, when representatives of the international clothing industry came to Paris. Anticipation ran high, and negotiations about wages and piece rates were still possible. Tailors and seamstresses who made "models" demanded a role in pricing them, arguing that they knew more about the labor, fabric, and trimmings in various fashions than did those setting the prices.[7] When they were rebuffed, they walked out.

The strike spread with unprecedented rapidity. It moved through the elite dressmaking shops of the rue de la Paix, then east to the "second order" wholesale enterprises clustered around Sentier, in the central third arrondissment, then into the hills of Montmartre, which were crowded with sweatshops and the dwellings of immigrant and French homeworkers. The variegated social geography of the strike made it a particularly Parisian affair. It also made it a striking departure from usual job actions, which had heretofore been confined to male cutters and "pumpers" (those in charge of alterations), with women in, at most, a supporting role.[8]

---

[6] On the strike, see Archives of the Prefecture of Police (hereafter APP), BA 1394 "Grèves: tailleurs, 1901–1918"; Office du Travail, *Statistique des grèves*, 1901, pp. 74–75; and Nancy Green, "Eléments pour une étude du mouvement ouvrier juif à Paris au début du siècle," *Le Mouvement Social* 110 (January–March 1980): 51–75.

[7] These shopworkers functioned much like subcontractors.

[8] The meeting at which the strike was called involved men and women, though the tailors were first to strike.

Thus the strike was widely perceived as a women's movement, defying expectations about womanly quiescence. "Will the *petites couturières* really drop their thimbles and needles?" asked a skeptical article in the *Echo de Paris*. The answer, apparently, was yes. By the fourth and fifth days of the strike, more than a thousand strikers, nearly half of them women, were meeting in the Bourse du Travail (the Parisian labor exchange) and had elected a strike committee with ten men and ten women. Women speakers took the podium in public meetings, many for the first time. They urged seamstresses and, especially, the women "assistants" to formulate their *own* demands rather than simply to support those of the tailors. At meetings women workers demanded that tailors respect their grievances, angrily recalling earlier strikes when, once the tailors' demands had been met, their strike had ended.[9]

The strike's gender dimensions were magnified by the burgeoning feminist movement. The feminists grouped around Marguerite Durand and *La Fronde* were eager to support the strikers and to interpret their demands; these women spoke at rallies, demonstrated, and produced some of the best journalistic coverage of the strike's progress. At the Bourse du Travail, speakers closely linked to feminism shared the podium with union leaders from the Parisian clothing trades. *La Fronde* saw the strike as a feminine *prise de parole*, a demonstration of working women's seriousness of purpose and capacities for public action and speech. As one journalist put it, naysayers who believed that women could "gossip," but were incapable of "speaking out," would now be forced to rethink their position. Cultural stereotypes were being shattered by the "joyous bands of seamstresses" with their "elegant bearing" and "truly Parisian chic."[10] As the depth of seamstresses' involvement in the strike became clear, *La Fronde* announced that "from now on, the success of the strike lies in the hands of women." The mainstream press agreed. Although the tailors insisted this was their strike, and although the majority of the strikers were men, the lion's share of the press coverage went to the women.[11]

Much about the strike had wide public appeal. The press dwelt on the street festival atmosphere created by the "courageous girls" on the boulevards, on the densely varied social landscape in which the strike unfolded, on the cross-class dimensions of the demonstrations, and on the "new womanly" character of the seamstresses' protest. The government's use of troops against the demonstrators and the manufacturers' willingness to lock

[9] Police reports on meetings, January 31, February 8, 10, and 11, 1901. APP, BA 1394. Demands included application of labor laws (especially those on night work), an eight-hour day, ten francs a day for the tailors, six for the first hands; five francs for the second hands; two and a half for *petits mains*.

[10] *La Fronde*, February 18, 1901.

[11] See, for instance, *Le Siècle*, February 24, 1901. APP, BA 1394. By February 13, the press was treating this as a women's strike.

women workers in the shops at lunch gave the events overtones of a
women's suffrage battle. That the clothing industry was so bound up with
the capital's self-image as the arbiter of European fashion raised the stakes;
that seamstresses in the haute couture shops (the so-called *midinettes*) represented Parisian artistry gave them a certain claim on public sympathies.[12]
The strike was rich in historical echoes as well as scenes from "modern"
Parisian life. Under Louis XVI, tailors and seamstresses had battled each
other for the right to make women's clothing, wrote a journalist in *Le
Figaro*; but now these young women had put aside the war between the
sexes and historic antagonisms between guild tailors and seamstresses in
order to stand, shoulder to shoulder, against their employers. When students flocked across the river to join the demonstrations (many of them for
right-wing nationalist reasons), papers waxed romantic about the revival of
"la vie de Bohème" and student-grisette relations.[13]

The dark aspects of the strike, however, were equally characteristic of
turn-of-the-century politics in the capital. Anti-Semitism unmistakably
contributed to aligning mainstream sympathies and to the relatively favor-
able coverage afforded the *midinettes*. The right-wing press cast the strike as
a battle between, on the one side, French women and Parisian artistry and,
on the other, Jewish clothing manufacturers, whose links to large retailing
concerns like the Bon Marché made them doubly easy targets of the nationalist and anti-modernist wrath of small shopkeepers. The Jewish clothing
manufacturer Paquin, head of the clothing firm Isodore Jacob, was not only
a Dreyfusard; he had connections to the socialist minister Millerand. This
compounded the right's fury. Paquin and others were confronted by nationalist gangs as well as striking workers, and by cries of "death to the Jews,"
and "down with the Jews."[14] The anti-Semitic aspects of attacks on immigrant subcontractors for unscrupulously preying on vulnerable (and implicitly, French) women, as some papers put it, were also obvious. These calls
to arms involved multiple distortions. Although ethnic tensions were potentially explosive, they did not neatly follow the strike's fault lines. The
conviction that immigrant workers undercut their French counterparts was
unfounded.[15] To the contrary, the strike provided ample evidence of the
tenacity and militancy of women, immigrants, and homeworkers.

[12] As the anti-Semitic and nationalist press put it, "Partout où il faut du goût, de l'élégance,
de la dexterité, du fine, n'est-ce pas l'artisan parisien qu'on est habitué à voir triompher?" But
Parisian high fashion was "crawling" with foreigners: "pittoresques, babeliques . . . peu de
français." *La Libre Parole*, February 7, 1901. See also APP, BA 1394.

[13] *Le Figaro*, February 19, 1901; *La Fronde*, February 20; and other press clippings in APP,
BA 1394.

[14] See police reports and press clippings in APP, BA 1394.

[15] Anti-immigrant newspaper articles were usually repudiated by striking workers in meetings the next day. On immigrant labor and Jewish community involvement in the 1901 strike,
see Green, *The Pletzl of Paris*, pp. 128–30; and *La Fronde*, February 27, 1901, "La physionomie
de la grève."

From the beginning of the strike, workers from the Center of Paris (the area around Sentier) had to contend with the manufacturers' threat to bypass them completely and to break the strike by simply giving all work out to homeworkers scattered throughout the city. Thus when strikers learned that a group of tailors, seamstresses, and their assistants in Montmartre were meeting to support them, their spirits soared. The high point of the strike came on February 14, when a delegation of women and men from Montmartre marched down the hill to join workers from central Paris, calling for an eight-hour day, the abolition of piece rates, and a general strike.[16] At a dramatic meeting that night at the Bourse du Travail, seamstresses from different parts of the city stood up group by group, identifying the houses for which they worked, and vowing to carry the strike further. "When we have purged Montmartre of the exploiters, we will head for Grenelle and Montrouge [other centers of garment industry subcontracting] and do the same there."[17]

The better-paid workers of the Center nonetheless were reluctant to cast their lot with downtrodden homeworkers and immigrant *apiéceurs* (subcontracting tailors), who were customarily seen as the enemy. The *midinettes* from the rue de la Paix were young; the women workers of Montmartre were older, married, and came to meetings with their children in tow. The *midinettes* were paid by the day, while almost all the Montmartre workers were paid by the piece, and the latter worked in tiny sweatshops or out of their homes, often doing inexpensive ready-made lines for the same houses that employed the others. The importance of community-based radicalism was particularly apparent in the Montmartre section of the strike, where the neighborhood offered moral and financial support. The Montmartre workers were not the only representatives of the other world of the needle trades, however; they were joined by similar groups of older women from the northern suburbs. *La Fronde*, which ran an excellent series of articles on the Montmartre strikers, underscored the different worlds of female experience.[18]

The 1901 strike spilled over the previous boundaries of clothing industry actions and shook many preconceptions. The left-wing press applauded the outburst of feminine militancy, hailing the "energetic strikers who have carved out their place in the family of workers, and taken their position for future struggles" and commending these women for "joining the forward march of history in the twentieth century."[19] In many respects, the Mont-

---

[16] These Montmartre workers were on contract to the same firms that were on strike.

[17] Police report, February 14, 1901. APP, BA 1394.

[18] On relations between the groups of strikers, see police reports and *La Fronde*, February 23, 1901.

[19] See press clippings from *Le Petit Sou*, February 18, 1901; *L'Intransigeant*, February 19; *La Fronde*, February 19. APP, BA 1394.

martre *apiéceurs* and seamstresses proved more radical than their counter-parts in the shop, remaining out on strike while the workers in the Center were unhappily accepting a settlement regarding the tailors' demands.[20]

The multiplication of contradictory demands was one of the most ob-vious problems to confront strikers. Piecework and subcontracting gave rise to bitter dispute. All the striking seamstresses and tailors called for the "abolition of piecework." For subcontractors and homeworkers in Mont-martre and elsewhere, the demand represented an effort to negotiate collec-tive contracts directly with the manufacturers and to regularize wages. For workers in the Center, the slogan meant eliminating competition from homeworkers.[21] Many subcontractors, however, refused to join the strike unless demands for elimination of piecework were dropped. In moments of enthusiasm and élan, workers from the Center and Montmartre could agree on "purging" neighborhoods of "exploiters." Yet many homeworkers in the areas to be purged considered this a declaration of war rather than of solidarity.

The 1901 strike lasted thirty-five days and involved fifty-five shops. As it wound down, weakened by diminished funds and support, recriminations began. Groups of tailors blamed women workers for the strike's failure. Women strikers indignantly protested such charges—the more so because when, in the last days of the strike, the workers' committee met with manu-facturers, it focused on tailors' demands, virtually ignoring the women's.[22] In the end, the clothing manufacturers made concessions on shopworkers' rates and hours, but refused to consider the elimination of piecework or subcontractors. Women workers gained virtually nothing. Still, they joined the union by the hundreds, and the strike was an eye-opener, a benchmark of a shifting politics of protest in the clothing trades.

In 1909, the different organizations of tailors, cutters, seamstresses, and lingerie workers in the Paris region joined their forces in the General Union of Clothing Workers of the Seine. This burst of syndicalist unity was critical to a pair of strikes that hit the Parisian clothing industry, this time the men's clothing trade, in the summer of 1910 and again in the winter of 1911. The target of an increasingly effective organizing drive was the Esders enter-prise, which manufactured inexpensive ready-made men's clothing for Pari-sian retailers and export. In Paris, Esders ran at least four large workshops and contracted out to a dozen large-scale entrepreneurs in Montmartre and suburban Montrouge and Vanves. In both 1910 and 1911, the strikes began

[20] That settlement involved a nine-hour day at eleven francs, with no concessions on piece-work and putting out. The Office du Travail called the result a "half-victory." *Statistique des grèves*, 1901, pp. 74–75.

[21] See Green, "Eléments pour une étude du mouvement ouvrier," pp. 68–70; Mény, *Le travail à domicile*, pp. 202–4.

[22] Police report, March 2, 1901. APP, BA 1394.

at Esders workshops but spread quickly to other manufacturers in the city
and the garment-making suburbs. The first strike, in July 1910, lasted little
more than a month, but it enrolled many new members in the union. The
second, building on those rising numbers, found much wider support and
created a more protracted battle, lasting from November 1911 to February
1912.[23]

In 1910 and 1911, unlike 1901, women composed the majority of the
strikers and were incontestably the strikes' leaders. The labor force in men's
ready-made clothing had been increasingly feminized since at least the
1830s. That trend accelerated at the turn of the century, multiplying the
numbers of women homeworkers and shopworkers. The women workers in
this branch of the industry were also distinctly less artisanal than the *midinettes* of 1901. As one newspaper put it, these were not the "sprightly and
elegant seamstresses of the rue de la Paix, they are *faubouriennes*."[24]

Most of the 1910–11 strikers were young and worked in shops. Their
grievances involved not only conditions in their own workshops, but the
subcontractors in the suburbs who undercut their rates and women who
worked at home. In 1910, workers sent delegations to Montmartre, and out
to the suburbs in Vanves, to "hunt foxes," or ferret out subcontractors and
women homeworkers who were continuing to accept work from the firms
whose main workshops had been shut down by the strikers.[25] In 1911,
similar delegations persuaded several large Esders subcontractors in Montrouge and Montmartre to support their strike. On several occasions, however, confrontations between strikers and subcontractors turned violent,
windows were broken, the police were called in, and more scuffles en-
sued.[26] Confrontations around the workshops were also explosive, and
women strikers' skirmishes with the police attracted sympathetic crowds.
The syndicalist press denounced "cowardly attacks" on "courageous," "tenacious," and "ardent" women. "It is unacceptable and revolting to see
women hit in this cowardly way."[27] THEY ARE BEATING WOMEN! AND WHAT
ARE MEN DOING ABOUT IT? ran a headline of *La Bataille Syndicaliste*. The
article below the banner lamented that men were not around to "teach the
police a lesson."[28] The relative quiet of the centrist press, less sympathetic

[23] See Guilbert, *Les femmes et les organizations syndicales*, p. 233; and Archives Nationales
(hereafter AN), series F7 13880 and 13881.
[24] Women outnumbered men five to one, according to the police. The 1911 strike had many
more union members participating. Police report, January 1911. AN, F7 13881.
[25] AN, F7 13740.
[26] Police reports and press clippings, 1911. AN, F7 13881.
[27] *La Voix du Peuple*, December 1911. AN, F7 13881.
[28] ILS BATTENT LES FEMMES!! QUE FONT DONC LES HOMMES? AN, F7 13881. See also clippings
from the *La Voix du Peuple* and *L'Humanité*. The syndicalist press was quite sympathetic to the
English suffragettes and found echoes of suffragism in the strikes.

in 1910 and 1911 than they had been in 1901, further incensed the voices of syndicalist opinion.

Both strikes failed.[29] They nonetheless marked the emergence of militancy in the branch of ready-made men's clothing, a branch whose quiescence had been the object of tailors' scorn and rage since the 1830s. They were widely interpreted as an awakening of women workers. "Women are beginning their spiritual emancipation," proclaimed *L'Humanité*. This was "a movement with important consequences . . . in feminine milieux."[30]

The Esders strikes of 1910 and 1911 put women's work at the top of the agenda of the Federation of Clothing Workers. The strikes "posed the question [of women's work] in a new area, undergoing rapid industrialization." The question was demonstrably "délicat"—tricky, or complicated. The Federation of Clothing Workers found itself confronted with "an enormous female proletariat—unorganized and traditionally unorganizable."[31] It was far from clear, however, how the federation would contend with the newly vociferous and militant female presence. How would unions organize women and keep them in unions? And how would this incorporation fit with the larger cultural and political construction of "women's" interests?

THE CHANGING POLITICS OF CLOTHING WORKERS' UNIONS

Dramatic social changes of the late nineteenth century brought many trades unions face to face with women's industrial labor. In typography, where women made inroads into hitherto unchallenged male monopolies, unions brooked no compromise with those they plainly considered the female invaders. Tin makers stated flatly that "a woman never comes into [the shop] as a comrade, but always as a competitor."[32] In the guild tradition, many of these trades excluded women from apprenticeship programs and vowed to sanction anyone giving women technical training. Madeleine Guilbert has shown that on these issues many late-nineteenth-century unions were virtually armed camps.[33]

---

[29] The second strike was over by the end of January 1912. Dumas accused the union of abandoning the Esders workers. APP, BA 1423 and AN, F7 13881. The only other notable strike before the war came in the Galeries Lafayette, in February–March 1913. It was led by skirt and blouse workers, most of them women immigrants and homeworkers. The strike, though, did not spread, and failed. AN, F7 13881 and APP, BA 1394.

[30] *L'Humanité*, August 27, 1910 and September 1, 1910. See also the police reports in AN, F7 13740.

[31] *La Bataille Syndicaliste*, August 17, 1912, reporting on Congrès de l'habillement. AN, F7 13740.

[32] Cited in Gemahling, *Travailleurs au rabais*, p. 158.

[33] Examples in ibid., pp. 161–62. The best-known instance of opposition to women's work came when the Fédération du Livre refused to admit a printer, Emma Coriau, to the union, and expelled her husband for allowing her to work. Historians disagree about whether or not the

Tailors' politics do not fit this picture. Unlike other unions, the tailors' unions had a long history of contending with fellow women workers. Unlike other trades unions, moreover, they had very few resources, whether economic, corporate, or ideological with which to resolve dilemmas posed by gender relations in the trades. Tailors' scorn for women workers notwithstanding, most tailors' skills did not fundamentally differ from those of their women competitors and assistants.[34] Cutters had constituted a privileged elite since the seventeenth century; they worked in shops, were given specialized training, and were entrusted with valuable materials. They maintained their status, excluding virtually all women, through the nineteenth century.[35] Tailors did not. Formal apprenticeship, never very strong, had been weakened by the decline of workshop production, the slow separation of the design and fashioning of clothing from its production, the rise of ready-made and the cheapening of labor, and the rapid proliferation of small jobbing tailors, too strapped to give young men and women more than the essential training.[36] When organized clothing workers discussed the need to shore up craft skills and improve technical training, creating some nineteenth-century substitute for apprenticeship traditions, they proposed courses in cutting, not sewing. Tailors retained much control over small workshop production, in the hiring and contracting process. But they were quite unable to prevent the increased use of female labor.

Moreover, nearly all tailors' wives worked, many in the garment industry. This complicated any outright ideological opposition to women's work. To talk about sending women in the labor force "home" would have been nearly meaningless. Women could scarcely be expected to stop earning wages, and homework simply created competition for shopworkers. Tailor activists murmured darkly about the dangers of women's "industrial" work. In the 1870s, they gave full play to medical warnings about the dangerously sensual side effects of sewing machine work—when it was done by women. They deplored the poor quality of work done in the rapidly feminizing sections of the trade.[37] They were bereft of other tactics.

"affair" was representative of unions' gender politics. Cf. Marilyn Boxer, "Foyer or Factory: Working-Class Women in Nineteenth-Century France," *Proceedings of the Second Meeting of the Western Society for French History* (1974); Guilbert, *Les femmes et les organizations syndicales*; Marie-Hélène Zylberberg-Hocquard, *Femmes et féminisme dans le mouvement ouvrier français* (Paris, 1981); and Charles Sowerwine, "Workers and Women in France before 1914: The Debate over the Coriau Affair," *Journal of Modern History* 55 (September 1983): 411–41.

[34] Jacques Rancière was the first to raise questions about the tailors' self-presentation as skilled workers. See "The Myth of the Artisan: Critical Reflections on a Category of Social History," *International Labor and Working-Class History* (1983); and Scott, *Gender and the Politics of History*, chap. 5.

[35] Cutters were the first section to unionize in the lingerie industry. See APP, BA 151.

[36] On apprenticeship, see Faraut, *Histoire de la Belle Jardinière*, pp. 28–29.

[37] Tailors' jury reports trumpeting the quality of French tailoring and deploring the shoddi-

In the 1860s, tailors' groups had been notoriously Proudhonist: anti-Church, anti-state, anti-capitalist, and staunch defenders of working-class patriarchy.[38] Their outlook on women's work was nourished by the long-standing and bitter competition between women and men within tailoring, and by the historic rivalries between tailors, lingerie workers, and seam-stresses. Since it was clearly impossible to eliminate women's work in their trade, maintaining strong patriarchal authority and moral disciple seemed the next best alternative. They fought to preserve their prerogatives as heads of (laboring) households, directing their family members' labor.

Conditions in the trade, however, were not the principal determinant of tailors' gender politics. Common rhetorical conventions, whose relation-ship to tailors' daily lives was hardly self-evident, powerfully shaped their discourse on women's work. As we saw in chapter 2, by the 1860s the exploitation of working womanhood had become a popular metaphor for capitalism's assault on nature and morality. Thus tailors like others in-veighed against capitalists for deforming "femininity" and portrayed work-ing women as lambs sacrificed at the altar of capitalism.[39] Speeches at tai-lors' meetings nostalgically harked back to a preindustrial golden age when a tailor's wife and daughters had occupied themselves with domestic chores while the male head of household supported the family. The picture of a well-ordered family shop with clearly defined and gendered roles was a deeply misleading portrait of the past, though it clearly appealed as a vision of the future. By the tailors' account, the rise of ready-made and sub-contracting had corrupted male authority, requiring jobbers and sub-contractors to "sweat" their wives and daughters. Changes in the trade, in other words, were corrupting honorable and longstanding patriarchal authority—the kind of authority that had once been upheld by the guilds.

Women, in this scenario, only participated in the trade by virtue of their membership in the family. They were the assistants and underlings in what tailors plainly considered a male enterprise. The Tailor's Union, formed in 1862, stipulated that *apiéceurs* could only employ their wives and children—an effort to limit the numbers of women and assure their mem-bers' control of the trade.[40] In 1868, when the union was officially "toler-ated" and beset by a rush of new members, it decided to admit women. But it banned them from speaking at assemblies; if women had "observations" or "proposals," those had either to be placed in writing or offered by one of the regular, male members. Such rules were hard to sustain, and they came

---

ness of foreign work drew fire in union meetings. Dissenting union members accused the reporters of self-defeating complacency as well as exclusivity. APP, BA 151.

[38] On Proudhon, see Magraw, *A History of the French Working Class*, 1:78–82.

[39] For characteristic reports on women's work in the 1870s, see press clippings in APP, BA 151.

[40] Office du Travail, *Les associations professionelles ouvrières*, 2:617–20.

under attack as well from increasingly self-confident women. In 1874, the union struck down the ban on women's speech, though over objections that public and political deliberation were inappropriate for women.[41]

Through the 1870s and 1880s, the gender politics of the clothing workers continued, fitfully, to change. As female subsections of the trade multiplied, their representatives—vest makers, breeches makers, pumpers, tailors' assistants, seamstresses, seamstresses in ready-made—figured more regularly at meetings. New political strategies, particularly what Michelle Perrot calls "la syndicalization de la grève" (the long and slow process by which unions took control over strikes) also brought changes.[42] Syndicalist leaders repeatedly urged the union to begin organizing women in the rapidly feminizing clothing trades and bring them into job actions. But as strikes were discussed more openly, and as strikes became part of regular union tactics, women's alleged "passivity" emerged as a key issue. The majority seems to have been persuaded that women would never join unions.[43]

From the mid-1880s to the mid-1890s, debates on these issues were overshadowed by political disputes.[44] Just as the Tailors' Union was officially legalized in 1884, it nearly collapsed from wrangling. By 1892, however, in the same spirit of unity that would establish the Confédération générale du travail (CGT) (General Confederation of Labor) three years later, the Parisian tailors' group joined in creating a national federation of all clothing workers.[45] Within ten years the federation grouped together representatives from a wide range of clothing trades: tailors, seamstresses, shirtmakers, and the makers of collars, corsets, gloves, furs, and artificial flowers.[46]

During this same period, the tone of artisanal self-defense was waning. Like the CGT, the Federation of Clothing Workers saw itself as an alliance of industrial rather than craft workers, and likewise its theory was informed

[41] Rescinding the ban on women's speech may have been an effort to improve the union's image at a time when its numbers and effectiveness were particularly low. It may have been encouraged by currents of republican feminism. See press clippings in APP, BA 151.

[42] Perrot, *Les ouvriers en grève*.

[43] APP, BA 152.

[44] On political divisions, see Office du Travail, *Les associations professionelles ouvrières*, 2:631–32.

[45] By 1901, the Parisian union was enrolling new members, operating seven sections in Paris and the suburbs, and publishing a regular newspaper, *L'Ouvrier Tailleur*, in several different languages. Ibid., pp. 642–44.

[46] Member organizations included: Cutters in Shirtmaking, Cutters in Tailoring; Tailors and Seamstresses of the Seine; Cutters in Collars and Ties; Flower-Makers; and Seamstresses in Collars and Ties. By 1910, the Parisian Tailors and Seamstresses had joined with the cutters to form the General Federation of Clothing Workers of the Seine. Seamstresses and Lingerie Workers of the Seine remained a separate group. By 1912, there was also a General Union of Shirtmaking of the Seine. See the *Comptes rendus* of the trade union congresses of the Federation of Clothing Workers in 1906, 1908, 1910, and 1912.

by overlapping strains of Marxism, evolutionism, and positivism. The logic of industrial development made craft skills and the politics of defending them obsolete. The CGT was committed to organizing the unskilled and to a spirit of inclusiveness that, in theory at least, sought to unite men and women, immigrants and French, skilled and unskilled under the banner of class. Many industrial unions adopted these political goals, but for garment workers, they were practical imperatives. The gender politics of the past had hardly proved effective. By 1900, a combination of doctrinal changes and socioeconomic developments had shaken the openly patriarchal politics of the tailor-dominated unions. The strike of 1901, and then those of 1910 and 1911, dramatized the importance of women's militancy and the urgency of bringing women into unions. The results were changing policies, heightened ambivalences, and new conundrums.

Women's Work and *Travail à Domicile*

Of all the issues confronting the Federation of Clothing Workers in the twentieth century, the most critical were women's work and homework. Syndicalist calls to cast aside destructive competition between workers and to recruit from the ranks of the unskilled made both issues central. So did the labor legislation of the 1890s and 1900s, which focused attention on the alleged distinctiveness of women's industrial work and which granted exemptions to "familial" home industries. As strikes became a more formal part of union politics, how to organize homeworkers (whether men or women) became central to union strategy.

Industrial homework involved a complex of questions and practices: subcontracting, piecework, artisanal autonomy, and the regulation of the labor market. It was not solely, or even primarily a gender matter. To the contrary, much union concern focused on male *apiéceurs*: jobbing tailors who worked at home, sometimes contracting out to others. The elimination of *apiéceurs* and piecework had been one of the tailors' central demands in the 1901 strike. The clothing workers' unions asked members to refuse piecework and homework; national union campaigns sought to stamp out what were seen as residues of Proudhonism and to instruct workers in the dangers of "individualism." "Although homework seems to leave more room for initiative and individual liberty," warned one Parisian delegate to the annual meeting of the Federation of Clothing Workers in 1897, "in reality it merely encourages *marchandage* [bargaining], backbiting, and destroys any feeling of solidarity."[47] Tailors who ran small shops or contracted to homeworkers were "exploiters in the real sense of the word, and must be com-

[47] Comité de la Seine, report to Congrès des travailleurs de l'habillement, 1897, cited in *Les associations professionelles ouvrières*, 2:658. The glove makers launched a similar campaign.

bated. They contribute to overproduction. They are worse than the bosses, for they force their colleagues work for next to nothing."[48] Every meeting of the Federation of Clothing Workers brought a resolution against piecework and industrial homework. These resolutions were not directed primarily at women, but rather at men who ran or worked in little shops, strategically located in crucial points of clothing manufacturing networks, and considered more open to union appeals.

Many local clothing workers' unions considered these campaigns utterly self-defeating. What was the point of making the elimination of homework a central plank of the Federation of Clothing Workers' platform when so many tailors plainly preferred to work at home? Repeated proposals to build collective workshops run by unions met with sarcastic rebukes. Even if manufacturers were to build "luxurious" shops, workers would not go to them.[49] Tailors who disagreed with the federation's official policy considered industrial homework, in the form of the family shop, an important source of autonomy and protection. Many also questioned the political wisdom of anti-homework campaigns. Denouncing the "individualism" of jobbing tailors could only estrange workers who were, in other respects, fiercely political, determined to defend their rates, and open to union propaganda. The 1901 strike, when many Montmartre apiéceurs went out, proved a case in point, when misunderstandings about the slogan "down with piecework" had helped to sour relations between the groups of strikers.

The dilemma was obvious. Through much of the nineteenth century, tailors and cutters had cast apiéceurs and their assistants (male or female) as the miserable, bottom-dwelling, chaotic element of the trade. Yet those apiéceurs were crucial to any successful organizing or strike. The Federation of Clothing Workers' campaign against homework, which involved distributing anti-homework brochures to Parisian apiéceurs, struck many as a futile exercise. Why not organize instead around working conditions, the eight-hour day, or wage legislation?[50] Those who supported the anti-homework campaigns argued that wages and hours could not be extricated from the social organization of labor, dismissing as "platonic" calls for reforms that ignored deep structures. Time and time again, however, anti-homework resolutions met with defiance or resignation. As one union leader wryly commented after listening to one of many speeches on the subject, "You will never eliminate homework and piecework. Do you understand that? We are more likely to make the Revolution."[51]

[48] Compte rendu officiel des travaux du sixième congrès, 1906, p. 48.

[49] Compte rendu officiel des travaux du septième congrès, 1908, p. 54.

[50] Compte rendu, 1906, pp. 48–50. See also L'Humanité's coverage of the meeting, August 22, 1906.

[51] Faure, in Compte rendu, 1908, p. 55.

Gender aside, then, homework would have been a difficult issue. Yet the discussions also framed the question of women's needs and grievances in a particularly tangled way. Women who spoke at the clothing workers' congresses considered homework one of their premier concerns. They repeatedly linked homework and contracting to the conditions of female employment and women's distinctive vulnerabilities, to very low wages and grueling fourteen- to sixteen-hour days in high season, to the "tyranny" of contractors, and to the abuses of family industry. They charged that *apiéceurs* sweated their wives and daughters and underpaid their assistants under the pretext that these were not "real" workers.[52] Reports at many clothing workers' meetings also brought up what they considered women's preference for working at home, a preference in many respects analogous to jobbing tailors' desire for autonomy. The issue nonetheless posed gender-specific problems. And since much of this was married women's work, it also pressed on the boundaries of labor's understanding of the role of women in the family and their labor in the family economy.

Women representatives first attended the Federation of Clothing Workers' national congress in 1906, amid proclamations that any successful working-class action depended on the "presence and aid of women."[53] Still, the speech welcoming the new delegates was a revealingly awkward one. It paid tribute to the women's militancy while underscoring their powerlessness.

> We men, the so-called strong sex, we vote and make laws. But the women, even those who compete with us—What do they have? Nothing but their pluck, their vision of a better future for all—and still, they hardly complain.
>
> That the representatives of the so-called weak sex are present at this Congress is for us a precious guarantee that our exploited sisters, like us, are willing to demand the rights to which we all are legitimately entitled.[54]

The urgency of organizing women workers mounted quite rapidly in the next few years. Tailors' and cutters' unions merged with those of seamstresses and lingerie workers, bringing a particularly energetic female presence into the larger regional federations.[55] The imperative was also pressed on the national federation by its new secretary, Pierre Dumas, a former tailor whose views tended toward anarcho-syndicalism.[56] Dumas' style was confrontational and his analysis of the "woman question" tinged with an anarchist-style feminism. "The first task at hand," he announced, "is to rid ourselves of union men's prejudices." Men organize for their own interests

---

[52] *Compte rendu*, 1906, pp. 64–65; 1910, pp. 87, 92; and 1912.

[53] See press clippings on 1906 meeting, AN, F7 13740.

[54] Opening speech, *Compte rendu*, 1906, p. 7.

[55] Police reports and press clippings, December 1908–January 1909, and October 1909. AN, F7 13740.

[56] Police biographies and reports in AN, F7 13740 and AN, F7 13881.

and they strike for their own demands, he said, but they consider union membership a male prerogative and duty, and would never imagine bringing their wives and daughters into unions.[57] Dumas also broke with precedent by addressing women directly, observing that "the evolution of society has moved women beyond the secondary role that nature assigned them," and encouraging them to defend themselves.[58] This approach soon met its limits. Like the union speaker who had welcomed the "so-called weaker sex" to the congress of 1906, Dumas tried to be sympathetic and generous, but constantly underscored women's distinctive vulnerability, and he returned repeatedly to the theme that women had been dragged from their "natural" state by the relentless forces of modernity. Moreover, his repeated requests that union men bring their wives to meetings, enthusiastically seconded by countless other speakers, were unlikely to change the fundamentally male culture of the union, to challenge male union members' convictions that women's grievances could be adequately represented by the male head of household, or to draw out women's independent grievances.

Part of the problem, as many historians of the labor movement have pointed out, lay in the custodial impulses and convictions of laboring men. In the Federation of Clothing Workers, as in the earlier tailors' unions, women workers were almost invariably discussed as wives of working men. There was much rhetoric about how women were "enslaved" by their husbands, cruelly forced to work and to neglect their natural home tending roles. Such speech making evinced more concern with the master than the slave. It was aimed at a male audience and sought to dramatize the corruption of patriarchal authority in the sweated family workshop. It also highlighted the contrast with more "modern" domestic arrangements represented by the eight-hour day, leisure, and domesticity.

Another part of the predicament among the clothing workers, ironically, lay with the anarchist-tinged syndicalism that made Dumas eager to rally women behind the banner of revolutionary action. His impatience with "male prejudice" went hand in hand with a withering scorn for female "reformism," an impulse that he detected in several of the women's unions belonging to the federation. In 1910, when the Esders strike made questions about how to recruit women particularly pressing, Dumas' politics collided with those of several women leaders in the Federation of Clothing Workers. Madame Augier of the Marseilles lingerie workers' union, for instance, considered her organization's role to be the "social education" of women—a goal best achieved by separate, female unions. Dumas was determined to distance the Federation of Clothing Workers from "reformist" politics. For him, the benchmark of a union's strength was its ability to lead

[57] *Compte rendu*, 1910, p. 80.
[58] Police report on Dumas speaking in La Rochelle, 1912. AN, F7 13740.

a strike, and by this measure most women's unions hardly deserved the title.[59]

By the end of the century, women's allegedly inherent "reformism" had become a set topic in left-wing circles. In the 1898 series of articles mentioned at the beginning of this chapter, Aline Valette had demonstrated how the vulnerability of women workers and the urgency of their demands shaped what they expected from a union. "Most women who go the seamstresses' union to sign up only do so because they are hoping for some immediate gain—a job, advice, or some kind of help." If a union did not respond to that particular need at that particular time, the women disappeared. Needleworkers' grievances, articulated as needs rather than demands, were dismissed in union circles as "reformist or individualistic."[60] Official union hostility to such ventures compounded the difficulties of creating an independent and secure female presence in groups like the Federation of Clothing Workers. In sum, then, changing policies made unions increasingly eager to organize women workers, but also impatient with separate female initiatives.

In analyzing union policy, however, we cannot assume the existence of a readily identifiable "women's interest," one that the union leadership obtusely ignored. We need instead to examine the process by which workers' claims were gendered, and "women's" interests identified and articulated. Historians usually argue that women themselves accomplished that identification. In this case the process was more complex.

To be sure, leaders like Madame Augier located both specific zones of conflict between women and men and distinctively female difficulties: women's unions could not absorb the costs of the federation's organizing literature and drives, the Conseil des Prudhommes (Arbitration Board) barred women, men dominated local meetings, and so on. As a woman speaker at one of the congresses pointed out, a man would go to a union meeting even if his wife complained about his absence, but the reverse was nearly unthinkable, and many husbands refused to let their wives leave home alone.[61] Most, though not all, union women wanted separate female unions, assuring that women would hold leadership positions. Madame Jousselin, of the Seamstresses and Lingerie Workers of the Seine, argued that in specialties like corset making, women should "naturally" be organized separately. Jousselin was trying to fend off the representative of the overwhelmingly male shirtwaist cutters, who intended to bring all the lingerie workers into one "mixed" union. The logic of industrial syndicalism

[59] *Compte rendu*, 1910, p. 81. Syndicalists, especially anarcho-syndicalists, scorned electoral parties and legislative action as reformist; they placed their hopes in very broad-based industrial unions and in strikes.

[60] "Le travail des femmes," *La Fronde*, July 10, 1898.

[61] *Compte rendu*, 1910, pp. 74–75.

supported his position; so too did his view of women as the wives and
mistresses of male union members. "Many of our cutters' wives are also
shirtwaist workers. These women will come much more easily to a mixed
union, arm in arm with their husbands or lovers, than they would to a
union specifically for them."[62] Jousselin's union rejected these advances and
declined to merge with either the shirtwaist cutters or the general clothing
workers of the Seine.[63] Such clearly marked conflicts aside, clothing
workers were uncertain what constituted "women's" interests and how they
could be effectively articulated. It was one thing to identify women's grievances against men within the union. It was another to come up with a
campaign that would mobilize women workers—without antagonizing
men—in larger circles and bring them into unions. Women union members
were no more confident than their male counterparts about how this could
be accomplished.

GENDERING WOMEN'S DEMANDS

The 1910 Esders strike forced the issue. At this point, two narratives, one of
long-term shifts in clothing workers' politics, and the other of an explosion
of militancy in the garment trades, intersect. The strike broke out just a
month before the clothing workers convened for their national conference,
located that year in Paris. Suddenly, as *La Guerre Sociale* put it, women
workers seemed to be taking matters into their own hands.[64] The crowds
outside the workshops of "A Reaumur" in the thirteenth arrondissment, the
wide press coverage, and the unusually large numbers of women representatives who attended the congress underscored the urgency of the issues.
Neither the local union nor the federation controlled the Esders strike. Indeed the federation seems to have been hard-pressed to keep up with it and
argued bitterly about how much support the strikers should be given. Parti-
sans of action believed that the strikers could be brought into the union and
their energies harnessed to a broad-based union campaign. They also believed that the federation should appeal to women as women—not as wives
and daughters of tailors and cutters, and not simply as female needleworkers. Others argued that the union should not squander its sparse resources on strikers whose union loyalties were tenuous at best.[65] Debate
ranged over a series of contentious topics, and tempers flared. Dumas railed
against male condescension toward women, but he also berated some
women's unions for their cautiousness and for their reluctance to stake all

[62] Ibid., p. 82.
[63] The national federation was displeased. Ibid., p. 12.
[64] Ibid., p. 10, opening speech. Press clippings, BA 1394.
[65] *La Voix du Peuple*, August 28, 1910, and reports on strike in AN, F7 13880. Unplanned
strikes depleted the union's funds and, if unsuccessful, diminished the union's stature in a
trade that was extremely difficult to organize.

on a strike. Whether or not separate union sections for women would encourage or dampen female militancy sparked angry exchanges, many men testily arguing that women could never fend for themselves, and women retorting that men had an interest in their passivity. Whether or not women's unions might provide services and education for their members (a "reformist" program) proved another bone of contention.

The only point on which those present at the divisive 1910 federation meeting could agree involved a propaganda brochure, aimed specifically at women, about the rising cost of living and falling wages. Such a brochure, said several speakers, would appeal to women as housekeepers, the ones most acutely aware of the cost of food and charged with balancing the budgets of strapped working-class families.[66] This kind of propaganda would be directed not at striking workers per se, but at a broader constituency of working-class women, tapping into "feminine" sympathies. A woman is less selfish than a man, said the (women's) group making the proposal: "among women, generous ideas germinate and grow with remarkable rapidity."[67] The Federation of Clothing Workers quickly endorsed the proposal, optimistic that this was one effective means to "appeal to the womanly spirit" even if they were unsure how women would eventually be integrated into the union.[68]

The other issue rapidly being defined as a tool for recruiting women was the "English week," a proposed reform that would guarantee a day and a half off per week, Saturday afternoon and Sunday. The measure had been promoted by activists of various political stripes, from social catholic to socialist, since the 1890s. In 1906 a narrow "weekly rest" bill had passed into law, although it was bitterly resisted by retailers and (like the Millerand-Collier hours bill of 1900) so riddled with special provisions and exemptions that it did more to anger than appease workers. The CGT had kept a wary distance from this particular reform movement, suspicious of social catholic moralism and conservative intentions and preferring, in any case, to press for time in the more secular form of an eight-hour day.[69] But by 1910 the labor movement had embraced the demand, despite its official skepticism about the value of any state legislation. During the Esders strikes of 1910 and 1911, the English week figured prominently in the list of demands.

There is no evidence that the Esders seamstresses as women found any special resonance in either the English week or in "consumerist" demands like those spelled out in the Federation of Clothing Workers' brochure.

[66] *Compte rendu*, 1910, p. 76.

[67] Ibid.

[68] The phrase was "frapper l'esprit féminin." Ibid.

[69] In the wake of a wave of strikes in 1905–6, the Chamber of Deputies had hastily cobbled together the *repos hebdomadaire*. See Cross, *A Quest for Time*, pp. 92–102.

Wages, hours, and industrial homework—either competition from outworkers or the grinding conditions of labor in tiny sweatshops—were the
striking women's principal grievances. These were tailors' grievances as
well. Time demands found predictably strong support, irrespective of the
gender of the worker. The clothing industry's flouting of the meager labor
laws that were on the books helped to make militants and strikers of
workers of both sexes. Yet the "awakening of working women" that both
strikes seemed to herald was interpreted as confirmation that the English
week was a "woman's" demand. The clothing workers assumed a leading
role in organizing the English week campaign, trying at once to bring more
women into the union and to involve the union in an ongoing, broad-based
international reform movement centering on hours as well as safety legislation, consumer organization, and, increasingly, minimum wage demands.
Nominally hostile to "reformist" initiatives, the Federation of Clothing
Workers nevertheless embraced this issue as their own.

In 1912, in the aftermath of the Esders strikes, membership in the Federation of Clothing Workers rose more than 30 percent. As federation secretary Dumas put it, "Never before has our central organization given such a
brilliant account of itself." [70] Militants found disturbing signs, however, that
these increases were evanescent. Women seemed unwilling to stay in the
union, and women's unions that had been formed during other strikes had
dissolved. Discouraged by the persistent difficulties of sustaining female
membership and organizations within the Federation of Clothing Workers,
its members turned their hopes toward reform campaigns. The delegation
of Parisian seamstresses and lingerie workers had been among the early
sponsors of resolutions for the English week. Yet federation secretary
Dumas took the opportunity to elaborate on what he saw as the reform
measure's gendered logic. Men wanted money; women wanted time; the
English week was the way to recruit women.

> Men only want to earn money, and since their physical strength permits it, they
> will accept long days of work. Women, on the other hand, are held by domestic
> arrangements and caring for the house. They would rather have a shorter day,
> which would leave them more leisure for their interior, than higher wages.
> When the issue is posed in that way, we will be able to reach groups of women
> whom we could not reach otherwise. [71]

That women would choose shorter days over higher wages was a curious
formulation. Women worked long days (industry-wide, much longer than
men) precisely because their wages were so low, a calculus that they would
have happily modified. Shorter days could as easily be understood as a
means to higher wages rather than an *alternative* to them. Such was cer-

---

[70] *Compte rendu*, 1912, pp. 15–16.
[71] Ibid., p. 52.

tainly the logic of the CGT's eight-hour day campaign, aimed at men as well as women. If the seamstresses' delegation that proposed the resolution to the Federation of Clothing Workers understood its meaning in this way, they did not say so—and neither did the striking Esders seamstresses. Yet Dumas approached the issue with the zeal of the converted; as if casting time and money as two opposing and gendered sets of demands suddenly illuminated long-troublesome puzzles. Women who worked in tailoring, he explained, often left the trade after marrying, and so would never be interested in "union issues," but they would be drawn to reform campaigns. Likewise, he continued, the daughters of the "demi-bourgeois," young women sent by their parents to get training in a *maison de couture*, would never be concerned with wages. Yet they would care about leisure time.[72]

Much in the English week campaign was popular among working women as well as men. The campaign evinced real reflection about the double duty of waged and unwaged work and the singular way in which that weighed upon women. The wave of militancy in 1910–12, combined with the influence of syndicalist thought about women's work, forced the clothing workers' unions to reckon with a strong female presence. Yet that presence was quickly pressed into a womanly mold and given a very specific logic. And the clothing workers' unions increasingly differentiated between single women, whose wages they acknowledged to be important (if only temporarily), and married women, whose earnings were inevitably and unalterably secondary and whose real interests lay in an enhanced domesticity and a family economy supported by a male breadwinner.

The English week reforms had limited reach. They could only apply to shopworkers. "Family shops" were officially exempt from all labor legislation, and those in clandestine shops stood beyond the reach of the law. Thus, how homeworkers fit into these campaigns was not entirely clear. The clearly identified "feminine" interest in domesticity and the union consensus that women should be organized as housewives, however, also shaped union appeals in their direction. From 1910 on, clothing workers' unions increasingly posed the issue as how women might be weaned from industrial homework. They increasingly presented the answer in depictions of an uncluttered and well-kept home, attemping to mobilize the imagery of respectable and modern domesticity against the kinds of "chaotic" family economic arrangements represented in homework. Brochures published by the Federation of Clothing Workers tried to show homeworkers that a house littered with scraps of clothing and sewing machine parts could not be a "real family home." Women, they argued, needed to be persuaded to send their children to school instead of dispatching them, unsupervised, on

---

[72] Ibid., p. 53; and AN, F7 13740. By 1912 the term "demi-bourgeois" appeared frequently, and so did the contrast between these workers, for whom labor was considered a "distraction," with those the unions considered truly needy.

errands around the city. They tried to correct what they considered women's shortsighted vision of their husbands' interests. A homeworker would invariably be distracted from preparing dinner, and her husband, instead of finding "a warm appetizing bowl of stew, which allows a man to replenish his forces," would have to cook dinner himself—a prospect that would drive him immediately to the nearest cabaret.[73] Women's alternative, particularly as posed in this last scenario, was not to work at all. Dissuading women from doing industrial homework meant persuading many women (at any rate, married women) to shun wage labor entirely.

Such campaigns were unlikely to mobilize many homeworkers. This is not to deny their broad appeal in the labor movement or reform circles. The picture of serene, well-tended and well-organized interiors struck very deep chords in a working class eager for space and decent housing, and in a group of laborers whose working days were among the longest in Europe. It harmonized as well with the celebration of consumer goods, modernity, and the "home" marketed by stores like the Grands Magasins Dufayel, and evidence suggests that both had real resonance. That picture could provide an important point of accord between some bourgeois reformers and sections of the labor movement; each group could invest its hopes (whether natalist, hygienic, moralist, or economic) in family life, public health, temperance, and respectability.[74] The reformers put the emphasis on the breadmaking, or domesticity; the labor movement on the breadwinning, on the male-earned "family wage" needed to underwrite these social arrangements.

Yet aspirations to idealized domesticity did not bind women home-workers to their homes in the first place, and were therefore unlikely to alter their families' economic strategies. The increasingly common attacks on the "demi-bourgeois" women working at home were, likewise, hardly pitched to garner much support in those quarters. The failure of these anti-homework campaigns was simple: nothing in them spoke to homeworkers' interests and needs, and it was, not surprisingly, impossible to mobilize homeworkers while arguing that their work should be abolished. At this point, labor's reflections on gender issues ground to a halt. Insofar as working women had legitimate separate interests, a point grudgingly recognized by the 1910s, they were represented in the English week, moral reform, and quality of family life. A sharp increase in women's militancy had forced a response from a reluctant male labor leadership. But even the most sympathetic leaders found their views shaped by the mold of gender complementarity and gender as a division of labor. When a response was at last framed,

[73] *Compte rendu*, 1912, p. 55. See also 1910. The corruption of working-class family life was an old theme in tailors' politics, but these appeals were addressed to women.

[74] Cross, *A Quest for Time*; Magraw, *A History of the French Working Class*, 2:35; Guilbert, *Les femmes et les organizations syndicales*; Perrot, "L'éloge de la ménagère"; Sowerwine, *Sisters or Citizens?*; Boxer, "Protective Legislation," pp. 45–65; and Stewart, *Women, Work, and the French State*.

it sidestepped the question of wages and centered instead on a reduction of working hours. The aim was not to value women's work but to make it easier for women to earn a "secondary wage" while still fulfilling traditional household functions.

Jeanne Bouvier: Feminism, Syndicalism, and Reform

Jeanne Bouvier (1876–1935), seamstress, feminist, and longtime union militant in the Shirtwaist-Lingerie Union, was bitterly disappointed by her experiences in the French labor movement. Indeed, in her view, between the 1890s and the 1920s both women and feminism had made inroads in every sector of French public life *except* the trade union movement.[75] Like the women who spoke up from the floor of the Federation of Clothing Workers' congresses, Bouvier emphasized how hard it was for women to pay union dues, to find time for meetings, and to fit into union culture. She also wrote as a woman who had hovered on the edges of union leadership, pointing in exasperation to the self-defeating aspects of union policy. Unions first excluded women from leadership posts and important meetings and committees, she wrote, and then taxed them with ignorance about social and political issues. Ostracized by an overwhelmingly male union culture, women workers found themselves charged with passivity and reactionary politics.[76] Bouvier had worked her way up through the world of the Parisian needle trades into the elite and relatively well-paid ranks of seamstresses in women's couture. Fired from at least one such job for her openly pro-union stance, she then worked by days for private customers and turned to union activities. Deeply committed, hard-working, and single, Bouvier rose through the ranks of the trade union movement, eventually becoming the only woman on the administrative council of the CGT. Yet she never believed that the union shared her concerns, particularly her lifetime engagement with women's work.[77]

Bouvier's brand of politics often put her at odds with syndicalist leaders. She embraced "reformism" with a passion. She worked closely with other feminists on issues involving working women. She helped put together the 1902 International Exposition on Women's Arts and Trades, intended to display women's skills and to underscore women's contribution to the national economy. She joined several anti-sweating organizations to work for a minimum wage bill.[78] Bouvier happily accepted appointments to the state

[75] Bouvier, *Mes mémoires*, p. 147. See also Bouvier's papers in the Bouglé Collection at the Bibliothèque Historique de la Ville de Paris.

[76] Bouvier, *Mes mémoires*, p. 103.

[77] Her autobiography contrasts the enthusiasm with which the CGT tried to recruit women in 1900 with its growing defensiveness and indifference after the war. Ibid., pp. 110–11. Bouvier says nothing about her early days in the union, the union's local activities, or strikes.

[78] Bouglé Collection, Bouvier papers, box 18, folder 3.

bureaucracy, uninhibited by concerns about cooperating with the state or middle-class women. Unlike Aline Valette (who had once been a school-teacher), Bouvier had virtually no education, and she never thought of herself as a Marxist or tried to theorize her feminism in Marxist terms. Yet like Valette and many feminists of her generation, she threw herself wholeheartedly into social research. She wrote three books: a study of the lingerie and shirtmaking trade for a series called "The Social Library of Trades"; a history of women during the French Revolution (inspired, she said, by the formidable role of the revolutionary legacy in turn-of-the-century syndicalist circles); and her memoirs. Between 1913 and 1914, she conducted her own study of homework, applying her findings to her work on behalf of a minimum wage bill.[79] Her writings emphasized the long traditions of independent female labor and the development of women's skills. Women workers, she was at pains to point out, were not simply men's underpaid competitors. Unlike Valette, Bouvier did not believe that women had been drawn into "men's" work by capitalism and mechanization. In the same vein, she was proud of her own patiently acquired expertise about wage rates, hours, and family budgets in different regions and specialties and her mastery of complicated legal issues involved in wage legislation. Technical competence, put at the service of administrative reform, was fundamental to her personal and political outlook—much more so than class politics.

Bouvier cast a slightly wistful eye on reform groups in other countries, particularly the American Women's Trade Union League. She admired their attention to "concrete social programs" and "social education," their commitment to mobilizing working women through labor legislation, and their attempts to bridge the gap between middle-class reformers and the trade union movement. In France, she said, the absence of large and independent groups of women within the trade unions, combined with syndicalist opposition to reformism, made such efforts impossible.[80] Bouvier's particular anger had much to do with her long advocacy of a bill proposing minimum wages for women who worked at home. She had been closely involved with the formation of a French Office on Homework, charged with gathering material and keeping abreast of anti-sweating laws in other countries.[81] As a member of the CST, she participated in long hearings on the bill. She energetically strove to keep the bill from being gutted as it moved from one committee to the next, and, once it was passed in 1915, to make sure that its provisions would be enforced, a process that required unions to be vigilant and active, bringing violations of the law to the state's attention. The labor movement—the CGT in general and the clothing workers in particular—offered nothing more than tepid support for the bill. Although

[79] *Mes mémoires*, p. 230.
[80] Ibid., p. 136.
[81] Bouglé Collection, Bouvier papers, box 18, folder 18.

they lamented the plight of homeworkers, Bouvier argued, they found it impossible to treat these workers as full-fledged members of the labor force or envision them making a "living" wage.[82]

Conclusion

The bleak portraits of sweated labor in the needle trades have helped to obscure the often boisterous politics of seamstresses. Women did strike; as the garment trades continued their rapid feminization, women's presence in labor actions quickly became decisive. Most but not all of the strikers were young; most but not all were shopworkers. Most of their demands echoed the tailors: better wages, more regular hours, and an end to the fearsome competition encouraged by subcontracting and piecework. Insofar as women were worse paid, worked longer hours, and sat out longer periods of unemployment, their strike demands, petitions, and speeches in clothing workers' congresses had a distinctive edge.[83] That distinctiveness, however, is less striking than the union's efforts to press women's demands into a mold of gender complementarity. Pierre Dumas' extemporizing on women's need for time as opposed to men's need for money is an excellent example of the larger process whereby the trade unions tried to assimilate women while holding onto their essentially male constituency.

As far as gender politics were concerned, neither the clothing workers' unions nor the labor movement in general were simply obtuse or defensive. To the contrary, rapid doctrinal and organizational changes were characteristic of this period. Through the turn of the century, the Federation of Clothing Workers was dominated by tailors and cutters and their often contradictory needs and politics; it was a decidedly male organization. The commitment to organizing women workers grew increasingly serious as the twentieth century opened, encouraged by bracing examples of female militancy, the emergence of national reform movements, and the indisputable evolution of syndicalist thinking about gender. Frustrated with their apparent inability to sustain a strong female membership—a problem exacerbated by their impatience with what they considered feminine "reformism" and resistance to separate women's organizations—they turned to other,

---

[82] *Mes mémoires*, p. 153.

[83] Historians used to speculate that women had a "weak work identity" because they were consigned to the ranks of casual labor or withdrew from the labor force upon marriage. Tilly and Scott, *Women, Work, and Family*; and Davis, "Women in the Crafts in Sixteenth-Century Lyon." But there is a growing body of evidence that women organized as workers, that they struck as often as they participated in food riots, and that they responded eagerly to socialist initiatives. See inter alia, Godineau, *Citoyennes tricoteuses*; Hilden, *Working Women*; Canning, "Gender and the Politics of Class Formation"; Harden-Chenut, *La formation d'une culture ouvrière*.

non-workplace strategies, riding groundswells of public opinion in favor of labor legislation and restrictions on hours.[84]

Many in the union movement found the simplest way to navigate the shoals of the "woman question" was to differentiate between single women, who might be conceived of as independent, and married women, whose work conflicted directly with the ethos of a male breadwinner. This view became the grid through which workingmen's representatives read the government's studies of industrial homework. The stories of hours spent at the sewing machine for pitifully low wages while the children cried and the house fell apart confirmed deeply rooted convictions that women's work simply was not and could never be productive. Such accounts seemed to confirm that the squalor of industrial homework destroyed family life, by contrast with the kind of modern domesticity and separation of gender roles that might be achieved through male breadwinning. Such social arrangements were only aspirations for the vast majority of French workingmen, just as household authority had been for guildmembers in the eighteenth century. Yet they were increasingly central aspirations as labor and, as we will see, social science researchers, reformers, and government policymakers focused their attention on the relationship between production, consumption, and the search for a social peace.[85]

[84] *Compte rendu*, 1906, 1908.
[85] Stone, *The Search for Social Peace.*

Chapter Seven

SOCIAL SCIENCE AND THE POLITICS
OF CONSUMPTION

LABOR'S urgent debates about women's work formed part of an unprece-dented groundswell of reform opinion on the subject. At the turn of the century, a small army of sociologists, political economists, and legal commentators—male and female, amateur and expert, working- and middle-class threw themselves into the fray. So, too, did all those concerned with what was then called the "woman question." The debate over women's industrial work and the range of literature it created would have been unim-aginable but for the energies unleashed by late-nineteenth-century femi-nism. The nexus of economic and cultural concerns that this topic repre-sented compelled attention from a very broad range of parties. And the debate provided a critical occasion for a broader reappraisal of women's role in the labor force, the household, and the economic order in general.

This groundswell of interest also marks an important moment in the history of the social sciences. If the late eighteenth century had been the age of "political economy," observed a writer in 1906, the late nineteenth was the age of "social economy."[1] The new authority of the social sciences, established in the state bureaucracy, helped frame the discussion. Economic and social crises drew reform-minded advocates of new research methods into increasingly pressing and concrete discussions about public policy. Sta-tistics, wage series, and family budgets became the approaches of choice. Thus the politics of the anti-sweating movement need to be understood alongside the origins and repercussions of these new ways of seeing.

THE ORIGINS OF THE ANTI-SWEATING CAMPAIGN

"Sweating" was not simply a labor or workplace issue. Heightened middle-class and elite concerns arose from an intersection of developments. The deceleration of the economy in the last quarter of the century combined with specific anxieties about the family, the falling birthrate, and industrial

---

[1] Gonnard, *La femme dans l'industrie*. On the state during the early Third Republic, see Stone, *The Search for Social Peace*; Sanford Elwitt, *The Making of the Third Republic: Class and Politics in France, 1868–1884* (Baton Rouge, La., 1985); Mitchell, *The Divided Path*; Stewart, *Women, Work, and the French State*; Jacques Donzelot, *The Policing of Families* (trans., New York, 1979); and François Ewald, *L'état providence* (Paris, 1986).

vitality. As American and German industrialists forged successfully into erstwhile French domains in the world market, the French worried about their country's competitiveness and possible decline. Aspects of this crisis cast a particular spotlight on Paris, the "female" trades, and large-scale commerce. Sweated labor in the clothing trades brought these concerns together.

In the 1880s and 1890s, foreign competition began to seriously undermine the Parisian luxury trades, which had long been strongholds of the economy and important sources of French pride. Conservatives and socialists alike repeated a common lament: artisanal trades and skilled workers (usually described, incorrectly, as male and native French) languished while department stores overflowing with cheap goods made by sweated women workers and immigrants flourished. The debasement of skill and quality had been a theme of organized tailors' politics since the eighteenth century, when guilds presented themselves as guarantors of aesthetic standards and craft. Now these issues were aired in a much wider literature. Since the eighteenth century, too, the capital's identity had been wrapped up in the production of luxury goods, artistry, and taste. Cultural critics and economists laid the blame for the "crise des métiers" (the collapse of artisanship) in Paris and the capital's accompanying woes at the feet of department stores like Dufayel. While commercial artists and advertisers promoted the promises of modernity and the pleasures of consumption, others charged that aggressive marketing assaulted the public with cheap merchandise, debasing taste and standards. While plebeian and middle-class Paris recklessly bought shoddily made clothes and furniture on credit, the city's artisanal trades deteriorated and the national reservoirs of craft knowledge dwindled. The problem was not simply that Paris was no longer the center of luxury or fine craft production, but that the city was losing (what the French considered) its position as the aesthetic capital of Europe.[2]

These were the reasons that led Pierre Du Maroussem to call large-scale commerce and its effects on the urban economy the "dominant economic question of the day," every bit as important as large-scale industry.[3] These

[2] See Auslander, *Taste and Power*; Berlanstein, *The Working People of Paris*; Louis Chevalier, *La formation de la population parisienne au XIXe siècle* (Paris, 1950); Centre de documentation d'histoire des techniques, *Evolution de la géographie industrielle de Paris et de sa proche banlieue au XIXe siècle* (Paris, 1976); Miller, *The Bon Marché*; Nord, *Paris Shopkeepers*; Silverman, *Art Nouveau*; and Williams, *Dream Worlds*.

[3] *Les halles centrales de Paris*, p. 100, cited in Nord, *Paris Shopkeepers*, p. 66. Du Maroussem headed several investigations into Parisian commerce and its effects on Parisian production, all grouped under the rubric of *La question ouvrière*, in four volumes (Paris, 1891–94): *Charpentiers de Paris* (1891), *Ebénistes du faubourg Saint-Antoine* (1892), *Le jouet parisien* (1894), and *Les halles centrales de Paris* (1894). His study of the Parisian clothing industry appeared as: Office du Travail, *La petite industrie*, vol. 2: *Le vêtement à Paris*. See also his "Les grands magasins tels qu'ils sont."

concerns also made women homeworkers in the clothing industry a significantly more common topic of social research than female factory laborers in sugar processing, match making, or other large enterprises.[4] They captured what contemporaries believed were important and disturbing social changes: the rise of large-scale commerce in the form of department stores, the victory of those stores and anonymous commercial capital over small familial industries and shops, the collapse of artisanship, and, most generally, the triumph of materialism, trumpeted by increasingly insistent advertising and display. What contemporaries were beginning to identify as an emerging consumer culture could be associated with one particular class of laborers: sweated women homeworkers. And in contemporaries' eyes, France's cultural superiority and artisanal reputation, so closely bound up with its national identity, were compromised by this debased form of production.

THE "SOCIAL FORCES OF CHRISTIANITY"

The anti-sweating campaign drew together reformers of very different political persuasions. Religious reformers found in homework an issue particularly congenial to their outlook and an issue almost guaranteed to mobilize their constituency. Much of the literature on the issue was written by social catholics. Social catholics in Parliament, fortified by the writings and actions of their supporters outside, were the principal supporters of the 1915 minimum wage bill for homeworkers. The revival of social catholicism during the Third Republic brought many new voices into the late-nineteenth-century debate on women's work and played a crucial role in shaping the discussion.

The parliamentary leader of social catholicism through the crisis-ridden decades of the fin de siècle was Count Albert De Mun, and his stance marked the changing political climate on the right. At the beginning of De Mun's career, his views were resolutely anti-interventionist. By the 1880s, he had moved in very different directions. His goals remained to reorganize labor along corporate lines, reminiscent of the Old Regime, and to wean the working class away from socialism. But he became persuaded that legislation alone, not private initiative, could achieve that goal.[5]

Labor legislation thus became central to De Mun's parliamentary activities. Beginning in 1885, he sponsored a variety of hours laws for men, women, and children, as well as early versions of the weekly day of rest

---

[4] On women's work in those industries, see Hilden, *Working Women*; Guilbert, *Les fonctions des femmes dans l'industrie*; and Judt, *Marxism and the French Left*.

[5] De Mun set himself in a Catholic tradition that reached back to the Vicomte de Villeneuve-Bargemont, proponent of the important social legislation of the 1840s. See Henri Rollet, *L'action sociale des catholiques en France, 1871–1901* (Paris, 1947), 1:208; Savoye, "Les continuateurs de Le Play," p. 328; and Caroline Ford, *Creating the Nation in Provincial France: Religion and Political Identity in Britanny* (Princeton, N.J., 1993), pp. 123–26.

(*repos hebdomadaire*) and the "English week," which would both permit Catholics to observe the Sabbath and allow workers a day for family life. On women's work, De Mun advocated radically restrictive measures. Echoing Simon, he denounced married women's work outside the home as "the utter destruction of domesticity." Uninhibited by Simon's liberal scruples about state power, De Mun proposed to ban that work completely. When anti-interventionist liberals in the Chamber of Deputies set themselves against hours bills for women, De Mun rose to the defense of reform. He thundered at his opponents that ten hours of labor in spinning and carding rooms, with their roasting temperatures, suffocating humidity, noxious fumes, and heavy dust, were already more than enough for anyone.[6]

De Mun's speeches bristled with indignation about the irreverence and moral decay that he considered the logical results of overwork and poverty. His first concern was the family's solidity and patriarchal authority. Following many other thinkers, he had initially believed that homework should be exempt from labor legislation on the grounds that the family was a sacred domain: "the law should interfere as little as possible between the father and children."[7] However, De Mun's politics grew increasingly intervention-ist. By the 1890s, he had changed his position on industrial homework. Persuaded that the family shop exemption simply allowed employers to skirt labor legislation, he sponsored the bill establishing minimum wages for homeworkers.[8]

De Mun's parliamentary activities, however, were only a small part of late-nineteenth-century social catholicism. The significance of the movement lay in its broader base and in its efforts to mobilize "the social forces of Christianity."[9] Encouraged by the papal encyclical of 1891, which seemed to endorse their course, social catholic groups flourished. By far the most radical of these was Le Sillon, formed in 1899 by a group of young Catholics. Le Sillon strayed too close to socialism, flirted with anticlericalism, and was annulled by the pope a decade later. In the interim, though, the group gained high visibility on issues ranging from peace among nations to the rights of women to labor legislation.

The "social forces of Christianity" also included important women's groups, many of them directly engaged with women's sweated labor. From the 1870s on, social catholics like De Mun had been trying to rouse Catholic women to their social duty, arguing that the revival of feminine philanthropy had a crucial role to play in the larger project of revitalizing French Catholicism and bringing it into the mainstream of Third Republic politics. Paradoxically, though, it was not philanthropy, but state-based reform and

---

[6] De Mun cited in Rollet, *L'action sociale des catholiques*, 1:200.

[7] Ibid., p. 204.

[8] See chapter 8.

[9] *Le Sillon*, June 25, 1909.

De Mun's support for labor legislation that succeeded in mobilizing Catholic women.

The first Catholic women's organizations in this period were predictably stodgy. With names like The Ladies of Charity, and an almost exclusively aristocratic board of organizers, it would be surprising if they had drawn any workers to their ranks. The Union of the Needle, a "mixed" union that aimed to join seamstresses, women employers and contractors, and representatives of charitable organizations, served up a familiar menu of hot meals, masses, placement bureaus, and small loans in hard times. When faced with the new outbursts of shop floor militancy, as in 1901, the organization recoiled, repudiating that part of the strike that involved male workers and warning women workers to remain dignified, eschew vulgar language, and avoid violence.[10]

More radical class-based initiatives, however, were forthcoming. Marie-Louise Rochebillard of Lyons stirred up considerable controversy in the Catholic women's movement by putting the emphasis on organizing workers rather than promoting harmony along corporate lines. The point of a union, as she saw it, was precisely to bring together those who "lived the same kind of life, and shared common experiences,"[11] a view closer to a class than a (social catholic) corporate outlook. The Catholic women's unions did not enjoy a very high profile in the world of work, but they did represent enough of a force and enough expertise to command an institutional presence in public administration and the emerging labor bureaucracy. They conducted studies of working conditions; campaigned in favor of the English week, an end to night work, and a minimum wage for homeworkers; and consulted with the CST (Conseil supérieur du travail). In their view, educating women was the means to reform. This commitment to education, along with De Mun's calls for the political engagement of women, coincided in the formation of the Ecole normale sociale in 1911, whose purpose was "to mobilize and train elites of women in all social strata for a broad ranging, authoritative, enlightened social action." It recruited professors from a variety of social catholic organizations, providing a bridge between male and female sections of the movement.[12]

One of the most interesting figures in this Catholic and feminine "go to the people" movement was Léonie Chaptal. Like other social catholics, Chaptal was concerned with preserving the family in the modern urban environment. Unlike others, she immersed herself in the daily lives of working families, took the measure of their forces in the battle against the debilitating effects of urban poverty, and set her sights on medical and social prevention rather than spiritual cure. She set up anti-tuberculosis infirm-

---

[10] Rollet, *L'action sociale des catholiques*, 1:569.
[11] Cited in ibid., 2:229.
[12] Ibid., p. 235.

aries and clinics in the slums of Paris and pioneered programs to provide large families with young children housing that was sanitary and well lit as well as inexpensive. She attacked infant mortality with a service designed to help poor women deliver their children at home—rather than in the night-marishly grim (and deadly) lying-in hospitals. Once the child was born, Maternal Assistance provided pediatric services, free milk to mothers who could not nurse, and free food to wet nurses who had taken on infants. And to enable mothers to stay at home and care for their children, Chaptal's group tried to find piecework that could be done in the home. Chaptal was unusually influential and well respected in broader circles. Her clinic was honored with awards and in 1907 was actually incorporated into the struc-ture of the French state. She represented France at world health congresses, and she worked easily with republican and government officials as well as social catholics. Of all the social catholic groups, Chaptal's strayed the fur-thest from the tradition of philanthropy and good works and instead ori-ented itself toward the women's movement. In Chaptal's view, women had a particular role to play in urban reform—not because (upper-class) women possessed any special moral or spiritual qualities, but because all women, especially mothers, felt the consequences of poor housing conditions, inad-equate medical care, and bad transportation. They were the victims of "our poorly built and badly organized cities." This common feminine condition demanded a commensurate political engagement. "Women must try to en-large their circle of activity into municipal affairs, an area in which they do not yet have any foothold." Nor did Chaptal believe that women should stop there. Although most of her activities involved Parisian social and health reform, like the English and American settlement workers, she used her base to publicize national issues. By raising a political agenda and ad-dressing herself to women of the people as well as those of the upper-middle class, Chaptal recast De Mun's call in a secular and feminist language. With other social catholic women like Jeanne Chenu, Paule Vigneron, and Henri-ette Brunhes, she became one of the fiercest proponents of labor legislation, especially the minimum wage for homeworkers.[13]

Social catholicism created no single politics. A diffuse movement, it con-tributed certain key voices and numerous reform campaigns and institu-tions to the debates and battles over sweating.

LE PLAY AND HIS HERITAGE:
FRENCH SOCIAL SCIENCE IN TRANSITION

Much of the energy galvanized by the anti-sweating movement went into sociological research. That research followed closely in the tradition of Fré-

---

[13] See the feminist encyclopedias in the Bouglé Collection. She also figures briefly in the *Dictionnaire de biographie française* and in Rollet, *L'action sociale des catholiques*, 2:153–60. The distinctive outlook of social catholic feminists is discussed in the next chapter.

déric Le Play, whose pioneering methodology was his most important contribution to nineteenth-century social thought and whose work left an indelible stamp on French sociology. But by the end of the century, Le Play's methodology had been altered in important respects, the changes in keeping with new preoccupations and imperatives.

Like many of France's Catholic thinkers, Le Play directed his methods and writings against the English school of political economy. Observing actual human situations, he argued, was both more "scientific" and more significant than pursuing immutable laws that were supposed to govern the economy. His followers both underscored and shared his opposition to the "abstractions" of both political economy and competing schools of sociology, particularly the German. Many also considered the antitheoretical bent of Le Play's writing particularly French. Emile Cheysson, for instance, one of his most influential followers, presented Le Play's method as the organic product of his native land: "He studied and built social science not from books and in libraries, but where he was, in the open air, in the village, the city, the family home, the industrial workshop, and the rural domain."[14]

Like earlier Catholic thinkers, Le Play also placed the family at the center of his social and political vision. In his view, the family was the human configuration toward which social science should direct its attention. It represented the seedbed of religious values, the center of social authority, and the most basic unit of economic life. But while others saw the family in cultural and psychological terms, Le Play saw it as a unit of production and a means of transmitting property.[15] He believed fervently in *la femme au foyer*. He calculated her value unsentimentally, however, in terms of her unwaged work: not just child-rearing or education, but laundry, house cleaning, sewing, and tending the garden or livestock.

Le Play joined his conservative ideas to a specific method of social observation. That method required detailed description of "family types," based on elaborate reconstruction of family economics. Alongside the income brought in by wage labor, he tallied earnings from rents and household production, from the sale of chickens, pigs, or butter. He tried to determine how, exactly, different "kinds" of families spent their resources—on land or housing, food, clothing—how much was saved, and, a common nineteenth-century preoccupation, how much went to drink. His claims for the value of this kind of accounting are startling indeed: "*Every action in the life of a working-class family* eventually becomes either a receipt or an expendi-

[14] Emile Cheysson, "Frédéric Le Play: L'homme, la méthode, la doctrine," *La Quinzaine*, January 15, 1896, p. 19. Cheysson conducted research with Le Play and remained the closest to that monographic tradition. See *Les budgets*. In the secondary literature, see Gay, *The Bourgeois Experience*, 1:422–38; Paul Lazarsfeld, *La philosophie des sciences sociales* (Paris, 1970); Perrot, *Enquêtes sur la condition ouvrière*; Catherine Silver, *Frédéric Le Play on Family, Work, and Social Change* (Chicago, 1982); and Savoye, "Les continuateurs de Le Play," pp. 315–45.

[15] Simon, by contrast with this school, defined it as "the intimacy of the hearth." *L'ouvrière*, p. 89.

ture."[16] Thus the budget "monograph" promised to open a window onto broader questions of religion, culture, and economics.

In the 1880s, as sociology was being formalized as a discipline, the monographic technique came under critical scrutiny. Both Le Play's focus on the family and his lengthy and largely descriptive budgets drew fire: the first because no family could be a "representative" microcosm; the second because the level of detail was thought to make comparisons and generalizations virtually impossible. His most influential followers, Pierre Du Maroussem and Emile Cheysson, developed the statistical aspects of the method. They strove to make the monographs shorter, and more analytic and quantitative, moving away from the long descriptions that their mentor prized.[17]

These changes followed cultural and political as well as social scientific imperatives. As Le Play's followers edged away from his staunch conservatism, they grew less interested in what the earlier monographs had revealed about religiosity, cultural values, and forms of property and inheritance. Instead, they turned to questions about a family's cash resources and their value—in short, standards of living and the family's place in the class structure. As the Third Republic grew more committed to social legislation and more troubled by social conflict, statistical analysis of earnings became key to developing a wage policy.[18] While much research continued to be closely linked with social catholicism and Le Playan journals, the transformation was significant. Le Play's deeply conservative chronicles of family life and relations, of property, and of waged and unwaged work, gave way to narrower studies of families' purchasing power.[19]

[16] Cited in Cheysson, "Frédéric Le Play," p. 17 (my emphasis).

[17] See Du Maroussem, "Les instruments," pp. 54–65; and idem, Enquêtes, esp. pp. 59–64.

[18] See Du Maroussem, "Les instruments," pp. 64–65, on the policy implications of his methods. On relations between sociology and the state, see Savoye, "Les continuateurs de Le Play," pp. 337–38.

[19] The short and "modernized" budget monographs that Du Maroussem developed in his research were only supposed to show the purchasing power of wages. Enquêtes, p. 64. As Du Maroussem said, the United States Trade Boards used the same techniques to the same ends. On related developments in American sociology, see Thomas Haskell, The Emergence of Professional Social Science: The American Social Science Association and the Nineteenth-Century Crisis of Authority (Urbana, Ill., 1977); Daniel Horowitz, The Morality of Spending: Attitudes toward the Consumer Society in America, 1875–1940 (Baltimore, Md., 1985); Martha May, "The 'Good Managers': Married Working-Class Women and Family Budget Studies, 1895–1915," Labor History 25, no. 3 (Summer 1984): 351–72; and Sklar, Florence Kelley. On England, see Seebohm Rowntree, Poverty, A Study of Town Life (London, 1901); Mrs. Pember Reeves, Family Life on a Pound a Week (London, 1912); and Seth Koven, "Culture and Poverty: The London Settlement House Movement, 1870–1914" (Ph.D. diss., Harvard University, 1988). Some of the most interesting theoretical discussions of standards of living and their relationship to class come from Maurice Halbwachs, whose research spanned four countries. See La classe ouvrière et les niveaux de vie (1913), and L'évolution des besoins dans les classes ouvrières (1933).

When the French Office du Travail was founded in 1891, the thus-revised Le Playan sociology found a powerful institutional base of support. Members of the Office du Travail hewed to a variety of political positions, but they worked closely with the Society of Social Economy, the leading organization of Le Play's followers. What was more, the Office hired as its chief researcher Pierre Du Maroussem, Le Play's most influential student and the most prominent adapter of Le Play's sociological method. The Office was mandated to gather general statistics on strikes, wages, hours, and standards of living. Under Du Maroussem's influence, it also began to turn its attention to the large-scale organization of urban commerce and production, and to sweating. And it did so using a combination of statistics and *monographs*, or budgets. The establishment of the Office du Travail both reflected and boosted the authority of the new tools of analysis.

ENQUÊTEURS AND FLÂNEURS: THE POPULARIZATION OF SOCIAL SCIENCE

The broad dissemination of these methods, however, flowed not only from "sociology in the service of the state," but also from their adoption by writers and social observers outside the government structure. Charles Benoist's *Les ouvrières de l'aiguille à Paris: Notes pour l'étude de la question sociale* (*The Needleworkers of Paris: Notes toward the Study of the Social Question*) provides an excellent example. The study was published serially in *Le Temps* in 1893 and two years later in book form.[20] Benoist drew heavily on De Mun's speeches and clearly intended to popularize De Mun's themes for a broader audience. Just as important, *Les ouvrières de l'aiguille* appeared almost simultaneously with the Office du Travail's study of the clothing industry (*La petite industrie à Paris: Le vêtement*), conducted by Du Maroussem. *Les ouvrières de l'aiguille* was a thoughtful layman's version of that investigation. Benoist's blend of Catholic concerns with social science research makes his study an important document; his language, metaphors, and imagery reveal a good deal of the process wherein a reforming social science was translated into a more popular discourse.

Although not a social catholic, Benoist did not hesitate to strike Catholic chords. In fact, the subject seemed well tuned to them. He opened his study with a sharp attack on what he called "dry abstractions" of government studies, burdened with wage charts, statistics, and budgets. He would not be satisfied with "impassive numbers"; he wanted the reader to "feel the stirring of muscles and nerves" and to experience the "suffering of human flesh." That suffering was all the more excruciating and significant, he continued, because it was endured by women. It involved ". . . that human flesh

---

[20] Benoist, *Les ouvrières de l'aiguille*. Benoist taught constitutional history at Sciences politiques. He went on to become a deputy, first associated with the Union républicaine and, later, turning sharply to the right, with royalism and the Action française.

already consecrated to so much suffering: the female body."[21] Almost any turn-of-the-century catalogue of typical Parisian scenes included *la sortie de l'atelier*: the moment when the shop doors in the garment district opened and hundreds of young girls poured into the streets of the capital. But Benoist gave this familiar scene a new twist, lingering over the girls' "wrinkled and threadbare" dresses and the way they stuck their needles into their blouses.[22] In a language strongly reminiscent of Catholic descriptions of the mortifications of saints, and tinged with eroticism, Benoist evoked the sensuous sufferings of labor and an image of modern female martyrdom.

Although critical of the abstractions of social science, Benoist committed himself to gathering the social facts of this martyrdom. Embracing sociological methods pioneered by Le Play and adapted by government researchers like Du Maroussem, he interviewed manufacturers, workers, and subcontractors throughout Paris and carefully reconstructed family budgets and wage scales. Benoist displayed an unusual methodological self-consciousness, doubtless related to his skepticism about sociology. Many investigators readily admitted an inability to describe the poverty they encountered; Benoist was one of the few to discuss and reflect on the problem of how to talk about "misery." He repeatedly apologized to his readers for leading them through page after page of wage charts and statistics. But what he saw as the alternative—telling tales of misery and privation, trying to "paint with words" (rather than numbers), risked lapsing very quickly into either "declamation," which was his favorite term of abuse for socialist writing, or the kind of grandiose and shrill indignation characteristic of writers like Simon.[23] He refused any theoretical framework for his study in the name of preserving its sincerity and spontaneity. He called his articles "studies" and "simple observations." They were, of course, much more than that: they offered both a lively version of social science findings for a wider audience and a timely set of reflections on the analytic and descriptive merits of the new sociology.

The reflections concerned the relationship between the "material misery" and "moral misery" of women's lives. Benoist moved back and forth between tallying budgets and chronicling the life stories of his Parisian subjects, between a language of social science and a more popular genre of urban sketches. The seamstresses' days were a series of "adventures" quickly leading to "falls." Here is Benoist's description of a *gargote*, or cheap restaurant reputedly frequented by seamstresses at lunchtime:

> The shop is painted bright red. In the first room, sitting in the place of honor in front of the glistening copper counter, is a large, hoarse, red-faced man. In the

[21] Benoist, *Les ouvrières de l'aiguille*, p. 17.
[22] Ibid., p. 122.
[23] Ibid., p. 85.

back there is another room, filled with the noise of glasses and bottles. From that same room come bitter fumes of burnt fat and tobacco—a thick, bluish steam which overpowers you as soon as you enter.[24]

The restaurant resembled a brothel, and, not surprisingly, Benoist believed that "the worst poison" in these places was not the food, which the girls could barely afford, but the masons, carpenters, and "messieurs" whom they encountered. Flirtations led to affairs, and affairs to illegitimacy. The arrival of children sealed a woman's fate. "With the first child, he beats her, with the second he leaves," was how he laconically summarized the unraveling of a "Parisian marriage." It was impossible to eliminate the moral perils of the capital. As he put it, that would "take Paris out of Paris."[25] Despite the grimness of some chapters, Benoist had a *flâneur*'s appreciation for his subjects, their flirtations, and the character they imparted to the city's streets and culture. The combination of social indignation and urban adventure story was probably what lent the book its wide appeal.

Still, it was the relationship between " moral" and "material" misery that most concerned Benoist and gave these life stories their significance. He clearly intended *Les ouvrières de l'aiguille* to dramatize his critique of political economy, of the "natural laws" of wages, and the supposedly self-regulating powers of the economy. He sarcastically proposed a new "theory" of wages: that a woman's wage would always fall just below what she needs to make a living. It would be up to her to fill that gap, he continued, "remembering that she is a woman."[26] In a passage characteristic of his mode of thinking and argument, he tried to connect shop-floor culture, theories of wages, and Catholic issues of morality. Were the needleworkers of Paris heroines or strumpets? How could a social observer explain the apparent moral disarray of his subjects' lives? The answer involved how, in his view, wages were experienced and interpreted. "Low wages are not the only cause [of prostitution, or vice generally], but they are the most important one; they weaken resistance and make the final collapse seem inevitable and also legitimate."[27] In other words, the seeming naturalness and immutability of "laws" of wages became part of the way in which working women constructed their possibilities and necessities. In his view, ideas about why women's wages were so low constituted at once an aspect of lived experience and a crucial ideological battleground. This process made the subject of Parisian needleworkers "grand social theory." Concern about whether economic phenomena were "natural" and whether society was run by laws

---

[24] Ibid., pp. 123–24. The passage was striking enough to be repeated by Haussonville, *Salaires et misères de femmes*, p. 18; and in Vernières, *Camille Frison*.

[25] Benoist, *Les ouvrières de l'aiguille*, p. 143.

[26] Ibid., p. 20

[27] Ibid., pp. 127–28.

that stood beyond human agency—and beyond the claims of justice—
rendered the issue of women's wages "the core of the social question."[28]

Les ouvrières de l'aiguille à Paris drew honors from the Academie des
sciences morales. Benoist's portrait of Parisian seamstresses was widely borrowed. But the book also set a methodological precedent, helping to popularize the *enquête*. Benoist's model proved particularly important to persons
often taxed with ignorance on social questions: members of the clergy and
women. Like him, they entered "the terrain of observation" to confront
"doctrine" (either socialism or political economy) with "facts."[29] Benoist's
combination of Christian rhetoric and social science probably appeared as a
heartening alternative to the secular "abstractions" of the state's ongoing
publications and the radicalism of socialist writings. The role of social investigators gave them credentials in policy debates increasingly structured
by statistical definitions and sociological research.

The next decade and a half brought a spate of works blending sociology
and fiction in an effort to capture the social texture of turn-of-the-century
Paris. One of the many hundreds of studies of women's work published
during this period was André Vernières' *Camille Frison, ouvrière de la couture* (1908), a barely fictionalized account of the life and loves of a Parisian
seamstress. The author tells Camille's story, beginning in her garret apartment in Montmartre and moving through her first workshop experiences
on the rue de la Paix, her (inevitable) seduction, and then, as a result of her
duties as a mother, out of the shop and back to the garret apartment as a
homeworker. The preface explains that Camille represents "Jenny the working girl" of the early twentieth century. She and her story are very different
from heroines and romances of the past. In the 1850s, the narrator con-
tends, "Jenny only had to tell her moving tale." But contemporary readers,
he continues, want something other than sentimental fiction. Today's Jenny
"gives us every detail on her wages, her budget, and her relations with
bosses and subcontractors." The history of her work is compelling of itself,
"without any twists and turns of the plot."[30] And indeed the plot is rudi-
mentary: Camille's life story closely traces the outlines of any number of
stories recorded in the official *enquêtes*. The author takes his set scenes,
including one in a *gargote*, directly from Benoist. Other "twists and turns of
the plot" steer Camille into encounters with representatives of virtually
every political party and social organization: a social catholic priest, a union
organizer, a socialist, and a feminist, "Fanny Mortal," clearly modeled on
Léonie Chaptal.

The same year that *Camille Frison* was published, a French economist
commented on the new genre and the concerns of his time: ". . . Modern

[28] Ibid., p. 20.
[29] See Mény, *Le travail à bon marché*, preface by Abbé Lemire, deputé du nord, p. vii, and
chap. 1, p. 3.
[30] Vernières, *Camille Frison*, p. ii.

readers have a passionate interest in studies, or even minutely detailed monographs . . . which retrace the common, everyday gestures of anonymous working people."[31] The outpouring of literature on sweating in the decades around the turn of the century did represent an important moment in the history of social science. As we have seen, a wide variety of researchers and writers (from novelists to Catholic priests) embraced the *enquête*. As a prominent social catholic woman said, "'Social science' is no longer a strange term; it has passed into common usage."[32] Benoist's *Les ouvrières de l'aiguille*, Vernières' *Camille Frison*, and the many other stories and studies by journalists, priests, reformers—many of whom had no formal training or position—reflect that common usage. To some, it seemed that the tradition of urban fiction was being swamped by a wave of statistics. Two other considerably more old-fashioned sketches of seamstresses in belle époque Paris, tellingly titled *Les cousettes* (*The Little Dressmakers*) and *Les reines de l'aiguille* (*The Queens of the Needle*), defended the glories of needlework and Parisian artistry. They bitterly denounced the new fashion for numbers and sociology. The Parisian *flâneur* (or stroller), they feared, had been transformed into an *enquêteur* (or sociologist).[33]

They were right. The strategies of social observation elaborated by Du Maroussem, Benoist, and Vernières contested the *flâneur*'s view of Paris. They turned their attention to the industry and commerce that formed the backbone of the city rather than at the varieties of human nature the metropolis embodied and displayed in the tradition of Balzac and Zola. The newly sociological literature also refused to look at these Parisian tradeswomen in the way that conservative boulevard fiction traditionally represented seamstresses—as exquisite objects producing exquisite cultural artifacts. The women were no longer aestheticized, no longer artists, no longer artisans. Sociology had brought new ways of seeing to the literature of the city. The *enquête* had transformed even boulevard fiction.[34]

The Pathology of Production

Benoist's 1895 study, like the Office du Travail's volume *La petite industrie à Paris: Le vêtement*, treated both shop hands and homeworkers.[35] Benoist

---

[31] Gonnard, *La femme dans l'industrie*, p. ii.

[32] Marie Gahery, head of Union familiale, in *Françaises*, a social catholic brochure, cited in Fayet-Scribe, "Les associations féminines catholiques." p. 110.

[33] Morin, *Les cousettes*; and Arsène, *Les reines de l'aiguille*.

[34] Vernières was as self-conscious about his method as Benoist had been. *Camille Frison* was written in the first person, and the narrator actually tracked his subject and questioned her in the manner of a social scientist. The narrator also remarked on the "voyeuristic" aspects of conducting social research and seems to be unsure about whether he is a *flâneur*, prospective lover, or social scientist. Zola voiced some of the same concerns about his writing and research. So did Du Maroussem. See *Enquêtes*, pp. 19, 74–75, and 79.

[35] Unlike *Le vêtement à Paris*, Benoist's *Les ouvrières* treated women garment workers only.

made no particular effort to distinguish one from the other. Their worlds overlapped, but increasingly reformers' efforts and the literature on women's work focused on what the author of *Camille Frison* called "the hell of homework."

Constant legislative hearings and debates fueled reformers' sense of urgency. In 1909, De Mun proposed a bill establishing a minimum wage for homeworkers in the clothing trades. Studies in support of his initiatives multiplied. Supporters held workshops in Paris on the question. The Catholic press kept up a steady stream of coverage—through brochures published by "L'Action populaire," scholarly work in *Le Mouvement Social*, and articles in papers like *L'Eveil Démocratique*. Secular-minded reformers and academics did much of their work under the auspices of the Association nationale française pour la protection légale des travailleurs (ANFPLT) (National Association for the Legal Protection of Workers), which held hearings on outwork and published their members' individual studies. As interest in the issue crested, social investigators, doctors and urban health and housing experts, interested politicians, legal experts, and union representatives of different political persuasions gathered at international meetings on homework in 1910 and 1912. By the 1910s, then, the particular issues raised by homework dominated the discussion of female labor.

The first of those issues was what reformers considered appallingly low wages. Indeed homework figured prominently in general studies of wages written during the period. Many writers began to claim that wages of homeworkers revealed an anomaly of women's work in general: it was not subject to any of the market equilibrations that political economy held to govern the wage relationship. As Georges Mény, author of some of the most widely respected studies, put it, women's wages constituted "a peculiar economic phenomenon."[36] There seemed to be no relationship between a woman's earnings and her skills, productivity, or most basic needs. And there seemed to be no downward limit, no bottom, to the depths to which women's wages could be driven. Cases from the Office du Travail's study of homework and countless private investigations were repeatedly used to disprove the maxim that earnings would never fall below subsistence.[37] As in Benoist's work, Christian images filled the space cleared by razing liberal economic laws. The Comte d'Haussonville, for example, called the government study "a kind of martyrology, which catalogues every variety of suffering."[38] The

---

The conventions of boulevard fiction and the concerns of economists dictated this focus. In this study as in others, tailors virtually vanished.

[36] Mény, *Le travail à bon marché*, p. 68.

[37] Maurice Guerrier, *Le salaire de la femme: Ses conséquences sociales et économiques* (Paris, 1912) p. 80.

[38] Haussonville, *Le travail des femmes à domicile*, p. 28. See also Reverend Père du Lac, "Couturières et modistes." p. 79.

appropriate points of reference for understanding the misery of home-workers' lives were not the principles of political economy, but the lives of the saints.

Descriptions of homes and family life among homeworkers made it clear that the reformers considered them the antithesis of a well-organized and efficient household. Images of disorder abounded, of naked children lying on unmade beds next to packages of finished clothing, of windows darkened by dirt and hung with filthy, tattered curtains, and of walls plastered with "vulgar lithographs from *Le Petit Journal* and *Le Petit Parisien*."[39] Furniture was pawned, sometimes to make the three-franc-a-week credit payment on the family's sewing machine. Families lived on only potatoes and dried vegetables, supplemented by little bits of sugar and coffee—hallmarks of urban life, even among the poor. Horror-stricken journalists claimed that homeworkers' quarters served simultaneously as "living room, bedroom, kitchen, workshop, birthing room, sick room, and mortuary."[40] The jumbling of these separate spaces testified to the disarray of those who inhabited them. The method of describing interiors in vivid detail derived from Le Play's tradition of family monographs; here it blended with muckraking journalism. The mingled images of machinery, dirt, and sick children recall writings on factories from the 1840s. But the scene is now the home and, as we will see, the factory enjoys a corresponding revaluation. The following description ran in a newspaper under the title "Misères sociales":

> The slum is black and smelly; torn wallpaper is peeling off the humid walls. . . .
> There is a large bed and a crib, covered with filthy sheets, a dusty placard, two
> beat-up chairs, piles of old clothes on the floor—empty bottles and, of course,
> the sewing machine, which is seven years old. . . . The woman is at her work. In
> the crib, a four-month-old baby is whimpering. The baby is barely alive:
> skinny, anemic, with a large boil on his head. On the double bed three children
> are crawling around, whining. Their clothes are in tatters, their hair unkempt.
> Two have the whooping cough, the other has a fever—probably the beginning
> of scarlet fever. The fifth child is at school.[41]

One reformer put the case brusquely, chiding those who defended the inviolability of industrial homework. "Do you call this a 'family'? . . . a poor hovel, turned into a shop, where human beings are packed for fifteen to sixteen hours at a time?"[42]

The reform literature grew frankly morbid, particularly where health was concerned. Here reform sociologists and social catholics found allies among

---

[39] Mény, *Le travail à bon marché*, pp. 134–35.

[40] *Gazette de Lausanne*, April 11, 1903.

[41] Cahen, "Misères sociales," p. 637. Here the reform literature on homework most clearly echoed that on depopulation and infant mortality.

[42] Henriette Brunhes before a social catholic meeting in Paris, 1901. Cited in Mény, *Le travail à bon marché*, p. 129.

a growing group of doctors studying the urban environment. Metaphors of disease and pathology joined the tropes of martyrdom. And here too, issues involving production started to merge with concerns about consumption. In hygienists' eyes, homework created special dangers. The first was to the workers: crowded, damp, and unventilated homes, along with overwork and exhaustion increased vulnerability to disease. Thus one writer called attention to Plaisance, "the unhealthiest neighborhood in all of Paris. Mortality is unusually high. Tuberculosis and frequent epidemics ravage the population. Not surprisingly, it is one of the centers of homework."[43] The image of jumbled spaces reappeared, as physicians condemned the "indescribably smelly packing together of furniture, food, working materials, and finished goods, which create *a breeding ground for germs*."[44] Doctors identified a second danger—this one to consumers, for workers could spread disease via the clothes, toys, and cardboard boxes they produced. Reformers admonished middle-class readers, when they saw a delighted baby putting a new toy in his mouth, to think of the conditions under which that toy was made—of the germs and the filth at homeworkers' quarters.

Writers repeatedly evoked a grisly image of home laborers, too old or sick to be at a shop, working until their death, and spreading germs all over the fruits of their labor. "Only in homework is it possible to exploit invalids who have utterly exhausted their resources; they labor on their deathbed, until the last minutes of their lives."[45] Perhaps the most vivid example comes from a pamphlet by a Parisian doctor named Rist. He warned that the public should be wary, not of the worker herself, but of her family, her children with diphtheria, scarlet fever, and smallpox—"everyone who shares her tiny, dark, and dirty home." Rist's pamphlet concluded with a memorable portrait of a seamstress incurably ill with pulmonary tuberculosis, who continued to work, "coughing and spitting from morning to night."[46] The images could have been from *La Bohème*; investigators now saw them through the lens of Pasteur.

Such pictures left even Benoist's relatively affectionate portrait of seamstresses far behind. That was precisely the point. Anti-sweating publicists intended their work to counter the "bowdlerized verse of boulevard literature" and "the fantasies published by the press on 'midinettes,' the 'fairies of the workshop,' and so on."[47] The portrait they sketched, though, was not simply pitiable. Disgust broke through their accounts of journeys through poor neighborhoods. Mény wrote of being "obsessed" with his memories of

[43] Cahen, "Misères sociales," p. 636.

[44] Mény, *Le travail à bon marché*, p. 163.

[45] Report of section on hygiene, *Exposition du travail à domicile*, 1:38–44.

[46] Edouard Rist, *Travail à domicile et salubrité publique* (Paris, 1914), p. 9. See also Robert Nye, *Crime, Madness, and Politics in Modern France: The Medical Concept of National Decline* (Princeton, N.J., 1984) on the "medical model" of cultural crisis.

[47] Gonnard, *La femme dans l'industrie*, p. 132; Mény, *Le travail à bon marché*, p. 188.

visiting homeworkers' houses.[48] Georges Cahen, in the widely read *Revue Bleu*, remembered "gagging on the stench." Economist René Gonnard, too, choked on his recollections of the "stale and nauseating odor of working women's rooms."[49] Revulsion helped to shape the "miserabilist" portrait of homeworkers. It encouraged investigators to imagine themselves as doctors, visiting a diseased patient. And it encouraged them to see their subjects as "pathological."

That clinical judgment shifted easily to an economic one. Just as writers moved from the moral disarray of homeworkers' lives to the health hazards that disarray posed, so their diagnosis merged medical and economic pathology. Homework was not simply unhealthy, it was unproductive. According to Dr. Rist (whose views distilled those of many), homework brought "physical and moral impoverishment, high infant mortality, and the degeneration of the race." It was "a painful sore on the body social," and "*a criminal waste of human life and effort*." [50] His medical opinion rejoined points made in the more strictly economic literature and the discussion of wages presented earlier: homework seemed to transgress the economists' law that wages could not fall below subsistence.

Images of wasted humanity, indeed, recurred constantly, and not only in writing. Social catholic women helped to stage exhibits that traveled through neighborhoods of Paris and the provinces displaying sweated work. They were called "Expositions of Economic Horrors," and as the name suggests, they shared the sensationalist and voyeuristic aspects of the reformist literature. The exhibits were intended as parodies of the great international expositions, which celebrated progress and consumer goods. Juxtaposing the marvels of industry with the miseries of sweating dramatized what reformers saw as the failures of technology and the social costs of unregulated industrialization. The lists of prices consumers paid for various articles of clothing, presented alongside hours workers spent making those same items and the appallingly low rates they were paid, were designed to drive home the squandering of human labor power in early-twentieth-century consumer culture. One scene showed a sewing machine powered by a baby running on a squirrel cage trying to reach its bottle.[51] This kind of labor, such images proclaimed, was not only exhausting, but futile. It more closely resembled punishment than productive labor.

[48] Mény, *Le travail à bon marché*, p. 136. See also p. 164.

[49] Cahen, "Misères sociales," p. 636; Gonnard, *La femme dans l'industrie*, p. 158.

[50] Rist, *Travail à domicile et salubrité*, p. 6 (my emphasis).

[51] The exhibit was called "The latest advance in family industry." Described in Rollet, *L'action sociale des catholiques*, 2:332–33; see also pp. 18–30 on *Le Sillon*. For very similar views on women workers as slaves, beasts of burden, and unproductive workers, with an emphasis on physical suffering, see Turmann, *Initiatives féminines*, pp. 153, 213. Descriptions of the exhibits can be found in Le Sillon's newspaper, *L'Eveil Démocratique*; Marie-Louise Compain, "Le féminisme au 20e siècle," *Les Idées Modernes* (May 1909): 337–39; and *Exposition du travail à domicile*, vol. 3.

Such images evoked older, biblical views of labor as a curse, as ceaseless physical travail and suffering. Thus they clashed dramatically with nineteenth-century political economy's view of work as a source of wealth and virtue—and of industry as a scene of efficiency and value creation.[52] Such discordant imagery made industrial homework seem that much more out of place in the modern industrial world.

Almost all of these studies took the "micro" approach of recounting individual stories. They nonetheless hinted at the political and cultural context in which these stories took place: the commercialization of Paris and the seeming decline of the family, of craft standards, and of Paris as the world center of fashion.[53] Against what right-wing critics in particular saw as the materialism and individualism of modern times, these women represented the last shards of family life. What these critics were beginning to identify as "consumer culture" had sapped the energies of women and poisoned the family. An engraving by Adolphe Willette, who had extreme right-wing sympathies and political ambitions, illustrates these themes rather well. Called "The Woman Worker," it shows a seamstress in her garret room. She has fallen asleep, her body slumped over the sewing machine, her scissors dropped on the floor. The candle has gone out, and the wisps of smoke curl past her head; they may represent her dreams, or the spirit of French artisanship. In any event, the artist made the context quite clear. Over the horizon looms the Eiffel Tower, an instantly recognizable symbol of the new Paris.[54] The seamstress had become an icon of urban modernity and exhaustion.

For the better part of the nineteenth century, many reformers had considered homework an attractive alternative to factory labor—at least when women were concerned. The anti-sweating literature played a key role in eroding that judgment. The demonization of industrial homework helped to reappraise its opposite: efficient and productive factory work. Dr. Rist, in his characteristic style, raised the stakes, contending not only that shopwork was better paid and healthier, but, more generally, that " . . . groups civilize and cultivate the mind."[55] The claim echoed through scores of arti-

[52] Kaplan and Koepp, *Work in France*, introduction.

[53] See the very stimulating discussion of boulevard literature and the cultural crisis of the late nineteenth century in Nord, *Paris Shopkeepers*, chap. 9.

[54] Willette's fellow right-wing nationalists loathed the Eiffel Tower and all that it symbolized. One nationalist paper said it stood over the Champs de Mars like "some foreigner." Quoted in Nord, *Paris Shopkeepers*, p. 452. Its presence in the engraving is probably a direct reference to such sentiments.

[55] Rist, *Travail à domicile et salubrité*, p. 4. Similar comparisons may be found in Haussonville, *Salaires et misères des femmes*; Cahen, "Misères sociales"; Louis, "Le travail à domicile"; Gonnard, *La femme dans l'industrie*; and Aftalion, *Le développement de la fabrique*. Reformers frequently contrasted the "barbarism" and lawlessness of outwork with "civilization." "Aussi vit-on dans le *travail à domicile* des conditions de vie indignes d'un peuple civilisé." Odry, *Application de la loi*.

Adolphe Willette, "L'ouvrière." Color stone lithograph from *Le Courrier Français*, March 6, 1898, used to advertise iron treatments for anemia.

cles and books. In groups, workers could organize themselves; women homeworkers were isolated and dependent on others. Shops and unions taught skills; women cloistered in their homes could not acquire those skills. Factories could be regulated; the anarchy of home production made it a breeding ground for disease and poverty. Like labor leaders, forward-looking reformers compared the purposefulness and efficiency of men working in factories with the distractedness of women working at home.[56]

This was a vivid set of contrasts: order and chaos, productivity and waste, male and female. They were set out in strong language, and the images that accompanied them were riveting. The accumulation of such powerfully constructed horror stories fortified the arguments of those like the socialist who said: "I have come to hope for the disappearance of homework as soon as possible, for workers in the factory are less unhappy."[57] But most reformers were passing judgment on the value of industrial homework to the national economy rather than assessing the happiness of homeworkers. Unlike shopwork, home labor was chaotic and, therefore, irrational, unproductive, and wasteful. It depleted the energies of not only the individual and the family, but the nation.

The discussion of sweating, in sum, was two-edged. On the one hand, it provided an occasion for criticizing the sentimental glorification of *la femme au foyer* and home industries. Self-consciously "modern," many of the writers attacked traditional ideas about appropriate work for men and women. The realities of homework should prove a salutary lesson for girls (and their teachers), showing them the bleak future awaiting those who were fortified only with needlework lessons. Benoist, for example, thought French schoolgirls should be required to read the verses of Thomas Hood's "The Song of the Shirt" rather than *Emile* and Rousseau's raptures on sewing and femininity.[58] At the same time, however, the discussion laid out rather strict ideas of what the home should be: well organized, controlled by carefully planned budgets, and, most important, separate from work. It also defined work more narrowly, as full-time factory labor. Much of the literature powerfully suggested that homeworkers were simply not productive. In this emerging vision of gender and work relations, women's economic role was recast as consumption.

[56] The following passage from Guerrier's *Le salaire de la femme* is a good example. "Men are interested, above all, in the wages that they earn from their work. . . . They pursue only one goal: to earn their living." Women, by contrast, worked in what Guerrier called a "meandering" way, for they did not need to support their families (p. 79).

[57] Cited in Fagnot, *La réglementation du travail en chambre*, pp. 35–36.

[58] Echoed approvingly by Gonnard, *La femme dans l'industrie*, pp. 154–55. Haussonville made the same point in *Le travail des femmes à domicile*, pp. 33–34.

CONSUMPTION AS POLITICS AND VALUE

Students of the "woman question" found much of interest in the enormous literature on sweated labor.[59] First, the government's studies of industrial homework, which documented both the range and resilience of the sweated trades, demonstrated that the vast majority of working women remained unprotected by the Third Republic's labor laws. Second, the research made abundantly clear that in one of the largest "female" trades, it was becoming virtually impossible for a woman to support herself with her work. Many had said as much long before. But by the 1890s, that argument, and the discussion of women's wages in general, was unavoidably and controversially linked with pressing feminist claims on the state and society. Third (and most pertinent here), many women considered ending sweating to be a particularly "feminine" mission—not because of the composition of the labor force, but rather because of the alleged gender of consumption.

The groups that pushed this last argument the furthest were the Consumers' Leagues. Many late-nineteenth-century reformers, including De Mun, credited the leagues with making sweated labor a public issue. Closely related to the developments in social catholicism sketched earlier, they stand at an important juncture of social science and the discussion of women, the value of their labor, and the family.

The Consumers' Leagues were born in the United States, where they drew on the forces of the labor movement, middle-class concern, and a powerful tradition of female reform that reached back to the antislavery movement. In England, the anti-sweating forces arose from already powerful groups of women—the Women's Labor League and the Women's Industrial Council, who cooperated in staging the Daily News Exhibition of Sweated Industry in 1906. Like all those involved in the new wave of female activism at the turn of the century, they believed that it was "not required that women should possess the franchise before beginning to make their influence felt."[60]

The leagues' purpose was twofold: to develop the public's awareness of

[59] See Karen Offen, "Depopulation, Nationalism, and Feminism in Fin-de-Siècle France," *American Historical Review* 89, no. 3 (June 1984): 648–76; idem, "Defining Feminism: A Comparative Historical Approach," *Signs* 14, no. 1 (Autumn 1988): 119–57; and the extensive bibliographies in Offen and Bell, eds., *Women, the Family, and Freedom*, vol. 2. On definitions of feminism and their relationship to the more broadly defined "woman question," see the exchange between Offen, Ellen Dubois, and Nancy Cott in *Signs* 15, no. 1 (Autumn 1989): 195–209. Among contemporary sources, Turgéon, *Le féminisme français*, provides a useful, though hostile, survey of the terrain.

[60] On England, see Schmiechen, *Sweated Industries*; and Ellen Mappen, "Strategies for Change: Social Feminist Approaches to the Problems of Women's Work," in Angela John, ed., *Unequal Opportunities: Women's Employment in England* (Oxford, 1986).

and sense of responsibility toward the condition of workers, and to bring
political pressure on manufacturers and the state for changes in those conditions. Their targets ranged across a spectrum of workers' grievances: low
wages, piece rates, long hours, arbitrary fines, unsanitary working conditions, and child labor. The leagues lobbied for stricter enforcement of labor
legislation, publicizing abuses and illegalities. They rode herd on the government and its newly created agencies, doubling the efforts of official
workplace inspectors with their own inquiries. Finally, they published
"white lists" of manufacturers who met their standards. The leagues' "label"
of approval was intended to alert potential buyers to the difference "between the product of the sweatshop and that of the well-ordered factory."[61]

The French Consumers' Leagues were founded in 1902 by a group of
Parisian women who intended to conduct social research and investigate
working conditions in the Paris clothing industry. While the association
eschewed any formal political or religious affiliation and gathered a diverse
group of reformers to its ranks, it was very closely associated with social
catholicism. Many of the female founders were married to prominent social
catholics. Catholic newspapers, unions, and groups like Le Sillon embraced
their work and cause. Wealthy and well-connected, the founders found it
easy to gather the support needed to launch their organization. They enrolled prominent men on their advisory committees, and by 1908 leagues
were established in the provinces as well as Paris.[62]

The leagues reflected broader changes in women's associations, changes
that had helped transform social catholicism in the last decades of the century: an impatience with traditional charity, a new engagement with social
questions and working people, and an eagerness to participate in the development of social legislation. The leagues were determined to pull middle-
class women from the shelter of their homes and give them "a more social
conception of their role." What was more, they tried to approach these issues
afresh, departing from the constraining tradition of *oeuvres*, or "good works."

Sociological research proved crucial to this change and to breaking with
the accustomed female voice and image. The leagues' work provides another
revealing glimpse of the extraordinarily rapid dissemination of social science among nonspecialists during this period. Study, observation, and gathering statistics were the underpinnings of their politics. "Il faut avoir vu de
ses yeux" [You have to have seen with your eyes] became one of their watch-
words, and the phrase captures nicely the combination of personal witness
and social investigation that characterized the leagues' approach. To see

---

[61] It was also intended to support union shops. The First Annual Report of the Consumers'
League, 1900, cited in Shallcross, *Industrial Homework*, p. 35.

[62] The original membership of the French leagues was thoroughly aristocratic. See Maurice
Deslandres, *L'acheteur: Son role économique et social* (Paris, 1911), pp. 28–41 for a description
of the leagues' circles and first activities.

meant to be aware, but it also enabled one to make arguments, and to prove. "In order to make demands and get reforms you have to have *seen* the shops of the garment industry . . ." their pamphlets declared.[63] They published copies of questionnaires from the Office du Travail's study of homework in the lingerie industry, and they drew up questionnaires of their own, which could be distributed to anyone interested in investigating other trades. As if to formalize their interest in social research being conducted by the state, they invited Du Maroussem from the Office du Travail to give a series of lectures on sociological method to their groups. In effect, they urged their members (who were much more completely excluded from university life than their Anglo-American counterparts) to become amateur sociologists.[64] Just as the *flâneur* and priest had become *enquêteurs*, so now did the politically active woman.

Training in social investigation was meant to enable women to join in contemporary discussions of social policy. In the United States and England, conceptions of women's moral authority gave them considerable legitimacy in the public realm. In the political climate of the Third Republic, the opposite was the case. Fierce anticlerical sentiment led to deep fears of and opposition to religious, charitable, and "feminine" initiatives, which republicans and radicals viewed as being all of a piece. The idea that women formed an obscurantist mass, blocking the modernization of French society was a particularly resilient aspect of the revolutionary tradition and a republican commonplace. It posed a real obstacle to the political and intellectual mobilization of middle-class women. In the slightly condescending words of one male member of the Consumers' Leagues, women needed to demonstrate that their organization was not merely "a group of sensitive women expressing their good will." Or, as one of the leagues' brochures, written by a woman, remarked self-deprecatingly, "women have to learn to think before they act."[65] Such apologetic sentiments hint at the barriers Consumers' Leagues confronted in France and are revealing about the agency of women in the political culture of the Third Republic. A weak system of girls' education, the virtual exclusion of women from the academy, and the complete absence of women's colleges were some of the obstacles; in addition to depriving French women of an education, they narrowed women's access to political and academic circles, making the kinds of networks that were so important in American reform movements impossi-

[63] *Bulletin de la Ligue Sociale d'Acheteurs* 1 (1905).

[64] If it had been woman's traditional role to educate, now it was her duty to gather information in order to educate others. See Zylberberg-Hocquard and Diebolt, eds., *Femmes et travail au XIXe siècle*, introduction, on women in social research during the nineteenth century. Kathryn Kish Sklar's discussion of women in social science in the United States provides an excellent point of comparison. See *Florence Kelley*.

[65] Deslandres, *L'acheteur*, p. 33.

ble. The French Consumers' Leagues, like French women's organizations in general, did not establish the same high profile as their American or English equivalents.

The leagues shared the broader cultural investment in "social scientific" approaches. But their work and politics are also important in other respects, notably the changing image of women as consumers. The leagues boldly designated sweated labor in the retail trades a "feminine" issue, but not chiefly because the workers in those trades were female. It is true that the largely female clothing trades remained one of their most consistent targets. Their pamphlets demanded that manufacturers not keep seamstresses after 9:00 at night, not give work to take home in the evening, and close on Sundays. They strongly supported a minimum wage bill for home-workers.[66] They were particularly attentive to cases of discrimination against women and conducted a long campaign against the grocer Felix Potin when they discovered that he dismissed women workers if they married. But they proved equally concerned with other "consumer" trades, like hairdressing and baking, most of which employed men. Their self-definition came not from identifying with the producers of retail goods (though clearly that entered into it) but from adopting the redefinition of women's new role as consumers.

In contemporary society, wrote one member in the leagues' bulletin, every Parisian woman, no matter what her social class, was a consumer. The question was simply whether she would follow the leagues' "ethics of spending": distinguishing between "true" and "false" needs; paying reasonable prices rather than hunting for bargains, which drove down wages; and settling her bills on time.[67] Other writers pressed further theoretically—beyond ethics to questions of changing gender roles and the social value of womanhood. In their eyes, the politics of the Consumers' Leagues arose from the historical transformation of women's social activity. Industrialization, they argued, had drawn many household labors, from soap making to baking and, above all, making clothes, into the cash nexus—"from the home to the factory."[68] So women encountered the former products of their labor as consumers rather than producers. That historical transformation, however, need not render women powerless, for women could "direct the organization of consumption." The leagues' politics and self-understanding aimed to shatter the boundaries between production and consumption.

[66] Henriette Brunhes, *La ligue sociale d'acheteurs*, brochure published by ANFPLT (Paris, 1903), p. 12.

[67] Brincard, "Le prix des bonnes occasions," *Bulletin de la Ligue Sociale d'Acheteurs* 3 (1905): 163–75. The Felix Potin campaign is covered in 2 (1904): 86.

[68] Maude Nathan, president of the New York Consumers' League. Speech at the International Congress of Women, Berlin, 1904. Translated and reprinted in *Bulletin de la Ligue Sociale d'Acheteurs* 3 (1905): 180. Brincard's article made similar points.

Their analyses often struck out along uncharted paths. History shaped and reshaped the ways in which societies organized and understood consumption, argued one article in the *Bulletin*. Contemporary culture designated consumption a "female" realm and understood it as a passive activity. But women could reappropriate both the term and the activity for their own purposes. The most radical redefinition came from the head of the Consumers' Leagues: "Buyers create what they buy. Women, and society at large, should think of *consumption, along with production, as a value-creating process*."[69]

The Consumers' Leagues did not stake out this social and conceptual terrain alone. The end of the century brought a new valuation of consumption in economic theory and a new attention to consumers, purchasing power, and their relationship to social order and economic expansion. It also encouraged a self-conscious theorizing of women's potential role as consumers.[70]

Some of this theorizing came from very conservative quarters. Anna Lampérière, prominent antifeminist and author of many books and articles, provides an illuminating example of how this argument could be developed. She argued fervently that men and women had different moral characters, intellectual capabilities, and physical capacities, and so therefore belonged in different economic domains. Women competed with men at their peril, and at grave social and economic disadvantage; their work, Lampérière believed, simply was not comparable. It was, however, complementary. In common with many feminists of her time (though for very different purposes), Lampérière grounded her theories in the history of civilization and gender roles. Men's historical task was wage earning, or, as she more grandly put it, exploring "new productive resources." History charged women, on the other hand, with using and distributing what men brought home. They paid the debts, bought food and clothing, and, through prudent purchasing and good taste, created the setting that constituted the home. "A woman's duties, understood in this way, have a decisive and incalculable value," wrote Lampérière. The economical organization of a home raised the value of a man's earnings; women's aesthetic talents could create "infinite joy." She repeated several times her most important point: women's role in modern society was "the systematic organization of consumption." "The woman's role is not to earn a wage, but to raise the 'purchasing power'

[69] Nathan, *Bulletin de la Ligue Sociale d'Acheteurs* 3 (1905): 176–77, my emphasis. See also p. 148, and the interesting article by E. Rivière, "Producteurs et Consommateurs," in the same issue, pp. 98–107.

[70] Long indifferent, even hostile, to theories that valued consumption over production, French economists began to change their positions in the 1870s and 1880s. Doing so involved breaking with eighteenth-century century convictions about productive and unproductive wealth and a deeply rooted suspiciousness about luxury and consumption. See Williams, *Dream Worlds*, pp. 222–33.

of her husband's wage."[71] Her unabashedly conservative sentiments put her out of the mainstream. But her language—the repeated references to "value," "consumption," and "production"—were strikingly modern, and anchored in the social science of her time. Like many others, she pointed to the enormous literature on homework as proof that women were both inefficient and debased in production and wage labor.[72]

Augusta Moll-Weiss offers a final and more representative illustration of these conceptual shifts and how they reshaped interpretations of the family economy. Moll-Weiss did not share Lampérière's politics, but she thought about gender and the division of social tasks in much the same way. From the turn of the century through the interwar period, she led a movement to reorganize housework and reeducate housewives. Her countless domestic manuals all shared a curious feature: children—their birth, diapering, feeding, education, sicknesses, and emotional needs—were tucked into a cursory last chapter. Not for her the sentimental image of la femme au foyer. The focus of Moll-Weiss's self-consciously modern approach to the home was the "science" of domesticity and the household economy. She approached that household in the manner of a social scientist; in fact, she worked in tandem with Emile Cheysson, using his model of the household and budget. Moll-Weiss's working-class budgets could not help but document the crucial importance of women's wage earning in various French family economies. Her interpretation of the data, however, imposed a more orderly and gendered division of economic roles on it: the man earned; the woman spent. In her view, and no matter what her research showed, women's most important task—and their value to the family—was not wage earning but the efficient ordering of consumption. "Each era has a new conception of things," she observed. In the past, women raised chickens and made pot au feu. Today's educated women balanced receipts and expenses and was concerned above all with her family's "purchasing power."[73] Moll-Weiss understood her work to involve applying sociological methods of analysis. She was also, and quite openly, reproducing the assumptions of the new sociology. She was interested in women as household managers and in the family as a unit of consumption rather than production.

Lampérière and Moll-Weiss provide just two examples of the broader currents on which the women in the Consumers' Leagues drew. Arguments that centered on consumption and purchasing power became more frequent, popular, and powerful.[74] The leagues also borrowed freely from the

[71] Lampérière, La femme et son pouvoir, esp. chap. 5, "Valeur économique du travail féminin." See also her Le rôle social de la femme (Paris, 1898), p. 47.

[72] Le role social de la femme, p. 48.

[73] She used the phrase, as did Lampérière. Moll-Weiss, Le livre du foyer.

[74] Duchêne, "Le relèvement du salaire," speech at Congrès international des oeuvres et institutions féminines, June 2–7, 1913.

literature generated by the anti-sweating movement, some of which simply blamed the *grands magasins* and modern commerce for destroying French industry and society. The leagues warned against the bad taste that was spread by marketing cheap goods and against the ruinous effects of living beyond one's means and buying on credit. "La vie à bon marché est une catastrophe," ran the title of one article in the *Bulletin*, disclosing the leagues' archly middle-class hostility to plebeian spending and materialism. At their worst, then, the leagues offered nothing more than an antimodern critique of commercial culture, with strongly nationalist overtones.[75] But the most revealing aspect of their politics may lie in the remarkable discursive fit between, on the one hand, the portrait of the inefficient woman worker taking shape in the investigations and journalism on sweating and, on the other, an emerging new understanding of consumption and an assessment of women's value in this realm. The leagues' mode of political action arose from a cultural redefinition of middle-class women's role as consumers, their "miserabilist" portrait of sweated labor made it difficult to imagine women as producers.

CONCLUSION

The late-nineteenth-century enthusiasm for "social economy" enrolled new members in the ranks of social science and provided a new forum for the battles over women's work. Ironically, though, the new and narrower monographic approach, pioneered by those eager to break with Le Play's traditionalism and conservative politics, provided a singularly impoverished framework for studying the family economy or female labor. Le Play's deliberate tallying of how families combined paid and unpaid labor, the economic value of *la femme au foyer*, and how culture and region shaped these variables was, despite its obvious shortcomings and thoroughgoing conservatism, more revealing on that score. The project of compiling information on standards of living dominated public attention, and the focus on purchasing power and the family's cash resources blurred and elided those earlier issues. Although the research was voluminous, the debate about sweating generated more heat than light. The directions in which the earlier research pointed remained uncharted.

As we will see in the next chapter, social catholic proponents of a minimum wage for outworkers hoped that the measure would revitalize home industries and the family economies they allegedly supported. People like De Mun and Chaptal believed that reinvigorated family industries would safeguard against socialism. But the dominant tone of the social research

[75] Du Maroussem, for instance, called department stores "palaces built to satisfy women's cravings." "Les grands magasins tels qu'ils sont," p. 923. On the relationship between nationalism, class, and taste, see Silverman, *Art Nouveau*; and Auslander, *Taste and Power*.

conducted at the time was much more pessimistic and, like the central themes and imagery of the reform literature, suggested that homework was hopelessly debased.

The meldings of inherited religious images and biblical tropes with newer languages of secular authority, medicine, and political economy made the characterization an extremely potent one. Thus the discussion of sweating contributed to narrowing notions of productive work. It also narrowed ideas about the family. The "pathology" of homeworkers' households helped to define the functions of their healthy counterparts—leisure and consumption. Here the anti-sweating reform literature reproduced and echoed the ideals promoted by the labor movement in its campaign for the eight-hour day: the separation of home and work, domesticity underwritten by a family wage, an uncluttered, well-ordered home alongside clean, well-ordered, and regulated factories. As in the labor movement, reformers found the kind of chaotic compromise of wage earning and household labor that homework represented increasingly "backward" and incompatible with their vision of both modern industry and modern family life.[76]

The "modernist" view of the family as a unit of consumption was also a product of late-nineteenth-century social sciences, particularly the school firmly ensconced in the state bureaucracy. The Office du Travail sociologists identified the family's buying power as the crucial information to supply to policymakers, and their new modes of analysis converged with state interest in settling strikes and promoting social peace. Still, beyond the world of officialdom, the work of Charles Benoist, novels like *Camille Frison*, the Consumers' Leagues' *enquêtes*, and Moll-Weiss' domestic manuals testify to a wider dissemination of new categories of analysis and perception, at least in circles committed to the "modernization" of France. As the issue of wage legislation became unavoidable, the gender politics of this modernizing vision would have to be spelled out.

---

[76] For more examples, see Cross, *A Quest for Time*.

Chapter Eight

THE MINIMUM WAGE BILL:
WORK, WAGES, AND WORTH

In France, across Europe, and in the United States, the early-twentieth-century crisis over women's work and sweating created the context for a critical milestone in social legislation—the first minimum wage bills. Previous reform efforts had focused on working conditions and hours. After 1900, and largely as a result of the anti-sweating campaigns, reformers began to urge intervention in the wage itself. The French state edged toward new policies reluctantly, worried about the implications of its undertakings. For if the social science literature had helped erode older certainties, it had also created new conundrums. The Office du Travail's studies of industrial homework threatened to shatter nostalgic images of French family industry. How the state might reform homework was far less evident. Would reforms eliminate homework? With what consequences for women, men, or industry? Progressive reformers, social catholic deputies, feminists from across the political spectrum, and clothing manufacturers had enormous stakes in this debate. Codifying a wage policy entailed examining deeply rooted assumptions about market culture, family organization, gender interests, and the very nature of economic progress.

Feminists, the State, and "Protection"

Late-nineteenth-century commentators hostile to the women's movement saw only an ironic relationship between the crisis over sweated labor and the contemporaneous rise of feminism. One writer contrasted the "noisy feminism" of a troublesome few women with the quiet sufferings of the vast working majority, whose isolation hid their miseries from public view.[1] The Comte d'Haussonville could barely believe that feminists (whom he abhorred) and sweated workers (whom he pitied) came from the same female "species." It was common to assert that the "orators in skirts" preoccupied with women's rights had nothing to say about women's labor.[2]

Historians, too, have argued that women and feminism played a peripheral role in debates about labor and legislation during the French Third Republic. This is misleading. True, by comparison with its counterparts in

[1] Guerrier, Le salaire de la femme, preface.
[2] Haussonville, Salaires et misères de femmes, pp. vii, 22–23, and 306.

England and the United States, French feminism was cautious and narrowly based. As we saw in the last chapter, Third Republic feminists were also hobbled by a political culture that made female initiatives particularly difficult.[3] Strong Catholic and equally powerful anticlerical currents churned the waters in which women reformers had to navigate.[4] Nevertheless, social catholic activists and reformers created a remarkably strong and influential network of reform associations—a "female dominion" comparable to the American and English ones in its institutional strategies and its politics. While the French women's movement had relatively weak liberal and socialist branches, its social catholic one was considerably stronger. Once these social catholic groups are taken into account, women hardly seem marginal to the crucially important debates about state-based labor reform in the Third Republic. In France as elsewhere, it is hard to imagine the furor about sweated labor and labor legislation without the social forces mobilized by the women's movement and the pointed questions raised by feminists.

Social catholic women were not the only ones to endorse reform campaigns. Feminists—and a surprisingly wide group of women were willing to adopt the identification—poured their energies into questions about sweating, labor legislation, and wage laws. Although they did not see themselves as carrying forward a tradition, their efforts fit with longstanding concerns. Feminist claims for women's citizenship rights had always argued as much from women's contribution to society as from "natural rights."[5] From the petitions of the eighteenth-century guild seamstresses and linen drapers down through the writings of several generations of nineteenth-century feminists—Flora Tristan, Jeanne Deroin, Louise Michel, and Hubertine

[3] Mary Lynn Stewart argues that women played a peripheral role in these debates. *Women, Work, and the French State*, pp. 55–57. So does Allan Mitchell: "No feminist concerns animated these discussions." *The Divided Path*, p. 99. For a different view, see Coons, "'Neglected Sisters.'" On the relative strength of women in French and German socialism, see Sowerwine, *Sisters or Citizens?*; and Steven Hause, *Women's Suffrage and Social Politics in the French Third Republic* (Princeton, N.J., 1984), on the French suffrage movement in comparative perspective.

[4] Historians are only beginning to consider how the institutional and ideological presence of the Catholic church shaped women's role in French political culture. See Anne Marie Sohn, "Catholic Women and Political Affairs," in Judith Friedlander, ed., *Women in Culture and Politics* (Bloomington, Ind., 1986); Caroline Ford's work on the feminization of religion, "Private Lives and Public Order in Restoration France: The Seduction of Emily Loveday," *American Historical Review* 99, no. 1 (February 1994): 21–43; and Fayet-Scribe, "Les associations féminines catholiques." For comparisons, see Sklar, *Florence Kelley*; Boris and Daniels, eds., *Homework*; Mappen, "Strategies for Change"; Schmiechen, *Sweated Industries*; Martha Vicinus, *Independent Women: Work and Community for Single Women, 1850–1920* (Chicago, 1985); Koven and Michel, eds., *Mothers of a New World*; and Pedersen, *Family, Dependence, and the Origins of the Welfare State*.

[5] Much historical literature to the contrary, the discontinuities of nineteenth-century feminism are one of its signal characteristics. On the narrowness of the natural rights tradition and the nineteenth-century retreat from it, see Fraisse, *Muse de la raison*; and Riley, *Am I That Name?*

Auclert—a central theme was echoed: women's activities were undervalued, and their capacity for productive labor was being squandered by political and social inequalities. As French feminist Louise Compain claimed at the beginning of the twentieth century, no issue was more urgent to feminists than the value and dignity of women's work.[6] Throughout this period, the related issues of women's wages, sweated labor, and the organization of production and consumption mobilized countless women and supplied the context for new forms of public and political engagement.

Gender by no means assured unanimity on these subjects. When the Consumers' Leagues began to lobby for laws regulating working conditions in the sweated trades, they set on a collision course with many influential feminists. As the leagues' president, Henriette Brunhes, bitterly commented about opponents of state intervention, "You know that the most ardent defenders of economic liberalism are still women."[7] Feminists disagreed fiercely about what "women's" interests were and about whether and how the government should intercede in the labor market.

The most notorious feminist battles involved gender-specific or "protective" laws covering women's industrial work. From 1848 through the 1880s, the French state had refused to regulate women's labor on any special basis, passing, instead, health, safety, and hours laws that covered all workers. In that period, the French government was more willing to regulate the labor of children than that of adult women. Unlike the British state, it did not group women and children as minors for the purposes of labor legislation—a measure of the greater acceptance of women's wage work in France, and of an idealized image of "family" shops and farms. Not until 1892 and the Millerand-Collier bill of 1900 did French laws specifically limit women's working hours, ban their night work, and bar them from hazardous trades. Doing so brought France labor law closer to its English and American counterparts; the British reformer Elizabeth Hutchins said that the 1892 law brought France, once "decidedly backward" on women in industry, "into line with the requirements of the modern industrial state."[8] Hutchins interpreted the new French laws as a humanizing of the industrial world, a bow to feminism, and a measure of concern for women. But the laws also represented a nod to a more gendered vision of the industrial world wherein male work was the norm and women's deviant.

These laws sparked furious debate in the women's movement. Socialist

---

[6] Louise Compain, "Le féminism au 20e siècle," four-part article in *Les Idées Modernes* (March, April, May, and June 1909).

[7] Henriette Brunhes, "La ligue sociale d'acheteurs" (Paris, 1903).

[8] Elizabeth Leigh Hutchins, *Labour Laws for Women in France*, pamphlet published by the English Women's Industrial Council (London, 1907), p. 2. Boxer, "Protective Legislation," pp. 45–65; Sowerwine, *Sisters or Citizens?*; Stewart, *Women, Work, and the French State*; and Cross, *A Quest for Time*, pp. 47–49.

and trade union women were the most consistent supporters of protective legislation. While they would have preferred laws covering men as well as women, they found narrower provisions amply justified on the grounds that half a loaf was better than none. Support also came from social catholic women like Léonie Chaptal, who believed in special treatment for the vulnerable and whose first priority was the protection of mothers and children, and from conservative natalists whose concerns about population and "protection of the race" forced them to compromise their conservative distaste for state intervention of any kind.[9] All three groups accused opponents of protective legislation of being willfully blind to the realities of working-class life—a blindness that revealed an incorrigibly "bourgeois" outlook and mindless allegiance to liberal principles of equality. To reject the regulation of women's work was to recklessly ignore basic class and gender issues. "If you do not protect women workers, who are so much more exploited than men, the bosses will know no limits." Since men and women lived in "different industrial worlds," another representative of this position argued, they required different treatment.[10] Women's distinctive vulnerabilities— their lower wages, longer hours, and double duties—made their needs urgent.[11]

Opposition to "protective" laws was equally impassioned, and this was the majority position in French feminist congresses. In 1900, just as Millerand-Collier was about to go into effect, the two most prestigious meetings of the French women's movement defiantly voted for "liberté du travail" and against regulation.[12] Feminists found abundant evidence that trade unions considered special labor laws a way to remove women from the workplace altogether. The 1898 Rennes resolution that men should be the household's breadwinners was repeatedly cited at feminist congresses and greeted by hissing and angry shouts.[13] The small female presence in the union movement added to the difficulty of establishing any sense of common purpose between feminist groups and labor leaders. Open antisocial-

[9] *Congrès . . . droits des femmes*, 1900, pp. 48–49. These positions were not hard and fast. For trade union women's views, see Bouvier, *Mes mémoires*; and Stephanie Bouvard at *Congrès . . . oeuvres et institutions*, 1913, p. 511.

[10] Eliza Vincent, at *Congrès . . . droits des femmes*, 1900, p. 48; and Compain at *Congrès . . . oeuvres et institutions*, 1913. See Sowerwine, *Sisters or Citizens?*, pp. 67–80.

[11] For the arguments about gender-specific regulation, see *Congrès . . . oeuvres et institutions*, 1900, plenary session on "liberté du travail de la femme," 1:81–91, and the working session on the same topic, 3:339–54; *Congrès . . . droits des femmes*, 1900, pp. 46–55; Ligue Belge du droit des femmes, *Actes du Congrès féminist international de Bruxelles*, pp. 67–76; *Congrès . . . oeuvres et institutions*, 1913, sec. 5 ("Travail"), sess. 1, pp. 233–36, 313–15, 511–20.

[12] *Congrès . . . oeuvres et institutions*, 1900; and *Congrès . . . droits des femmes*, 1889, p. 121. The resolutions passed almost unanimously.

[13] *Congrès . . . oeuvres et institutions*, 1900, 3:353–54.

ism animated some of the opposition to labor laws for women.[14] Although liberal feminists claimed they only objected to laws infringing *women's* right to work, many clearly refused any interference in the "free" labor market. Marguerite Durand, the colorful and well-connected French feminist leader, publisher of *La Fronde*, and prominent supporter of the women garment workers' strikes, offered a case in point. Her efforts to introduce women into jobs previously dominated by men and her opposition to any restrictions on women's industrial work had run her afoul of the labor movement in the past, and her well-founded worries about the consequences of protective legislation were now articulated in a language that made her seem like an apologist for the manufacturers. "Once employers are released from the shackles of our present law, they can simply chose between good and bad workers, no matter what their sex, and pay them the same price." Such free-market rhetoric infuriated feminists who considered their purpose to be the emancipation of women rather than the deliverance of capitalists. Durand insisted she would support laws that covered both sexes, but these assurances rang predictably hollow.[15]

As the exchanges grew more heated, the burgeoning literature on sweated labor became a point of reference for both sides; indeed, that literature contributed to miring feminists in futile and acrimonious debate. The grim realities of sweating seemed to provide a case study of liberal (i.e., antiprotectionist) feminist concerns. If working women were marginalized by a hostile labor movement, restrictive apprenticeship rules, and laws that limited their participation in factory labor, they could only languish in the unregulated, largely female sweated home industries.[16] Durand called "protective" legislation "the surest cause of women's low wages." She characteristically overstated the case, but the claim had merit: such legislation had exacerbated the crowding of the needle trades and other poorly paid industries.[17] At the same time, the anti-sweating literature seemed to confirm the protectors' arguments about women's distinctive vulnerabilities. The miserabilist portrait of women's work that emerged from that literature made the economic individualism promoted by liberal feminists like Durand seem utopian at best.

The feminist debate about protection peaked at the turn of the century, with the passage of the Millerand-Collier hours bill of 1900. Still, whether

[14] See the attacks on the "socialist mania for minute regulation of conditions of labor." *Congrès . . . oeuvres et institutions*, 1900, 3:336.

[15] At *Congrès . . . droits des femmes*, 1900, p. 52. The fascinating contradictions in Durand's politics warrant further study. Whether or not the congress would have supported gender-neutral labor legislation is ambiguous. See *Congrès . . . oeuvres et institutions*, 1900, 1:91.

[16] *Congrès . . . oeuvres et institutions*, 1900, 1:81.

[17] Durand at *Congrès . . . droits des femmes*, 1900, p. 52. See also *Congrès . . . oeuvres et institutions*, 1900, 1:81; the testimony of Mme Pégard before the CST, *Rapport sur le travail des femmes à domicile*, p. 78; and Compain, "Le féminism au 20e siècle."

state intervention should target women in particular, and whether feminists could support legislation that singled out women's vulnerabilities and confirmed their special status remained anguishing questions, and placed considerable obstacles in the path of the minimum wage bill.[18]

HOMEWORK AND THE FAMILY ECONOMY

Historians have focused much attention on feminist debates about protection and their views of class differences and market culture. They have said much less about issues that were directly relevant to the discussion considered here: the economic role of married women, the acceptability of part-time work, and how different models of the family economy could facilitate women's participation in the labor force. On this terrain again, feminists clashed with each other. Although these arguments are less familiar, they were equally fundamental, and have proved of even more enduring importance.

One strong current of French feminist opinion had always favored women's work in the home. That school of thinking, dominated by social catholics, valued women's participation in the labor force, prized women's contribution (waged and unwaged) to the household's budget, and considered viable "family industries" the best way to organize the family economy and national labor force. The 1900 Congrès des oeuvres et institutions féminines (Congress of Women's Charities and Associations)—the more moderate of two feminist congresses held in that year—devoted a whole session to "ways of encouraging women's work in the home."[19] Social catholics— male and female—wrote on this subject in journals like La Réforme Sociale. Léonie Chaptal, Gabrielle Duchêne, and other social catholic women followed through on these convictions, founding groups that distributed homework to young mothers. The prominence of social catholic women in the anti-sweating organizations was a measure of the importance they attached to rejuvenating and reforming homework.

This first school of thought fully embraced the more general feminist concern with valuing women's productive activities. They firmly believed that work conferred dignity and worth on an individual as well as putting more food on the table. But family was the fundamental building block of social catholic (corporatist) thought and politics. Social catholics thus accented women's contribution to the *family's* well-being and particularly applauded the self-sacrificing woman who managed to be both a wage earner

---

[18] For more debates, see Compain, Durand, Misme, and Brunschwig, at *Congrès . . . oeuvres et institutions*, 1913, pp. 510–11, 515, 519.

[19] At that session, however, Lampérière's conservative resolution that women should endorse a "family wage" was promptly voted down. *Congrès . . . oeuvres et institutions*, 1900, 3:487–90.

and a good mother. Making it possible for working women to reconcile their wage labor and family responsibilities topped social catholics' list of priorities.

For these reasons, social catholics considered the deterioration of home industries (homeworkers' falling wages, ferocious competition among women for jobs, the faster pace of labor set by sewing machines, and so on) a disaster for working women. But homework could not be eliminated. To declare war on *travail à domicile*, as social catholics saw it, was to overlook the needs of the nation's working women. "Despite the opinions of the collectivist school, we believe that women's work in the home can be organized in a way that comports with social, moral, and industrial progress."[20] An artisanal world of women homeworkers could be reconstructed; the means for this included regulation of housing conditions, better apprenticeship programs, laws against child and prison labor, unions of homeworkers, elimination of machines, and, by 1909, minimum wage laws.[21]

Both socialist and liberal feminists fiercely disagreed with such strategies. Labor spokeswomen like Stephanie Bouvard, who represented the flower workers' union at the 1900 Congrès des oeuvres et institutions féminines, led the battle against social catholic resolutions. Like other militants in the clothing workers' unions, or socialist women like Aline Valette, Bouvard despaired of organizing women homeworkers. Homeworkers would never come to meetings, never educate themselves, and never break out of the cycle of underpaid, unskilled work. ". . . Only in workshops . . . will we move towards the emancipation of women."[22] Women shopworkers, like their male counterparts, resented the competition from homeworkers; differences in age and marital status deepened the gulf between the two groups. As Marie Bonnevial explained, "Homework creates competition for the woman working in the factory; it drives down wages. . . . It represents the backward spirit of resignation, the polar opposite of moving forward, of revolt."[23] Women could no longer be relegated to the *foyer*, their productive capacities constrained by the walls of their homes.

Liberal feminists like Bonnevial and Durand also found the social catholic attachment to family industry utterly misguided. Durand was a thor-

[20] *Congrès . . . oeuvres et institutions,* 1900, 3:481, and also Vigneron, "Les métiers de famille." Vigneron's comments were directed against Lampérière's resolution that women should withdraw from the labor force. Vigneron rejected the prospect of a family economy in which women did not work for wages, yet she opposed the "decasualization" of female labor that pushed women into full-time, uninterrupted, and better paid jobs. She also argued that homework was key to the survival of poor and underdeveloped regions of all the industrial countries.

[21] *Congrès . . . oeuvres et institutions,* 1900, 3:483–84.

[22] Ibid., p. 486. These differences also surfaced at the Exposition of Women's Crafts in Paris in October 1902. Bouvier, *Mes mémoires,* p. 110.

[23] *Actes du Congrès féministe internationale de Bruxelles,* p. 72.

oughgoing individualist, scornful of dominant conceptions of femininity and impatient with feminists who idealized family and womanly sacrifice. When social catholic feminists offered resolutions urging married women to work at home (or to work part-time), sparks flew. Durand and other liberals charged that such proposals repudiated the fundamental principles of the women's movement: women and men participated in the public sphere on the same terms—in politics as in the labor force.[24] While social catholic feminists deferred to what they deemed an immutable division of labor between the sexes, liberals contested that immutability. Social catholics' fundamentally corporatist outlook (however modulated toward women's rights) clashed with the arch individualism of feminists like Durand, who suspected her opponents were simply acquiescing to natalism. For social catholics, homework preserved women's contribution to the family economy; it accommodated women's particular vulnerabilities; and it fit into the larger project of fighting economic disenfranchisement and underscoring women's contribution to the nation.[25] For both trade union and liberal feminists, homework seemed a galling example of women's fatalism and their acceptance of the double burden of paid and unpaid labor. Accepting the double duty of home and work, whether in homework or part-time employment, would only further women's marginalization, just as would demanding "special treatment" from the law.

Behind this conflict lay a clash between different models of the family economy and gender roles within it. Social catholics embraced a somewhat nostalgic model of a family economy that mixed the waged and unwaged contributions of all family members. The general vision of industrial modernity that inspired male liberals and socialists, on the other hand, included less casual labor, more separation of home and work, and (rhetoric about gender equality and companionship notwithstanding) more differentiation of gender roles. Liberal and socialist feminists called for mandatory maternity insurance and payment for housework so that women (and men) could focus on one task at one time. There was no room in their vision of household organization for the messy combination of housework and paid labor. Instead, they envisioned the separation of household, childrearing, and workplace; men and women as individuals could freely chose how to allocate their time.

With such fundamentally different views, little feminist consensus was

---

[24] See Durand's angry speech in *Congrès . . . oeuvres et institutions*, 1913, p. 315.

[25] *Congrès . . . oeuvres et institutions*, 1900, 3:486. In 1913, one resolution proposed to reduce the work week in the "women's trades," sparking angry retorts that "no such thing existed." Another resolution urged feminists to study—and, implicitly, promote—married women's part-time work, a proposal that also enraged many at the congress. Those on each side of the debate accused the others of being out of touch with "new" developments in feminism. *Congrès . . . oeuvres et institutions*, 1913, pp. 512–18.

possible. Leaders like Durand and Bonnevial could often summon majorities in feminist congresses. Their disproportionate influence in feminist circles, however, disguised the weakness of both liberal and socialist feminism in the larger political culture. Pulled by the strong social catholic strand, the French women's movement was often swallowed up in natalist currents.

A WOMAN'S WAGE—FEMINIST CONCEPTIONS

Until the turn of the century, labor legislation had focused on working conditions—regulating night work and sanitary standards, setting maximum hours, and requiring days off for rest. After 1900, reformers began to urge intervention in the wage itself. Raoul Jay, professor of law and an important player in government and international reform circles, explained the new consensus this way: poor housing, unsanitary workshops, and long hours should be seen as symptoms of a more basic problem. "Wages are the heart of the question."[26] The Office du Travail's statistical studies of wages and standards of living underscored the shifting emphasis and acknowledged state interest in wage policy as a means to social peace. As this new interest became clear, feminists began to articulate their views on the subject, asserting the centrality of gender concerns and trying to change the terms of discussion.

The first statement of a feminist understanding of these issues came from Marie Bonnevial in a wide-ranging and brilliant report from the labor section of the 1900 Congrès international de la condition et des droits des femmes (International Congress on the Condition and Rights of Women). The question that so preoccupied policymakers, she argued, had been wrongly posed. The "problem" with women's work was not the corruption of morals, the collapse of the family, or, as the natalists saw it, the falling population and "decline of the race." Female labor was simply grossly underpaid.[27]

Bonnevial urged her audience to make women's wages *the* central feminist issue. In the labor force, wage inequality between men and women created corrosive competition between the sexes. In the family, it deepened women's dependence on men, corrupting the marriage relation and love.[28] Above all, women's wages were the principal measure of women's devalued worth. Bonnevial contested all of the political economists' various explanations for wage inequality: women's alleged lower productivity, their intermittent participation in the labor force, their secondary role in the family, the mechanization of women's traditional tasks, and so on. Wage inequality,

[26] ANFPLT, *Le minimum de salaire dans l'industrie à domicile* (Paris, 1912), pp. 79–80.
[27] *Congrès . . . droits des femmes*, 1900, pp. 29, 42.
[28] Ibid.

she argued instead, had been produced by social definitions of women's needs and aspirations: the notion that women were supported by men, that women had limited needs, and that feminine virtue consisted of resignation and martyred self-sacrifice. Bonnevial suggestively linked the latter assumptions to a residual combination of early modern corporate distinctions between "noble" and "servile" work and Catholic images of work as punishment.[29] In twentieth-century culture, a wage had become the accepted benchmark of value. She put it bluntly: "The individual is only worth as much as the producer."[30] But the wage expressed nothing more than cultural assumptions. Feminists thus had to contest their culture's undervaluing of women by raising women's wages.[31]

The 1900 Congrès international de la condition et des droits des femmes gave its ringing endorsement to Bonnevial's call for wage parity; other feminists made similar points in speeches and writings; and the point registered in larger political circles. Feminist arguments squarely challenged theories that a woman's wage was "secondary." They likewise contested trade union men's demands for a "family wage," which both assumed and prescribed female economic dependence. Charles Poisson, author of one of the cascade of books on women's earnings in the first decade of the twentieth century, called "equal pay for equal work" the "war cry of feminists."[32] He understood the stakes of the debate: codifying a new wage policy involved spelling out assumptions about family, gender, and individuality, as well as about class and social hierarchies.

In 1900, a minimum wage seemed perilously close to socialism.[33] Over the next ten years, however, the political terrain shifted dramatically, and feminist stances changed accordingly. By 1910, feminists like Gabrielle Duchêne and Jeanne Bouvier emerged as the strongest supporters of minimum wage legislation, making arguments that strongly echoed Bonnevial's. Duchêne was head of the French Office on Homework, active in the Consumers' Leagues, and head of the "work" section of the National Council of French Women—an organization with twenty-one thousand members and, by 1910, one of the leading feminist advocates of minimum wage legislation. Like Bonnevial, Duchêne emphasized the wide-ranging repercussions of wage inequality and female poverty. Reforms centering on hours and hygiene, or restricting access to "dangerous" trades had proven ineffective.

[29] Ibid., pp. 30, 34.

[30] "La femme et la question économique," *Actes du Congrès féminist international de Bruxelles*, p. 73.

[31] *Congrès . . . droits des femmes*, 1900, p. 42. See her other speech in *Actes du Congrès féminist international de Bruxelles*, p. 73.

[32] Poisson, *Le salaire des femmes*; Haussonville, *Salaires et misères de femmes*; Gonnard, *La femme dans l'industrie*; and Guerrier, *Le salaire de la femme*.

[33] The congress to which Bonnevial spoke rallied behind the slogan of "equal pay for equal work," but voted down a state-imposed minimum wage. *Congrès . . . droits des femmes*, 1900, pp. 42–44.

Traditional nostrums, like consumer education, apprenticeship and technical education, and union organization did not go to the heart of revaluing women's work. Wages, Duchêne argued, were the core issue.[34] Duchêne's report occupied two sessions at the 1913 Congrès des oeuvres et institutions féminines. With very little controversy that congress endorsed a resolution calling for the regulation of homework and a broad minimum wage bill guaranteeing a "living" wage for both sexes.[35]

By the 1910s, feminists of clashing political persuasions could agree on a minimum wage bill. Liberal feminists, once vociferously opposed to protective legislation, agreed with the principle of revaluing women's work, raising all wages to a new minimum. They were also willing to back away from the orthodox liberalism of earlier decades. Social catholics had long been less wary of state intervention per se. They hoped a minimum wage bill would raise the earnings of homeworkers, humanizing a kind of work they considered morally superior and in grave jeopardy. A third group of women, closer to socialism (one that included Bonnevial, Bouvard, Bouvier, and Pelletier), was eager to champion any measure that offered to challenge, at long last, the class and gender dogmas of political economy. Like the liberals, this group hoped that a minimum wage would help to eliminate homework and female casual labor. Consensus behind the resolution, in short, masked important disagreements on matters of principle as well as clashing expectations about the measure's practical effects.

Despite their disagreements, feminists helped turn debates about women's wages into a broader examination of the relationship between work, needs, and value. As most feminists conceived it, a minimum wage for women (or women and men) fit into the larger feminist project of restoring the social value of womanhood and female economic independence. Promoting as they did a minimum *living* wage, they explicitly challenged assumptions that women were lesser producers, unskilled workers, and dependent beings, with fewer needs than men. Yet internal discord inhibited feminists' efforts to carry this vision outside the halls of their congresses. And outside of those halls, criss-crossed alliances, political and social caution, and a powerful manufacturers' lobby made reform anguished and difficult.

THE MINIMUM WAGE BILL

Feminist debates offered a microcosm of French political culture. Marie Bonnevial, Stephanie Bouvard, and Jeanne Bouvier hewed to a trade union

[34] Duchêne, "Le relèvement du salaire"; *Le travail à domicile* (brochure published by French Office of Homework, 1914). *Le droit à la vie et le minimum de salaire* (pamphlet published by the Shirtwaist-Lingerie Union, 1917). On Duchêne's work with Bouvier, see their papers in the Bouglé Collection at the Bibliothèque Historique de la Ville de Paris.

[35] "Le relèvement du salaire," pp. 45–46. This session dealt with a bill then being considered in the Chamber of Deputies (of which more in the next section), and feminists specifically demanded that homeworkers' wages be raised to the same level as shopworkers'.

perspective; Gabrielle Duchêne and Léonie Chaptal represented social catholicism; and Marguerite Durand was moving, in turn-of-the-century fashion, from liberalism toward solidarism. Just as feminist support for a minimum wage bill brought together different currents of thought, so the bill
that finally passed represented mixed constituencies and intentions. The
same dilemmas that tangled feminist debates also vexed policymakers and
legislators: Should state legislation regulate women's work separately?
What gender assumptions lay behind different wage proposals? What
would eliminating homework mean for the nation's industries, French family life, or gender roles?

By the turn of the century, a combination of domestic and international
forces had increased the pressure for some kind of measure reforming
homework.[36] Groups like the Consumers' Leagues and ANFPLT lobbied
internationally for the extension and enforcement of labor laws everywhere.
In 1901, the government established a French Office on Homework to link
up with these larger efforts, report back from international conferences, and
recommend French initiatives. The Office brought together interested parties and experts, like Pierre Dumas of the Federation of Clothing Workers,
Jeanne Bouvier from the shirtmakers, feminists Louise Compain and Gabrielle Duchêne, and various legislators to discuss reform proposals. In the
1890s, the English House of Lords' investigation of sweating had pressed
the more conservative French into studying homework; in 1909 the English
Trades Boards Act, which set minimum wages for all workers in sweated
industries, made French advocates of reform measures more adamant.[37]

The history of the French minimum wage bill is a tangled one. The measure that passed into law in 1915 began as a social catholic proposal, sponsored by Albert De Mun. The proposed measure was broadly conceived, at
least compared to the bill that eventually passed. It covered all homeworkers, male and female, in all industries where they were employed, and
it required that homeworkers be paid a "living wage." Although it was modeled on the English Trades Boards Act of 1909, De Mun's bill rose from
specifically French and social catholic concerns. It aimed to rescue home
industries from deteriorating conditions and to put them on the kind of
footing envisioned by the social catholic feminists.

In this as in his other reform initiatives, De Mun's concern with family
and patriarchal authority was palpable. But his bill was not gender-specific.

[36] Laws on tenement manufacturing were the American strategy, but the international reform movement preferred minimum wage measures. See Boris, *Home to Work*.

[37] New Zealand and Australia (Victoria) had established wage boards in the 1890s. In 1900,
Germany passed a bill requiring employers with homeworkers in their labor force to keep wage
books. On international legislation, see Shallcross, *Industrial Homework*. On the French Office
du Travail, see Bouvier papers in the Bouglé Collection at the Bibliothèque Historique de la
Ville de Paris.

Intervention in wage contracts was justified by a broader critique of market society.[38] Social relations could not be entrusted to the vagaries of the free market, and human labor could not be appraised by the laws of supply and demand. "Work is not simply another commodity," De Mun said.[39] Christian principles of human worth and dignity trumped the precepts of laissez-faire. Social catholic notions of economic justice decidedly did not involve fundamental redistribution of wealth. Still, De Mun pegged the minimum wage to Catholic versions of demands for a "living" or "just" wage— demands that had been articulated with some ambiguity in Leo XIII's papal encyclical of 1891. Such a wage, the pope said, would enable a hard-working man to support his family; justice should reward virtue and promote paternal authority.[40]

De Mun's bill was a far cry from longstanding, bolder socialist proposals. Socialist deputies in France had been proposing such a universal minimum wage since the 1890s. Their proposals were not limited to homeworkers; to the contrary, socialists hoped that better wages industry-wide would help eliminate the kind of casual labor that they associated with homework. Socialists also had a more expansive vision of workers' needs and, thus, of what constituted a "living wage." In their view, the purpose of a minimum wage was not simply to assure daily bread for the deserving poor. It was part of a larger effort to redistribute the benefits of modern technology and industry, giving workers security, shorter working days, and access to leisure, culture, and the "wealth that they [the workers] had helped to create."[41] Socialists saw a minimum wage, alongside the eight-hour day and "English week" as the elements of a new, modern, industrial order.[42] De Mun's 1909 proposal was not their bill.[43]

[38] De Mun later accepted gender-specific legislation, but he started with this broader position.

[39] De Mun quoted in Duchêne, "Le relèvement du salaire," p. 5.

[40] De Mun could hardly invoke the pope on women's wages; the encyclical asserted that women's role and destiny were motherhood. See Pedersen, *Family, Dependence, and the Origins of the Welfare State*, p. 63; and Pic, *Traité élémentaire*, p. 641. The Catholic Church opposed trade unions and strikes, and social catholics like Henriette Brunhes contrasted their version of a minimum wage with the "illegal minimum" set by labor action. See Bouvier papers.

[41] Levasseur, *Questions ouvrières*, chap. 8 generally and p. 456 on socialist "minimum d'existence." See also Willoughby, *La situation des ouvrières*, p. 158; Pic, *Traité élémentaire*, p. 641; Boyaval, *La lutte contre le sweating-system*, p. 342.

[42] The logic of socialist wage demands was less overtly patriarchal than that of social catholics, but it was nonetheless inextricable from demands for a family wage paid to a male breadwinner, the elimination of casual labor, and a vision of a social order in which working-class wives would devote themselves to family and domesticity. See Paul Lafargue, *Le droit à la paresse* (1892), and chapter 6 above.

[43] In 1907, the socialists proposed their own bill for a universal "minimum existence," or "living wage," which explicitly tied wages to workers' needs and also required that piece rates be replaced by hourly wages. See Mény, *Le travail à domicile*, p. 317. In the 1913 Chamber of

Social catholic sponsorship of their own minimum wage bill seemed a calculated effort to shore up their credentials as a party of change, bidding for wider audiences and presenting themselves as the party of moderate reform. "You do not have a monopoly on social questions," angry social catholic deputies shouted at their socialist rivals during the debates on the minimum wage bill.[44] By taking up the cause of sweated homeworkers, social catholics could claim to be remedying the *limited* failures of the market, representing the interests of workers neglected by the union movement, expressing concern for women, and working on the urgent problem of declining fertility.

Different wage proposals found support among very different constituencies. Trade unions, like the socialist deputies, pressed for universal or classwide wage legislation and a generously defined living wage, although in practice they envisioned working-class men as the beneficiaries of such a measure. They mustered little enthusiasm for a narrower measure covering homeworkers—except insofar as it raised a minimum wage high enough to reduce competition from homeworkers or made homeworkers less attractive to employers. When clothing manufacturers warned that wage legislation would lead to the disappearance of homework, trade union leaders were unperturbed.[45] Likewise, socialist and liberal feminists wanted to set minimums high enough to discourage homework, pushing women out of what they considered casual labor and into the mainstream of the labor force. Social catholic intentions were different. Their critique of political economy and the free market in labor echoed the socialists'. But their objective was to revive homework and strengthen precisely the kind of family economy and social order that socialists and many feminists wanted to leave behind. And for the last group of reformers, a broad-based group of radicals and solidarists tied into the ANFPLT and international movements for labor law reform, minimum wage legislation involved a balancing act. They wanted to bring France into line with the other industrial nations, remedying the worst abuses of sweated labor. Could they change the wage structure without transforming the organization of either industry or family labor?

Intentions and interests behind the bill, then, were not only mixed, but contradictory. De Mun's bill shuttled between legislative committees from

Deputies debate on the bill, socialists tried to reassert their version of the minimum wage, calling for much wider coverage and casting the minimum wage as a class rather than a gender issue. Bouvier papers, box 18, folder 1.

[44] Bouvier papers, box 18, folder 1.

[45] Keufer, at the hearings of the CST, *Rapport sur le travail des femmes à domicile*, pp. 67–68. On the CGT's relative indifference to this particular bill, see Bouvier, *Mes mémoires*; and Willoughby, *La situation des ouvrières*, p. 151.

1909 to 1913. During this time, in classic Third Republic fashion, different interests threatened to cancel each other out.

Women's Work? A Women's Bill?

In committee, the most vigorous debate centered on whether or not the law on homework should cover both sexes. The strategy of manufacturers and conservatives was to stave off any broad intervention in wage policy by narrowing the bill to women and keeping the minimums very low. Several clothing manufacturers spoke against any measure, arguing that home-workers were already perfectly well paid for labor that was unskilled and casual. Nearly all warned that state intervention would eliminate home-work, with disastrous moral and social consequences for women and the fabric of family life. At the CST's hearings on the bill, one manufacturer after another testified that low "secondary" wages were the inevitable result of accommodating the industrial world to the rhythms of family life.[46] The only homeworkers of significance were women, and insofar as wages were low, that was because the workers were women. Homework—they were adamant on this score—was only a gender issue.

The CST met the manufacturers' lobby more than halfway, radically revising De Mun's proposal. The CST report was penned by the committee's ranking conservative, also a former director of the Magasins du Louvre, one of the oldest department stores in Paris. His report urged that the law apply only to women, and only to clothing workers, whose case was deemed "the best known, the most touching, the most moving."[47] The CST also reduced fines, altered grievance procedures so as to favor the manufacturers, and dropped the minimum rate.[48]

De Mun and a diverse handful of allies continued to argue for the original proposal that covered all homeworkers. At ANFPLT hearings, deputies and union representatives from Saint-Etienne, center of the ribbon weaving industry, were particularly adamant about the need to regulate all homework, regardless of the sex of the worker. Many pointed out that the lingerie workers of Paris and Argenton were no worse off than homeworkers in

[46] CST, *Rapport sur le travail des femmes à domicile*, pp. 22–35; and Edouard Payen, *La réglementation du travail*, brochure published by Society of Merchants and Manufacturers (Paris, 1913); Motteau quoting Jules Simon and Emile Cheysson on behalf of manufacturers at ANFPLT, *Le minimum de salaire*, p. 89.

[47] ANFPLT, *Le minimum de salaire*, pp. 93–94. The law did not cover the knitting industry of the Aube; the silk industry, which spread out over five or six departments; workers in the mountains of the Jura; handkerchief makers in the Cambresis; and many others.

[48] The minimum wage was set at the rate of "an unskilled female laborer doing common sewing work." On the law, see Boyaval, *La lutte contre le sweating system*; Lupiac, *La loi du 10 juillet*; and Odry, *Application de la loi*.

other industries. Liberal feminists also tried to have the classwide provisions reinstated. "As women, we should want to protect men's work as well
as women's. As feminists, we demand equality in protection as well as in
rights," testified the prominent feminist Cécile Brunschwig, to the exasperation of others who accused her of trying to subvert any chance of reform. "The logical conclusion of your argument, Madame," responded one
member, "would be to do nothing for women because we do nothing for
men."[49] When Louise Compain remarked that the English minimum wage
bill covered men as well as women, and asked why the French republic
would not follow suit, the president of the ANFPLT snapped, "Because the
French Republic has more difficulties, because we are less advanced than
England."[50] Women trade union representatives from the Seamstresses and
Lingerie Workers of the Seine underscored how many men worked at
home. The deputies' emphasis on women's preferences for homework ob-
scured the role of manufacturers' calculations in its tenacity. Constant reference to women's secondary role in the family and to their "weakness" or
"passivity" as the reason for low wages ignored the importance of other
factors, like competition from large workshops and convent and prison labor, as well as from crowded labor markets. The solution lay in minimum
wages for all workers, not special measures for women.[51] Last, a series of
sociologists and legal experts also argued against seeing the issue solely in
gender terms. They recognized that doing so ran against powerful currents
of conviction. At hearings before the ANFPLT, Cécile Brunschwig, Georges
Alfassa, and Georges Mény insisted, despite the obvious skepticism of their
colleagues, that many men worked in the same home industries as women
and that male homeworkers were as poorly paid as their female counterparts.[52] "There are men, young fellows, and even more often old men who
are working at exactly the same task as women," said Raoul Jay, who openly
challenged the assumptions informing the public debate on labor legislation. Why were people so certain that men could defend themselves and
women could not? Why did they believe that women undercut men and
never vice versa? Why did they insist on seeing women's work as an entirely

[49] ANFPLT, *Le minimum de salaire*, p. 127.

[50] See ANFPLT, *Le minimum de salaire*, pp. 48, 81–87, 101–2, and 129. The feminist *Congrès . . . oeuvres et institutions* meeting in 1913 demanded that that the bill cover men. But
Brunschwig, Compain, and Duchêne, all of whom had testified before various government
committees and clearly were discouraged by the hostility they encountered, advised fellow
feminists to defer to public opinion and accept a lesser measure. *Congrès . . . oeuvres et institutions*, 1913, pp. 512, 516.

[51] ANFPLT, *Le minimum de salaire*, p. 159; and CST, *Rapport sur le travail des femmes à
domicile*, p. 38. In other contexts, however, the labor movement was willing to support gender-
specific legislation.

[52] See testimony in ANFPLT, *Le minimum de salaire*, pp. 101–2, 117–19, 121, 124, 155.

distinct form of labor, following different principles and requiring separate regulation?[53]

Jay's opponents were quick to reaffirm traditional gender certainties. The Christian Democrat Lémire indignantly demanded the discussion return to first principles. It would plainly be ludicrous to see men and women in the same way: men did not need to be in their homes. "In no country in the world would a woman want a man to stay at home," he asserted confidently. The minimum wage bill was self-evidently "a law intended for women; we should not even be talking about men."[54] Léonie Chaptal concurred, disagreeing with liberal feminists who were holding out for a broader bill. "We have a very great victory to win for women; we cannot compromise our chances by fighting for men. . . . What is more, frankly, I am not interested in the wages of men who work at home. . . . Men can go to the shop."[55] No one denied that thousands of male furniture makers, ribbon weavers, tailors, and shoemakers worked at home. But whatever its social realities, male homework, as one reformer put it, had no "social significance."[56] If men worked at home, so the dominant thinking went, that was incidental to their role and duties in the family. As a matter of social policy, it did not warrant further discussion.

Conventions of economic thought, buttressed by turn-of-the century social research, also played a decisive role in narrowing the bill's provisions to women. Women's wages, as we have already seen, were repeatedly cast as an economic anomaly, one that did not challenge the paradigm of classical economics. As one lawmaker put it, rehearsing the justification for intervention, "Women's work is not subject to the law of supply and demand."[57] Women's nature, double duty, and position in the family prevented them from being competitive bargainers in the marketplace. To extend minimum wage provisions to men, who were conceived as freely contracting individuals, was a considerably more radical proposal—"an absolutely different goal."[58] Women and men did not do the same jobs, and women worked at home because they were women. With these certainties intact, a far more modest bill, setting minimum wages for women homeworkers in the clothing industry, went through the Chamber of Deputies and Senate.

As the bill was narrowed to women, its definitions of a "minimum" wage contracted.[59] De Mun's original bill called for a "living" wage. De Mun,

---

[53] Ibid., pp. 101–3.
[54] ibid., p. 123.
[55] Ibid., p. 121.
[56] Coupat, at ibid., p. 129.
[57] ANFPLT, *Le minimum de salaire*, p. 151.
[58] Fagnot, at ibid., p. 99.
[59] Willoughby, *La situation des ouvrières*, Odry, *Application de la loi*; Lupiac, *La loi du 10 juillet*.

trade union leaders, and various social researchers recommended defining the minimum as the rate of an average shop hand in the same branch of the clothing industry. Doing so would reduce competition between the different groups of laborers and be seen as a gesture toward the trade unions. It would also establish that homework was not inherently "cheap" and poor quality labor.[60] Manufacturers found De Mun's proposal outrageous, insisting that the home industries were the refuge of women without craft or skill, that high wages would ruin France's industry, and (backpedaling) that in any case national minimums were unworkable.[61] At the other end of the political spectrum, Jeanne Bouvier and Gabrielle Duchêne considered De Mun's proposal to use the average shopworker's wage as a minimum too cautious. Bouvier was one of the few to suggest that the minimum should correspond to a working woman's *needs*, by which measure shop hands' rates should be raised as well. Bouvier's position was in line with feminist conceptions of a minimum "living" wage for women as a means of economic independence, the conception specifically endorsed by the feminist congress of 1913.[62]

None of the more sweeping views prevailed.[63] Deputy Berthod, a radical republican (centrist) who sponsored the bill in the Chamber of Deputies in 1913 pointedly distanced his legislation from any "vague" or socialist demands.[64] Berthod's bill did not represent any concession to socialist or even social catholic aspirations for a "living," "just," or "family" wage, with all that those aspirations might entail; he explicitly repudiated that language.[65] Expectations and hopes embodied in socialist (and, to a lesser extent, social catholic) proposals—supporting a household, sharing in the nation's wealth, gaining access to the "good society," leisure, and culture—were utterly absent in this measure and the debate surrounding it. That the bill applied only to women made it easier to retreat from the broader minimum wage projects, with their gender-bound objectives and imagery. As Marie Bonnevial had pointed out thirteen years earlier, social definitions of a woman's needs and expectations were far more constricted. To earn the bare

---

[60] De Mun and Mény, ANFPLT, *Le minimum de salaire*, pp. 55–58.

[61] CST, *Rapport sur le travail des femmes à domicile*, 22–35.

[62] During her time on the CST, Bouvier did her own survey on homework, drawing up budgets. Bouvier papers, box 19.

[63] Berthod and some social catholics remarked that some legislators would doubtless find these wages too high. Their apologies were greeted with hoots of derision from the socialists. Bouvier papers, box 18, folder 1. On how the wage committees worked, see Willoughby, *La situation des ouvrières*, pp. 119–22.

[64] Clippings and notes in Bouvier papers, box 18, folder 1.

[65] The question of whether or not a working *man's* wage should enable him to support a family was adjourned. On these matters, see Pedersen, *Family, Dependence, and the Origins of the Welfare State*.

necessities, avoiding misery and prostitution seemed enough. The vast majority of legislators considered such larger objectives irrelevant in a bill directed at women. As one legislator explained, the law established "a *minimum* wage, not a *living* wage."[66] Berthod made it explicit. "We are restricting this bill to homeworkers, and to women. We are not introducing new principles into legislation, but rather extending the application of well-established principles: these poor women are legally considered minors for whom we may pass protective measures."[67] Speeches that underscored women's simple needs and their solely domestic desires brought enthusiastic applause from most deputies.[68]

It is difficult, then, to find more than faint traces of bolder aspirations in the 1915 minimum wage bill. Nothing could have been further from the feminist goals of asserting the dignity of women's work and valuing their contribution to the national and family economy. The bleak and miserabilist portrait of homeworkers painted in much of the reform literature legitimated state intervention in the free market of labor. Yet the same convictions that justified intervention foreclosed setting a decent minimum; that such miserable women could aspire to independence or sharing in a world of plenty became, in the context of this debate, nearly unimaginable. The minimum wage to which they were entitled was envisaged as charity rather than justice.[69] The principle of wage parity between the sexes was tersely rejected; the law pegged women homeworkers' wages to those of *women* (not men) in the shop. Last, it was clear that the law did not bring homeworkers out of their limbo as regards labor law. Jeanne Bouvier, who along with Gabrielle Duchêne worked indefatigably to pass the bill and to enforce it once it became law, optimistically hoped that the new law would confer new status on homeworkers: entitled to a minimum wage, they no longer would be seen as casual laborers. She was frustrated when the postwar legislature refused to include homeworkers in laws establishing insurance against work-related accidents, and angry at the CGT for refusing to protest these exclusions and, she charged, largely ignoring its role in enforcing the 1915 law. More than ten years after the law passed, Bouvier and others were still campaigning for revisions that would give it some teeth.[70]

---

[66] Bouvier papers, box 18, folder 1.

[67] Quoted in Willoughby, *La situation des ouvrières*, p. 82. Natalist concerns ran through the debates as well, with one senator asking how the nation could continue to squander "ce capital admirable de la France, la jeune fille capable de devenir une honnête et une féconde mère de famille" [our national capital, a young girl able to become an honest and fertile mother of a family]. Cited in Bouvier, *La lingerie et les lingères*, p. 309.

[68] *Journal Officiel*, November, 13–14, 1913. Bouvier papers, box 18, folder 1.

[69] This was Brunschwig's analysis. *Congrès . . . oeuvres et institutions*, 1913, p. 512.

[70] Bouvier, *Mes mémoires*, p. 153; and Bouvier papers, box 18, folder 1 and box 19, folder b.

The English Trades Boards Act

A brief comparative analysis will highlight the distinctively French features of this legislation and the class and gender politics that lay behind it. The English Trades Boards Act, passed in 1909, set minimum wages in all industries where the Minister of Labour deemed wages substandard. It applied to shop as well as homeworkers, and to both sexes. The strength of the English trade union movement was a crucial factor in the English statute's passage. The act aimed to create something like a trade union model in the seemingly unorganizable sweated industries, and the "trades boards" that set wages worked by a process much like collective bargaining.[71] The act reflected a trade union perspective in another respect: it aimed to reduce casual labor and to encourage labor that paid a family wage. Families that scraped together a living from the meager earnings of husbands, wives, and children, and in which all family members worked at household chores— families, in other words, that fit an older model of the family economy— were to become part of the past. English labor reformers, like the "modernizing" French reformers considered in chapter 7, envisioned a society where technology and better wages would make workers more productive; schooling would make working-class children better laborers; higher earnings would enable working-class women to withdraw from the labor force; and heightened domesticity would moralize the working-class families and improve the standard of living. In sociological terms they hoped for a model of the family economy with more gender (and age) differentiation. The English alliance of trade unions and social democracy, in which women reformers played an important role, was an effective one, and the British state, as Susan Pedersen has demonstrated, could be pressed toward upholding such a model of family life and a "breadwinner" wage for men.[72]

By contrast, the French labor movement and French socialism were small and politically fragmented, unable to impose their vision in a political culture increasingly dominated by nationalism and natalism. French feminists were less elitist and marginal than many historians have implied. But social catholics had the strongest base of support, and they were willing to settle for a narrow measure offering a minimum to women. Their original proposal, as we have seen, refused the neat packaging of gender and was considerably more generous in its allowances, but they refused to ally with socialists or

[71] Comparisons may be pieced together from Cross, *A Quest for Time*; Pedersen, *Family, Dependence, and the Origins of the Welfare State*; Rose, *Limited Livelihoods*; Shallcross, *Industrial Homework*; Willoughby, *La situation des ouvrières*; Bythell, *The Sweated Trades*; and Schmiechen, *Sweated Industries*.

[72] The English Trade Boards Act did not guarantee a living wage, though it gave the boards wide latitude in determining how to set the minimum. Willoughby, *La situation des ouvrières*, pp. 83–88.

labor to press through a universal minimum. In France, conservative business opposition to labor reform ran deep. Although many manufacturers in other industries were eager to end the clothing industry's virtual exemption from labor laws, and, like their British counterparts impatient with the "backward" behavior of sectors of the economy, they fought hard against setting any broader precedents for state intervention in wage matters.[73]

Conclusion

Wage policy is also family policy and gender policy.[74] These other matters were never far from the surface of debates on a minimum wage and anti-sweating measures. Did the interests of "family life"—variously defined as natalism, patriarchal authority, the viability of the family economy, leisure and consumption—dictate the separation of home and work, protecting the family from the corrosive forces and rhythms of the industrial world? Or did the home and the family need to be preserved as an economic unit? How would the state establish a minimum wage, and what social calculations and gender assumptions would be embedded therein? The French answers to these questions were extremely cautious, and the political majority was clearly reluctant to break with its view of "French" family industry and its concomitant gender relations.

Georges Mény was one of several French reformers who tried to ease his contemporaries' fears that a minimum wage would encourage factories and destroy "traditional" home industries. Worries that homework would disappear were groundless, he said; dispersed production was fundamental to the manufacturing strategies in many industries. But even if homework were to contract, Mény continued, the social consequences might be beneficial. Agriculture could absorb the surplus of female labor that might be produced by the reduction of homework. Mény suggested that women might be able to find "other kinds of work," though his imagination did not stray very far on this subject. But he also proposed a different view of gender relations and the family economy, the one preferred by labor leaders, modernist social scientists, and the English reformers. Women could save their families money by doing chores well, by cooking inexpensive meals, and by investing time in their households rather than adding earnings to the family economy. "If then, regulation of small industry would lead to its reduction (and we do not think that it will) that would be no cause for sorrow."[75]

[73] See Cross, A Quest for Time; and Payen, La reglementation.

[74] Kessler-Harris, A Woman's Wage; and Pedersen, Family, Dependence, and the Origins of the Welfare State.

[75] Mény, Le travail à domicile, pp. 259–60. For summaries of this view, see also Keufer in CST, Rapport sur le travail des femmes à domicile; Paul Leroy-Beaulieu, Le travail des femmes au XIX siècle; Aftalion, Le développement de la fabrique; Boyaval, La lutte contre le sweating system, pp. 100–104.

Across the Channel, in England, such views were embedded in wage policy. In France they were not. The torrent of anti-sweating literature had made pure nostalgia for a Le Playan world of family industry impossible. Still, few could agree on an alternative vision of the family economy.[76] Women were vital to the French labor force and family economies. French industries depended on longer hours and, therefore, cheaper labor. Opposed to a broader wage policy, reluctant to abandon familiar gender certainties, and concerned not to disrupt the fragile equilibrium of the family economy, the French legislature settled for a singularly narrow bill. From this perspective, the 1915 minimum wage bill for homeworkers can be seen as a revealing example of Third Republic gridlock on gender relations and industrial modernity.

As the Third Republic moved hesitantly toward increasing the interventionist powers of the state, wage policy and the assumptions embedded in it became the subject of intensive research and impassioned polemic. For all the parties to the debate—solidarists, socialists, social catholics, and feminists of varying political persuasions—wage policy was key to their vision of a social harmony, industrial order, and gender relations. Disputes over these questions, for all their technicalities, thus cast a searching light not only on the different ways of understanding how the "problem" of women's work could be framed, but also on clashing conceptions of the industrial future in prewar France.

[76] In the postwar period, the French government's family policy was expressed in the paternalist, corporatist form of family allowances rather than higher wages to male "heads of households." This policy provided French mothers with more resources, but French women with fewer rights. Pedersen, *Family, Dependence, and the Origins of the Welfare State*.

CONCLUSION

THE MINIMUM WAGE bill dramatizes crucial changes that occurred in the decades around the turn of the century. Under the weight of a protracted economic recession and rising nationalism, liberal, laissez-faire certainties collapsed. A secular and newly authoritative social science stepped into the breach, identifying questions and supplying data to a newly interventionist state. The groundswell of labor, socialist, and feminist militancy brought a new urgency to the debates. Economic difficulties along with a cultural crisis created real dilemmas for conservatives—dilemmas about the character of the French economy, the central role of women therein, and the future of the working-class family. The debate over wage policy unfolded against the backdrop of deteriorating international relations, intensified nationalism, and anxiety about depopulation and decline of the "race." By the time the bill was passed, of course, France was at war; the outbreak of hostilities encouraged French legislators to close debate and agree on a compromise reform meant to shore up French family industries. But the 1915 bill also fits into a larger context and offers an opportunity to consider the road traveled from the world of the late eighteenth century to that of the twentieth.

The central importance of wage issues gives one indication of the changes. By the turn of the century, wage policy had become the fulcrum of the new relationship between government, labor, and gender that we now call the welfare state. Wages and household budgets took center stage in government sociological studies. In the place of the laws of the market, the new "social economy" of the late nineteenth century offered statistical studies of earnings and their relationship to social and economic stability. The late-nineteenth-century labor movement invested its hopes and visions of the good society in wage demands. The concerns for patriarchal authority and household governance so forcefully advanced by the eighteenth-century tailors' guilds were rearticulated as demands for a family wage for men. Labor leaders, like many secular reformers, saw the family wage as a mark of modern family arrangements and a route to a better standard of living.

The significance and very meaning of gender had also changed. In the debates over the minimum wage bill, homeworkers were women workers; *travail à domicile* was *travail féminin*.[1] This had not always been so. In the eighteenth century, outwork was usually referred to as "false" or "clandestine" work. Le Play and other mid-nineteenth-century sociologists used the

---

[1] Guilbert and Isambert-Jamati, *Travail féminin*.

term "dispersed production." The late-nineteenth-century term of choice, "homework," was a relatively new phrase. It was more strongly associated with home as the province of women—tied to a nineteenth-century conception of gender as a division of labor, social spheres, and responsibilities.[2]

In the eighteenth-century discussions, the gender of what the guild world called "false" workers was not necessarily relevant. In the forging of early-twentieth-century social policy, by contrast, the gender of homeworkers frequently seemed the *only* relevant factor or category of analysis. As the reformer cited in the last chapter so strikingly put it, male homeworkers had "no social significance." Between the two moments we have seen the erosion of gender as a relationship of authority and its construction as a division of labor. In this paradigm, which defined gender as a division of labor and spheres, male homeworkers were an anomaly. That outworkers were women served to explain their presence in the home and to naturalize what might otherwise disturb: women's low wages, long hours, and inferior position in the world of wage labor. Third Republic labor legislation worked squarely within this analytic framework; it operated on the dual assumption that women's work was readily distinguishable from men's and that "home" could be meaningfully distinguished from "shop."

In the last three chapters we have seen the labor movement, fin-de-siècle sociology, and many reformers trying to press a variety of issues into this paradigm of gender complementarity. These efforts did not always illuminate the issues. Casting men as producers and women as consumers, men as breadwinners and women as secondary wage earners, men's sphere as the shop and women's as the home distorted perceptions of women's role both in the family and in France's labor force, constricting interpretations of what working-class families needed and how they operated. Lingering over the distinctive pathologies of women's work distracted economists from equally important issues, like the crowded labor markets, economic fluctuations, and manufacturers' strategies that also cheapened labor.

Late-nineteenth-century feminism contributed to framing homework as a women's issue—calling *travail à domicile*, for instance, "the disease that is slowly killing the female labor force."[3] In doing so they tapped reservoirs of political energy by providing a sense of common purpose among women across class lines. They created a forum for debating conceptions of femininity, the basis for female economic well-being, and the respective roles of family and individualism in women's lives. At the same time, the literature of the anti-sweating movement in which women activists were so important

[2] The government studies of *travail à domicile* made a point of studying male homeworkers in the shoe industry. The more narrowly gendered understanding applied in discussions of government intervention, when the labor in question was considered a "problem."

[3] Mme Pégard, commenting on the government's 1911 study of homework. CST, *Rapport sur le travail des femmes à domicile*, p. 78.

contributed to constructing the image of women's work as pathological and undermined other feminist arguments about women's needs and rights as producers and citizens. What I have called the "miserabilist" portrait of women's work legitimated state intervention in the late nineteenth century, but limited that intervention to women and helped to seal the image of women as unskilled and casual workers, as dependent family members with correspondingly lesser needs, and as charity cases rather than deserving producers.

As the multitudes of workers in the garment trades—seamstresses in lingerie or ready-made men's clothing, collar-and-tie makers, vest makers, and so on—came to be seen as "homeworkers" or "women workers" and as their life stories were incorporated into the drama of cultural crisis, national decline, or the economic disenfranchisement of women, their specific interests fell from view. The enormous late-nineteenth-century literature on female labor—the spiraling numbers of treatises and articles bearing some version of the title "Women's Work and Wages"—also displaced discussion of still more general and troubling questions: How did society divide labor? Why were some jobs paid better than others? Questions about the sources of class hierarchies and economic inequality were transmuted into discussions of the social roles of the sexes. In short, the social question had become the question of women's work.

Let us once more put the garment industry in a larger perspective. The textile and garment industries (the two largest employers of women workers) are often portrayed as a study in contrasts. The textile trades supplied the most striking landmarks of nineteenth-century industrial modernity: mills, machines, and quintessential proletarians.[4] In historical narratives that centered on the drama of nineteenth-century industrialization wrenching women and their work from the home, the textile industry seemed to provide the best case in point. Garment making, in these accounts, was depicted as a tradition-ridden backwater, slow to adopt new technologies and modern forms of industrial organization. This conventional contrast is misleading. By the second half of the century, the garment trades were not only the largest, but also the most rapidly growing sector of female employment, vigorously expanding and modernizing. In an economy that was deeply and increasingly dependent on female labor (and the French economy has consistently had among the highest rates of female labor force participation in the industrial world), the garment trades were a pivotal economic sector. Between 1866 and 1906, when the number of women in the labor force rose by one million, an extraordinary 80 percent

---

[4] See Hilden, *Working Women*; Reddy, *The Rise of Market Culture*; Kathleen Canning, *Gender and the Changing Meanings of Work: Structures and Rhetorics in the Making of the Textile Factory Workplace in Germany, 1850–1914* (Ithaca, N.Y., forthcoming).

of that expansion went into the garment industry.[5] We have seen the crucial historical developments behind those figures: the gendering of the sewing machine; manufacturers' urgent needs for labor that was at once skilled, flexible, and inexpensive; and the expansion of networks of home laborers in the 1890s, when easy and aggressively promoted credit payment and small machines made it possible for women to move from declining sectors into the expanding garment industry.

More generally, though, the points underscored in this study of the garment industry apply to other industries, including textiles. Nowhere did the logic of technological change or industrial efficiency doom dispersed production or homework. Technological innovation was always and everywhere uneven, and industrial organization was shaped by an array of social and cultural forces. And neither men nor women's experiences took shape around the twin poles of home and work.

"Separate spheres" and "domesticity," then, are inadequate descriptions of nineteenth-century social developments. They have also been ill-understood as nineteenth-century prescriptions or norms. This study has suggested how we might reinterpret what these concepts meant, the expectations they conveyed, the aspirations they distilled, and the cultural authority they commanded. In an economy so reliant on female labor, France's conservatives, like Albert De Mun, did not invest their hopes in a "woman's sphere" sealed off from the world of labor, but instead in orderly and well-governed family economies. The problems arose when, in the 1890s, it became clear that homework did not match an idealized portrait of family industry. Secular, modernizing reformers like Augusta Moll-Weiss promoted a rationalized domesticity directed by a well-informed housewife, but with little effect. French working men did not expect their wives to withdraw from the labor force; instead they confronted the more difficult problem of reconciling their competing desires and claims on women's time and labor. From the point of view of working women in the late nineteenth century, to do piecework in the home was not to genuflect before cultural ideals of domesticity. Moreover, "domesticity" did not stand for womanly virtue and industriousness. Its range of meanings arose from a nascent consumer culture; it meant a higher standard of living and access to the goods that this new culture associated with the "home." These could only be at-

[5] Cottereau, "The Distinctiveness of Working-Class Culture," in Katznelson and Zolberg, eds., *Working-Class Formation*; Guilbert, *Les fonctions des femmes dans l'industrie*, pp. 42–43; idem, *Les femmes et les organizations syndicales*, pp. 13–14; and Levasseur, *Questions ouvrières*, pp. 271–75. For international comparisons, see Daric, *L'activité professionelle des femmes*; and Deldycke et al., *La population active et sa structure*, pp. 3, 29. The rates of female labor force participation were highest in Paris, not because of the diversity of employment opportunities, but because of the concentration of clothing trades in the capital. Statistique générale de la France, *Résultats statistiques du recensement générale: 1911*, 1:60–61, and *Résultats statistiques du recensement des industries . . . 1896*, 1:xx–xxi, 207–8.

tained by a combination of earning money and investing time and energy in the household.[6] It meant being able to either buy things or make them, which required skills as well as time. This is what gave the sewing machine, as both emblem and tool, its real appeal for working-class women. As a hybrid of waged and domestic labor, as a means of production and an object of consumption, it distilled key dimensions of their emergent modern identities.

World War I marks a watershed in this history in several important respects. In the short run, the departure of men for the front and the mustering of replacement female labor threw a particularly harsh light on the discrepancy between men's and women's earnings, exploded the fiction that women were "secondary wage earners," and sparked a wave of strikes in the clothing industry. The Shirtwaist-Lingerie Union turned both the shortcomings of the 1915 minimum wage bill and the gap between male and female wages into an effective organizing device, eventually winning a broader measure.[7] In the longer run, the postwar years saw a contraction of employment in the garment trades and the expansion, in particular, of clerical work. While homework in the clothing trades rose sharply in the immediate postwar period, it declined steadily afterward as married women sought and found better paid work. As it became clear that France could not "bring back the world that the war destroyed,"[8] and the seismic shifts of the war made possible a thoroughgoing reconsideration of the French economy, society, and the state, the discourse on modern, rationalized domesticity that we have seen emerging in the prewar decades came into its own. Yet even then, economic insecurity and the instability of working- and lower-middle-class incomes continued to undermine any such gender arrangements in the family.[9] Then as now, domesticity cannot be understood apart from changes in patterns of production and consumption, waged disentangled from unwaged labor, or participation in the labor force separated from the modernity of the home.

French women's livelihoods are no longer bound up with fabrics, fash-

---

[6] For a different calculation of time-money interests, but a similar view of domesticity and working women's identity, see Joanna Bourke, "Housewifery in Working-Class England, 1860–1914," *Past and Present* 143 (May 1994): 171–73.

[7] "Are women inferior to men?" "Is life less expensive for women than for men?" Federation of Clothing Workers' posters in Bouglé Collection, Henriette Coulmy papers, boxes 1 and 2. The minimum wage bill was extended to other trades in 1922 and to workers of both sexes in 1928. See also Bouvier papers, boxes 18 and 19, in the same collection.

[8] Roberts, *Civilization without Sexes*, p. 187.

[9] Robert L. Frost, "Machine Liberation: Inventing Housewives and Home Appliances in Interwar France,"*French Historical Studies* 18, no. 1 (Spring 1993): esp. 127–29; Martin, "Ménagère: Une profession?," pp. 89–109; Françoise Werner, "Du ménage à l'art ménager: L'évolution du travail ménager et son écho dans la presse féminine française de 1919 à 1939," *Le Mouvement Social* 129 (October–December 1984); and de Grazia, "The Arts of Purchase."

Adolphe Willette, "Journée du poilu." Poster for soldiers' leave, December 1915. The twentieth-century Penelope. The sewing chair has been kicked over in the surprise and delight of the reunion. The sewing machine has settled into a place alongside the dog, as an emblem of faithfulness in the iconography of domestic life.

ions, and sewing machines. But the very familiarity of the images in Adolphe Willette's poster for a soldier's day of leave in 1915—the comely modern woman at a machine, the sewing machine as icon of domesticity, and the suggestion of a timeless (non)history in which women have always made clothes and men have always fought wars—show that the images and understandings of gender and femininity that we have seen slowly take shape in the nineteenth century have proved remarkably enduring in our own.

BIBLIOGRAPHY

NATIONAL ARCHIVES

F 12 commerce and industry
    781 a b–e Paris: corporations d'arts et métiers
AD XI
    10–11 communautés d'arts et métiers: règlements et statuts
    20 édits, arrêts, lettres patentes, etc.
C parliamentary
    3019 enquête sur la situation des classes ouvrières, 1872–75
F 22 industrial statistics
F 7 police
    13740 Congrès national de la Fédération de l'habillement, 1910, 1912, 1914,
        1929, notes and press clippings
    13741 Habillement, 1920–29, and Chapeliers, 1906–21
    13880 Habillement, grèves des ouvriers: chemisiers, lingères, tailleurs, 1909–10
    13881 Habillement, Galeries Lafayette, Esders, 1911–14
    13882 Habillement, 1919–23, grève générale, 1923
    13883 Habillement, grève générale

ARCHIVES OF THE PREFECTURE OF POLICE

Lamoignon Collection

BA 151 Chambre syndicale des tailleurs, 1872–78
BA 152 Chambre syndicale des tailleurs, 1879–93
BA 173 Grèves—tailleurs, 1885–89
BA 182 Grèves: . . . dossier #206
BA 1376 Grève de l'habillement
BA 1394 Grèves: tailleurs, 1901–18
BA 1406 Grèves: tailleurs, 1876–1919, Seine
BA 1411 Chambre syndicale des brodeuses, lingères, couturières, 1874–83
BA 1423 Chambre syndicale de l'habillement, 1909–18
BA 1708–10 Cercles russes
BA 1711 Cercles polonais

BIBLIOTHÈQUE NATIONALE

Manuscripts

Joly de Fleury Collection 1776, volume 462, folios 117, 128–29, 154, 173; volume
    596, folios 73, 89–91, 96

Service Recueil

Journal illustré des Grands Magasins Dufayel

Palais de la nouveauté: affichage national 1889, 1892, 1893 (pamphlets describing Dufayel's advertising service)

Palais de la nouveauté: catalogues

Singer (compagnie) Paris: documents techniques et publicitaires

BIBLIOTHÈQUE HISTORIQUE DE LA VILLE DE PARIS: MARIE-LOUISE BOUGLÉ COLLECTION

Jeanne Bouvier Papers

Henriette Coulmy Papers

Gabrielle Duchêne Papers

MUSEUMS AND LIBRARIES WITH COLLECTIONS OF ENGRAVINGS, POSTCARDS, POSTERS, AND ADVERTISEMENTS

Bibliothèque Forney, Paris

Bibliothèque du Musée des Arts Décoratifs, Paris

Bibliothèque Nationale, Cabinet des Estampes, Paris

Conservatoire National des Arts et Métiers, Paris

Musée Crozatier, Le-Puy-en-Velay, Haute Loire

Musée de la Chemiserie et de l'Elégance Masculine, Argenton-sur-Creuse, Indre

Musée de la Mode et de la Costume, Paris

Musée de la Publicité (in Musée des Arts Décoratifs)

GOVERNMENT REPORTS AND DOCUMENTS

Chambre de commerce de Paris

Enquête sur les conditions du travail en France pendant l'année 1872. Paris, 1875. In AN, C3019.

Statistique de l'industrie à Paris, résultant de l'enquête faite par la Chambre de commerce, 1847–1848. Paris: Guillaumin et Cie, 1851.

Statistique de l'industrie à Paris, 1860. Paris: Guillaumin et Cie, 1864.

Ministère du commerce, de l'industrie, des postes et des télégraphes

CONSEIL SUPÉRIEUR DU TRAVAIL

Rapport sur le travail des femmes à domicile, session de 1910. Paris: Imprimerie nationale, 1911.

OFFICE DU TRAVAIL

Les associations professionelles ouvrières. 6 vols. Paris: Imprimerie nationale, 1899–1904.

Enquête sur le travail à domicile dans l'industrie de la chaussure. Paris: Imprimerie nationale, 1914.

Enquête sur le travail à domicile dans l'industrie de la fleur artificielle. Paris: Imprimerie nationale, 1913.

Enquête sur le travail à domicile dans l'industrie de la lingerie. 5 vols. Paris: Imprimerie nationale, 1907–11.

La petite industrie (salaires et durée de travail). Volume 2, *Le vêtement à Paris*, by Pierre Du Maroussem (Paris, 1896).

Rapport sur l'application des lois réglementant le travail. Paris: Imprimerie nationale, annual, 1896–1914.

Salaires et dureé du travail dans l'industrie française. Paris: Imprimerie nationale, 1893.

Statistique des grèves et des recours à la conciliation et à l'arbitrage. Annual. Paris: Imprimerie nationale, 1894–1914.

STATISTIQUE GÉNÉRAL DE LA FRANCE

Résultats statistiques du recensement général de la population. Paris: Imprimerie nationale, 1896, 1901, 1906, and 1911.

Résultats statistiques du recensement des industries et des professions: Dénombrement général de la population du 29 mars 1896. 4 vols. Paris: Imprimerie nationale, 1901.

EXPOSITION REPORTS

Musée industriel. *Description complète de l'exposition des produits de l'industrie française faite en 1834.* Paris: Société polytechnique, 1834.

Exposition universelle de 1855: Rapports du jury mixte international. 2 vols. Paris: Imprimerie imperiale, 1856.

Exposition de Londres en 1862: Rapports des délégués des ouvriers parisiens. Paris: Imprimerie Poupart-Davyl et Cie, 1862–64.

Exposition universelle de 1867: Rapports des délégations ouvrières. 3 vols. Paris: A. Morel, 1869.

Exposition universelle de 1867 à Paris: Rapports du jury international. Presented by Michel Chevalier. Paris: P. Dupont, 1868. Class 35, "Habillement des deux sexes," by Auguste Dusautoy.

Exposition universelle de 1873 à Vienne: Rapports de la délégation ouvrière française. Paris: A. Morel & Cie, 1874.

Exposition universelle de 1878: Rapports du jury international. Paris: Imprimerie nationale, 1880. Class 58, group 6, "Matériel et procédés de la couture," by Emile Bariquand.

Exposition universelle de 1889 à Paris: Rapports du jury international. Presented by Alfred M. Picard. Paris: Imprimerie nationale, 1891. Class 36, "Materiel et procédés de la couture."

Exposition universelle de 1900: Rapports du jury international. Paris: Imprimerie nationale, 1902.

Musée rétrospectif de la classe 79, matériel et procédés de la couture et de la fabrication de l'habillement, à l'Exposition universelle de 1900, à Paris. Saint Cloud: Bélin, 1901.

FEMINIST CONGRESSES

Actes du premier Congrès international des oeuvres et institutions féminines, Paris, 1889. Paris: Bibliothèque des annales économiques, 1890.

Congrès français et international du droit des femmes. Paris: E. Dentu, 1889.

Congrès international des oeuvres et institutions féminines, Paris, 1900. 4 vols. Paris: Imprimerie C. Blot, 1902.

Exposition universelle de 1900: Congrès international de la condition et des droits des femmes. September 5–8, 1900. Paris: Imprimerie des arts et manufactures, 1901.

Congrès international des oeuvres et institutions féminines, Paris, 1913. Paris: Girard et Brière, 1914.

Ligue Belge du droit des femmes. *Actes du Congrès féministe international de Bruxelles*. Brussels:. Bulens, 1912.

TRADE UNION CONGRESSES

Congrès national des syndicats ouvriers, tenu à Lyon en octobre, 1886. Compte rendu officiel. Lyon: Imprimerie nouvelle, 1887.

Compte rendu officiel des travaux du premier congrès de la Fédération des travailleurs de l'habillement. Nîmes, 1893. Nîmes: Imprimerie Roger et Laporte, 1893.

Compte rendu officiel des travaux du deuxième congrès de la Fédération des travailleurs de l'habillement. Lyon, 1894. Lyon: Imprimerie nouvelle, 1894.

Compte rendu officiel des travaux du troisième congrès de la Fédération des travailleurs de l'habillement. Toulouse, 1897. Toulouse: Imprimerie Passemen et Alquier, 1898.

Compte rendu officiel des travaux du sixième congrès de la Fédération des travailleurs de l'habillement. Limoges, 1906. Grenoble: N.p. 1906.

Compte rendu officiel des travaux du septième congrès de la Fédération des travailleurs de l'habillement. Avignon, 1908. Avignon: Imprimerie Nillo, 1908.

Compte rendu officiel des travaux du huitième congrès de la Fédération des travailleurs de l'habillement. Paris, 1910. Avignon: Imprimerie Nillo, 1911.

Compte rendu officiel des travaux du neuvième congrès de la Fédération des travailleurs de l'habillement. Bordeaux, 1912. Bayonne: La Rénovatrice, 1913.

NEWSPAPERS AND PERIODICALS

Almanach des Femmes, 1853–54

L'Atelier, 1840–50

Bulletin de la Ligue Sociale d'Acheteurs

Gazette des Tribunaux

Journal des Demoiselles, 1855–57, 1864–65, 1865–70, 1872–73, 1878–82

Journal des Tailleurs

La Mode Illustrée

La Politique des Femmes. Journal Publié pour les Intérêts des Femmes et par une Société d'Ouvrières, nos. 1 (June 18–24, 1848) and 2 (August 1848)

La Publicité

La Publicité Moderne

La Réforme Sociale

Le Sillon

La Voix des Femmes: Journal Socialiste et Politique, Organe des Intérêts de Toutes, nos. 1–45 (March 20, 1848 to June 18–20, 1848)

OTHER PRIMARY SOURCES (TO 1930)

Abensour, Léon. *La femme et le féminisme avant la révolution.* Paris: Editions Ernest Leroux, 1923.

Aftalion, Albert. *Le développement de la fabrique et le travail à domicile dans les industries de l'habillement.* Paris: Larose & Tenin, 1906.

Arsène, Alexandre. *Les reines de l'aiguille: Modistes et couturières.* Paris: Théophile Belin, 1902.

Association nationale française pour la protection légale des travailleurs (ANFPLT). *Le minimum de salaire dans l'industrie à domicile.* Paris: Felix Alcan, 1912.

Audiganne, Armand. *Les populations ouvrières et les industries de la France dans le mouvement social du 19e siècle.* Paris, 1854.

Avenel, Vicomte Georges de. *Le mécanisme de la vie moderne.* Paris: Armand Colin, 1902.

Avril de Sainte-Croix, Ghenia. *Le féminisme.* Paris: Giard et Briere, 1907.

Barberet, J. *Le travail en France: Monographies professionnelles.* 7 vols. Paris: Berger-Lerrault, 1886–90.

Benoist, Charles. *Les ouvrières de l'aiguille à Paris: Notes pour l'étude de la question sociale.* Paris: L. Chailley, 1895.

Bibliothèque de la tante Marguerite. *La coupe et la couture à la maison et à l'école.* Circa 1900.

Black, Clementina, ed. *Married Women's Work.* London: G. Bell and Sons, 1915.

Boileau, Etienne. *Les métiers et corporations de la Ville de Paris, XIIIe siècle: Le livre des métiers d'Etienne Boileau.* Paris: Imprimerie nationale, 1879.

Bonneff, Léon and Maurice. *La vie tragique des travailleurs, enquêtes sur la condition économique et morale des ouvriers et des ouvrières de l'industrie.* Paris: M. Rivière et Cie, 1914.

Bouvier, Jeanne. *La lingerie et les lingères.* Paris: Gaston Doin et Cie, 1928.

———. *Mes mémoires: Une syndicaliste féministe, 1876–1935.* Originally published 1936; reissued with introduction by Daniel Armogathe and Maité Albistur. Paris: La Découverte/Maspero, 1983.

Boyaval, Paul. *La lutte contre le sweating système, le minimum légal de salaire, l'exemple de l'Australasie et de l'Angleterre.* Paris: Taffin-Lefort, 1912.

Buret, Eugène. *De la misère des classes laborieuses en Angleterre et en France.* 2 vols. Paris: Paulin, 1840.

Cahen, Georges. "Misères sociales: L'ouvrière en chambre à Paris." *Revue Bleu: Revue Politique et Littéraire* 19 (May 1906).

Cere, Paul. *Les populations dangereuses et les misères sociales.* Paris: Dentu, 1872.

Cheysson, Emile. *Les budgets comparés de cent monographies de famille.* Rome: Heritiers, 1890.

Cochin, Augustin. *Paris: Sa population, son industrie.* Paris: Durand, 1864.

Combat, Ed. *Le travail des femmes à domicile: Textes officiels avec commentaire.* Paris: Berger-Levrault, 1915.

Corbon, Anthine. *Le secret du peuple de Paris.* Paris: Pagnerre, 1863.

Cotelle, Théodore. *Le sweating système: Etude sociale.* Angers: J. Siraudeau, 1904.

Couture, Charles. *Des différentes combinaisons de ventes à crédit.* Paris: LaRose, 1904.

Dallier, G. *La police des étrangers à Paris et dans le département de la Seine.* Paris: Arthur Rousseau, 1914.

De Las Cazes. *Le féminisme d'après l'école socialiste et d'après l'école de la paix.* Paris, 1901.

Des Cilleuls, Alfred. *Histoire et régime de la grande industrie en France au 17e et 18e siècle.* Paris: Girard et Brière, 1898.

Descoust, René. *Marchandage et sweating-system.* Paris: Jouve & Cie, 1918.

Drouard, Charles. *Les écoles de filles.* Paris: Bélin, 1904.

Duchêne, Gabrielle. *Le droit à la vie et le minimum de salaire.* N.p.: Syndicat générale de la chemiserie-lingerie, 1917.

———. "Le relèvement du salaire." Offprint of speech at Congrès international des femmes, June 2–7, 1913.

———. *Le travail à domicile.* French Office on Homework, 1914.

Du Lac, Reverend Père. "Couturières et modistes." In *Quatre conférences blanches.* Rouen, 1897.

Du Maroussem, Pierre. *Les enquêtes, pratique et théorie.* Paris: F. Alcan, 1900.

———. "Les grands magasins tels qu'ils sont." *Revue d'Economie Politique* (November 1893): 922–62.

———. "Les instruments monographiques d'observation." *Revue d'Economie Politique* (January 1897): 54–65.

———. *Ouvrière mouleuse en cartonnage d'une fabrique collective de jouets parisiens.* Paris, Firmin-Didot, 1893.

———. *La question ouvrière.* 4 vols. Paris: A. Rousseau, 1891–94.

Dupin, Charles. *Les forces productives et commerciales de la France.* Paris: Bachelier, 1827.

———. *Rapport du jury central sur les produits de l'industrie française exposés en 1834.* Paris: Imprimerie royale, 1834.

Exposition du travail à domicile. 3 vols. First international congress at Brussels, 1910. Volume 1: *Compte rendu des séances.* Brussels: Misch and Thron, 1910.

Fagnot, François. *La réglementation du travail en chambre.* Paris: Alcan, 1904.

Franklin, Alfred. *Les corporations ouvrières de Paris du XIIe au XVIIIe siècle.* 13 pamphlets. Paris: Firmin-Didot, 1884.

Frégier, Honoré. *Des classes dangereuses de la population dans les grandes villes, et des moyens de les rendre meilleures.* 2 vols. Paris: J.-B. Baillière, 1840.

Gemahling, Paul. *Travailleurs au rabais: La lutte syndicale contre les sous-concurrences ouvrières.* Paris: Blond et Cie, 1910.

Gonnard, René. *La femme dans l'industrie.* Paris: Colin, 1906.

Guillot, Marie. "La femme hors du foyer." *La Vie Ouvrière: Revue Syndicaliste Bimensuelle,* July 5, 1913.

Halbwachs, Maurice. *La classe ouvrière et les niveaux de vie.* Paris: Alcan, 1913.

Hauser, Henri. *Ouvriers du temps passé.* Paris: F. Alcan, 1899.

Haussonville, Gabriel Paul, Comte de. *Salaires et misères des femmes.* Paris: Calmann-Lévy, 1900.

———. *Le travail des femmes à domicile.* Paris: Blond, 1909.

Jaubert, Pierre. *Dictionnaire raisonné universel des arts et métiers.* 4 vols. Paris, 1773.

Kim, Le Van. *Féminisme et travail féminin dans les doctrines et dans les faits.* Paris: Marcel Giard, 1926.

Koenig, Marie. *La couture en classe.* Paris: Hachette, 1901.

Lampérière, Anna. *La femme et son pouvoir.* Paris: Girard et E. Brière, 1909.

Lauzel, Maurice. *Ouvriers juifs de Paris: Les casquettiers.* Paris: Edouard Cornély et Cie, 1912.

Le Play, Pierre Guillaume Frédéric. *Les ouvriers européens.* 2d ed. 6 vols. Paris: Dentu, 1877–79.

Leroy-Beaulieu, Paul. "Les ouvrières de fabrique autrefois et aujourd'hui." *Revue des Deux Mondes* 157 (February 1872).

————. *Le travail des femmes au XIX siècle.* Paris: Charpentier, 1873.

————. "Le travail des femmes dans la petite industrie." *Revue des Deux Mondes* 160 (May 1872).

Lespinasse, René de. *Les métiers et corporations de la Ville de Paris.* 3 vols. Paris: imprimerie nationale.

Levansier, Gabriel, ed. *Syndicat de l'aiguille: Papiers de famille professionnelle, l'ancienne communauté des couturières de Paris et le syndicat actuel de l'aiguille, 1675–1896.* Blois: Grande imprimerie de Blois, 1896.

Levasseur, Emile. *Questions ouvrières et industrielles en France sous la Troisième République.* Paris: Arthur Rousseau, 1907.

Louis, Paul. "Le travail à domicile." *Revue Bleu* 15 (April 1905): 467–72.

Lupiac, J. *La loi du 10 juillet 1915 pour la protection des ouvrières dans l'industrie du vêtement.* Paris: Rousseau, 1918.

Mas, Emile. "La main-d'oeuvre étrangère en France." *Revue Politique et Parlementaire* (March 1904).

Mény, Georges. *Le travail à bon marché: Enquêtes sociales.* Paris: Blond et Cie, 1907.

————. *Le travail à domicile: Ses misères—les remèdes.* Paris: Marcel Rivière, 1910.

Mercier, Louis Sebastien. *Les tableaux de Paris.* 12 vols. Amsterdam, 1782–88.

Meyssin, Jean. *Histoire d'une invention: La machine à coudre.* Lyon: Rey et Sézanne, 1866.

Milhaud, Caroline. *L'ouvrière en France. Sa condition présente. Les réformes necessaires.* Paris: Alcan, 1907.

Millet-Robinet, Cora. *Maison rustique des dames.* 13 editions, 1845–88.

Moll-Weiss, Augusta. *Le foyer domestique.* Paris: Hachette, 1902.

————. *Le livre du foyer.* Paris: Armand Colin, 1910.

————. *Le manuel du foyer domestique.* Paris: Armand Colin, 1923.

Morin, Louis. *Les cousettes: Physiologie des couturières de Paris.* Paris: Librarie de la Conquête, 1895.

Odry, Jeanne. *Application de la loi du 10 juillet 1915 sur le salaire minimum des ouvrières à domicile.* Paris: Dubois et Bauer, 1924.

Office du travail de Belgique. *Bibliographie générale des industries à domicile.* Brussels: Dewitt, 1908.

Payen, Edouard. "L'industrie à domicile et la réglementation du travail." *L'Economiste Français* 31 (July 30, 1904): 161–63.

Pelloutier, Fernand. *La vie ouvrière en France.* Paris: Schleicher, 1900.

Philippe, A. "Les décisions corporatives: Le travail de la femme dans l'industrie." *La Voix du Peuple,* June 16, 1901, p. 2.

Pic, Paul. *Traité élémentaire de legislation industrielle: Les lois ouvrières.* Paris: Rousseau, 1909.

Picard, Alfred M. *Le bilan d'un siècle, 1801–1900*. 6 vols. Paris: H. Le Soudier, 1906–7.

Piffault, Eugènie. *La femme au foyer: Education ménagère des jeunes filles*. Paris: Delagrave, 1908.

Poisson, Charles. *Le salaire des femmes*. Saumur: P. Godet, 1906.

Rapport du jury d'admission des produits de l'industrie de département de la Seine. Paris: Ballard, 1819.

Rapport du jury sur les produits de l'industrie française. Paris: Imprimerie royale, 1806.

Savary des Bruslons, Jacques. *Dictionnaire universel de commerce*. 3 vols. Paris: Estienne, 1741.

Schirmacher, Kaethe. *La spécialisation du travail par nationalité à Paris*. Paris: Arthur Rousseau, 1908.

———. "Le travail domestique des femmes: Son évaluation économique et sociale." *Revue d'Economie Politique* (May 1905): 353–79.

———. *Le travail des femmes en France*. Paris: Arthur Rousseau, 1902.

Schweidland, Eugen. "Comment est-il possible d'organiser les ouvrières en chambre?" *Revue d'Economie Politique* (1902).

———. "La répression du travail en chambre." *Revue d'Economie Politique*. 3 parts. (June–September 1897).

Scott, John. *Genius Rewarded; Or, the Story of the Sewing Machine*. New York: J. Caulon, 1880.

Simon, Jules. *L'ouvrière*. Paris: Hachette, 1860. Reprint, Paris: Saint-Pierre de Salerne, 1977.

Turgéon, Charles. *Le féminisme français*. 2 vols. Paris: Larose, 1902.

Turmann, Max. *Initiatives féminines*. Paris: Lecoffre, 1905.

Valette, Aline. *Travaux manuels pour les filles (programme du 27 juillet, 1882)*. Paris: Delarue, 1882.

Verhaegen, Pierre. *Travail à domicile et sweating système*. Brussels: A. Dewitt, 1912.

Vernières, André. [Lucien-François Delpon de Vissec]. *Camille Frison, ouvrière de la couture*. Paris: Plon-Nourrit, 1908.

Vigneron, Paule. "Les métiers de famille." *La Réforme Sociale* 2 (1901): 824–29.

Viollet, Jean. *Le travail à domicile et les devoirs de la conscience*. Paris: Sociétés savantes, 1914.

Webb, Mrs. Sidney. *Socialism and the National Minimum*. London: A. C. Fifield, 1909.

Willoughby, Gertrude. *La situation des ouvrières du vêtement en France et en Angleterre, considérée plus particulièrement dans ses rapports avec la législation sur le minimum de salaire*. Paris: Presses Universitaires de France, 1926.

Selected Secondary Sources

Abdy, Jane. *The French Poster: Chéret to Cappiello*. London: Studio Vista, 1969.

Accampo, Elinor. *Industrialization, Family Life, and Class Relations: Saint Chamond, 1815–1914*. Berkeley and Los Angeles: University of California Press, 1989.

Alexander, Sally. "Women's Work in Nineteenth-Century London." In Juliet Mitchell and Anne Oakely, eds., *The Rights and Wrongs of Women*. Harmondsworth: Penguin, 1976.

Auslander, Leora. *Taste and Power: Furnishing Modern France.* Berkeley and Los Angeles: University of California Press, forthcoming, 1996.

Ballot, Charles. *L'introduction du machinisme dans l'industrie.* Original edition, 1923. Reprint, Geneva: Slatkine Reprints, 1978.

Baron, Ava, ed. *Work Engendered: Toward a New History of American Labor.* Ithaca, N.Y.: Cornell University Press, 1991.

Benabou, Erica-Marie. *De la prostitution et la police des moeurs au XVIIIe siècle.* Paris: Perrin, 1987.

Berg, Maxine. *The Machinery Question and the Making of Political Economy, 1815–1848.* Cambridge: Cambridge University Press, 1980.

———. "What Difference Did Women's Work Make to the Industrial Revolution?" *History Workshop Journal* 35 (Spring 1993): 22–44.

Berg, Maxine, and Pat Hudson. "Rehabilitating the Industrial Revolution." *Economic History Review* 45 (1992): 24–50.

Bergeron, Louis. *Banquiers, négociants et manufacturiers parisiens du Directoire à l'Empire.* Paris: Mouton, 1978.

Berlanstein, Lenard R. *Rethinking Labor History: Essays on Discourse and Class Analysis.* Urbana: University of Illinois Press, 1993.

———. *The Working People of Paris, 1871–1914.* Baltimore: Johns Hopkins University Press, 1984.

———. "Working with Language: The Linguistic Turn in French Labor History." *Comparative Studies in Society and History* 33, no. 2 (April 1991): 426–40.

Boris, Eileen. *Home to Work: Motherhood and the Politics of Industrial Homework in the United States.* Cambridge: Cambridge University Press, 1994.

———. "Homework and Women's Rights: The Case of the Vermont Knitters, 1980–1985." *Signs* 13, no. 1 (Autumn 1987).

Boris, Eileen, and Cynthia Daniels, eds. *Homework: Historical and Contemporary Perspectives on Paid Labor at Home.* Urbana: University of Illinois Press, 1989.

Bourdieu, Pierre. *Distinction: A Social Critique of the Judgement of Taste.* Translated by Richard Nice. Cambridge, Mass.: Harvard University Press, 1984.

Boxer, Marilyn. "Protective Legislation and the Marginalization of Women Homeworkers in Late-Nineteenth- and Early-Twentieth-Century France." *Journal of Social History* 20 (Fall 1986): 45–65.

———. "Women in Industrial Homework: The Flowermakers of Paris in the Belle Epoque." *French Historical Studies* 17, no. 3 (Spring 1983).

Boydston, Jeanne. *Home and Work: Housework, Wages, and the Ideology of Labor in the Early Republic.* New York: Oxford University Press, 1990.

Brandon, Ruth. *A Capitalist Romance: Singer and the Sewing Machine.* New York: Lippincott, 1977.

Braudel, Fernand, and Ernest Labrousse. *Histoire économique et sociale de la France.* 4 vols. Paris: Presses universitaires de France, 1970–82.

Bythell, Duncan. *The Sweated Trades: Outwork in Nineteenth-Century Britain.* New York: St. Martin's Press, 1978.

Canning, Kathleen. "Feminist History after the Linguistic Turn: Historicizing Discourse and Experience." *Signs* 19, no. 2 (Winter 1994): 368–404.

———. "Gender and the Politics of Class Formation: Rethinking German Labor History." *American Historical Review* 97, no. 3 (June 1992): 736–68.

Coleman, William. *Death Is a Social Disease: Public Health and Political Economy in Early Industrial France*. Madison: University of Wisconsin Press, 1982.

Coons, Lorraine. "'Neglected Sisters' of the Women's Movement: The Perception and Experience of Working Mothers in the Parisian Garment Industry, 1860–1915." *Journal of Women's History* 5, no. 2 (Fall 1993): 50–74.

———. *Women Home Workers in the Parisian Garment Industry, 1860–1915*. New York: Garland, 1987.

Cooper, Grace Rogers. *The Sewing Machine: Its Invention and Development*. Washington, D.C.: Smithsonian Institution Press, 1976.

Coornaert, Emile. *Les corporations en France avant 1789*. Paris: Gallimard, 1941.

Cottereau, Alain. "L'usure au travail, destins masculins et destins féminins dans les cultures ouvrières en France, au XIXe siècle." *Le Mouvement Social* 124 (July–September 1983).

Cox, Donald, and John Vincent Nye. "Male-Female Wage Discrimination in Nineteenth-Century France." *Journal of Economic History* 49 (1989): 903–20.

Cross, Gary. *A Quest for Time: The Reduction of Work in Britain and France, 1840–1940*. Berkeley and Los Angeles: University of California Press, 1989.

Dalotel, Alain, Alain Faure, and Jean-Claude Freiermuth. *Aux origines de la Commune: Le mouvement des réunions publiques à Paris, 1868–1870*. Paris: Maspero, 1980.

Daric, Jean. *L'activité professionelle des femmes en France*. Paris: Presses universitaires de France, 1947.

Daumas, Maurice, and Jacques Payen. *Evolution de la géographie industrielle de Paris et sa proche banlieue au XIXe siècle*. Paris: Centre de documentation d'histoire des techniques, 1976.

Daumas, Maurice, ed. *Histoire générale des techniques: L'expansion du machinisme*. Paris: Presses universitaires de France, 1976.

Davies, Robert Bruce. *Peacefully Working to Conquer the World: Singer Sewing Machines in Foreign Markets, 1854–1920*. New York: Arno Press, 1976.

Davis, Natalie Zemon. "Women in the Crafts in Sixteenth-Century Lyon." In Barbara A. Hanawalt, ed., *Women and Work in Preindustrial Europe*. Bloomington: Indiana University Press, 1986.

de Grazia, Victoria. "The Arts of Purchase: How American Publicity Subverted the European Poster, 1920–1940." In Barbara Kruger and Phil Mariani, eds., *Remaking History*. Seattle, Wash.: Bay Press, 1989.

Deldycke, T., H. Gelders, and J. M. Limbor. *La population active et sa structure*. Brussels: Institut de sociologie, 1969.

Devance, Louis. "Femme, famille, et morale sexuelle dans l'idéologie de 1848." In *Mythes et représentations de la femme au XIXe siècle*. Paris, 1977.

Downs, Laura Lee. "If 'Woman' Is Just an Empty Category, Then Why Am I Afraid to Walk Alone at Night? Identity Politics Meets the Postmodern Subject." *Comparative Studies in Society and History* 35, no. 2 (1993): 414–37.

Doyen, Marcel. *Thimonnier, 1793–1857, inventeur de la machine à coudre*. Lyon, 1968.

Evans, Richard, and W. R. Lee, eds. *The German Family: Essays on the Social History of the Family in Nineteenth- and Twentieth-Century Germany*. London: Croom Helm, 1981.

Fairchilds, Cissie. "A Comparison of the Consumer Revolution in 18th-Century England and France." Paper presented at Economic History Meeting, Boston, 1992.

―――. "Government Support for Working Women in Old Regime France." Paper presented at the French Historical Studies Bicentennial Conference on the French Revolution, Washington D.C., 1989.

―――. "The Production and Marketing of Populuxe Goods in Eighteenth-Century Paris." In John Brewer and Roy Porter, eds., *Consumption and the World of Goods*. London: Routledge, 1993.

Faraut, François. *Histoire de la Belle Jardinière*. Paris: Bélin, 1987.

Farge, Arlette. "Dix ans d'histoire des femmes." *Le Débat* 23 (January 1983): 161–70.

―――. *Miroir des femmes, textes de la Bibliothèque bleue*. Paris: Montalba, 1982.

Farge, Arlette, and Cécile Dauphin. "Culture et pouvoir des femmes: Essai d'historiographie." *Annales E.S.C.* (March–April 1986).

Faure, Alain, and Jacques Rancière. *La parole ouvrière, 1830–1851*. Paris, 1976.

Fayet-Scribe, Sylvie. "Les associations féminines catholiques d'éducation populaire et d'éducation sociale de rerum novarum (1891) au front populaire." 2 vols. Thèse de troisième cycle, University of Paris, 1988.

"Femmes et techniques." Special issue of *Pénélope: Pour l'Histoire des Femmes* 9 (Autumn 1983).

Ferree, Myra. "Between Two Worlds: German Feminist Approaches to Working-Class Women and Work." *Signs* 10, no. 3 (Spring 1985).

Folbre, Nancy. "The Unproductive Housewife: Her Evolution in Nineteenth-Century Economic Thought." *Signs* 16, no. 3 (Spring 1991).

Fraisse, Geneviève. "Les femmes libres de 48." *Les Révoltes Logiques*, no. 1.

―――. *Muse de la raison: La démocratie exclusive et la différence des sexes*. Aix-en-Provence: Alinéa, 1989.

Fuchs, Rachel G. *Poor and Pregnant in Paris: Strategies for Survival in the Nineteenth Century*. New Brunswick, N.J.: Rutgers University Press, 1992.

Gay, Peter. *The Bourgeois Experience: Victoria to Freud*. Volume 1: The Education of the Senses. New York: Oxford University Press, 1984.

Giedion, Siegfried. *Mechanization Takes Command*. New York: Oxford University Press, 1948.

Godineau, Dominiqe. *Citoyennes tricoteuses: Les femmes du peuple à Paris pendant la révolution française*. Paris: Alinéa, 1988.

Granger, Jean. *Thimonnier et la machine à coudre*. Paris: Les publications techniques, 1943.

Green, Nancy. *The Pletzl of Paris: Jewish Immigrant Workers in the Belle Epoque*. New York: Holmes and Meier, 1986.

Groppi, Angela. "Le travail des femmes à Paris à l'époque de la révolution française." *Bulletin d'Histoire Economique et Sociale de la Révolution Française* (1979).

Guilbert, Madeleine. *Les femmes et les organisations syndicales avant 1914*. Paris: Centre national de la recherche scientifique, 1966.

―――. *Les fonctions des femmes dans l'industrie*. Paris: Mouton, 1966.

Guilbert, Madeline, and Vivianne Isambert-Jamati. *Travail féminin et travail à domicile*. Paris: Centre national de la recherche scientifique, 1956.

Gullickson, Gay. *Spinners and Weavers of Auffay: Rural Industry and the Sexual Division of Labor in a French Village, 1750–1850. Cambridge: Cambridge University Press, 1986.

Hafter, Daryl M. "Gender Formation from a Working-Class Viewpoint: Guildswomen in Eighteenth-Century Rouen." Proceedings of the Annual Meeting of the Western Society for French History 16 (1989): 415–22.

Harden-Chenut, Helen. Formation d'une culture ouvrière féminine: Les bonnetières troyennes, 1880–1939. Thèse de troisième cycle, University of Paris, 1988.

Harris, Ruth. Murders and Madness: Medicine, Law, and Society in the Fin de Siècle. Oxford: Clarendon, 1989.

Hausen, Karin. "Technical Progress and Women's Labour in the Nineteenth Century: The Social History of the Sewing Machine." In George Iggers, ed., The Social History of Politics: Critical Perspectives in West German Historical Writing since 1945. Dover, N.H., 1985.

Hilden, Patricia. Working Women and Socialist Politics in France, 1880–1914: A Regional Study. Oxford: Clarendon Press, 1986.

Hounshell, David. From the American System to Mass Production: The Development of Manufacturing Technology in the United States. Baltimore, Md.: Johns Hopkins University Press, 1984.

Howell, Martha C. Women, Production, and Patriarchy in Late Medieval Cities. Chicago: University of Chicago Press, 1986.

Hudson, Pat, and W. R. Lee. Women's Work and the Family Economy in Historical Perspective. Manchester: Manchester University Press, 1990.

Hufton, Olwen. "Women and the Family Economy in Eighteenth-Century France." French Historical Studies 9 (Spring 1975): 1–22.

———. Women and the Limits of Citizenship in the French Revolution. Toronto: University of Toronto Press, 1992.

Hunt, Lynn, and George Sheridan. "Corporatism, Association, and the Language of Labor in France, 1750–1850." Journal of Modern History 58 (December 1986): 813–44.

Johnson, Christopher. "Economic Change and Artisan Discontent." In Roger Price, ed., Revolution and Reaction: 1848 and the Second French Republic. London: C. Helm, 1975.

———. "Patterns of Proletarianization: Parisian Tailors and Lodève Workers." In John M. Merriman, ed., Consciousness and Class Experience in Nineteenth-Century Europe. New York: Holmes and Meier, 1979.

Jones, Jennifer. "Repackaging Rousseau: Femininity and Fashion in Old Regime France." French Historical Studies 18, no. 4 (Fall 1994).

Joyce, Patrick. The Historical Meanings of Work. Cambridge: Cambridge University Press, 1987.

Judt, Tony. Marxism and the French Left: Studies in Labor and Politics in France, 1830–1981. Oxford: Oxford University Press, 1986.

Kalaora, Bernard, and Antoine Savoye. Les inventeurs oubliés: Le Play et ses continuateurs aux origines des sciences sociales. Seyssel, France: Champ Vallon, 1989.

Kaplan, Steven L. "Les 'faux ouvriers' et le Faubourg Saint-Antoine." Annales E.S.C. 43, no. 2 (March–April 1988).

Kaplan, Steven L., and Cynthia J. Koepp. Work in France: Representations, Meaning, Organization, and Practice. Ithaca, N.Y.: Cornell University Press, 1986.

Katznelson, Ira, and Aristide R. Zolberg, eds. *Working-Class Formation: Nineteenth-Century Patterns in Western Europe and the United States*. Princeton, N.J.: Princeton University Press, 1986.

Kessler-Harris, Alice. *A Woman's Wage: Historical Meanings and Social Consequences*. Lexington: The University Press of Kentucky, 1990.

Koven, Seth, and Sonya Michel, eds. *Mothers of a New World: Maternalist Politics and the Origins of Welfare States*. New York: Routledge, 1993.

Laqueur, Thomas. *Making Sex: Body and Gender from the Greeks to Freud*. Cambridge, Mass.: Harvard University Press, 1990.

Levy, Marie Françoise. *De mères en filles: L'éducation des françaises, 1850–1888*. Paris: Calmann-Levy, 1984.

Liu, Tessie. *The Weaver's Knot: The Contradictions of Class Struggle and Family Solidarity in Western France, 1750–1914*. Ithaca, N.Y.: Cornell University Press, 1994.

Magraw, Roger. *A History of the French Working Class*. 2 vols. Oxford: Blackwell, 1992.

Martin, Martine. "Ménagère: Une profession? Les dilemmes de l'entre-deux-guerres." *Le Mouvement Social* 140 (July–September 1987): 89–109.

———. "La rationalisation du travail ménager en France dans l'entre-deux guerres." *Culture Technique* 3.

Martin-Fugier, Anne. *La bourgeoise: Femme au temps de Paul Bourget*. Paris: Bernard Grasset, 1983.

Meacham, Standish. *A Life Apart: The British Working Class, 1890–1914*. Cambridge, Mass.: Harvard University Press, 1977.

Medick, Hans. "The Proto-Industrial Family Economy." In Peter Kriedte, Hans Medick, and Jurgen Schlumbohm, eds., *Industrialization before Industrialization: Rural Industry in the Genesis of Capitalism*. Cambridge: Cambridge University Press, 1981.

Milkman, Ruth. "New Research in Women's Labor History." *Signs* 18, no. 2 (Winter 1993): 376–87.

Miller, Michael. *The Bon Marché: Bourgeois Culture and the Department Store, 1869–1920*. Princeton, N.J.: Princeton University Press, 1981.

Mitchell, Allan. *The Divided Path: The German Influence on Social Reform in France after 1870*. Chapel Hill: University of North Carolina Press, 1991.

Moses, Claire. *French Feminism in the Nineteenth Century*. Albany: State University Press of New York, 1984.

Nord, Philip. *Paris Shopkeepers and the Politics of Resentment*. Princeton, N.J.: Princeton University Press, 1986.

O'Brien, Patrick, and Cagler Keyder. *Economic Growth in Britain and France, 1780–1914: Two Paths to the Twentieth Century*. London: G. Allen and Unwin, 1978.

Offen, Karen. "'Powered by a Woman's Foot': A Documentary Introduction to the Sexual Politics of the Sewing Machine in Nineteenth-Century France." *Women's Studies International Forum* 11, no. 2 (1988): 93–101.

Offen, Karen, and Susan Bell, eds. *Women, the Family, and Freedom: The Debate in Documents*. 2 vols. Stanford, Calif.: Stanford University Press, 1983.

Parker, Rozsika. *The Subversive Stitch: Embroidery and the Making of the Feminine*. London: Women's Press, 1984.

Pedersen, Susan. "The Failure of Feminism in the Making of the British Welfare State." *Radical History Review* 43 (Winter 1989.)

————. *Family, Dependence, and the Origins of the Welfare State: Britain and France, 1914–1945.* Cambridge: Cambridge University Press, 1993.

Pellegrin, Nicole. "Femmes et machines à coudre: Remarques sur un objet technique et ses usages." *Pénélope* 9 (Autumn 1983): 65–71.

————. *Les vêtements de la liberté: Abécédaire des pratiques vestimentaires en France de 1780 à 1800.* Aix-en-Provence: Alinéa, 1989.

Pellegrin, Nicole, Jacques Chauvin, and Marie-Christine Planchard. *L'aiguille et le sabaron: Techniques et production du vêtement en Poitou, 1880–1950.* Poitiers: Musée de la Ville de Poitiers et de la Société des antiquaires de l'ouest, 1983.

Perrot, Michelle. "L'éloge de la ménagère." *Romantisme, Revue du Dix-neuvième Siècle* 13–14 (1976).

————. *Enquêtes sur la condition ouvrière en France au 19e siècle.* Paris: Microeditions Hachette, 1972.

————. *Les ouvriers en grève: France 1871–1890.* 2 vols. Paris: Mouton, 1974.

Perrot, Philippe. *Les dessus et les dessous de la bourgeoisie: Une histoire du vêtement au XIXe siècle.* Paris, 1981.

Peyrière, Monique. "Recherches sur la machine à coudre en France, 1830–1889." Mémoire de DEA, Histoire des techniques, Ecole des hautes études en sciences sociales, directed by Patrick Fridenson. October 1990.

Pierrard, Pierre. *La vie ouvrière à Lille sous le Second Empire.* Paris: Blond-Gay, 1965.

Pinchbeck, Ivy. *Women Workers and the Industrial Revolution, 1750–1850.* London: Routledge, 1930. Reprint, London: Virago Press, 1981.

Quataert, Jean H. "The Shaping of Women's Work in Manufacturing: Guilds, Households, and the State in Central Europe, 1648–1870." *American Historical Review* 90 (December 1985): 1122–48.

Rancière, Jacques. "Histoire 'des' femmes entre subjectivation et répresentation (note critique)." *Annales E.S.C.* 4 (July–August 1993): 1011–19.

————. *La nuit des prolétaires: Archives du rêve ouvrier.* Paris, Fayard, 1981.

Reddy, William. *The Rise of Market Culture: The Textile Trade and French Society, 1750–1900.* Cambridge: Cambridge University Press, 1984.

Riley, Denise. *Am I That Name? Feminism and the Category of "Women" in History.* Minneapolis: University of Minnesota Press, 1988.

Robert, Hélène. *Le machinisme et le travail féminin au 19ième siècle.* Thèse de troisième cycle, University of Paris, 1980.

Roberts, Mary Louise. *Civilization without Sexes: Reconstructing Gender in Postwar France.* Chicago: University of Chicago Press, 1994.

Roche, Daniel. *La culture des apparences: Une histoire du vêtement.* Paris: Fayard, 1989.

————. *Le peuple de Paris.* Paris: Aubier, 1981.

Rose, Sonya O. *Limited Livelihoods: Gender and Class in Nineteenth-Century England.* Berkeley and Los Angeles: University of California Press, 1992.

Rougerie, Jacques. "Remarques sur l'histoire des salaires à Paris au XIXe siècle." *Le Mouvement Social* 63 (1968).

Sabean, David Warren. *Property, Production, and Family in Neckerhausen, 1700–1870.* Cambridge: Cambridge University Press, 1990.

Sabel, Charles, and Jonathan Zeitlin. "Historical Alternatives to Mass Production: Politics, Markets and Technology in Nineteenth-Century Industrialization." *Past and Present* 108 (August 1985): 133–76.

Samuel, Raphael. "The Workshop of the World: Hand Power and Steam Technology in Mid-Victorian Britain." *History Workshop Journal* 3 (1977).

Savoye, Antoine. "Les continuateurs de Le Play au tournant du siècle." *Revue Française de Sociologie* 22 (1981): 315–44.

Schmiechen, James. *Sweated Industries and Sweated Labor: The London Clothing Trades, 1860–1914.* Urbana: University of Illinois Press, 1984.

Scott, Joan. *Gender and the Politics of History.* New York: Columbia University Press, 1988.

———. "The Woman Worker." In Geneviève Fraisse and Michelle Perrot, eds., *A History of Women in the West*, vol. 4. Cambridge, Mass.: Harvard University Press, 1993.

Scranton, Philip. "Market Structure and Firm Size in the Apparel Trades: Philadelphia, 1890–1930." Paper presented at conference on "L'habillement et ses entreprises," Argenton-sur-Creuse, June 1993.

———. *Proprietary Capitalism: The Textile Manufacture at Philadelphia.* Cambridge: Cambridge University Press, 1983.

Sewell, William H., Jr. *Structure and Mobility: The Men and Women of Marseilles, 1820–1870.* Cambridge: Cambridge University Press, 1985.

———. *Work and Revolution in France: The Language of Labor from the Old Regime to 1848.* Cambridge: Cambridge University Press, 1980.

Shallcross, Ruth Enalda. *Industrial Homework: An Analysis of Homework Regulations, Here and Abroad.* New York: Industrial Affairs Publishing Co., 1939.

Silverman, Deborah. *Art Nouveau in Fin-de-Siècle France: Politics, Psychology, and Style.* Berkeley and Los Angeles: University of California Press, 1989.

Sklar, Kathryn Kish. *Florence Kelley and the Nation's Work.* Volume 1: *The Rise of Women's Public Culture, 1830–1900.* New Haven, Conn.: Yale University Press, 1995.

Smith, Bonnie. *Ladies of the Leisure Class: The Bourgeoises of Northern France in the Nineteenth Century.* Princeton, N.J.: Princeton University Press, 1981.

Sonenscher, Michael. *The Hatters of Eighteenth-Century France.* Berkeley and Los Angeles: University of California Press, 1987.

———. *Work and Wages: Natural Law, Politics, and the Eighteenth-Century French Trades.* Cambridge: Cambridge University Press, 1989.

Sowerwine, Charles. *Sisters or Citizens? Women and Socialism in France since 1876.* Cambridge: Cambridge University Press, 1982.

Stewart, Mary Lynn. *Women, Work, and the French State: Labour Protection and Social Patriarchy, 1879–1919.* Kingston, Ont.: McGill-Queen's University Press, 1989.

Tabet, Paola. "Les mains, les outiles, les armes." *L'Homme* 19, nos. 3–4 (July–December 1979): 5–61.

Talbot, Margaret. "An Emancipated Voice: Flora Tristan and Utopian Allegory." *Feminist Studies* 17, no. 2 (Summer 1991): 219–40.

Taylor, Barbara. "Socialism, Feminism, and Sexual Antagonism in the London Tailoring Trade in the Early 1830s." *Feminist Studies* (Spring 1979).

Thomas, Edith. *Les femmes de 48.* Paris: Presses universitaires de France, 1948.

———. *Pauline Roland*. Paris: Rivière, 1956.

Tilly, Louise A. "Connections." *American Historical Review* 99, no. 1 (February 1994): 1–20.

———. "Gender and Jobs in Early-Twentieth-Century French Industry." *International Labor and Working-Class History* 43 (Spring 1993): 31–47.

———. "Gender, Women's History, and Social History," with comments and debate by Gay L. Gullickson and Judith M. Bennett. *Social Science History* 13, no. 4 (Winter 1989): 439–80.

———. "Women and Work in French Cities." In John M. Merriman, ed., *French Cities in the Nineteenth Century*. New York: Holmes and Meier, 1981.

Tilly, Louise, and Joan Scott. *Women, Work and Family*. New York: Holt, Rinehart and Winston, 1978.

"Travaux des femmes." Special issue of *Le Mouvement Social* 105 (October–December 1978).

Truant, Cynthia. "The Guildswomen of Paris: Gender, Power, and Sociability in the Old Regime." *Proceedings of the Annual Meeting of the Western Society for French History* 15 (1988): 130–38.

———. "Parisian Guildswomen and the (Sexual) Politics of Privilege." In Dena Goodman and Elizabeth C. Goldsmith, eds., *Going Public: Women and Publishing in Early Modern France*. Ithaca, N.Y.: Cornell University Press, 1995.

Vanier, Henriette. *La mode et ses métiers: Frivolités et luttes des classes, 1830–1870*. Paris: Armand Colin, 1960.

Vardi, Liana. *The Land and the Loom: Peasants and Profit in Northern France, 1680–1800*. Durham, N.C.: Duke University Press, 1993.

Verdier, Yvonne. *Façons de dire, façons de faire: La laveuse, la couturière, la cuisinière*. Paris: Editions Gallimard, 1979.

Walton, Whitney. *France at the Crystal Palace: Bourgeois Taste and Artisan Manufacture in the Nineteenth Century*. Berkeley and Los Angeles: University of California Press, 1992.

Williams, Rosalind. *Dream Worlds*. Berkeley and Los Angeles: University of California Press, 1982.

Zylberberg-Hocquard, Marie-Hélène. *Féminisme et syndicalisme en France*. Paris: Editions Anthropos, 1978.

Zylberberg-Hocquard, Marie-Hélène, and Evelyne Diebolt, eds. *Femmes et travail au XIXe siècle: Enquêtes de la Fronde et de la Bataille syndicaliste / Aline Valette, Marcelle Capy*. Paris: Syros, 1984.

INDEX

women's unions and, 205; minimum wage and, 241; De Mun and, 204

engravings, 20, 48n.4, 88–89, 94–95. *See also* fashion plates

Enlightenment, the, 21, 36, 40, 41, 45

entrepreneurs. *See* subcontractors

Epinal engravings, 48n.4

Esders strike, 181–83, 187, 190, 192–94

Espagne, Adelphe, 108

Europe: anti-sweating campaigns in, 138; fashion in, 179; guilds in, 25n.23; home industry studies in, 173; immigrants from (*see* immigrants); industrialization in, 15, 121, 130n.34; minimum wage bills in, 229; reformers in, 164, 174; social science in, 15

"European system," 78

Eveil Démocratique, L' (newspaper), 214

exhaustion. *See* overwork

"Expositions of Economic Horrors," 217

fabrics. *See* textiles

factories: Aftalion on, 122; family shops and, 129; homework coordination with, 131–34; labor laws evaded by, 127, 194; mechanization of, 62, 123, 124; minimum wage bill and, 243, 246, 248–49; multiplication of, 125n.13; 1901 strike and, 181; production coordination in, 57; reform advocacy of, 218, 220; sewing machine distribution by, 128; sexual arousal in, 110–11; Simon on, 66–67; specialized sewing machines for, 79; "white lists" of, 222. *See also* assembly lines

Fagnot, François, 141n.3

family life. *See* domestic life

family shops, 129; immigrant-owned, 137–38; labor legislation and, 126, 127–28, 195, 204; tailor favor for, 188. *See also* homeworkers

fan making, 32n.48

Farge, Arlette, 20n.2

fashion. *See* couture

fashion magazines, 115, 116

fashion plates, 91

Faubourg Saint-Germain, 161n.72

Fédération du Livre, 183–84n.33

Federation of Clothing Workers: CGT and, 186–87; "English week" issue and, 194, 195; Esders strikes and, 183, 192–93;

homework issue and, 187–92, 195–96; male domination of, 199; mentioned, 197

feminists, 12, 15, 16, 201, 221; Dumas and, 189; economic theorists and, 65; English, 16; homework issue and, 233, 234–37, 252, 253; labor movement and, 176, 197; minimum wage bill and, 13, 229, 248; 1901 strike and, 178; Tailor's Union and, 186n.41; wage issue and, 237–39

Ferrand, M., 47n.2

Ferry, Jules, 115

fiction, 212–13, 216

fiefs, 32

Figaro, Le (newspaper), 179

financial institutions, 82. *See also* capital; credit

fine lingerie, 143

fine work, 61, 132. *See also* embroidery

finishing work, 132

flower making. *See* artificial flower industry

Folies Bergères, 97

folklore, 20, 21, 99

Fontaine, André, 168n.104

Forces productives et commerciales de la France, Les (Dupin), 50, 51, 64

foreign competition, 144, 173, 174, 202

foreign immigrants. *See* immigrants

foreign workmanship, 184–85n.37

framework knitting, 134

Franco-Prussian War, 69

free trade treaty (1860), 56, 66

"French" looms, 123

French Sewing Machine Company, 91, 92

Fronde, La (newspaper), 175, 178, 180, 233

Furet, François, 36n.62

fur making, 160

furniture industry, 124n.10

Gaillard, Jeanne, 136

Galeries Lafayette, 183n.29

Gallic wedding ceremonies, 20–21

gas motors, 123

gas ranges, 113–14

Gemahling, Paul, 176

General Confederation of Labor. *See* Confédération générale du travail

General Federation of Clothing Workers of the Seine, 186n.46

General Union of Clothing Workers of the Seine, 181, 182